# NDS™ for NT

# NDS™ for NT

Jeffrey F. Hughes and Blair W. Thomas

IDG Books Worldwide, Inc.
An International Data Group Company

Foster City, CA ◆ Chicago, IL ◆ Indianapolis, IN ◆ New York, NY ◆ Southlake, TX

NDS™ for NT

Published by
**IDG Books Worldwide, Inc.**
An International Data Group Company
919 E. Hillsdale Blvd., Suite 400
Foster City, CA 94404

www.idgbooks.com (IDG Books Worldwide Web site)

Library of Congress Catalog Card No.: 98-70239

ISBN: 0-7645-4551-5

Printed in the United States of America

10 9 8 7 6 5 4 3 2 1

1B/RT/QU/ZY/FC

Distributed in the United States by IDG Books Worldwide, Inc.

Distributed by Macmillan Canada for Canada; by Transworld Publishers Limited in the United Kingdom; by IDG Norge Books for Norway; by IDG Sweden Books for Sweden; by Woodslane Pty. Ltd. for Australia; by Woodslane New Zealand Ltd. for New Zealand; by Addison Wesley Longman Singapore Pte Ltd. for Singapore, Malaysia, Thailand, and Indonesia; by Norma Communicaciones S.A for Colombia; by Addison Wesley/Intersoft for South Africa; by International Thomson Publishing for Germany, Austria, and Switzerland; by Toppan Company Ltd. for Japan; by Distribuidora Cuspide for Argentina; by Livraria Cultura for Brazil; by Ediciencia S.A. for Ecuador; by Addison-Wesley Publishing Company for Korea; by Ediciones ZETA S.C.R. Ltda. for Peru; by WS Computer Publishing Corporation, Inc., for the Philippines; by Unalis Corporation for Taiwan; by Contemporanea de Ediciones for Venezuela; by Computer Book & Magazine Store for Puerto Rico; by Express Computer Distributors for the Caribbean and West Indies. Authorized Sales Agent: Anthony Rudkin Associates for the Middle East and North Africa.

For general information on IDG Books Worldwide's books in the U.S., please call our Consumer Customer Service department at 800-762-2974. For reseller information, including discounts and premium sales, please call our Reseller Customer Service department at 800-434-3422.

For information on where to purchase IDG Books Worldwide's books outside the U.S., please contact our International Sales department at 650-655-3200 or fax 650-655-3297.

For information on foreign language translations, please contact our Foreign & Subsidiary Rights department at 650-655-3021 or fax 650-655-3281.

For sales inquiries and special prices for bulk quantities, please contact our Sales department at 650-655-3200 or write to the address above.

For information on using IDG Books Worldwide's books in the classroom or for ordering examination copies, please contact our Educational Sales department at 800-434-2086 or fax 817-421-5012.

For press review copies, author interviews, or other publicity information, please contact our Public Relations department at 650-655-3000 or fax 650-655-3299.

For authorization to photocopy items for corporate, personal, or educational use, please contact Copyright Clearance Center, 222 Rosewood Drive, Danvers, MA 01923, or fax 978-750-4470.

The IDG Books Worldwide logo is a trademark under exclusive license to IDG Books Worldwide, Inc., from International Data Group, Inc.

# ABOUT IDG BOOKS WORLDWIDE

Welcome to the world of IDG Books Worldwide.

IDG Books Worldwide, Inc., is a subsidiary of International Data Group, the world's largest publisher of computer-related information and the leading global provider of information services on information technology. IDG was founded more than 25 years ago and now employs more than 8,500 people worldwide. IDG publishes more than 275 computer publications in over 75 countries (see listing below). More than 60 million people read one or more IDG publications each month.

Launched in 1990, IDG Books Worldwide is today the #1 publisher of best-selling computer books in the United States. We are proud to have received eight awards from the Computer Press Association in recognition of editorial excellence and three from *Computer Currents'* First Annual Readers' Choice Awards. Our best-selling *...For Dummies*® series has more than 30 million copies in print with translations in 30 languages. IDG Books Worldwide, through a joint venture with IDG's Hi-Tech Beijing, became the first U.S. publisher to publish a computer book in the People's Republic of China. In record time, IDG Books Worldwide has become the first choice for millions of readers around the world who want to learn how to better manage their businesses.

Our mission is simple: Every one of our books is designed to bring extra value and skill-building instructions to the reader. Our books are written by experts who understand and care about our readers. The knowledge base of our editorial staff comes from years of experience in publishing, education, and journalism — experience we use to produce books for the '90s. In short, we care about books, so we attract the best people. We devote special attention to details such as audience, interior design, use of icons, and illustrations. And because we use an efficient process of authoring, editing, and desktop publishing our books electronically, we can spend more time ensuring superior content and spend less time on the technicalities of making books.

You can count on our commitment to deliver high-quality books at competitive prices on topics you want to read about. At IDG Books Worldwide, we continue in the IDG tradition of delivering quality for more than 25 years. You'll find no better book on a subject than one from IDG Books Worldwide.

John Kilcullen
CEO
IDG Books Worldwide, Inc.

Steven Berkowitz
President and Publisher
IDG Books Worldwide, Inc.

**Eighth Annual
Computer Press
Awards ≥1992**

**Ninth Annual
Computer Press
Awards ≥1993**

**Tenth Annual
Computer Press
Awards ≥1994**

**Eleventh Annual
Computer Press
Awards ≥1995**

IDG Books Worldwide, Inc., is a subsidiary of International Data Group, the world's largest publisher of computer-related information and the leading global provider of information services on information technology. International Data Group publishes over 275 computer publications in over 75 countries. Sixty million people read one or more International Data Group publications each month. International Data Group's publications include: **ARGENTINA:** Buyer's Guide, Computerworld Argentina, PC World Argentina; **AUSTRALIA:** Australian Macworld, Australian PC World, Australian Reseller News, Computerworld, IT Casebook, Network World, Publish, Webmaster; **AUSTRIA:** Computerwelt Österreich, Networks Austria, PC Tip Austria; **BANGLADESH:** PC World Bangladesh; **BELARUS:** PC World Belarus; **BELGIUM:** Data News; **BRAZIL:** Annuário de Informática, Computerworld, Connections, Macworld, PC Player, PC World, Publish, Reseller News, Supergamepower; **BULGARIA:** Computerworld Bulgaria, Network World Bulgaria, PC & MacWorld Bulgaria; **CANADA:** CIO Canada, Client/Server World, ComputerWorld Canada, InfoWorld Canada, NetworkWorld Canada, WebWorld; **CHILE:** Computerworld Chile, PC World Chile; **COLOMBIA:** Computerworld Colombia, PC World Colombia; **COSTA RICA:** PC World Centro America; **THE CZECH AND SLOVAK REPUBLICS:** Computerworld Czechoslovakia, Macworld Czech Republic, PC World Czechoslovakia; **DENMARK:** Communications World Danmark, Computerworld Danmark, Macworld Danmark, PC World Danmark, Techworld Denmark; **DOMINICAN REPUBLIC:** PC World Republica Dominicana; **ECUADOR:** PC World Ecuador; **EGYPT:** Computerworld Middle East, PC World Middle East; **EL SALVADOR:** PC World Centro America; **FINLAND:** MikroPC, Tietoverkko, Tietoviikko; **FRANCE:** Distributique, Hebdo, Info PC, Le Monde Informatique, Macworld, Reseaux & Telecoms, WebMaster France; **GERMANY:** Computer Partner, Computerwoche, Computerwoche Extra, Computerwoche FOCUS, Global Online, Macwelt, PC Welt; **GREECE:** Amiga Computing, GamePro Greece, Multimedia World; **GUATEMALA:** PC World Centro America; **HONDURAS:** PC World Centro America; **HONG KONG:** Computerworld Hong Kong, PC World Hong Kong, Publish in Asia; **HUNGARY:** ABCD CD-ROM, Computerworld Szamitastechnika, Internetto online Magazine, PC World Hungary, PC-X Magazin Hungary; **ICELAND:** Tolvuheimur PC World Island; **INDIA:** Information Communications World, Information Systems Computerworld, PC World India, Publish in Asia; **INDONESIA:** InfoKomputer PC World, Komputek Computerworld, Publish in Asia; **IRELAND:** ComputerScope, PC Live!; **ISRAEL:** Macworld Israel, People & Computers/Computerworld; **ITALY:** Computerworld Italia, Macworld Italia, Networking Italia, PC World Italia; **JAPAN:** DTP World, Macworld Japan, Nikkei Personal Computing, OS/2 World Japan, SunWorld Japan, Windows NT World, Windows World Japan; **KENYA:** PC World East African; **KOREA:** Hi-Tech Information, Macworld Korea, PC World Korea; **MACEDONIA:** PC World Macedonia; **MALAYSIA:** Computerworld Malaysia, PC World Malaysia, Publish in Asia; **MALTA:** PC World Malta; **MEXICO:** Computerworld Mexico, PC World Mexico; **MYANMAR:** PC World Myanmar; **NETHERLANDS:** Computer! Totaal, LAN Internetworking Magazine, LAN World Buyers Guide, Macworld Netherlands, Net, WebWereld; **NEW ZEALAND:** Absolute Beginners Guide and Plain & Simple Series, Computer Buyer, Computer Industry Directory, Computerworld New Zealand, MTB, Network World, PC World New Zealand; **NICARAGUA:** PC World Centro America; **NORWAY:** Computerworld Norge, CW Rapport, Datamagasinet, Financial Rapport, Kursguide Norge, Macworld Norge, Multimediaworld Norge, PC World Ekspress Norge, PC World Nettverk, PC World Norge, PC World ProduktGuide Norge; **PAKISTAN:** Computerworld Pakistan; **PANAMA:** PC World Panama; **PEOPLE'S REPUBLIC OF CHINA:** China Computer Users, China Computerworld, China InfoWorld, China Telecom World Weekly, Computer & Communication, Electronic Design China, Electronics Today, Electronics Weekly, Game Software, PC World China, Popular Computer Week, Software Weekly, Software World, Telecom World; **PERU:** Computerworld Peru, PC World Profesional Peru, PC World SoHo Peru; **PHILIPPINES:** Click!, Computerworld Philippines, PC World Philippines, Publish in Asia; **POLAND:** Computerworld Poland, Computerworld Special Report Poland, Cyber, Macworld Poland, Networld Poland, PC World Komputer; **PORTUGAL:** Cerebro/PC World, Computerworld/Correio Informático, Dealer World Portugal, Mac*In/PC*In Portugal, Multimedia World; **PUERTO RICO:** PC World Puerto Rico; **ROMANIA:** Computerworld Romania, PC World Romania, Telecom Romania; **RUSSIA:** Computerworld Russia, Mir PK, Publish, Seti; **SINGAPORE:** Computerworld Singapore, PC World Singapore, Publish in Asia; **SLOVENIA:** Monitor; **SOUTH AFRICA:** Computing SA, Network World SA, Software World SA; **SPAIN:** Communicaciones World España, Computerworld España, Dealer World España, Macworld España, PC World España; **SRI LANKA:** Infolink PC World; **SWEDEN:** CAP&Design, Computer Sweden, Corporate Computing Sweden, Internetworld Sweden, it.branschen, Macworld Sweden, MaxiData Sweden, MikroDatorn, Nätverk & Kommunikation, PC World Sweden, PCaktiv, Windows World Sweden; **SWITZERLAND:** Computerworld Schweiz, Macworld Schweiz, PCtip; **TAIWAN:** Computerworld Taiwan, Macworld Taiwan, NEW ViSiON/Publish, PC World Taiwan, Windows World Taiwan; **THAILAND:** Publish in Asia, Thai Computerworld; **TURKEY:** Computerworld Turkiye, Macworld Turkiye, Network World Turkiye, PC World Turkiye; **UKRAINE:** Computerworld Kiev, Multimedia World Ukraine, PC World Ukraine; **UNITED KINGDOM:** Acorn User UK, Amiga Action UK, Amiga Computing UK, Apple Talk UK, Computing, Macworld, Parents and Computers UK, PC Advisor, PC Home, PSX Pro, The WEB; **UNITED STATES:** Cable in the Classroom, CIO Magazine, Computerworld, DOS World, Federal Computer Week, GamePro Magazine, InfoWorld, I-Way, Macworld, Network World, PC Games, PC World, Publish, Video Event, THE WEB Magazine, and WebMaster; online webzines: JavaWorld, NetscapeWorld, and SunWorld Online; **URUGUAY:** InfoWorld Uruguay; **VENEZUELA:** Computerworld Venezuela, PC World Venezuela; and **VIETNAM:** PC World Vietnam. 3/24/97

# Credits

ACQUISITIONS EDITOR
Jim Sumser

DEVELOPMENT EDITOR
Stefan Grünwedel

TECHNICAL EDITORS
Michelle Hendry
DeeAnne Higley

COPY EDITORS
Ami Knox
Carolyn Welch

PRODUCTION COORDINATOR
Susan Parini

BOOK DESIGNER
Jim Donohue

GRAPHICS AND PRODUCTION
SPECIALISTS
Mario Amador
Linda Marousek
Hector Mendoza
Christopher Pimentel

QUALITY CONTROL SPECIALISTS
Mick Arellano
Mark Schumann

ILLUSTRATOR
Donna Reynolds

PROOFREADER
Sharon Duffy

INDEXER
Ty Koontz

# About the Authors

**Jeffrey F. Hughes,** Master Certified Novell Engineer, joined Novell in 1993. **Blair W. Thomas,** Master Certified Novell Engineer, joined Novell in 1986. Both authors are senior consultants for Novell Consulting Services and have designed and implemented NetWare 4.1 production sites around the globe. They have over 20 years of combined networking experience. Jeffrey Hughes holds a B.S. degree in Marketing from Brigham Young University. He lives in Sandy, Utah. Blair Thomas holds a B.S. degree in Computer Science and an M.B.A. from Brigham Young University. He lives in Orem, Utah.

*To our wives, Wendy and Pam, for their constant support and encouragement*

—JFH and BWT

# Preface

Novell's NetWare operating system has gained popularity as the system of choice for large and small organizations around the world because of its file and print capabilities. Among its many features, NetWare offers Novell Directory Services (NDS), which provides one of the most powerful Directory Services in the industry. Although NDS introduces a different paradigm to typical networking, its capabilities are significant once they are understood. NDS is unique because it enables you to organize your network resources, provide ease of access, and administer or manage your system centrally from one location. Additionally, NDS for NT, an add-on product for Novell Directory Services, provides you the capability to manage NT users and domains within the Novell Directory.

This book is written for all LAN administrators, system administrators, consultants, resellers, and any others who design NDS and need to know how to include NT domains in that design. This book is unique because it is completely written from Novell Consulting's experiences with its customers. Its primary objective is to outline and illustrate for the reader the correct principles for designing NDS trees and deploying the NDS for NT product. The design principles, with supporting rules and guidelines, apply to all companies regardless of their size. Both large and small companies with networks will gain an understanding of how to successfully design their own NDS trees.

While there is no absolute method to designing an NDS tree, these principles and rules have proven to be very efficient and useful. Efficiency is achieved when the NDS tree is stable before, during, and after synchronization and when the design provides for the least amount of NDS synchronization traffic.

Using this book, you will learn each of the essential principles, along with very specific rules that should drive the design of each NDS tree. Whether your interest lies solely in designing a highly efficient NDS tree or in just understanding the primary concepts, functions, and components of NDS, you'll find this book to be the definitive source.

This book is organized into five parts, in accordance with each essential step:

- ◆ **Design the NDS tree to represent the network infrastructure and its resources.** The chapters in this section describe the proper method of designing the NDS tree based on the network infrastructure. It is our experience that a well-designed tree has been based on the network infrastructure, whether it is a WAN or simply a LAN.

- ◆ **Divide NDS into partitions and replicas, providing scalability and fault tolerance.** We examine this principle by discussing the rules for properly partitioning and replicating the NDS tree to provide customers and users immediate access to NetWare information. These rules will enable you to provide quick access while maintaining efficiency and overall performance of the system.

◆ **Use NDS objects to establish the organization, administration, and user access for NT and intraNetWare.** In this section, we describe the specific procedures for using and maintaining NDS objects to provide organization within the NDS hierarchy and access for both the administrators and users.

◆ **Configure time synchronization to support NDS operations.** This section covers the information and rules relating to the configuration and proper setup of time synchronization. Here is where we provide step-by-step instructions on how to configure and set up time synchronization using the SET parameters for time.

◆ **Install and design NDS for NT.** The last section of the book describes how you design NDS to include NDS for NT with Domain objects. We also discuss the installation of NDS for NT and related products such as NDSManager, Workstation Manager, and the Novell Application Launcher.

Throughout the book, we have used a fictitious company named ACME as the basis for our examples. We chose to depict as an NDS tree a large company with wide area connections around the country. Our intent is not to preclude smaller companies, but to demonstrate as closely as possible the five essential principles of designing effective and efficient NDS trees. Regardless of the size of your NetWare installation, the design strategies are the same. You may have fewer wide area connections or no WAN at all. As you read through the chapters, you will understand how to design a tree that meets your particular needs.

As a supplement to this book, you can find valuable information regarding the design of directory trees on our Web site at http://www.directorydesign.com.

# Acknowledgments

We acknowledge the assistance of all the many talented individuals who have contributed and helped us with the creation of this book. We owe our thanks to several people.

We want to thank the staff at IDG Books Worldwide, specifically recognizing the talents of Jim Sumser, our acquisitions editor, who initiated this project and kept its focus. Jim has always been a good friend, providing keen insight and knowledge in a tough industry. We also thank Stefan Grünwedel, our development editor, and Ami Knox and Carolyn Welch, our copy editors, who have done an excellent job with this book. Thank you for your patience and tremendous attention to detail, which has made this book even better.

We also thank our technical editors, Michelle Hendry and DeeAnn Highley, for their efforts in making the content of this manuscript accurate and readable. Because NDS for NT is a new product, their knowledge and experience are rare and appreciated.

Next, we want to thank all the members of the Novell NDS for NT development team that have generously answered our questions and offered suggestions. Their talents applied through long working hours and weekends have made the NDS for NT product revolutionary in the industry.

Our appreciation is also extended to each member of the Novell Consulting staff. We appreciate the friendship and value our association with each consultant. The combined expertise of this group of dedicated individuals is unsurpassed in the industry.

Finally, we want to thank our families, who have offered encouragement and support throughout the entire project. We appreciate the sacrifice that they bore to grant us the gift of time to complete this book.

# Contents at a Glance

Preface . . . . . . . . . . . . . . . . . . . . . . . . . . . . . . . . ix

Acknowledgments . . . . . . . . . . . . . . . . . . . . . . . . . xi

Chapter 1    Introduction to NDS for NT Design . . . . . . . . . . . . . 1

First Step   Design the NDS Tree to Represent the Network
             Infrastructure and Its Resources

Chapter 2    Design the Top of the Tree Based on the Network . . 39
Chapter 3    Design the Bottom of the Tree to Represent
             Network Resources . . . . . . . . . . . . . . . . . . . . . . . . 83

Second Step  Divide NDS into Partitions and Replicas, Which Provide
             Scalability and Fault Tolerance

Chapter 4    Divide NDS into Partitions to Scale NDS
             Across Network Servers . . . . . . . . . . . . . . . . . . . 111
Chapter 5    Replicate for Fault Tolerance and
             to Reduce Synchronization Traffic . . . . . . . . . . . 143

Third Step   Use NDS Objects to Establish the Organization,
             Administration, and User Access for NT
             and intraNetWare

Chapter 6    Use NDS Objects to Define Organization,
             Administration, and User Access . . . . . . . . . . . . 189
Chapter 7    Apply NDS Access Methods . . . . . . . . . . . . . . . . 217

Fourth Step  Configure Time Synchronization to
             Support NDS Operations

Chapter 8    Design and Configure Time Synchronization . . . . 259
Chapter 9    Manage Time Synchronization Through
             SET Parameters . . . . . . . . . . . . . . . . . . . . . . . . . 303

**Fifth Step**    **Install and Design NDS for NT**

Chapter 10    Install NDS for NT . . . . . . . . . . . . . . . . . . . . . . . 331
Chapter 11    Design and Manage NDS for NT . . . . . . . . . . . . . 359

Index . . . . . . . . . . . . . . . . . . . . . . . . . . . . . . . . 395

# Table of Contents

Preface . . . . . . . . . . . . . . . . . . . . . . . . . . . . . . . . . ix

Acknowledgments . . . . . . . . . . . . . . . . . . . . . . . . . . . xi

Chapter 1     Introduction to NDS for NT Design . . . . . . . . . . . . . . 1

Advantages of NDS for NT . . . . . . . . . . . . . . . . . . . . . . . . . 2
How NDS for NT Works . . . . . . . . . . . . . . . . . . . . . . . . . . 3
Other NT Integration Tools . . . . . . . . . . . . . . . . . . . . . . . . 6
    Novell Application Launcher . . . . . . . . . . . . . . . . . . . . . . . . 6
    intraNetWare Client for Windows NT with Workstation
       Manager for NT . . . . . . . . . . . . . . . . . . . . . . . . . . . . . . . 8
    NetWare Administrator for Windows NT . . . . . . . . . . . . . . . . . 10
    Mail Box Manager for Exchange . . . . . . . . . . . . . . . . . . . . . . 11
NDS Design Principles . . . . . . . . . . . . . . . . . . . . . . . . . . . 11
NDS Design Objectives . . . . . . . . . . . . . . . . . . . . . . . . . . 11
    Organize the Network Resources in Your Company . . . . . . . . . . . 13
    Provide a Blueprint for the Consistent Rollout of NetWare 4 . . . . . 19
    Provide Flexibility to the Design to Reflect Corporate Changes . . . 20
The Five Essentials of NDS Design . . . . . . . . . . . . . . . . . . . . 20
    First Step – Base Your NDS Tree Design on Your Network
       Infrastructure . . . . . . . . . . . . . . . . . . . . . . . . . . . . . . . 20
    Second Step – Divide NDS into Partitions and Replicas
       to Provide Scalability and Fault Tolerance . . . . . . . . . . . . . . . 21
    Third Step – Use NDS Objects to Define Organization,
       Network Administration, and User Access . . . . . . . . . . . . . . . . 22
    Fourth Step – Configure Time Synchronization to
       Support NDS Operations . . . . . . . . . . . . . . . . . . . . . . . . . . 23
    Fifth Step – Install and Design NDS for NT . . . . . . . . . . . . . . . 24
NDS Design Tasks . . . . . . . . . . . . . . . . . . . . . . . . . . . . . 25
    Gather the Corporate Documents . . . . . . . . . . . . . . . . . . . . . 26
    Design the Top Level of the Tree . . . . . . . . . . . . . . . . . . . . . 31
    Define the Bottom Levels of the Tree . . . . . . . . . . . . . . . . . . . 33
    Make Modifications to the Tree Based on Your
       Organization's Needs . . . . . . . . . . . . . . . . . . . . . . . . . . . . 35

**First Step**　　**The NDS Tree Should Represent the Network Infrastructure and Its Resources**

**Chapter 2**　　**Design the Top of the Tree Based on the Network . . 39**
Design Rules for the Top of the NDS Tree. . . . . . . . . . . . . . 40
Naming the [ROOT] Object . . . . . . . . . . . . . . . . . . . . . . . 41
　　Using the NDS Tree Name to Locate a NetWare 4 Server . . . . . . . 42
　　Keeping the NDS Tree Name Unique . . . . . . . . . . . . . . . . . . . 43
　　Changing the NDS Tree Name . . . . . . . . . . . . . . . . . . . . . . . 45
Determining How the Country Object Will Be Used in
　　Your NDS Tree . . . . . . . . . . . . . . . . . . . . . . . . . . . . . . . . . 45
Naming the O=Organization for Your Company . . . . . . . . . 47
　　Using One Organization Object . . . . . . . . . . . . . . . . . . . . . . . 47
　　Using More Than One Organization Object . . . . . . . . . . . . . . . . 48
Determining Your Company's Network Infrastructure . . . . . 49
　　LAN-Based Network. . . . . . . . . . . . . . . . . . . . . . . . . . . . . . . 50
　　Campus or MAN Network . . . . . . . . . . . . . . . . . . . . . . . . . . . 50
　　Hub and Spoke Network. . . . . . . . . . . . . . . . . . . . . . . . . . . . 51
　　Meshed Network . . . . . . . . . . . . . . . . . . . . . . . . . . . . . . . . . 52
Using the First Level of OU=Organizational Units to
　　Represent the Network . . . . . . . . . . . . . . . . . . . . . . . . . . . . 53
Designing NDS for Each Type of Network Infrastructure . . . 55
　　Campus or Metropolitan Area Network . . . . . . . . . . . . . . . . . . 59
　　Hub and Spoke Network Design. . . . . . . . . . . . . . . . . . . . . . . 66
　　Meshed Network Design. . . . . . . . . . . . . . . . . . . . . . . . . . . . 78

**Chapter 3**　　**Design the Bottom of the Tree to Represent
Network Resources. . . . . . . . . . . . . . . . . . . . . . . . . 83**
Designing the Bottom of the Tree to Represent Your
　　Company's Organizational Units . . . . . . . . . . . . . . . . . . . . 83
　　Creating Containers at the Bottom of the Tree . . . . . . . . . . . . . . 85
　　Determining the Depth of the NDS Tree . . . . . . . . . . . . . . . . . . 86
　　Creating Common Resource Containers . . . . . . . . . . . . . . . . . . 88
Determining Your Design Criteria. . . . . . . . . . . . . . . . . . . 90
　　Administering the Network. . . . . . . . . . . . . . . . . . . . . . . . . . . 91
　　Placing Network Resources in Your Tree . . . . . . . . . . . . . . . . . . 96
　　Placing NT Users in the NDS Tree. . . . . . . . . . . . . . . . . . . . . . 100
　　Organizing Login Scripts . . . . . . . . . . . . . . . . . . . . . . . . . . . . 100
　　Bindery Services. . . . . . . . . . . . . . . . . . . . . . . . . . . . . . . . . . 102
　　Partitions and Replicas. . . . . . . . . . . . . . . . . . . . . . . . . . . . . 105

**Second Step    Divide NDS into Partitions and Replicas, Which Provide Scalability and Fault Tolerance**

**Chapter 4      Divide NDS into Partitions to Scale NDS Across Network Servers . . . . . . . . . . . . . . . . . . . . 111**

Designing NDS Partitions . . . . . . . . . . . . . . . . . . . . . . . . . . 112

Basing Your Partitions on the WAN Infrastructure . . . . . . . . . . . 115

Characteristics of NDS Partitions . . . . . . . . . . . . . . . . . . . . . . 117

Partitioning the Top Layers of the Tree. . . . . . . . . . . . . . . . . . . 119

Partitioning the Bottom Layers of the Tree. . . . . . . . . . . . . . . . . 120

Minimizing the Number of Replicas . . . . . . . . . . . . . . . . . . . . 121

Controlling the Partition Administration . . . . . . . . . . . . . . . . . . 121

Partitioning in the Shape of a Pyramid . . . . . . . . . . . . . . . . . . . 122

Not Spanning a WAN Link or Physical Locations with
a Partition . . . . . . . . . . . . . . . . . . . . . . . . . . . . . . . . . . . . 123

Partitioning Around the Local Servers in Each
Geographic Area . . . . . . . . . . . . . . . . . . . . . . . . . . . . . . . 124

Keeping the Partition Size Small . . . . . . . . . . . . . . . . . . . . . . . 125

Keeping the [ROOT] Partition Small . . . . . . . . . . . . . . . . . . . . . 126

Limiting the Number of Subordinate Partitions from 10 to 15 . . . 126

Managing NDS Partitions . . . . . . . . . . . . . . . . . . . . . . . . . . . 130

Understanding NDS Partition Operations . . . . . . . . . . . . . . . . . 131

Creating a Partition and Replica Matrix . . . . . . . . . . . . . . . . . . 140

**Chapter 5      Replicate for Fault Tolerance and to Reduce Synchronization Traffic . . . . . . . . . . . . . . . . . . . . 143**

Using Three Replicas for Fault Tolerance . . . . . . . . . . . . . . 144

Replicating Locally . . . . . . . . . . . . . . . . . . . . . . . . . . . . . . . 146

Replicas for Remote Offices with One Server . . . . . . . . . . . . . . 149

Replicas for Other Types of Remote Offices . . . . . . . . . . . . . . . 150

Remote Offices That Have Two NetWare 4 Servers. . . . . . . . . . . 150

Remote Offices That Have No Servers. . . . . . . . . . . . . . . . . . . . 151

Not Exceeding 7 to 10 Replicas per Partition . . . . . . . . . . . 151

Not Exceeding 15 Replicas per Server. . . . . . . . . . . . . . . . . 152

Replicating to Reduce Subordinate References . . . . . . . . . . 153

Example of Subordinate Reference Replicas. . . . . . . . . . . . . . . 154

Subordinate References' Effect on Partitioning Operations. . . . . . 156

Replicating to Provide Bindery Service Access . . . . . . . . . . 157

Planning Bindery Services . . . . . . . . . . . . . . . . . . . . . . . . . . . 157

Understanding the Server Bindery Context . . . . . . . . . . . . . . . . 157

Replicating to Improve Name Resolution . . . . . . . . . . . . . . 160

Using a Partition and Replica Matrix . . . . . . . . . . . . . . . . . 162

NDS Replicas . . . . . . . . . . . . . . . . . . . . . . . . . . . . . . . . . . 163

Replica Types ................................... 164
 Master Replica ....................................... 164
 Read/Write Replica.................................... 165
 Read-Only Replica .................................... 167
 Subordinate Reference Replica.......................... 169
Replica Synchronization ........................... 171
 Fast Synchronization ................................. 173
 Slow Synchronization ................................ 173
 How Replica Synchronization Works ..................... 173
 Scheduling the Replica Synchronization Process ............ 174
 Performing the Replica Synchronization ................. 175
 The Replica Synchronization Heartbeat ................... 176
 Replica Synchronization Cycle on a Server ............... 176
Managing NDS Replicas ........................... 178
 Add Replica Operation ................................ 180
 Remove Replica Operation ............................. 181
 Change Replica Type Operation ........................ 182
 Rebuild Replicas Operation............................ 183

**Third Step**        **Use NDS Objects to Establish the Organization, Administration, and User Access for NT and intraNetWare**

**Chapter 6**        **Use NDS Objects to Define Organization, Administration, and User Access** . . . . . . . . . . . . . **189**

Using a Naming Standard for NDS Objects. ........... 190
Goals for Creating Naming Standards. ................ 191
 Help NDS Browsing and Navigation. ..................... 191
 Help Maintain the Network and NDS ..................... 192
 Help Merge NDS Trees ................................ 193
 Help Keep NDS Object Names Unique ..................... 193
 Avoid Special or Reserved Characters..................... 193
Producing a Naming Standards Document ............. 195
 Determining the Naming Standard for Each Object Used
  in the Tree........................................ 195
 Providing an Example for Each Object Used ............... 196
 Specifying Properties for Each Object Class Selected ......... 197
 More Ideas for Naming Standards ....................... 198
Using Container Objects to Organize Network Resources . . 200
Using Leaf Objects to Provide User Access ............. 201
Using Leaf Objects to Place Physical Network
 Resources in NDS................................. 202
 Required Objects..................................... 203
 Commonly Used Objects................................ 206
 Less Commonly Used Objects .......................... 212

**Chapter 7**    **Apply NDS Access Methods** . . . . . . . . . . . . . . . . **217**

Using Client Software to Provide Network Connections . . . 218

DOS/Windows Requester (Virtual Loadable Modules). . . . . . . . . 219

NetWare Client 32 . . . . . . . . . . . . . . . . . . . . . . . . . . . . . . . . . 220

Client for Windows NT. . . . . . . . . . . . . . . . . . . . . . . . . . . . . . 221

Client Software Connection States. . . . . . . . . . . . . . . . . . . . . . . 223

Types of Client Connections: NDS and Bindery Services . . . . . . . 224

Establishing Bindery Services. . . . . . . . . . . . . . . . . . . . . . . . 225

Multiple Bindery Contexts . . . . . . . . . . . . . . . . . . . . . . . . . . . . 226

Objects in the Bindery . . . . . . . . . . . . . . . . . . . . . . . . . . . . . . . 226

Static Bindery Objects . . . . . . . . . . . . . . . . . . . . . . . . . . . . . . . 227

Dynamic Bindery Objects. . . . . . . . . . . . . . . . . . . . . . . . . . . . . 228

SafeGuard the Bindery Supervisor Account . . . . . . . . . . . . . . . . 230

Setting Up User Environments Using Login Scripts . . . . . . 232

Bindery-Based Login Scripts . . . . . . . . . . . . . . . . . . . . . . . . . . 233

NDS Login Scripts . . . . . . . . . . . . . . . . . . . . . . . . . . . . . . . . . 235

NDS Container Login Scripts . . . . . . . . . . . . . . . . . . . . . . . . . . 237

NDS Profile Login Scripts. . . . . . . . . . . . . . . . . . . . . . . . . . . . . 239

Setting Up Mobile User Access . . . . . . . . . . . . . . . . . . . . . . 245

Remote Users . . . . . . . . . . . . . . . . . . . . . . . . . . . . . . . . . . . . . 246

Mobile Users . . . . . . . . . . . . . . . . . . . . . . . . . . . . . . . . . . . . . 246

Supplying Network Applications Using NetWare

Application Launcher. . . . . . . . . . . . . . . . . . . . . . . . . . . . . 252

Minimizing the Need for Login Scripts. . . . . . . . . . . . . . . . . . . . 254

Setting Up Network Applications. . . . . . . . . . . . . . . . . . . . . . . . 254

Distributing Software Using NetWare

Application Launcher. . . . . . . . . . . . . . . . . . . . . . . . . . . . . 255

**Fourth Step**    **Configure Time Synchronization to**
**Support NDS Operations**

**Chapter 8**    **Design and Configure Time Synchronization** . . . . **259**

Time Synchronization Design. . . . . . . . . . . . . . . . . . . . . . . . 259

Single Reference Configuration . . . . . . . . . . . . . . . . . . . . . . . . . 260

Time Provider Group Configuration. . . . . . . . . . . . . . . . . . . . . . 260

Time Synchronization Communication. . . . . . . . . . . . . . . . 261

Service Advertising Protocol Communication. . . . . . . . . . . . . . . 261

Configured Lists Communication . . . . . . . . . . . . . . . . . . . . . . . 262

Purpose of Time Synchronization. . . . . . . . . . . . . . . . . . . . 263

Checking Time Synchronization. . . . . . . . . . . . . . . . . . . . . . . . . 264

Assigning Timestamps . . . . . . . . . . . . . . . . . . . . . . . . . . . . . . . 265

Setting the Network Time. . . . . . . . . . . . . . . . . . . . . . . . . . . . . 268

Time Server Types. . . . . . . . . . . . . . . . . . . . . . . . . . . . . . . . 269

Secondary Time Servers . . . . . . . . . . . . . . . . . . . . . . . . . . . . . . 271

Primary Time Servers. . . . . . . . . . . . . . . . . . . . . . . . . . . . . . . . 272

Reference Time Server . . . . . . . . . . . . . . . . . . . . . . . . . . . . . . . . 275
Single Reference Time Server. . . . . . . . . . . . . . . . . . . . . . . . . . . 280
Details About Time Synchronization Design Options . . . . . 281
Single Reference Configuration . . . . . . . . . . . . . . . . . . . . . . . . . 282
Time Provider Group Configuration. . . . . . . . . . . . . . . . . . . . . . 284
Multiple Time Provider Groups . . . . . . . . . . . . . . . . . . . . . . . . . 288
Time Synchronization Communication Methods. . . . . . . . . 290
Time Synchronization Using Service
    Advertising Protocol . . . . . . . . . . . . . . . . . . . . . . . . . . . . . . . . 290
Time Synchronization Using Configured Lists Method. . . . . . . . 290
Other Time Synchronization Design Rules
and Considerations. . . . . . . . . . . . . . . . . . . . . . . . . . . . . . . . 296
Configuring Secondary Servers to Follow Other
    Secondary Servers. . . . . . . . . . . . . . . . . . . . . . . . . . . . . . . . . 296
Having More Than One Reference Server. . . . . . . . . . . . . . . . . 298
Time Synchronization Traffic Considerations. . . . . . . . . . . . . . 299
Adding or Booting Time Servers . . . . . . . . . . . . . . . . . . . . . . . 300
Changing the Type of Time Server . . . . . . . . . . . . . . . . . . . . . . 301

Chapter 9      Manage Time Synchronization Through
               SET Parameters . . . . . . . . . . . . . . . . . . . . . . . . . . . 303
Periodically Viewing Time on All NetWare 4 Servers . . . . . 304
TIMESYNC Debug Commands. . . . . . . . . . . . . . . . . . . . . . . . 305
SET Parameters to Adjust Time Configurations. . . . . . . . . . 307
Additional TIMESYNC SET Commands . . . . . . . . . . . . . . . 321
Troubleshooting Time-Related Problems. . . . . . . . . . . . . . . 324
Booting Time Servers. . . . . . . . . . . . . . . . . . . . . . . . . . . . . . . . 325
NDS Time Not Synchronized . . . . . . . . . . . . . . . . . . . . . . . . . 325
Correcting Local Time on a Server. . . . . . . . . . . . . . . . . . . . . . 325
Synthetic Time. . . . . . . . . . . . . . . . . . . . . . . . . . . . . . . . . . . . . . 326
Synchronizing Time for NDS Operations . . . . . . . . . . . . . . . . 327

Fifth Step     Install and Design NDS for NT

Chapter 10     Install NDS for NT . . . . . . . . . . . . . . . . . . . . . . . 331
NDS for NT Core Components. . . . . . . . . . . . . . . . . . . . . . . 332
Bundled Administration Utilities. . . . . . . . . . . . . . . . . . . . . 332
NDS for NT Installation . . . . . . . . . . . . . . . . . . . . . . . . . . . 334
Installation Files. . . . . . . . . . . . . . . . . . . . . . . . . . . . . . . . . . . . 334
Running the WINSETUP.EXE Utility. . . . . . . . . . . . . . . . . . . . 334
Installing the NDS for NT Administration Utilities . . . . . . . . . . . 341
Novell Workstation Manager Configuration . . . . . . . . . . . 343
Workstation Manager Components. . . . . . . . . . . . . . . . . . . . . . 343
Workstation Manager Installation . . . . . . . . . . . . . . . . . . . . . . 344

Novell Application Launcher Installation . . . . . . . . . . . . . . 346
    Product Components . . . . . . . . . . . . . . . . . . . . . . . . . . . . . . . . . . 346
    Rights Requirements. . . . . . . . . . . . . . . . . . . . . . . . . . . . . . . . . . 349
    NAL Installation Files. . . . . . . . . . . . . . . . . . . . . . . . . . . . . . . . . 349
Mail Box Manager for Exchange Installation . . . . . . . . . . 352
    Components of the Mail Box Manager. . . . . . . . . . . . . . . . . . . . 353
    Installation Prerequisites . . . . . . . . . . . . . . . . . . . . . . . . . . . . . 354
Novell Administrator for Windows NT Installation. . . . . . . 356
    Installation Prerequisites . . . . . . . . . . . . . . . . . . . . . . . . . . . . . 356
    Easy Installation Wizard . . . . . . . . . . . . . . . . . . . . . . . . . . . . . 357
    Integrating and Synchronizing Users . . . . . . . . . . . . . . . . . . . . 357
    Compatibility Issues. . . . . . . . . . . . . . . . . . . . . . . . . . . . . . . . . 358

**Chapter 11    Design and Manage NDS for NT . . . . . . . . . . . . . . 359**
Designing NDS for NT . . . . . . . . . . . . . . . . . . . . . . . . . . . . 360
    Summary of NDS Design Guidelines . . . . . . . . . . . . . . . . . . . . . 360
    Designing the NDS Tree for NDS for NT. . . . . . . . . . . . . . . . . . 362
Managing NDS for NT . . . . . . . . . . . . . . . . . . . . . . . . . . . . 368
    Creating NT Users in NDS . . . . . . . . . . . . . . . . . . . . . . . . . . . . 369
    User Authentication and Single Login . . . . . . . . . . . . . . . . . . . 372
    Maintaining Password Synchronization. . . . . . . . . . . . . . . . . . 373
    NDS for NT and Windows NT Domain Controllers. . . . . . . . . . 374
Managing NDS Users with Other Novell Utilities . . . . . . . . 374
    Managing User Objects with NAL . . . . . . . . . . . . . . . . . . . . . . 375
    Inheriting Applications. . . . . . . . . . . . . . . . . . . . . . . . . . . . . . . 380
    Container Association Considerations . . . . . . . . . . . . . . . . . . . 381
    NDS Design Considerations . . . . . . . . . . . . . . . . . . . . . . . . . . . 382
    Application Object Properties. . . . . . . . . . . . . . . . . . . . . . . . . . 382
Managing NT Workstation Objects in NDS . . . . . . . . . . . . . 386
    Creating Associations. . . . . . . . . . . . . . . . . . . . . . . . . . . . . . . . 388
    Configuring Dynamic Local Users . . . . . . . . . . . . . . . . . . . . . . 389
    Volatile User Accounts . . . . . . . . . . . . . . . . . . . . . . . . . . . . . . . 390
    Defining Profiles and Policies. . . . . . . . . . . . . . . . . . . . . . . . . . 391
    Using Login Tabs . . . . . . . . . . . . . . . . . . . . . . . . . . . . . . . . . . . 392
    Using Login Scripts . . . . . . . . . . . . . . . . . . . . . . . . . . . . . . . . . 393
    The NWGINA Welcome Screen. . . . . . . . . . . . . . . . . . . . . . . . . 393
    Client Upgrades . . . . . . . . . . . . . . . . . . . . . . . . . . . . . . . . . . . . 393

**Index . . . . . . . . . . . . . . . . . . . . . . . . . . . . . . . . . . 395**

# Chapter 1

# Introduction to NDS for NT Design

IN THIS CHAPTER

- ◆ Advantages of NDS for NT

- ◆ How NDS for NT works

- ◆ Other NT integration tools

- ◆ The five essentials of NDS design

- ◆ NDS design principles, objectives, and tasks

NDS FOR NT IS a simple solution that makes it easier to manage the resources on your network, whether they are NetWare or Windows NT resources. If you use Novell Directory Service (NDS) to store and manage information about your network in one place or tree, you should also use NDS for NT to manage the NT domains.

You may have discovered that as Windows NT Servers are installed on your company's network, managing these servers in your existing intraNetWare environment has become more difficult. By default, no cohesive method exists for managing both systems. When making any change to intraNetWare and NDS, you must then make the same change in the Windows NT domains. For example, when a system administrator adds a new user, he or she would first check to see if the user name is unique within the NT domain. This is due to the flat file nature of Windows NT. The user is then created in NDS and added again in Windows NT via User Manager for Domains. As a result, a user must enter multiple passwords to log in to this environment. The user first enters his or her intraNetWare name and password and then the NT Server name and password. This causes confusion for users and increases the volume of support calls to the IS or support staff. If several hundred users need accounts in a domain and on NDS, the amount of work required to maintain those accounts can be prohibitive.

This problem gets worse if Microsoft Exchange is installed on your system. Your network administration is then spread over three platforms, and as such, you end up using NWAdmin for the intraNetWare and NDS environment, User Manager for Domains for the NT Server environment, and Exchange ADMIN for the e-mail users. Fortunately, Windows NT has a link to Exchange, which creates the user there automatically. However, ongoing management of the Exchange user is done from within the Exchange ADMIN utility. This whole process obviously creates extra work and can be prone to errors.

To alleviate these problems, install and configure NDS for NT, which integrates Windows NT domains directly into your NDS tree. This allows you to manage all aspects of the NT Server domain through NDS. The result is the inherent ability to provide a single login, which reduces user confusion, and a single point of administration for the entire network. Thus, if changes are made using the User Manager for Domains, those changes are automatically made in the NDS tree. If the changes are made first in NDS using NWAdmin, they are represented in the NT Server domain. Therefore, you can use either User Manager or NWAdmin to manage your network, and NDS remains consistent. This is significant if some system administrators primarily use the User Manager to administer objects.

# Advantages of NDS for NT

NDS for NT extends the normal advantages and benefits of Novell Directory Services. These benefits are extended to the Windows NT platform through the integration of NDS for NT. Some of the advantages NDS for NT offers are as follows:

♦ Gives you a single login to both NetWare and Windows NT servers

♦ Provides a single point of administration for your entire network

♦ Reduces the complexity and cost of managing domains

♦ Simplifies the deployment of NT applications

♦ Manages the Windows NT desktops

♦ Dramatically cuts the total cost of owning a network

Since NDS for NT gives you the ability to integrate Windows NT domains directly into your NDS tree, it allows you to administer all aspects of the NT domain through NDS. For example, NDS for NT has been designed so any application requiring Windows NT domain information receives that information directly from NDS. This is accomplished with no change to the application. NDS for NT is installed entirely on the Windows NT Servers. No workstation components or workstation configuration is required. From the perspective of the Microsoft clients or applications using that domain, nothing has changed. All workstations and applications continue to function as they always did before NDS for NT was installed.

Having a single login is one of the major benefits of integrating the NT domain into NDS. In this situation, a single login means that when a user needs to access network resources from intraNetWare or Windows NT, the user only enters one username and password. When an NT domain is migrated to NDS, the hashed user passwords are also migrated. This allows a user to log in to a recently migrated domain using the same password that was defined before the migration took place. NDS holds both hashed passwords for the user, one encrypted using the MD4 algorithm (Microsoft) and one encrypted using RSA (NDS).

Because no modification occurs to the workstation, the login process used to authenticate to NDS and the NT Server does not change. The login process hashes the user password with RSA and sends that directly to the intraNetWare server for authentication to NDS. The login process also hashes the password using MD4 and sends that to the Windows NT domain controller. The redirected domain controller retrieves the hashed user password from NDS and compares it to that sent from the workstation. If they match, the user is authenticated to the Windows NT domain.

You are now ready for the increased penetration of Windows NT Workstation into your intraNetWare network. NDS is the key to centrally manage all aspects of the Windows NT domains. By installing and configuring NDS for NT, you are upgrading the Windows NT domain system to a true directory service that gives you single login, single point of administration, and full NT application support for mixed intraNetWare and NT networks.

# How NDS for NT Works

NDS for NT works by integrating the Windows NT domains into NDS. This is accomplished by replacing the SAMSRV.DLL on each Windows NT Server that is designated as a primary domain controller (PDC) and a backup domain controller (BDC). Next, you need to install the Novell intraNetWare Client for Windows NT on all the Windows NT Servers. This enables the NT Servers to connect to the intraNetWare servers. The SAMSRV.DLL being replaced redirects all domain access calls to NDS. Figure 1-1 illustrates how the SAMSRV.DLL is replaced to redirect the domain access calls to NDS instead of the SAM database on NT.

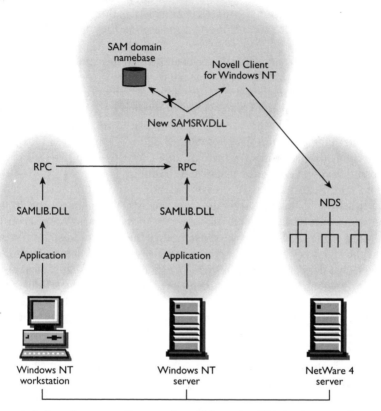

Figure 1-1: Domain access calls are redirected from the SAM database on NT to NDS.

When you configure the NDS for NT software, you select a specific context in the tree where the current NT Domain objects will be migrated. The migration is performed using the Domain Object Wizard. During the execution of the Wizard, you are asked to provide a name for the NT Domain object created in the selected context. This Domain object in NDS represents the NT domain. This object behaves similarly to a Group object: Not only does it hold information about the domain and its users, but it contains member objects such as computers and groups. This is illustrated in Figure 1-2.

The Domain object acts as a group with a list of domain members. The computers and groups associated with the domain are represented as objects contained within the NDS Domain object. By making User objects members of the domain rather than having them actually reside within the domain, administrators can place the NDS User objects anywhere in the tree and still give them access to specific domains. Because NDS stores each domain user's Relative Identifier (RID) in the NT Domain object and does not make it a property of the User object, one NDS User object can be a member of more than one NT Domain object. This provides a simple way for a single NDS user to access resources in multiple domains without having to set up complicated trust relationships.

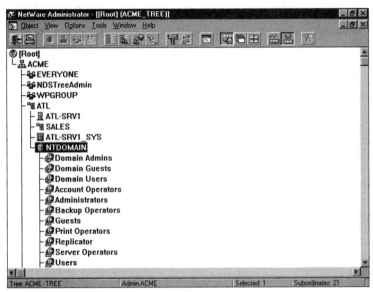

Figure 1-2: There is a Domain object (in this case, NTDOMAIN), created in the NDS tree, that represents the NT domain. Users added to the Domain object in NDS are immediately visible to the NT Server domain.

NDS for NT is installed completely on the NT Server. No workstation components or configurations are needed. To the workstation running normal Microsoft clients or applications using the domain, nothing has changed. All workstations and applications continue to function as they did before the installation. All clients and applications communicate to the servers using Remote Procedure Calls (RPC). Any request passed from the workstations using RPCs is extracted and passed to the SAMSRV.DLL layer. Normally, the SAMSRV.DLL accesses the Windows NT Security Accounts Manager (SAM), where the domain namebase is stored and performs the requested operation. By replacing the SAMSRV.DLL, however, the request is not forwarded to the local SAM namebase. Instead it gets passed directly to NDS. Thus, NDS becomes the single directory where everything is stored. Replacing the SAMSRV.DLL ensures the level of compatibility is 100 percent.

When you bring a Windows NT domain into the NDS tree, the NT domain controller must be able to authenticate to that tree. The NT server that is a PDC or BDC needs to store, modify, and retrieve domain information from the Domain object placed in NDS. In order for that NT server to authenticate, an NDS object is created for its use. This object is a *service account,* which must have administrative rights to create and modify all containers holding the NDS User objects of the domain membership. This may require you to grant trustee rights to the service account where future domain members may exist. The service account may be an existing NDS User object or a new User object created during the domain migration into NDS.

# Other NT Integration Tools

In addition to the base NDS for NT product, other NT integration products are included with NDS for NT. These products are provided to help you manage other aspects of your network. The other NT integration products include the following:

- ◆ **Novell Application Launcher** helps customers reduce the cost of software management by automating application distribution and updates to NT Workstations and other desktops via NDS.

- ◆ **intraNetWare Client for Windows NT with Workstation Manager** lets customers integrate and manage NT desktops with intraNetWare/NetWare environments without deploying NT servers and domains.

- ◆ **Novell Administrator for Windows NT** allows administrators to synchronize existing NT domains with NDS.

- ◆ **Mail Box Manager for Exchange** enhances NDS for NT by offering a single point of administration for Exchange mailboxes.

## Novell Application Launcher

The Novell Application Launcher (NAL) provides simple, powerful software application management and deployment. Instead of visiting every desktop each time an application needs to be installed or updated, NAL allows all applications to be managed from a single utility called NWAdmin. Built on Novell Directory Services (NDS), NAL allows you to deliver new and updated applications and data to users across your network quickly and easily. Using the Novell Application Launcher makes it easy to distribute new applications and application updates to your desktops. You can deliver applications from intraNetWare and NT servers to your Windows 3.1, Windows 95, and Windows NT Workstations running Novell's Client 32 for DOS/Windows, Windows 95, or Windows NT; or Virtual Loadable Module (VLM) client software 1.2. This greatly reduces the cost of managing your network and its services. The user of NAL gets applications that work every time and are always available.

The Novell Application Launcher has several major components that work together to create and manage NDS application objects in the NDS tree. The components are:

◆ Novell Application Launcher (NAL) Window program

◆ NAL Explorer

◆ NWAdmin Snap-In Module (APPSNAP.DLL)

◆ NAL snAppShot

◆ NAL Library (NWAPP)

The NAL program component is a user tool that allows users to run applications set up by a system administrator through NWAdmin. The APPSNAP.DLL is a snap-in to the NWAdmin utility that expands the NDS schema to include a new class of objects called Application and to provide descriptions of the attributes for application objects. It also provides additional functionality to your NWAdmin utility so you can create and define application objects in NDS. The NAL snAppShot is a subset utility that allows you to install complex applications on workstations requiring updates to a Windows Registry, .INI files, file system files, and CONFIG.SYS and AUTOEXEC.BAT files.

The NAL Window is the workstation component that delivers icons of the NDS application objects you have set up using the NAL Snap-In feature in NWAdmin. The NAL Explorer adds greater functionality for Windows 95 and Windows NT by delivering application objects to the Windows Explorer, Start Menu, System Tray, and desktop.

In addition to the other components, there is a special library, called NWAPP, which enables NAL Window, Explorer, Snap-In, and snAppShot to access Application objects in the NDS tree. This library provides a simple interface the developer can use to create and access NDS objects. Figure 1-3 illustrates how each of the NAL components uses the NWAPP library to access NetWare and NDS.

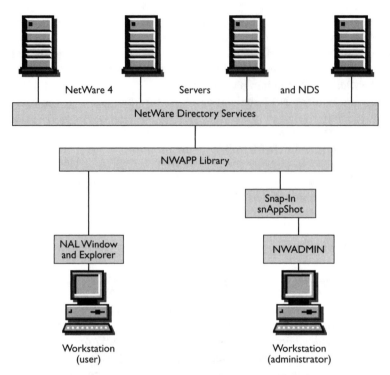

Figure 1-3: The NAL components use the NWAPP library interface to access the application objects stored in NDS and NetWare 4.

For a complete description on how to install, configure, and manage your network using the Novell Application Launcher (NAL), refer to Chapters 10 and 11.

## intraNetWare Client for Windows NT with Workstation Manager for NT

The intraNetWare Client for Windows NT with Workstation Manager makes managing NT Workstations simple, as it enables you to avoid the troubles of deploying domains. This solution is extremely useful if you have discovered that integrating Windows NT desktops into your current NetWare network can be a challenge. For example, a typical Windows NT user is required to first log in to the network and then the workstation. That's two accounts for just one user, with one for the NT Workstation and one for the network. In addition, you have to choose between managing all the Windows NT Workstation configuration settings manually or centrally using NT domains.

If you are like most NetWare administrators, creating and managing additional Windows NT domains is painful. Instead, we suggest you use your existing Novell Directory Services (NDS) structure to integrate the Windows NT desktops more easily and quickly into your current network without having to install Windows NT domains. This can be accomplished by installing your NT Workstations into NDS using a combination of Novell's intraNetWare Client for Windows NT and the Novell Workstation Manager utility. The client software (current version is 4.11) supports NT Workstations running both versions 3.5 or 4.0. It also supports all services over IPX or IP transport protocols. The Novell Workstation Manager works between the client software and NDS through a NWAdmin snap-in interface to store the NT Workstation configuration files for both local and roaming workstations.

After the client software has been installed on the NT Workstation, you can place the workstation in the NDS tree by creating a new Workstation object. The Workstation object is a new type of object in NDS called the NT Configuration object. This object holds the information necessary for the Novell client software to dynamically create a preconfigured user account on any NT Workstation. The object can grant security access to both the network and desktop PC. It controls individual desktop preferences, such as colors, shortcuts, cursors, backgrounds, and so on. Figure 1-4 shows the individual windows tabs in the NT Configuration object that are used to set up and control the various configurations and access.

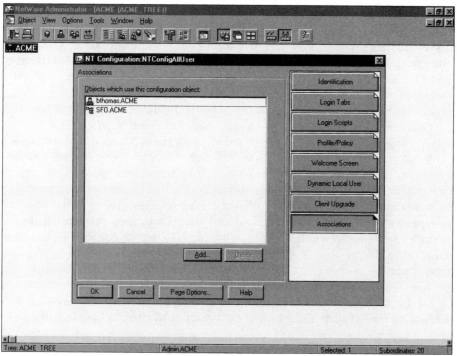

Figure 1-4: The NT Configuration object main screen showing the specific tabs central to NDS and Windows integration. Through NDS, the NT Configuration object allows you to centrally configure and control any number of Windows NT user desktops.

To associate an individual NT Configuration object with specific users, click on the Associations tab and choose country, organization, organizational units, groups, or users. When a user logs in from an NT Workstation, the client software uses these associations to find the appropriate NT Configuration object for each user. The influences of the NT Configuration object on the local desktop are applied after network login but before login to Windows NT.

The client software or NT requester is designed to expose the desktop to all of the available functionality in a NetWare environment, not just basic file and print options. Some of the most significant features are NetWare IP (NWIP) support, auto-reconnect, multi-tree support, customizable graphical pop-up login box (GINA), roaming profile support, policy support, and ODI or NDIS.

For a complete description on how to install, configure, and manage your network using the intraNetWare Client for Windows NT with Workstation Manager for NT, refer to Chapter 10 and Chapter 11.

# NetWare Administrator for Windows NT

The NetWare Administrator for Windows NT product provides you with a different method for integrating your Windows NT server with NetWare 4. This solution synchronizes your NT domains with the NDS tree. The NetWare Administrator for Windows NT differs from the basic NDS for NT method because it synchronizes domains and NDS and keeps two separate databases. All the user and group information is stored in both the Windows NT and NDS databases. You can use this tool if you want to synchronize your NT domains with NDS instead of redirecting the information.

Like NDS for NT, this product is designed to alleviate the dual administration necessary in managing NT domains and an NDS tree. With NetWare Administrator for Windows NT, all administration is done with the NWAdmin tool. NWAdmin stores all information necessary in the NDS tree, and a back-end process synchronizes the information to the appropriate NT domains. This solution ensures all changes in the tree are synchronized to the domain in a reliable, secure manner.

In addition, the Domain Object Wizard creates NT User objects in the NDS tree to represent the NT domain users. Administrators can then manage all the NT domain users from NWAdmin. Optionally, the NT User objects can be linked to standard NDS User objects. Objects linked in this manner are called hybrid User objects and are used to grant access to both the NT domain and the NDS tree. This provides a single point of administration for both worlds.

For a complete description on how to install, configure, and manage your network using the NetWare Administrator for Windows NT, refer to Chapters 10 and 11.

## Mail Box Manager for Exchange

The Mail Box Manager for Exchange is an extra utility included for you to use to manage the Exchange users on your network. This tool enhances NDS for NT by offering a single point of administration for Exchange mailboxes.

For a complete description on how to install, configure, and manage your network using the Mail Box Manager for Exchange, refer to Chapters 10 and 11.

# NDS Design Principles

Because NDS for NT depends on a well-designed NDS tree, we recommend that you learn and follow the basic design principles. There are five essential steps to designing NDS for NT, which, if followed, will give you an efficient and successful tree design regardless of the type and size of your network. If you learn and utilize these principles, you can confidently and easily design an NDS tree that meets the needs of any network environment.

No two trees will be exactly alike, and yet all trees have common characteristics that can be summarized in these five steps. The rest of this chapter briefly outlines and explains each principle along with the rules that support and substantiate it. In addition, this chapter discusses the actual application of the five steps and their rules. Chapters 2 through 11 cover in detail each principle, with clear examples and associated rules as well as exceptions.

# NDS Design Objectives

First, let's talk about the objectives for designing an NDS tree. What's the point of designing a tree before installing your NetWare 4 servers? What are the benefits of using a Directory structure as provided in NetWare 4? The basic NDS design can be done very quickly once the concepts are understood. An NDS design for companies large and small can be mapped out in literally hours. In addition, having a plan before beginning an installation will save you time in the long run. Your design can serve as your installation guide. A good design is important and provides the following benefits:

◆ It allows the tree to be used as a tool to find services more easily and efficiently so users and administrators can accomplish daily tasks, such as gaining access to and managing printers, e-mail, and other applications in a common way worldwide.

◆ Site/departmental containers will have a standard structure for applications, groups, mappings, printers, servers, and services. This structure provides a common look and feel throughout the tree.

◆ Publicly available objects, such as printers, Novell's GroupWise, Directory Map objects, and other applications can reside under each site container to facilitate public access for the regular and traveling user within the site.

◆ A partitioning and replication model can be created, providing increased processor power to incorporate Directory-aware applications in the synchronization process between these products and NDS without overall tree performance degradation.

◆ NDS is an information name service in NetWare 4 that organizes network resources, such as users, groups, printers, servers, volumes, and other physical network devices, into a hierarchical tree structure.

◆ The NDS tree, also known as the Directory tree, allows resources to be managed and displayed as a single view. In contrast, NetWare 3 provides only a server-centric view. You can manage the NDS tree, including objects and their various properties, by providing varying degrees of security access, which gives your network enormous flexibility as it expands and changes.

◆ NDS replaces the bindery found in NetWare 3 networks. A major difference between the two methods is that the Directory is distributed and can be replicated on multiple servers for increased fault tolerance. The bindery in NetWare 3 is a flat structure in which the resources belong to a single server that does not cooperate with other NetWare 3 servers. Compatibility of the bindery is available in NetWare 4 for applications requiring bindery emulation services. This feature in NetWare 4 is known as bindery services and is discussed in more detail in subsequent chapters.

◆ NDS provides a single point of login. Users log in to the network once using one username and password to access all authorized network resources. This means that the users log in to the network and NDS will process other connections to NetWare 3.1 and NetWare 4 servers if the username and password are the same.

◆ NDS provides easy administration of your network. NetWare 4 consolidates most NDS administrative functions into a single, easy-to-use graphical utility that greatly reduces the time you spend on network administration. The Novell utility called NWAdmin.EXE is a Windows-based utility that enables you to make changes to the Directory with an easy point-and-click of the mouse. You can get information about a particular object by double-clicking on its icon. The icon will bring up a dialog box that displays object details that can be modified.

◆ NDS is scaleable. It is an object hierarchy that can be divided into smaller sections, and the sections can be distributed to any number of network servers. We say it is scaleable because one server does not need to contain all Directory information. With NDS, the information can be distributed and also replicated on multiple servers to provide increased accessibility and reliability.

As a result of having spent many hours consulting for corporations large and small, we have formulated the following objectives for your NDS tree design:

◆ Organize the network resources in your company for ease of access.

◆ Provide a blueprint for a consistent rollout of NetWare 4.

◆ Provide flexibility in the tree to reflect corporate changes.

# Organize the Network Resources in Your Company

One of the primary objectives for installing and using an NDS tree is to organize the network resources in your company. The NDS tree should be arranged to reflect the location and placement of the network resources in the network. The network resources should also be placed in the tree to provide easy access to both the users and administrators. The goal of the NDS tree design is not to reproduce the organization chart of the company but to represent all users and resources in such a way that allows them to work efficiently and easily.

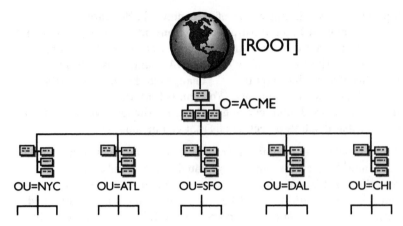

Figure 1-5: The ACME_TREE consists of five cities.

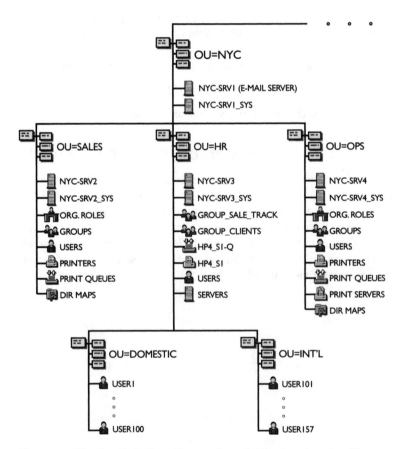

Figure 1-6: The New York City office consists of three departments with their separate resources.

At this point we introduce the ACME Tree, which serves as the sample tree for our discussion throughout this book. The ACME Company is an engineering and manufacturing firm with five main offices in the United States and is connected primarily via a T1 network to these sites. Figure 1-5 represents the ACME NDS tree with five main cities: New York City, Atlanta, San Francisco, Dallas, and Chicago. As we explain later in the book these cities make up the first level of organizational units for the ACME Tree and represent the company's network infrastructure.

The New York City office consists of Sales, Human Resources, and the Operations departments and is shown with its resources in Figure 1-6.

The Atlanta location, shown in Figure 1-7, is actually an FDDI network with four separate locations including the Key Road, Beltway, Airport, and Industrial facilities. This type of network is also included in the design and represents an additional definition of geographic locations.

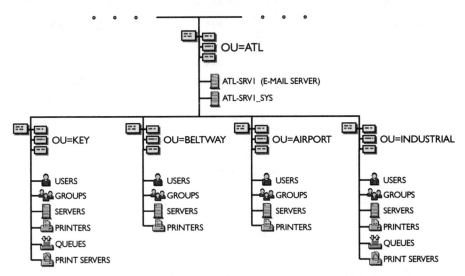

Figure 1-7: The Atlanta office includes multiple locations in the city of Atlanta using an FDDI network.

The San Francisco location includes multiple departments such as Finance, Sales, and Engineering along with their resources. San Francisco represents a single location with three departments. This location is represented in Figure 1-8.

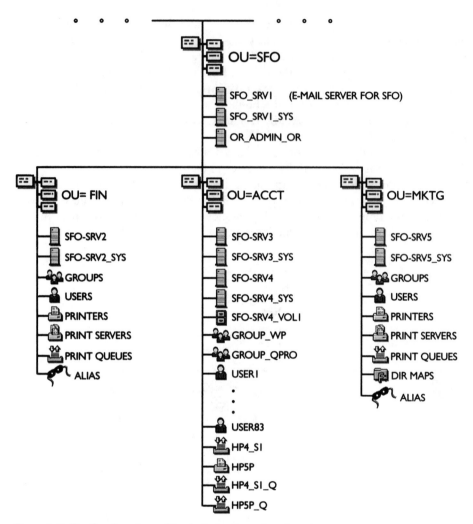

**Figure 1-8: The San Francisco office includes three departments.**

The Dallas office also consists of three departments: Communications, Accounting, and Marketing. The Accounting department is broken down into Accounts Payable and Accounts Receivable. An example of the Dallas location is shown in Figure 1-9.

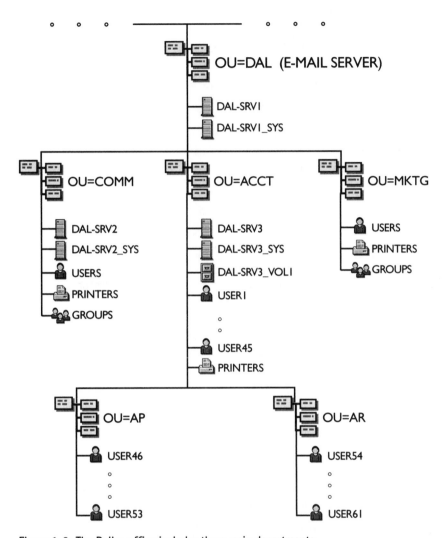

Figure 1-9: The Dallas office includes three main departments.

The Chicago office includes test, labs, and engineering departments and is shown in Figure 1-10.

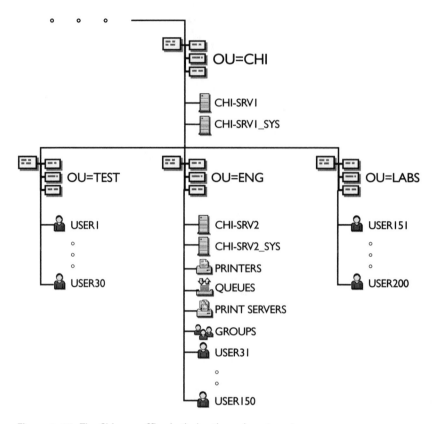

Figure 1-10: The Chicago office includes three departments.

Some users may need access to a particular printer or server, while the entire site will need access to an e-mail server. The e-mail server can be placed higher in the tree so all users needing that resource have easier access to it. Figure 1-11, as well as the previous six figures, shows how users, printers, and servers are grouped together in the same container where there is a common need. These figures also show an e-mail server at each location to serve the needs of the users in each city. Keep in mind as you design your tree that you are trying to make resource access easy for each user.

Sometimes grouping resources together may not be as simple as shown in these examples because of your network restraints or business functions. We discuss these variances later in the book. However, your objective should still be to provide the easiest access possible for your users by grouping them together.

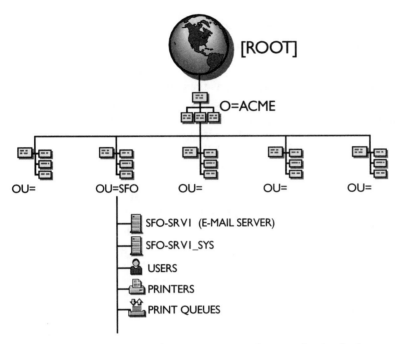

Figure 1-11: Users, printers, and servers are grouped near each other in the
ACME Tree. Some divisions will have a NetWare 4 server dedicated as an e-mail
post office, for example.

# Provide a Blueprint for the Consistent Rollout of NetWare 4

A blueprint can be published to all network administrators as a guide to creating
NDS resources in your tree properly. Your blueprint for NDS installation includes a
naming standard, an NDS tree design, and implementation/migration strategies.
With this information in hand, you will also have a guide for the installation of all
your NetWare 4 servers. For example, the tree design will give you the location
where an NDS server should be installed. An administrator can review the naming
standards and know exactly how a server should be named. During the rollout of
NetWare 4, some companies may be forced to implement more than one NDS tree
on the network, with the intent to merge them together in the future. This is made
much easier if the multiple trees are based on the same NDS tree design.

In addition, your blueprint gives you a clear map of how to migrate an entire
company to NetWare 4. Initially, your migration may begin with a few servers and
may eventually involve hundreds. Your design, regardless of the number of servers,
can be the master plan for the migrating of all servers to NetWare 4 and your NT
domains to NDS.

## Provide Flexibility to the Design to Reflect Corporate Changes

The last objective of the NDS tree design is to provide flexibility for both users and administrators. This simply means that as the corporation changes both organizationally and physically, you will be able to easily incorporate those changes into the tree without making large modifications to your tree structure. For example, you want a design that allows for easy moves of users and containers. This objective can be met by designing the NDS tree as described in the chapters presented here.

These three objectives are also very important in resolving some of the NDS design political issues. One classic example that seems to always come up is that different groups or individuals in an organization want the NDS tree designed to meet their specific situation. This kind of political issue can best be handled by referring back to your design objectives. If you have specific goals to fall back on, you can deal with the political issues by applying each question against your design objectives. Keep in mind that the network is installed to serve a business purpose, and your job as an administrator is to see that that purpose is being met. If you design your tree with this goal in mind, many of the political issues can be removed from this process.

# The Five Essentials of NDS Design

Understanding and applying the following NDS design principles will enable you to construct a Directory tree that provides network efficiency and information accessibility for your entire organization.

## First Step – Base Your NDS Tree Design on Your Network Infrastructure

The proper method for designing an NDS tree is to base it on your network infrastructure. Your network infrastructure may be only a local area network (LAN) with a single site or it may also include a wide area network (WAN) with numerous sites. Properly designed trees must be based on the network infrastructure to work efficiently because NDS, like any other protocol, rides on the network infrastructure. It makes sense that an efficiently designed tree is one that is optimized for its particular environment. An NDS tree design based on the network structure is easier to support and provides the greatest benefit for users and network administrators. The following rules are associated with this principle:

1. Name the [ROOT] object.

2. Determine the necessity of the Country object for your NDS tree.

3. Name the O=Organization for your company.

4. Determine the type of network infrastructure used by your company.

5. Represent the first level of OU=Organizational Units on the network infrastructure.

6. Determine the lower levels of your NDS tree around departments, workgroups, and so on.

## Second Step — Divide NDS into Partitions and Replicas to Provide Scalability and Fault Tolerance

A balance of replication for fault tolerance and performance can be achieved if the rules for partitioning and replication are followed as closely as possible. This principle states that the Directory can be scaled, if necessary, to meet the growth needs of your network environment. Partitioning is the method by which NDS can be logically segmented for greater efficiency across multiple NetWare 4 servers. Small LAN-only environments may not need any partitioning and can utilize the default partition known as [ROOT]. WAN environments should be designed with the following rules in mind:

1. Base partitions on the WAN infrastructure.

2. Do not create a partition that spans your WAN sites.

3. Partition around the local servers in each geographic area.

4. Keep the partition size small (1,000 to 1,500 objects).

5. Limit the number of subordinate partitions beneath a single parent from 7 to 10.

Replication is the physical placement of NDS partitions on various servers. Replication can provide fault tolerance and immediate information access to the NetWare 4 user community. The following rules for replication should be followed as closely as possible:

1. Maintain three replicas for fault tolerance.

2. Replicate locally at each site.

3. Maintain no more than 7 to 10 replicas per partition.

4. Maintain no more than 15 different replicas per server.

5. Replicate to provide bindery service access.

6. Replicate to improve name resolution.

The specific design rules for partitioning and replication of Directory Services can be separated into two different categories, depending on your specific implementation requirements, hardware, and knowledge level of your staff. The two categories defined for the partition and replica design rules are the Quick Design and the Advanced Design options.

## QUICK DESIGN

The Quick Design rules for partitions and replicas are simple, basic rules that can be applied in all companies and in almost every situation regardless of the WAN or LAN infrastructure. The Quick Design is highly recommended for designers and customers who want to operate their NDS tree structures as effectively and easily as possible. These design rules will minimize the impact of replica synchronization and will provide a good foundation for overall performance.

The Quick Design rules provide everyone with an easy and safe method to design and implement NDS in their network environments. This means that if you follow and stay within the recommendations we give you in Chapter 11, you will be successful in designing NDS. The system will also be much easier to service and maintain.

There will be only a few situations where the Quick Design rules will not apply. In the few portions of the tree where these rules cannot be followed, we introduce the Advanced Design rules.

## ADVANCED DESIGN

The Advanced Design rules are simply greater numbers for each of the partition and replica areas. Because these rules will exceed the numbers given in the Quick Design, they are going to be more costly in the efficiency of the replica synchronization process on the servers. For this reason, we strongly recommend, if not require, that you or your staff completely understand the effects or impact of the larger numbers. It is safe to say that the Advanced Design rules require that the individuals maintaining the system have a greater in-depth knowledge of NDS and NetWare 4.

For the most part, the Advanced Design rules are targeted at the consultant or administrator who understands the impact of moving past the Quick Design rules to the larger numbers.

We discuss the Advanced Design rules in more detail in Chapter 11.

# Third Step – Use NDS Objects to Define Organization, Network Administration, and User Access

One of the fundamental goals of NDS is to simplify the access to the network resources. NDS primarily accomplishes this goal by providing several key features, including a logical view to the network resources in a hierarchical tree, single login to the network, and a single point of administration using the GUI utilities, such as NWAdmin.

The building blocks of NDS are the objects that define the structure of the tree and allow for easier administration of the network. Regardless of the size of your network, you must learn how NDS objects function and how they can be used to enhance the usability of your tree. NDS objects provide organization within the NDS hierarchy and provide access to information for both the administrators and users. Some NDS objects are actually more efficient than their bindery-based counterparts and should be used to provide the best performance for your users. Keep the following rules in mind as you create NDS objects for your tree:

1. Use a naming standard for NDS objects that is short yet descriptive.

2. Use container objects to organize network resources.

3. Use container objects to provide distributed network administration.

4. Use leaf objects to provide user access.

5. Use organizational role objects to define network administrative responsibilities within your tree.

In addition to using the individual NDS objects to simplify access, there are other methods you can use to take even greater advantage of NDS and its capabilities. These methods include Novell's client software, login scripts, bindery services, NetWare Application Launcher, and others. In order to take complete advantage of NDS and make the access easier for both administrators and users, you can apply these methods in the following ways:

◆ Use client software to provide network connections.

◆ Set up user environments using login scripts.

◆ Establish bindery services.

◆ Set up mobile user access.

◆ Supply network applications using NetWare Application Launcher.

◆ Distribute software using NetWare Application Launcher.

# Fourth Step – Configure Time Synchronization to Support NDS Operations

The next step in an NDS design strategy is to define how time synchronization will be provided to the network. Time synchronization is necessary to the proper functioning of NDS and requires few changes after its implementation. Time synchronization can be managed through the MONITOR utility or by using a series of SET parameters at the server console. Your design of NDS time should provide stable and consistent time to all servers in the network. The following rules will help you configure time synchronization to your network.

1. If your network is LAN only and you have fewer than 30 servers, use the default configuration: Single Reference Server on one NetWare 4 server, all other servers are Secondary.

2. If your network has multiple sites or consists of 30 servers or more, use a time provider group: Reference server on one NetWare 4 server, two other servers are Primary, all other servers are Secondary.

3. Communicate time using the Service Advertising Protocol (SAP) for small environments or any network that can propagate SAP type 26Bh across a WAN network.

4. Use a configured list and/or turn SAPping off for any site that wants to reduce the SAP on its network.

5. Use Novell's SERVMAN (Monitor) utility to make changes to time configuration parameters, including any SET commands.

# Fifth Step — Install and Design NDS for NT

The last essential step is to install and design NDS for NT in your environment. Since NDS for NT gives you the ability to integrate Windows NT domains directly into your NDS tree, it requires you to design your NDS tree to accommodate these new objects.

New topics that are covered later in the book are:

♦ Designing NDS trees with NT domains

♦ Establishing the best approach to designing domains

The following guidelines are recommended in your NDS design:

1. Limit the number of members in the membership list of the NT Domain object to a maximum of 3,000.

2. Keep users associated with the NT domain in the same partition. This minimizes external references and its associated traffic.

3. Place each NT domain and its associated users in separate partitions.

4. Create the NT Domain object as its own partition when you exceed 1,500 objects in the container.

5. Always have the NDSDM.NLM running on the master replica of the partition holding the NT domain.

6. The NT domain PDC or BDC must be in the same SAP domain as the NDS domains supporting the User objects.

# NDS Design Tasks

The design of an NDS tree can be quite simple once you understand a few design tasks and apply them in the appropriate order. For example, we recommend that you have a naming standard before beginning your NDS design. This will simplify the naming of users, printers, and servers when the time comes during the installation to name them.

You should use the tree design tasks to apply the five essentials of NDS design. Once you have a design that meets your needs, you can begin the installation of or migration to NetWare 4. Keep in mind that you can always make changes to your tree later, but a properly designed tree will almost never need significant changes. Modifications may be necessary at some point to meet the needs of your changing organization.

In the following sections we will briefly discuss four tree design tasks:

- Gather the corporate documents

- Design the top level of your tree

- Design the bottom level of your tree

- Make modifications to the tree based on your organization's needs

While we recognize that there is no absolute or exact way to design an NDS tree, some methods are definitely more efficient than others in terms of performance and network traffic. Again, a more efficient NDS design takes into consideration the strengths or limitations of your network infrastructure. Efficiency is achieved when the tree is stable and the design provides for the least amount of NDS traffic possible.

These methods are presented in the following sections to help you design an efficient NDS tree. The methods presented here have been developed by Novell Consulting and have been successfully implemented for hundreds of large and small customers. The design guidelines presented here work for both small and large companies regardless of any unique requirements that will always be present at every company.

For purposes of this discussion it is important to define a small and large company. For the examples in this chapter, a small company consists of five servers or fewer with no (WAN) connections and fewer than 500 users. In contrast, a large network has more than five servers with a WAN connection and more than 500 users. A small network has fewer design issues than a network with thousands of users and a very complicated network infrastructure. NetWare 4 is extremely easy to design, configure, and install for small networks.

# Gather the Corporate Documents

Some company information or documentation is necessary to help you initiate an NDS tree design for your corporation. The following documents are listed below in order of importance:

◆ The wide area network (WAN) diagrams of your company

◆ The campus network maps for all your individual locations

◆ A list of sites or locations within your company

◆ A resource list that includes your file servers, printers, and other major network resources

◆ The organizational chart or similar document for your company

## THE WIDE AREA NETWORK (WAN) DIAGRAMS FOR YOUR COMPANY

For single server and LAN-only environments, you won't have a WAN diagram. However, you may have some documents that define the wiring of your LAN and also the location of current network servers, users, and printers. These documents are also very useful for the smaller NetWare 4 installations.

For the larger sites, WAN documentation is very important in the design process. Figure 1-12 shows the ACME WAN layout map. The WAN layout usually consists of all your major hub locations that are interconnected with routers and bridges. Notice in ACME's WAN layout map that all five main sites are shown with their router connections and the speed of these links in kilobits per second. Your WAN layout map may look similar to ACME's or it may include the link speeds of your satellite offices.

Your WAN documentation may consist of a single drawing or multiple pages of documentation. Don't worry if your documentation consists of many pages of information. These documents will help you to understand how your infrastructure is organized and where the major hub locations exist. These documents are also necessary for the design of the upper layer of your tree as we will explain in this book. Most companies have some sort of WAN diagrams available. Try to obtain the latest WAN map from your staff that manages your network infrastructure.

## THE CAMPUS NETWORK MAPS FOR ALL YOUR INDIVIDUAL LOCATIONS

LAN-only sites will not have any documentation of this type. If your company or organization is a LAN-only site, you can skip this section.

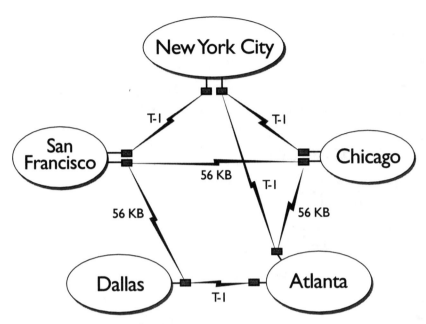

Figure 1-12: The ACME WAN layout map includes important information such as the major hub locations of its network, as well as router connections and link speeds.

Along with your WAN layout maps, campus diagrams will provide a further breakout of locations of your hub sites. This type of documentation varies from company to company. Some companies show the entire hub and campus diagrams together, while others separate the information because of the size of the network. A campus network map may show you a campus, such as the one illustrated in Figure 1-13.

The campus diagrams show information such as an FDDI ring and routers connecting this site's buildings. The campus diagram may also show buildings and their interconnections. Again, this information, along with the physical WAN map, describes your WAN/LAN infrastructure. This preliminary information is needed to build the foundation for your NetWare 4 environment.

## A LIST OF SITES OR LOCATIONS WITHIN YOUR COMPANY

LAN-only sites will not have any documentation regarding additional locations, so this section can be skipped.

Figure 1-13: The campus diagrams show a continuation of your physical WAN diagrams. Information can include connections between buildings such as FDDI, bridged token rings, 10baseT fiber, and so on.

An important aid in the placement of network resources is a list of sites or locations throughout your network. Sometimes this information is included with the other documentation previously discussed. Large companies usually have a list of sites with their locations. For example, the ACME network has a WAN site known as Atlanta with the site designator ATL. Within the ATL site, there are individual locations in the campus shown back in Figure 1-7. Further documentation, however, reveals that one of the locations within the ATL area is broken up into individual buildings. Figure 1-14 shows an example of the location called Industrial Parkway within the ATL. The Industrial Parkway location actually consists of multiple buildings called Foundry, Iron, and Main.

Notice that in the NDS tree back in Figure 1-7 the Industrial Parkway site is shown as one container and that the individual buildings are not used as containers to further break out the network resources.

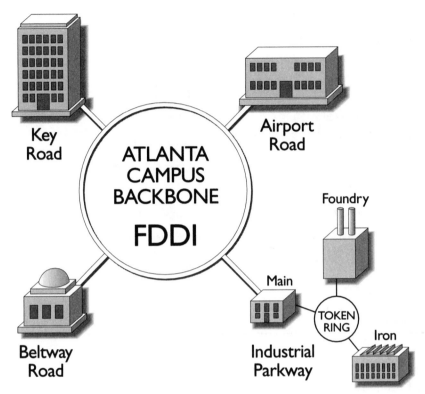

Figure 1-14: The Industrial Parkway location is actually multiple buildings called
Foundry, Iron, and Main.

## A RESOURCE LIST THAT INCLUDES YOUR FILE SERVERS, PRINTERS, AND OTHER MAJOR NETWORK RESOURCES

In a LAN-only site, the network resources currently in operation are probably available or are already known by the network administrator.

A resource list may be found with your LAN maps for each site. This list gives important information about the servers and printers found in each region, site, building, or department. This information is later used in your tree design for the placement of these resources into their proper containers. A resource list is really a list of the servers and printers that are currently in operation at your site as shown in Table 1-1. They could be NetWare 3 servers or servers that are running a different operating system that you plan to migrate to NetWare 4. Notice also that some of the naming standards shown here can be used in your NetWare 4 environment, while others may need some slight changes.

TABLE 1.1 ACME Resource List

| LOC/DIV | SERVER NAME | PRINTERS/QUEUES |
|---------|-------------|------------------|
| ATL | ATL-312 | 1 print queue, 1 printer |
| ATL | ATL-APPS | 1 print queue, 1 printer |
| NYC | NYC1-APPS | |
| NYC | NYC1-DATA | 1 print queue, 1 printer |
| NYC | NYC2-APPS | |
| DAL | DALLAS-SAAGW | |
| DAL | DALLAS-BUS1 | 1 print queue, 1 printer |
| CHI | CHICAGO-1 | 1 print queue, 1 printer |
| SFO | SFO-SALES1 | |
| SFO | SFO-SALES2 | 1 print queue, 1 printer |

## THE ORGANIZATIONAL CHART OR SIMILAR DOCUMENT FOR YOUR COMPANY

LAN-only companies may not have this document, which is fine because most LAN-only installations of NetWare 4 do not need to create many containers to represent departments.

However, this last piece of information is helpful in designing your tree in large network environments that need to base their tree on the company's organizational charts at the lower levels of the tree. Your company may have many pages of organizational charts or a very large chart. Your main purpose in obtaining the organization chart is to determine what divisions, departments, or other groups need to be created at the bottom layer of your tree. The organizational chart will assist you in defining the lower layers of the NDS tree. Figure 1-15 shows an example of the organizational chart for the ACME tree.

Typically, the most difficult task in designing the NDS tree is the task of gathering all these corporate documents. However, an even more difficult task is to try to design the tree without them. These documents are the inputs into the NDS tree design process. Obviously the larger the tree, the more effort should be spent in obtaining these documents. Small, LAN-only designs can simply focus on creating a few containers to meet their needs.

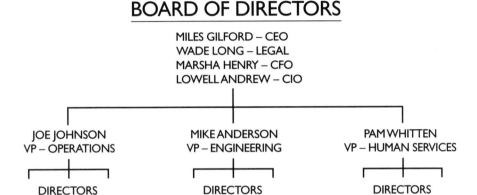

Figure 1-15: The organizational structure for ACME gives us information on departments, divisions, and workgroups that may need to be represented in your NDS tree structure.

Each of the input documents is used during different phases of the design process, and some documents are more important than others. The most important company document is the WAN layout or map. The WAN map is required before starting the NDS design for your company because it is used to design the top of the NDS tree. If your company has campus networks at one or more locations, documentation of the physical campus network is also needed. If you have a small network, you may not have a WAN map, but you will probably have an organizational chart.

The organizational chart is also an important document. But, as you will see, the organizational chart is used only during the design of the bottom of the tree. After you have gathered the corporate documents, you are ready to start the planning of the NDS tree.

## Design the Top Level of the Tree

An overall design concept before beginning an NDS design in a WAN environment is to have the tree resemble, to the extent possible, the shape of a pyramid or inverted tree. The pyramid design implies that you place most of the containers and objects at the bottom of the structure with fewer containers at the top. The pyramid shape of the tree is logically split into two sections. First, you design the top of the tree, with its appropriate containers. Then, you design the bottom of the tree. Figure 1-16 illustrates how the pyramid design is split into the top and bottom sections of the tree.

The advantage of a pyramid-shaped tree is that the top layers (the static layers) are the foundation upon which the bottom layers can be established. The bottom layers of the tree will be more dynamic and will allow for greater flexibility to change when your company changes. With this design approach you can easily make changes to your tree, such as moving users or subtrees.

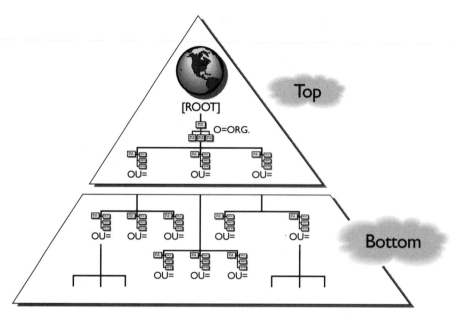

Figure 1-16: The NDS tree should be designed like a pyramid with a top and bottom portion of the tree.

An efficient NDS tree will have more organizational units at the bottom and fewer at the top. We recommend that each level not exceed 10 to 15 organizational units per parent partition in the tree. Even the largest companies with many branch offices will usually meet this recommendation as explained later in this chapter.

Another advantage of the pyramid tree design is that the partitioning of the NDS database is more natural. The alternative to the pyramid design is to create a flat tree layout or structure that places all the objects in the top layers of the tree. As shown in Figure 1-17, a very flat and wide tree is not an efficient design approach because of how NDS communicates with its subordinate levels.

Having all the objects in the top of the tree also makes the tree rigid and inefficient for most large companies. A flat tree is not recommended primarily because of the way it has to be partitioned and replicated. Synchronization traffic of NDS on all servers in the tree is increased considerably with this design approach. The tree partition and replica layout becomes extremely flat, which could cause many subordinate reference replicas to be created. Subordinate references are pointers between partitions and subordinate partitions and are automatically created by NDS. For more information about subordinate reference replicas refer to the "NDS Partitions and Replicas" section later in this chapter.

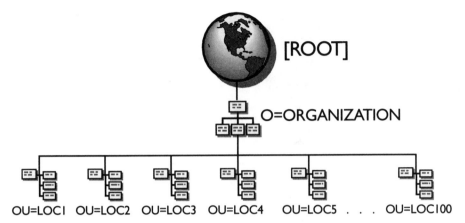

Figure 1-17: A very flat and wide tree is not as efficient as an NDS tree in the shape of a pyramid.

As seen in Figure 1-18, the tree begins with the [ROOT] object at the top followed by the O=Organization object. After the O=Organization object(s), the next level is a layer of OU=Organization Unit(s). Typically, only a selected set of users and network resources is located in the top layers of the tree. For example, the ADMIN User object is located in the O=Organization because the installation program automatically creates it.

# Define the Bottom Levels of the Tree

You should design the bottom level of the NDS tree along the organizational lines of your company using your company's organizational charts or similar documents. The bottom layers of the tree are made up of Organizational Unit (OU) containers that are based on the divisions, departments, workgroups, and teams under each of the various locations defined at the top of the tree.

The bottom layers of the tree should represent the network resources located in the LAN network of the location or site. Since the LAN supports a greater bandwidth or throughput of information than the WAN, the design of the bottom layers is extremely flexible. You, as the designer and administrator, can shape the bottom of the tree to meet your specific needs.

It is recommended that you design the bottom of the tree based on the organizational chart documents because the users and administrators are already familiar with that layout. Remember that the bottom section is flexible if it is designed around organizations. You will discover through experience that a tree designed with the organizations at the bottom can more easily change or adapt to the changing requirements of the corporation.

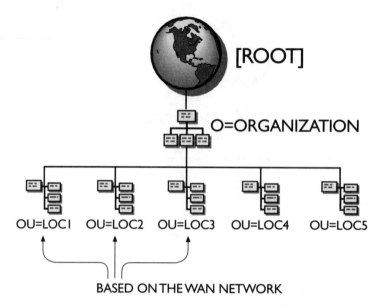

Figure 1-18: The top of the tree includes the [ROOT] object, O=Organization, and the first layer of OUs. The first layer of OUs should be based on the network infrastructure.

During the design of the bottom of the NDS tree, make sure that there is a place for every user and network resource currently in your company. Remember that one of the primary objectives for designing the NDS tree is to organize the network resources. This includes the users. If you do not have a place for all the users or network resources, you need to adjust your tree design. The bottom layers are typically the only ones affected.

As mentioned earlier, the bottom containers or OUs in the tree are typically the divisions, departments, workgroups, and teams of your company. Do not include as containers any individuals that appear as division or department heads in your company's organizational charts. You simply want to identify the functional groups or departments; the individuals become the users in each container.

The bottom of the tree is defined by the LAN and is based on the actual organization of your company from a departmental or divisional standpoint. See Figure 1-19. The bottom layers in the tree are most flexible if they represent the divisions, departments, and workgroups of your company. These bottom layer OUs (Organizational Units) will hold the majority of your leaf objects such as the users, file servers, printers, queues, and other network resources. This design approach provides the greatest flexibility because when you make changes to a department you will affect only the container(s) of that department. The rest of the tree is left unchanged. In contrast, if you make changes to an organization represented at the top of your tree, these changes can possibly affect your containers subordinate to the container you initially changed.

# BOTTOM OF THE TREE
### –BASED ON THE ORGANIZATIONAL STRUCTURE OF THE COMPANY

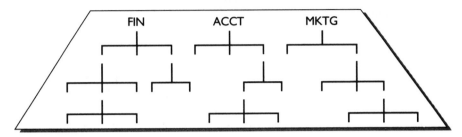

Figure 1-19: The bottom of the tree is based on the organization of the company. These lower layers offer flexibility to the tree design for moves and other changes.

# Make Modifications to the Tree Based on Your Organization's Needs

When you have completed your first draft design of the NDS tree, you are ready to apply some other design considerations as needed. This process greatly simplifies the tree design effort. Note that the design considerations impact only the design at the bottom and really do not affect the top of the tree. The greatest flexibility for changes in the design is supported at the bottom of the tree.

The design considerations that affect the bottom of the tree are:

- ◆ Network administration
- ◆ NDS partitions and replicas
- ◆ Login scripts
- ◆ Bindery services

## NETWORK ADMINISTRATION
One of the most important design considerations is how the NDS tree is going to be managed at your company. Are you going to manage the NDS tree as one Information System (IS) group (the centralized approach) or by several different IS groups or people (the decentralized approach)?

## NDS PARTITIONS AND REPLICAS

The next design consideration you need to address is how you will split the NDS hierarchy into partitions. You will need to consider the size of the partition (total number of objects), the total number of replicas, and where in the tree the partition is created. A container object is required for the creation of a partition and is designated the root-most object of the partition.

## LOGIN SCRIPTS

Another design consideration for the bottom of the tree is how the users will access the information in the tree. The users will access NDS primarily through the use of login scripts. Remember, the users need login scripts to map network drives and applications, capture to print queues, and set other variables. Thus, the login scripts become a very important design consideration. Typically, the users needing the same login script will be grouped together in the same OU container. You can then use the OU login script to provide users access to the NDS tree.

## BINDERY SERVICES

NDS is compatible with NetWare 2 and NetWare 3 using a feature called bindery emulation services. This feature allows bindery versions of NetWare applications and other third-party software that require the bindery to access the NDS database as if it were the bindery. For example, a client can use the NETX shell (NetWare 3 client) to log in to a NetWare 4 server and run any bindery-based application that may exist on the NetWare 4 server.

The five essentials of NDS design and the tasks that are associated with them are discussed in greater detail in the following chapters.

# First Step

## Design the NDS Tree to Represent the Network Infrastructure and Its Resources

**CHAPTER 2**

Design the Top of the Tree
Based on the Network

**CHAPTER 3**

Design the Bottom of the Tree
to Represent Network Resources

# Chapter 2

# Design the Top of the Tree Based on the Network

IN THIS CHAPTER

- ◆ Designing rules for the top of the NDS tree

- ◆ Naming the [ROOT] object and O=Organization for your company

- ◆ Determining the company's infrastructure

- ◆ Designing NDS for each type of network infrastructure

AS DISCUSSED IN CHAPTER 1, a primary objective in designing an NDS tree is to organize the network resources in your company for ease of access and management. The NDS tree should be designed and optimized to reflect the location and placement of the network resources in the network. The design of the top of the NDS tree is the first and most important step because it is the foundation of the NDS tree. The rest of the tree will branch downward from the top.

The goal of the NDS tree design then is not to reproduce the organization chart of the company but to represent all users and resources in such a way that allows them to work efficiently and easily. Designing your NDS tree design will be easier if you break it into two separate tasks:

- ◆ Design the top of the tree based on the network infrastructure, such as a local area network (LAN), campus or metropolitan area network (MAN), hub and spoke network, and a meshed network.

- ◆ Design the bottom of the tree based on the network resources (organizational units such as sales or accounting departments).

This chapter will focus on the design rules for the top of the NDS tree. Designing the upper levels of the NDS tree can be likened to laying a foundation before starting construction of a building. For small networks, creating a foundation may be quite simple, while larger networks will require more preparation.

# Design Rules for the Top of the NDS Tree

The top level of the tree starts with the tree name, which is represented by the [ROOT] object. Beneath the [ROOT] object is the O=Organization object and the first layer of OU=Organizational Units. This first layer of OUs should be based on your physical network infrastructure, especially if the network infrastructure is a WAN network with multiple locations or sites.

The top levels of the tree form the static portion of the tree, meaning that fewer changes will need to be made at these levels. Because any change made to the top of the tree affects the rest of the tree, you want to design the top of the tree so that few changes will be necessary. Once the top of the tree has been defined, minor corporate changes will rarely affect it because most of the changes will be enacted at the bottom levels of the tree. Figure 2-1 illustrates the top layers of a basic NDS tree, including [ROOT], O=Organization, and first level of OU=Organizational Units.

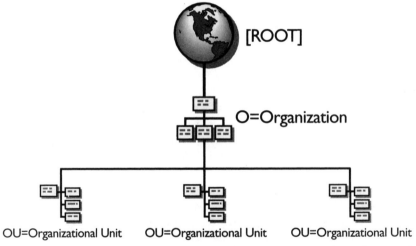

Figure 2-1: An example of a basic NDS tree design with each layer defined. The top of the tree includes the [ROOT] object, O=Organization, and first layer of OU=Organizational Units.

Each layer in the top of the NDS tree is important and should be considered before you implement your first NetWare server. In fact, there are some basic NDS design rules for each of the layers at the top of the tree. Take a moment before you begin your first NetWare installation to follow these rules to create the foundation for your NDS tree. The design rules are as follows:

1. Name the [ROOT] object.

2. Determine how the Country object will be used in your NDS tree.

3. Name the O=Organization for your company.

4. Determine your company's network infrastructure.

5. The first level of OU=Organizational Units should represent the network.

Your NDS design can be created by using a drawing package, a software model-ing tool, or simply a pencil and paper. We leave it up to you to decide the best method to create a representation of your NDS tree.

Once you have performed the preliminary design tasks such as gathering your corporate documents as explained in the previous chapter, you are ready to begin the NDS tree design by following the first design rule.

# Naming the [ROOT] Object

The first entity that needs to be named in NDS is the tree itself. The tree name is also the name of the [ROOT] object, which is defined as the top-most object in your tree. The NDS tree name is displayed in many of the current NetWare utilities such as MONITOR and DSREPAIR. You can also find the tree name by typing CONFIG at the NetWare server console. The tree name you choose can be more descriptive if it represents the company name plus _TREE. For example, the company we will use in most of the examples in this book is called ACME. Thus, the name of the NDS tree for ACME is ACME_TREE. Figure 2-2 illustrates how the [ROOT] object is prop-erly named by using the name of the tree (ACME_TREE). As with any other object type, keep the tree name short but descriptive.

The name of the tree should be a unique value on the network wire because the NDS tree uses the Service Advertising Protocol (SAP) to broadcast to the client or workstations where the tree can be found. The SAP information helps bootstrap the clients and all applications requiring NDS. The SAP information helps the client locate the nearest server with the NDS database very efficiently.

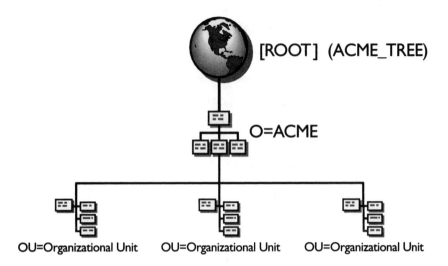

Figure 2-2: Another name for the [ROOT] object is ACME_TREE.

## Using the NDS Tree Name to Locate a NetWare 4 Server

Because NDS is a distributed name service with different information on each server, the client can use the NDS tree name to locate any network resources in the network. Once the client or workstation is attached to any NetWare server that holds the NDS tree, all the servers work together to locate the requested resource.

The NetWare servers that contain part of the NDS tree use the SAP to broadcast their location. The service type for the NDS tree SAP is 0x0278 hex (or 632 decimal).

Figure 2-3 illustrates how the client initially finds the first NetWare 4 server by broadcasting or making a service request indicating the SAP type 0x0278 and the tree name if it has been set by a preferred tree. Any NetWare 4 server receiving this request and storing NDS tree information for that tree will respond to the request.

If no preferred tree or server has been set, the client will use the first tree that responds to the request.

 The other SAPs that must be supported are type 0x0004 hex and type 0x026B hex. A normal NCP server or file server uses the SAP type 0x0004 for SAP broadcasts on the network. The SAP type 0x026B is used by time synchronization in a NetWare 4 environment.

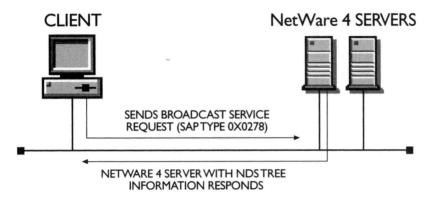

Figure 2-3: The client initially finds the first NetWare 4 server by broadcasting or making a service request indicating the SAP type 0x0278 and the tree name if a preferred tree is set.

## Keeping the NDS Tree Name Unique

In addition, using TREE to name the NDS tree clearly identifies the SAP broadcasts as shown in Figure 2-4. Each of the servers or devices that send out a SAP is displayed using the DISPLAY SERVERS command at the server console prompt. Notice the NDS tree SAP information for the ACME_TREE.

### Consulting Experience

Never filter Router Information Protocol (RIP) broadcasts, and be careful when filtering SAP broadcasts on your routers. It is very important that you do not use a RIP filter between any NetWare 4 server. Each NetWare 4 server needs to be able to see every other NetWare 4 server. Some people think that since a NetWare 4 server does not have replicas stored on it that it can be filtered out. This is not the case. The server needs to be able to perform a service request for type 0x0278 hex to find the NDS tree. In addition, the clients or workstations need type 0x0278 hex to boot up.

```
NYC-SRV1:display servers
  ACME_TREE___  0    ACME_TREE___  0    ACME_TREE___  1    ATL-SRV1    1
  NYC-SRV1      0    NYC-SRV1      0    SFO-SRV1      1    SFO-SRV1    1
There are 8 known servers
NYC-SRV1:
```

Figure 2-4: An example of an NDS tree SAP using the DISPLAY SERVERS feature of NetWare. Clearly naming the tree makes for easy identification of servers and NDS trees during troubleshooting.

Because the SAP does not support spaces in the name, the NetWare 4 installation utility will not let you enter spaces in the tree name.

If you need to install multiple trees on the same physical network, each NDS tree must be uniquely named. You need different tree names so that the SAP broadcasts are unique. If the tree names are not unique, the clients may not be able to find the appropriate NDS tree during initialization. Figure 2-5 illustrates how two different NDS tree names are uniquely displayed on the SAP list.

 **TIP** Keep in mind that the DISPLAY SERVERS command shows a limited number of characters. This is another reason to keep your NDS tree names short.

```
NYC-SRV1:display servers
  ACME_TREE1__  0    ACME_TREE1__  0    ACME_TREE1__  1    ACME_TREE2__  1
  ACME_TREE2__  1    ATL-SRV1      1    NYC-SRV1      0    NYC-SRV1      0
  SFO-SRV1      1    SFO-SRV1      1
There are 10 known servers
NYC-SRV1:
```

Figure 2-5: Two separate tree names ACME_TREE1 and ACME_TREE2 are shown using the DISPLAY SERVERS command from the server console.

The NDS tree always starts with the [ROOT] container object. However, the [ROOT] object is not counted as a layer in the tree. You begin counting from the Organization object layer downward.

## Changing the NDS Tree Name

In order to change the NDS tree name, the administrator must run the DSMERGE utility. From DSMERGE select the option Rename Tree. Although changing the name of the NDS tree is simple, it will impact the clients that depend on the PRE-FERRED TREE statement in their NET.CFG file or Registry. If the NDS tree name is changed, all of the PREFERRED TREE statements in these files must be changed in order for the users to log in to the new tree name.

For larger networks with more users, changing the name of the NDS tree will require more effort because it impacts more users. As an administrator, it is best to decide initially what your NDS tree name will be to avoid the work necessary to make a change later.

# Determining How the Country Object Will Be Used in Your NDS Tree

The use of the C=Country object in your private corporate NDS tree is optional. Although the C=Country object is used to specify a particular country code based on the X.500 standard, the public network providers own and use the C=Country object in their trees. If your company is using such a service, the C=Country object is not required for your corporate tree. The provider of the global network will use the C=Country object in their tree, and the customer connecting to the global network will participate through a subordinate organizational unit or through other means to their tree.

If your company is doing business in multiple countries and each country needs to be represented in the tree, you can use the OU=Organizational Unit objects to represent the countries below your Organization object. Figure 2-6 illustrates how the ACME company can represent offices in multiple countries using the OU=Organizational Unit object under the O=Organization object. In this example, there is an OU=MX, OU=US, and OU=UK representing Mexico, United States, and the United Kingdom, respectively. The reason for choosing this option instead of the Country object is to eliminate multiple Organization objects in the NDS tree. Most companies should use only one Organization object as discussed later in this chapter.

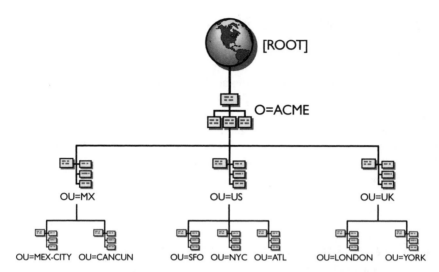

Figure 2-6: The ACME company can represent offices in multiple countries using the OU=Organizational Unit object under the O=Organization object. In this example, there is an OU=MX, OU=US, and OU=UK.

The use of OU=Organizational Units instead of the C=Country object is a cleaner approach because it enables you to have a single O=Organization container at the top of your tree to represent your entire company.

Some companies just simply want to include the C=Country object in their NDS design. Although you can use this object, keep in mind that it will add an additional layer to your NDS tree.

As discussed earlier, if using a C=Country object is absolutely necessary, you may have multiple NDS tree designators for your O=Organization object or company because of multiple countries as shown in Figure 2-7.

Another problem with using the C=Country object is that there is not a single identifier for the company. In the case of O=ACME, this will be a problem when you try to connect to a public data provider. The public data provider wants to have the company in the country where it is incorporated. In the example given above, it is not clear where the company O=ACME is incorporated. The outside user may have a difficult time finding all the network resources that belong to ACME.

Another problem with using the C=Country object is that there is not a single identifier for the company. In the case of O=ACME, this will be a problem when you try to connect to a public data provider. The public data provider wants to have the company in the country where it is incorporated. In the example given above, it is not clear where the company O=ACME is incorporated. The outside user may have a difficult time finding all the network resources that belong to ACME.

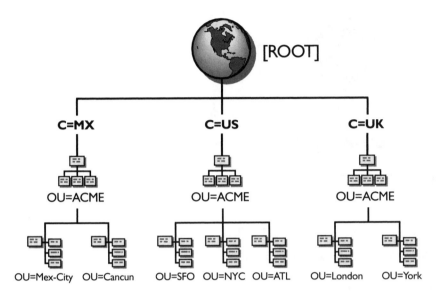

Figure 2-7: An example of using C=Country objects in the NDS design and
Organization objects

# Naming the O=Organization for Your Company

After placing the [ROOT] object at the top of the tree (and assuming you are not using the C=Country object), you will provide the NDS tree with at least one O=Organization object. At least one O=Organization object is required for all NDS trees. Subsequent layers in the tree – the OU=Organizational Units – will be placed directly below the O=Organization object.

## Using One Organization Object

We recommend that you name the O=Organization the same name as your company name or use an abbreviation of the company name. Most companies use an abbreviation for the company name because it is easier to type when setting a context, for example. For example, our company is the abbreviated ACME, which stands for A Consolidated Manufacturing Enterprise. The abbreviation of ACME is much easier to type than its full name. In almost every case, the O=Organization layer in the tree contains only one O=Organization object, which gives you a single object to represent the entire company. Figure 2-8 shows how we have named our organization to represent our company name.

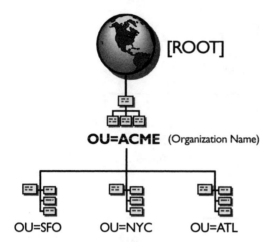

**OU=SFO**     **OU=NYC**     **OU=ATL**

Figure 2-8: The O=Organization is named ACME
(A Consolidated Manufacturing Enterprise), which
represents the entire company.

## Using More Than One Organization Object

Your company may want to use more than one O=Organization object if your corporation has multiple companies that do not share the same network infrastructure.
You may also want to use more than one O=Organization if you need to represent
separate business units or organizations. For example, the large conglomerate illustrated in Figure 2-9 uses multiple O=Organization objects because there are two
separate companies included under a single NDS tree.

In addition, other factors may influence you to use multiple organizations, such
as company policies or other internal guidelines. However, most companies will
use a single O=Organization because they want to represent all resources under the
same organization.

A single NDS tree with two or more O=Organization objects is rarely used
because the main design goal discussed in Chapter 1 is to represent the
entire corporation in a single tree with the same organization name.

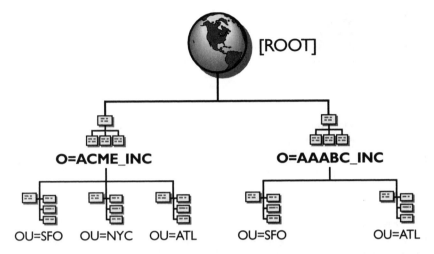

Figure 2-9: A large conglomerate company with multiple O=Organization objects. Each O=Organization represents a different network infrastructure or major business unit.

# Determining Your Company's Network Infrastructure

After you have completed the previous steps of naming the [ROOT] and O=Organization objects you are ready to design the next layer of the NDS tree, the OU=Organizational Units. This layer of OUs should be based on your physical network infrastructure. So the next design rule is to define the type of network infrastructure installed at your company.

The following sections will help you define the various types of networks that are in use. In some cases your network may consist of a combination of several of the network types. For the most part, there are only a few network infrastructures and a combination of them. They can be defined as follows:

- ◆ Local Area Network (LAN)

- ◆ Campus or Metropolitan Area Network (MAN)

- ◆ Hub and Spoke Network

- ◆ Meshed Network

## LAN-Based Network

Figure 2-10 illustrates a simple example of a local area network infrastructure. The LAN network has three segments connected by either a bridge or router.

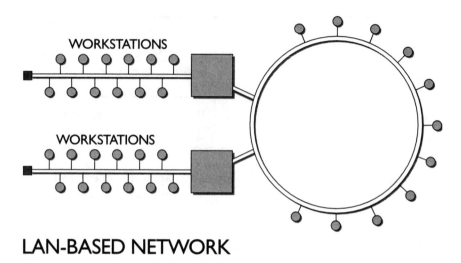

## LAN-BASED NETWORK

Figure 2-10: An example of a local area network (LAN) infrastructure. The LAN has three segments connected by either a bridge or router.

## Campus or MAN Network

Figure 2-11 illustrates a campus or metropolitan area network (MAN) infrastructure. The campus has four sites that are connected by a high-speed campus backbone. The four sites are: Key Road (the headquarters), Beltway Road, Airport Road, and Industrial Parkway. The sites are geographically dispersed buildings.

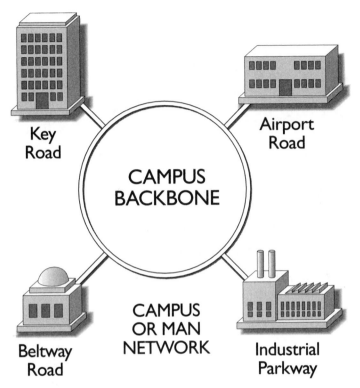

Figure 2-11: An example of a campus or metropolitan area network (MAN) infrastructure. Each of the sites is a separate building in a separate location.

# Hub and Spoke Network

Figure 2-12 illustrates a hub and spoke network infrastructure. The hub and spoke locations are specifically WAN sites that have been connected using common WAN links. In this example, the three major hub sites are: New York City (the main office), Atlanta, and San Francisco. In addition, the San Francisco hub has spokes that connect several other sites. These additional sites are: Los Angeles, San Jose, Seattle, and Salt Lake City.

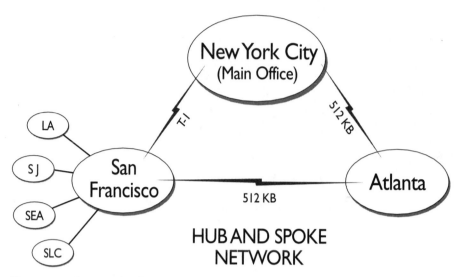

Figure 2-12: An example of a hub and spoke network infrastructure

## Meshed Network

Figure 2-13 illustrates a meshed network infrastructure that adds redundancy between each of the major WAN locations. Each physical site has been connected using WAN links. In this example, several major hub sites have multiple WAN links connecting them. In addition, there are several more spokes (WAN locations) that have only one connection to the main meshed network.

If your company has a small network infrastructure, it probably meets one of the network categories described above. However, each of the different types of network infrastructures can be part of a larger network. For example, most of the larger networks are just combinations of the different network types working together to provide a complete infrastructure solution.

In order to properly represent the network infrastructure in the NDS tree, you must determine which network type or types you have currently implemented at your company.

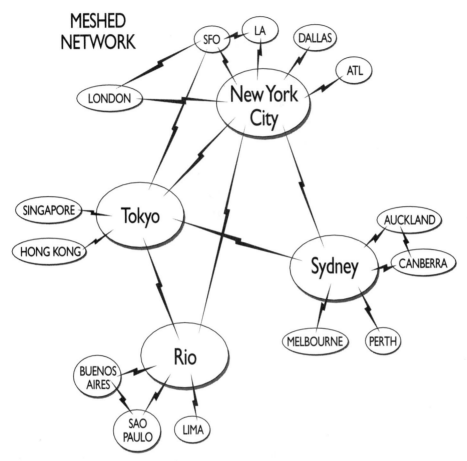

Figure 2-13: An example of a meshed network infrastructure

# Using the First Level of OU=Organizational Units to Represent the Network

The last design rule for the top of the NDS tree is the most significant. You should represent your network infrastructure in the top of the tree. This means that you use the first level of OU=Organizational Units to define the LAN or WAN locations depending on your infrastructure. These OU=Organizational Units will be created immediately below the O=Organization as shown in Figure 2-14.

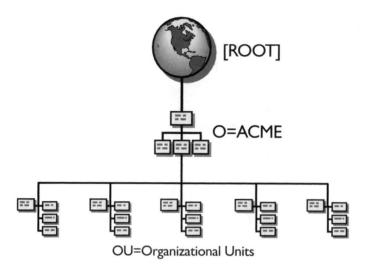
[ROOT]

O=ACME

OU=Organizational Units

Figure 2-14: The first layer of organizational units is based on the
network infrastructure. These OUs are created immediately below the
O=Organization in the NDS tree.

Because the network infrastructure is the most important design consideration
in developing the top layers of the NDS tree, a complete understanding of your
network's physical structure is crucial. You need to start with your physical network maps in creating a design that provides the greatest efficiency and flexibility.

If you do not have current physical network maps or documentation for your
company, you must try to obtain them. It is extremely difficult to create a good
design for the top of the tree if you do not have the proper documentation. If you
have a LAN-only network, you most likely do not have this type of documentation and can design your tree based on your LAN topology as discussed later in
this chapter.

The corporate documentation required are the LAN maps, the campus or MAN
layouts (if any), and most importantly, the WAN maps if your network type war-
rants them. Each of these network diagrams should include the speed of the links
between each WAN location or site. A list of the locations or sites in the physical
infrastructure should accompany the physical network maps.

Using this information, you can easily represent the physical network infrastructure, such as the WAN, in the top of the tree. Figure 2-15 shows how we are
taking the information from the WAN diagrams (network infrastructure) and
designing the top of the tree. You should begin by representing each of the physical network locations as OUs. In the example below, the ACME hub and spoke network is represented by the first level of OU=Organizational Units. The hub and
spoke network depicted is a simple WAN network with only three hubs (San
Francisco, New York City, and Atlanta) and no spokes. Each of the hubs on the
WAN will become OUs in the NDS tree.

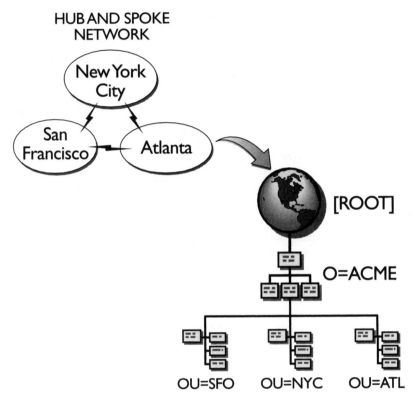

Figure 2-15: Use the first level of OU=Organizational Units to represent the ACME hub and spoke network locations. This example depicts a simple WAN network with only three hubs (San Francisco, New York City, Atlanta) and no spokes. Each of the hubs on the WAN will become OUs in the NDS tree.

# Designing NDS for Each Type of Network Infrastructure

Whether your network infrastructure is a LAN or a WAN, the top of the tree design should represent this infrastructure. Typically, a WAN connects the individual sites or locations of your company. These sites or locations will become the first layers of containers or OUs in your NDS tree.

For some network infrastructures the design may need to represent only a LAN and thus will constitute few peer OUs. Other installations may need to represent WANs, which require more design and attention to the physical network. In all cases, the network infrastructure should be the first and only design consideration when developing the top layers of the NDS tree.

Each of the different network types will be discussed here with examples to help you identify the best design solution for each environment. If your network infra-structure is a combination of several different network types, you can take ideas from each of the examples and build an NDS tree that meets your specific needs. Your NDS design may not match up exactly with the examples, but you can still follow the guidelines outlined below.

The first and most simple type of network is the LAN. By definition a LAN is a grouping of workstations and servers through a common network system without the use of a WAN. This type of network is used by small companies and typically consists of 5 to 250 users with one or more file servers and no interconnections between sites. A company may have multiple LANs in place that function as islands that do not share information. Figure 2-16 shows an example of a LAN system using both the ethernet and token ring topologies.

## LAN-BASED NETWORK

Figure 2-16: An example of a LAN network that utilizes ethernet and token ring topologies

## LAN-ONLY NETWORK RESOURCES
Because LAN-based networks with a single site network are not dependent upon the geographic locations, the design for these networks will not include physical locations. Thus, the first layer of OU=Organizational Units will not represent the locations but rather the departments, divisions, and workgroups of your company.

Using the departments, divisions, and workgroups as the first layer of OUs will help you quickly represent the network resources in the LAN. Some companies with just a few servers and users may not even need to create OU=Organization Unit containers at all. Rather, they can place all the network resources (NDS objects) under the single O=Organization. You must determine if it makes sense to have multiple containers for a small company. In most cases, small companies can place all the users, servers, and printers in the same container.

Figure 2-17 shows how an NDS tree design can be very simple for a small company. If ACME had only a few servers in a single location, their tree could appear as shown. You may still want to subdivide the tree a little if you have a need for separate groups. Usually this need is based on assigning users different rights or using different login scripts.

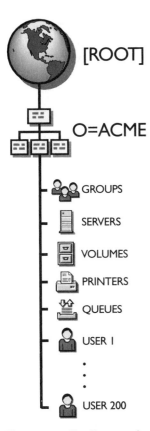

Figure 2-17: Small companies can group all their network resources in a single O=Organization container if they have a small LAN and a single network administrator managing all resources.

This type of network will typically have limited corporate or network documentation. Because there is no WAN network to incorporate in your design at the top of the tree, the LAN-based design can use virtually any type of design that suits the administrator's needs. In many cases the tree design for a LAN-only network can be finished very easily and work extremely well because most servers, users, and other resources can be placed in the single O=Organization container without creating any more containers. If you are the network manager responsible for all users, printers, and servers, you can simply group everyone in the same O=Organization container.

Again, this type of tree design is easy and works well for a network with a single server or a couple of servers. As the number of servers grows, the demands of the users grow. This may mean that the users want access to departmental resources and have different access rights to each server. The basic design, then, could consist of a [ROOT] object, O=Organization, and possibly a few department organizational units below the Organization object.

Figure 2-18 shows an example of an NDS tree design with a single LAN using a few organizational units defined as departments within the company. The reason for creating these additional containers would be to define separate container login scripts or to have separate administrators manage each organizational unit.

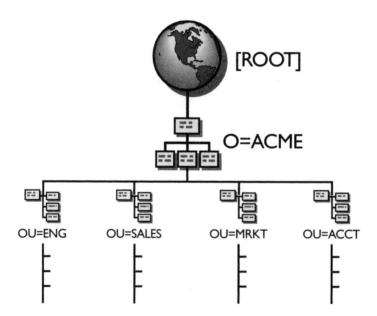

Figure 2-18: The NDS tree design for a single LAN uses organizational units to define some departments for user access or for administrative purposes.

---

## LAN–Only Network Design Guidelines (Top of the Tree)

The following guidelines will help you design a LAN-only network:

1. Name the [ROOT] of your tree based on your company's abbreviated name plus the TREE, such as ACME_TREE. If you use the simple installation method, the tree name is the same name you give the Organization object during installation.

2. Name the O=Organization using the name of your company's abbreviated name, such as O=ACME.

3. Decide whether you need additional containers defined under the O=Organization to provide departmental access for the user or to separate administrative roles.

4. Place all the network resources in the NDS tree design. Make sure there is a place for all the users, groups, NT Domain objects, servers, printers, queues, and other network resources.

---

# Campus or Metropolitan Area Network

The campus or metropolitan area network (MAN) can be defined as a group of LANs and their network resources combined on a high-speed backbone such as 16MB Token Ring, FDDI, or 100baseT. A campus is usually a group of geographically close buildings that do not employ the use of a WAN. An example of a campus network depicting the ACME corporation is shown in Figure 2-19. In this example there are four buildings in the campus or MAN network: Key Road (headquarters), Beltway Road, Airport Road, and Industrial Parkway.

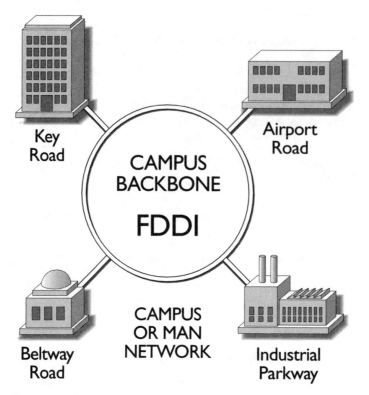

Figure 2-19: An example of a campus network depicting a corporation
that includes multiple buildings geographically close and connected by
a fiber (FDDI) campus backbone

When designing a campus network layout, such as a research park or university, consider first the speed of the links between the buildings of the campus network. The locations in the campus network, such as the buildings, can be used to
represent minor sites in the network infrastructure and in the NDS tree. The buildings in the campus network can be useful container objects if they help organize
your network resources and the NDS tree. The ability to effectively organize network resources is one of your design goals. Figure 2-20 illustrates how the NDS
tree representing the campus or MAN network for ACME may be designed. Each
of the locations in the campus network becomes organizational units immediately
under O=ACME.

Another example using the same campus or MAN network for ACME is to use names that represent the functional assignments of each building in the network instead of the geographic assignments. This means that each of the physical locations or sites will have a functional name as opposed to the name of the building or road. For example, let's assume that each building in the campus also has a specific functional assignment. The building or location of Key Road is functionally the headquarters for ACME. In addition, Beltway Road houses the Accounting Services department. Airport Road performs Marketing and Sales functions, while Industrial Parkway is Engineering and Manufacturing.

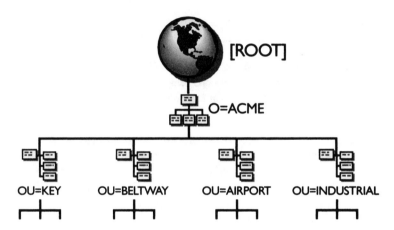

Figure 2-20: The NDS tree design representing the campus or MAN network for ACME

Thus, the functional designators or assignments for each of the physical locations or sites in the campus are as follows:

◆ KEY ROAD – HQ (headquarters)

◆ BELTWAY ROAD – AS (Accounting Services)

◆ AIRPORT ROAD – MS (Marketing and Sales)

◆ INDUSTRIAL PARKWAY – EM (Engineering and Manufacturing)

Figure 2-21 illustrates how the NDS tree design would appear representing the functional designators instead of using building names for ACME. Each of the physical locations in the campus network has been given specific functional names that become organizational units under the O=ACME.

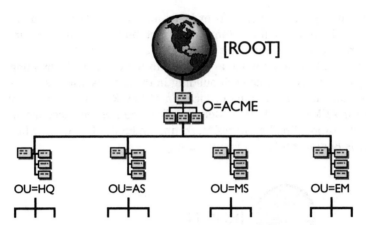

Figure 2-21: The NDS tree design representing the campus or MAN network for ACME. The first layer of organizational units uses the functional names for each site instead of the physical location name.

Although it looks as if the OUs under O=ACME are departments and that the entire tree is based on organization instead of location or geography, this is not the case. Actually, each of the OU containers represents physical locations or sites on the campus or MAN network, even though each container is named functionally. The names just happen to be organizational names. Using department names to represent a physical site on the network is acceptable as long as the department name does not include network resources from other locations. Remember, effectively organizing network resources is the primary design goal of NDS. This goal has been met.

Many companies choose to use geographic containers even though they have very high speed links in their campus or MAN networks. A particular company for which we did consulting had a MAN running FDDI connecting 12 buildings together across a large metropolitan area. This company based their decision to use geographic sites at the top of the tree on the following criteria:

♦ For administrative purposes, the company wanted each site to be supported by a single administrator. The sites gave the tree a good place to break out security and network administration.

♦ The company was installing an e-mail application on their servers at each geographic location. The geographic tree design was the best way to organize and place the e-mail servers, which were geographically based.

So, even though a company has high speed links between separate locations, it may choose to design the NDS tree using the geographic sites.

## REPRESENTING THE NETWORK INFRASTRUCTURE
## IN THE NDS TREE FOR A UNIVERSITY

Another example of the campus type network is a university that has buildings connected together via a fiber backbone. As shown in Figure 2-22, this university has eight major buildings in the campus network represented as organizational units in the tree.

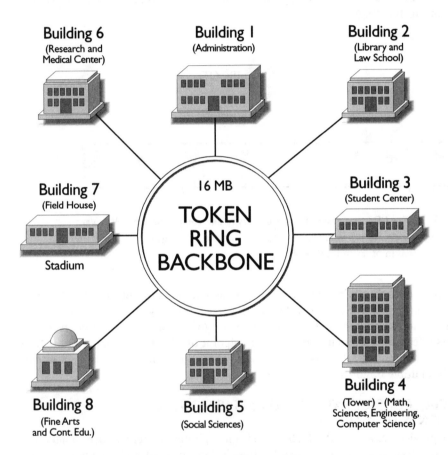

Figure 2-22: A university has eight major buildings on its campus network that are represented as organizational units in the tree.

Figure 2-23 depicts the best NDS tree design that would represent the network infrastructure of the campus network. Although the university has a high-speed backbone that appears to favor an organizational design approach, we still use the geographic approach of separating the university by its buildings. The reason we want to separate the network infrastructure by its building, even though there is a high-speed backbone, is to localize NDS traffic. This localization of the NDS traffic based on buildings can be accomplished more easily by dividing the NDS tree into locations or buildings.

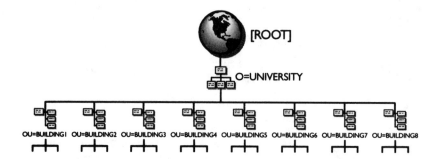

**Figure 2-23: The NDS tree design for the university and campus network. We want to design the network infrastructure by representing the buildings of the university as separate OUs in order to localize NDS traffic.**

Several of the buildings contain multiple departments or colleges. For this reason, it is not a good idea to divide the NDS tree according to departments or colleges within the university. If the NDS tree design is based on departments, it will be less effective and efficient from the standpoint of NDS traffic. Dividing the NDS tree according to departments within a university could put one department or college in multiple buildings or locations.

## SPECIAL CONSIDERATIONS FOR REPRESENTING STUDENTS OF A UNIVERSITY

In the previous example, the NDS tree design supports the general user population for a university work force. However, this design does not address students who want access to the network. If the university needs to provide network access to students, you can build special OU containers directly below the O=Organization (or university) to accommodate the mass of the student body. Figure 2-24 illustrates how the student body of a university would be represented in the NDS tree.

This type of NDS design provides a special OU container, plus subordinate containers for the placement of individual students according to their last names. Having a separate container to manage the student body enables the administrators to make large changes more effectively even if there are thousands of students.

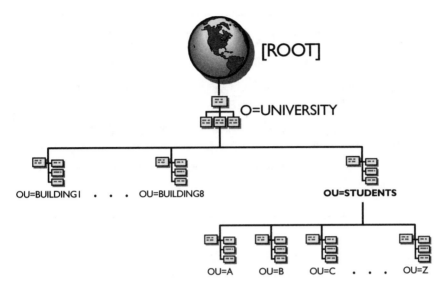

Figure 2-24: The individual students of a university should be placed in a special OU container directly below the O=UNIVERSITY container.

The special OU=STUDENTS container can and definitely should be subdivided A through Z or by using some other logical indicator. For example, the students could be divided according to the department or college in which they are registered or according to the individual classes they are taking. Figure 2-25 illustrates how the OU=STU-DENTS container can be subdivided according to the departments in the colleges.

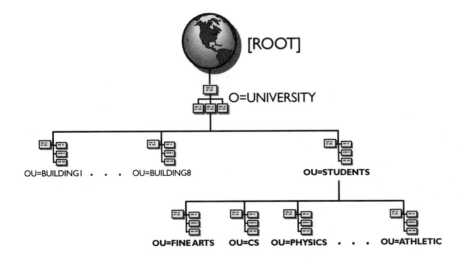

Figure 2-25: The OU=STUDENTS container should be subdivided according to the departments in the colleges.

---

### Campus or MAN Network Design Guidelines

The following guidelines will help you design a campus or MAN network:

1. Name the [ROOT] of your tree based on your company's abbreviated name plus the _TREE, such as ACME_TREE.

2. Name the O=Organization using your company's abbreviated name, such as O=ACME or O=UNIVERSITY.

3. Use your building or location names as the first level of organizational units in the top portion of the tree.

---

Access to the servers and network resources throughout the campus network is not affected, since the users can access information from any server anywhere in the network.

# Hub and Spoke Network Design

The most common WAN configuration is the hub and spoke network in which several different geographic locations are connected by various link speeds. In general, each of the geographic sites or locations connected by the hub and spoke should be represented in the top layers of the NDS tree as a container or OU named for the location. The organizational structure (departments, divisions, and workgroups) for each location will become the subtree structure under each of these locations.

### TOP OF THE TREE BASED ON HUBS ONLY

Figure 2-26 illustrates a basic hub network with WAN connections or links between each of the geographic locations. In this example, there are only three locations or hubs in the ACME company: New York City (NYC), San Francisco (SFO), and Atlanta (ATL).

Using this physical network map, you can properly design the top of the NDS tree for the ACME company. In this case, the three hubs or locations on the WAN need to be represented in the NDS design. Figure 2-27 shows how the top layer of containers directly beneath the O=ACME will match each of the WAN locations. In this case, OU=NYC, OU=SFO, and OU=ATL. It is convenient to name the hub locations with short descriptive names.

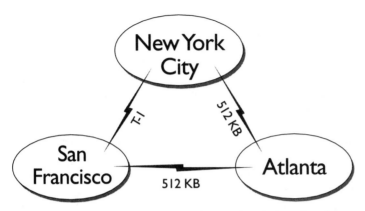

Figure 2-26: Basic WAN layout for ACME with three hubs or locations:
New York City (NYC), San Francisco (SFO), and Atlanta (ATL)

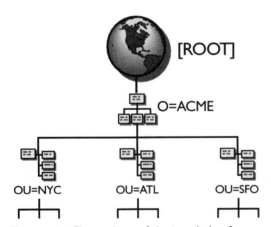

Figure 2-27: The top layer of the tree design for
ACME is based on the physical or geographical WAN
sites. The containers are OU=NYC, OU=SFO, and OU=ATL.

Keep in mind that our primary design goals for the NDS tree are to organize and represent the network resources and to design a flexible tree where changes are easily made. These two goals can be accomplished through this design because the NDS tree provides you the proper structure to adequately organize the network resources geographically. This is correct because the physical resources have already been organized geographically.

The top of the tree depicting the WAN locations becomes the foundation for the rest of the tree and will not change frequently. This foundation is required in order to provide flexibility at the lower layers. The flexibility of the design is achieved under each of the location containers where the departments, divisions, and workgroups can be defined and easily adjusted to reflect corporate changes. Changes to the lower layers of the tree will not affect the top of the tree, which again provides stability to the overall tree design.

## TOP OF THE TREE BASED ON BOTH HUBS AND CAMPUS SPOKES

Another example of a hub and spoke network design is illustrated in Figure 2-28, in which there are three major hubs: NYC, SFO, and ATL. The Atlanta (ATL) hub, however, has spokes to the physical sites within a metropolitan area network (MAN). The WAN connections or links between each of the major hubs are established with additional connections to the individual sites on the MAN. The site names on the MAN are specifically: Airport Road, Key Road, Industrial Parkway, and Beltway Road.

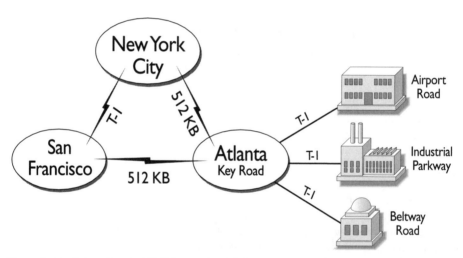

Figure 2-28: Hub and spoke WAN layout for ACME with locations New York City (NYC), San Francisco (SFO), and Atlanta (ATL). In addition, there are sites within the Atlanta (ATL) area called Airport Road, Key Road, Industrial Parkway, and Beltway Road.

In order to properly design the top of the NDS tree for ACME, you need to use the physical network map, which includes the metropolitan area network for Atlanta. In this case, three hubs or locations on the WAN need to be represented first in the NDS design. However, the Atlanta (ATL) location is not a single hub; instead it is a MAN. So in the case of Atlanta, you need to first represent the WAN connection to the Atlanta hub (OU=ATL) and then the individual spokes of the metropolitan area network.

Figure 2-29 shows how the top containers in the NDS tree match each of the WAN locations, including the MAN sites for Atlanta. In this case, OU=NYC, OU=SFO, and OU=ATL are the major hubs. Beneath OU=ATL are the MAN sites of OU=KEY, OU=AIRPORT, OU=BELTWAY, and OU=INDUSTRIAL, which represent the spokes from the major hub.

Notice in this example that each MAN site is assigned the name of the road or street address of the building. This naming convention may not be convenient to all users and administrators. We recommend that you establish the naming conventions for each NDS object before you finalize the NDS design as discussed in Chapter 6. Also, notice that each of the sites in the MAN is a physical location with a WAN link connecting it to the infrastructure.

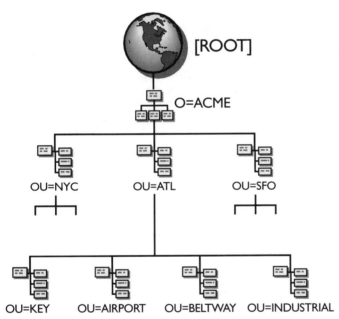

Figure 2-29: The top layer of the tree design for ACME is based on the physical or geographical WAN sites.

In some cases, the campus portion of a network is part of a larger network infrastructure. You may have a combination of a campus network at the corporate offices and a hub and spoke network supporting the rest of the company across the country or around the world. An example of a network that uses a combination of a campus and a hub and spoke is shown in Figure 2-30.

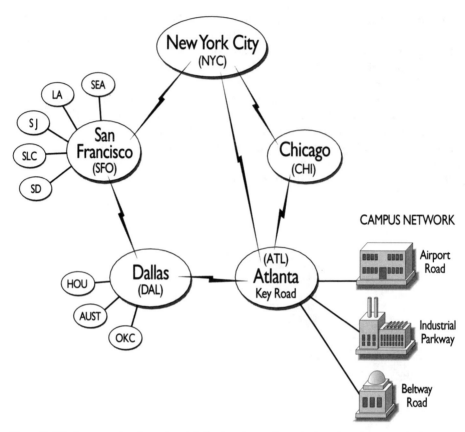

Figure 2-30: An example of a network infrastructure using a hub and spoke network that includes a campus network at one of the hubs

## TREE DESIGN BASED ON HUBS AND SPOKES TO CONNECT OTHER CITIES

Using the previous example, the hub and spoke network infrastructure includes spokes that connect cities from some of the hubs with a campus network at another hub. This WAN layout is illustrated in Figure 2-30, where major hubs (NYC, SFO, DAL, ATL, and CHI) are connected. Notice how the San Francisco and Dallas hubs spoke or connect directly to other cities. A WAN connection or link between the San Francisco and Dallas hubs and the other cities represents remote sales offices. The names of the sales offices that are connected specifically to San Francisco (SFO) are as follows: Los Angeles (LAX), San Diego (SD), San Jose (SJ), Seattle (SEA), and Salt Lake City (SLC). In addition, the sales offices that are connected to Dallas (DAL) are: Houston (HOU), Austin (AUS), and Oklahoma City (OKC). The Atlanta hub is a campus network.

The design of the top of the NDS tree for ACME will represent the hub and spoke network map, which includes the sales offices attached to the San Francisco, Atlanta, and Dallas hubs. In this case, there are a total of five major hubs on the WAN plus the individual sales offices.

The natural impulse in designing the NDS tree is to first represent the major hubs and then move down in the tree to include the remote sales offices beneath their appropriate hub. If we designed the NDS tree based strictly in this way, we may have a design that does not logically make sense as illustrated in Figure 2-31. For example, the distinguished name for a user in the Los Angeles sales office would be:

```
USER.LAX.SFO.ACME
```

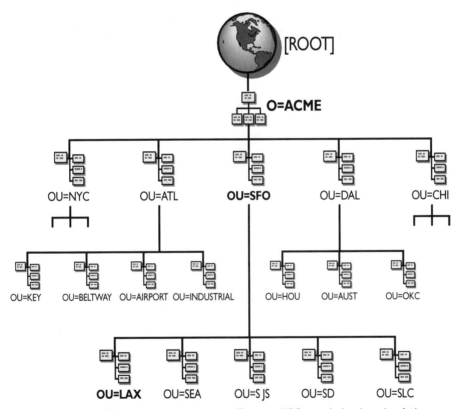

Figure 2-31: If the NDS tree has remote sales offices, an NDS tree design based strictly on network infrastructure connections may not make logical sense.

To resolve this situation, you should use placeholder (or super set) containers that will help distribute the peer locations under one single container. This means that the hub sites and sales offices will be placed at the same layer. In Figure 2-32 the SFO and DAL hubs have been placed beneath their appropriate placeholder containers. The place holders are OU=WEST and OU=SOUTH. These place holders contain not only the hub sites but the sales offices or cities as well. This type of NDS tree design resolves the distinguished name conflict for the users. The user in the Los Angeles sales office would now have a distinguished name of:

USER.LAX.WEST.ACME

Remember that the Atlanta (ATL) location is not a single hub; instead it is a MAN. So in the case of the Atlanta hub, the individual campus or MAN locations are placed beneath the OU=ATL designator. OU=ATL is really just a placeholder container that identifies the logical placement in the tree of the campus network. Beneath OU=ATL is the representation of the campus or MAN network, which consists of OU=KEY, OU=AIRPORT, OU=BELTWAY, and OU=INDUSTRIAL.

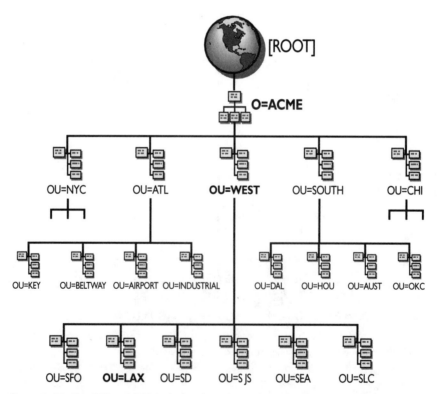

**Figure 2-32:** The SFO and DAL hub sites have been placed beneath their appropriate placeholder containers.

## USING PLACEHOLDER CONTAINERS OR REGIONAL CONTAINERS TO HELP DISTRIBUTE PHYSICAL LOCATIONS

In some cases, it will be necessary to use place holders or regional containers directly below the O=Organization in the NDS tree to more fully distribute the total number of locations or geographic sites. Using place holder or regional OUs under the O=Organization but before the actual location OUs will increase NDS operating efficiency (in terms of subordinate reference distribution) and give the tree a shape closer to pyramid.

As an example, consider the case company ACME as we change the WAN layout to include more offices or cities around the world. Figure 2-33 illustrates both the regional hubs and the offices or cities that are connected via WAN links. Each of the cities added to the WAN layout is connected to its appropriate regional hub. The major hubs in each region are: New York City (NYC), Rio de Janeiro (RIO), London (LON), and Tokyo (TOK).

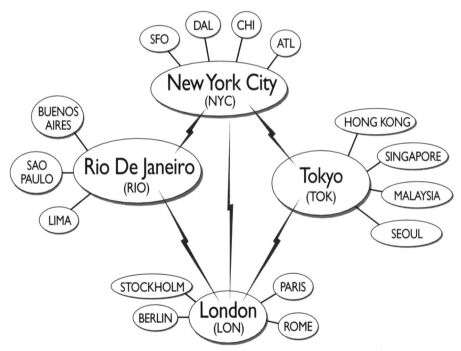

Figure 2-33: The network infrastructure for ACME with regional hubs and cities throughout the world

Using the WAN infrastructure diagram, the NDS tree can be designed using regional place holders. The regional place holder helps to properly distribute NDS traffic and makes the NDS design more efficient. Figure 2-34 depicts the tree design, which includes the regional OUs named North America (NA), South America (SA), Europe (EUR), and Asia (ASIA). These regional OUs are the place holders that group the appropriate cities together and help keep the NDS tree design closer to the pyramid shape.

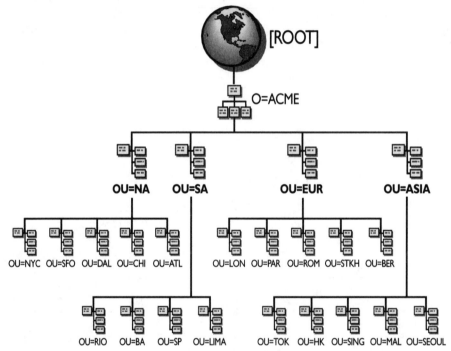

Figure 2–34: The NDS tree design contains the regional OUs: North America (NA), South America (SA), Europe (EUR), and Asia (ASIA).

## USING REGIONAL CONTAINERS TO HELP DISTRIBUTE REMOTE OR BRANCH OFFICES

You can use the same principle of regional containers or placeholder containers to help you distribute a lot of remote offices or branch offices on the network. These offices are also commonly called field offices because they are remotely located from the headquarters of the company.

The remote or branch offices typically are smaller offices with fewer users. For example, a branch office may have 5 to 100 users. The office may belong to only one department or several departments. A company that is organized with several large hubs or headquarters and a large number of sales offices should place those offices in specific containers to help distribute them. Figure 2-35 illustrates how ACME could design their NDS tree to accommodate many field offices by creating special containers just for the field offices. In this case, the field office containers are the regional containers OU=WEST, OU=EAST, and OU=SOUTH.

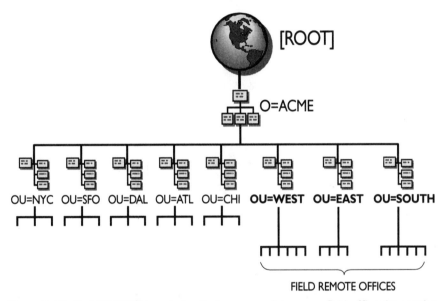

Figure 2-35: An ACME NDS tree design that accommodates many field offices by creating special containers just for the field offices

## DESIGNING FOR BANKS AND SIMILAR COMPANIES

Another example is a bank institution with many remote or branch offices. A successful NDS tree design for a bank would follow the guidelines previously discussed of grouping the remote sites according to their geographic location or region. Figure 2-36 and Figure 2-37 illustrate how the top layer of the ACME tree can be designed if there is a large number of remote or branch offices. Figure 2-36 illustrates the physical WAN layout for ACME (which could be a bank), and Figure 2-37 applies the NDS design principles for the top of the tree to represent each physical site beneath regional place holders.

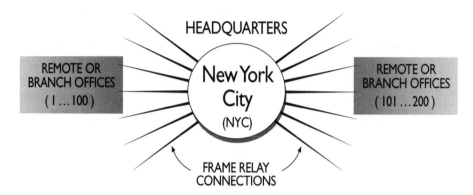

*All remote or branch offices are located within
the 48 contiguous states.

Figure 2-36: Physical WAN layout for ACME, which could be a bank with hundreds of remote or branch offices

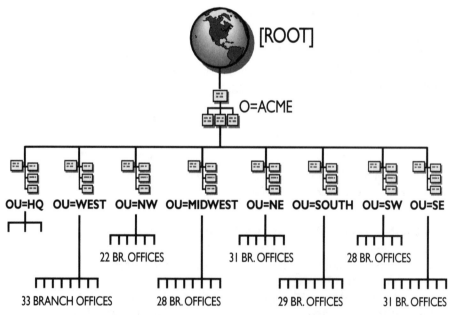

Figure 2-37: The NDS tree design for ACME uses the regional containers to distribute the 200 branch offices or geographic WAN sites.

Another possible NDS tree design that would meet the needs of the network infrastructure is illustrated in Figure 2-38. This solution uses an OU=STATE designator for each of the states that have branch offices. It is unlikely that all states will have a branch office for ACME. You must decide which NDS design works best for your particular circumstances.

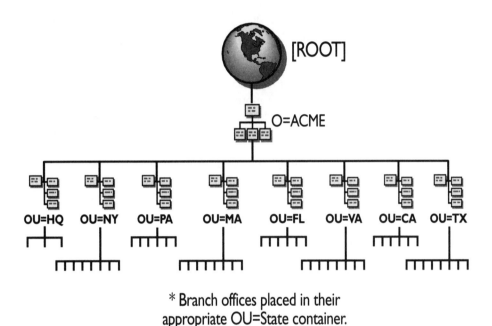

\* Branch offices placed in their
appropriate OU=State container.

Figure 2-38: The NDS tree design for ACME uses OU=STATE containers as the place holders to distribute the 200 branch offices or geographic WAN sites.

## MAXIMUM NUMBER OF SUBORDINATE CONTAINERS

There is a specific guideline for the number of OUs or containers that can exist beneath any one single parent OU. We are assuming that the subordinate OUs or containers that exist in the top of the tree will be created as partitions. The following rules apply to the number of subordinate containers:

1. Always try to have fewer than 10 to 15 subordinate OUs under any single OU in the tree. The fewer subordinate OUs that will become partitions the better.

2. If your NDS tree design absolutely dictates that you need more than 10 to 15 subordinate OUs, never go beyond 35 to 40. See Chapters 4 and 5 for more details.

3. If you exceed 15 subordinate OUs, you must understand the impact or ramifications of a higher number of OUs as explained in Chapters 4 and 5.

Although the current utilities do not enforce a strict rule for the number of subordinate containers, we have found that companies following these guidelines have implemented NDS trees that perform more efficiently. Most companies can maintain the most efficient NDS synchronization if they stay at or below the 10 to 15 subordinate OU range. However, for exceptionally large companies with thousands of fields and remote or branch offices, you may have no choice but to exceed this recommendation. But, you should first try to insert layers of regional organizational units to distribute the subordinate branch offices among those containers. Figure 2-39 illustrates how the number of subordinate containers may look in an NDS tree design.

Most companies will be able to work within the guideline of 10 to 15 subordinate OUs regardless of their size. If you need to exceed this number, you must pay special attention to partitioning and replication guidelines as presented in the later chapters.

# Meshed Network Design

A meshed network is similar to the hub and spoke design; however, the WAN infrastructure is built with more redundancy between the individual WAN sites. This configuration is a specialized WAN with multiple links to each of the locations or hubs in the network. If each of the locations on the network has redundant links to other sites, then essentially there would be no spokes. This means that each WAN site effectively becomes a hub that is simply connected to the other hubs using several WAN links. Figure 2-40 depicts a meshed network infrastructure for the ACME tree.

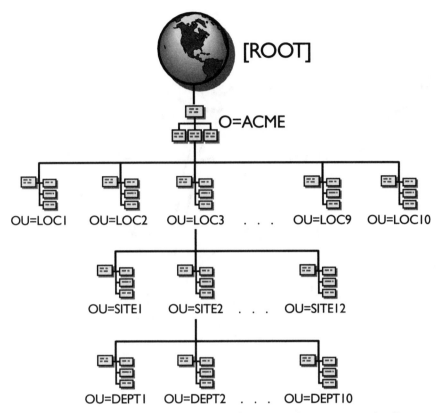

Figure 2-39: The NDS tree design should maintain no more than 10 to 15 subordinate organizational units beneath any single OU in the tree. Beyond this number you should consider adding additional layers in your tree to distribute the subordinate containers.

The important point to remember when designing the NDS tree based on a meshed network layout is that the meshed network is still trying to represent the physical WAN locations or sites. That is the whole purpose of the meshed WAN network, to make the physical locations or sites more important, not less. Some individuals believe that since the network is meshed, the individual WAN sites become less important in an NDS design. In reality, the opposite is actually true.

With the WAN locations being represented in the meshed network, the NDS tree design can be quite simple. As illustrated in Figure 2-41, each of the geographic sites or locations on the meshed WAN is connected by redundant hub and spoke links and should be represented as OUs in the top layers of the NDS tree. Each of the containers should be named for the location. The organizational structure (departments, divisions, and workgroups) for each location will become the subtree structure under each of these locations.

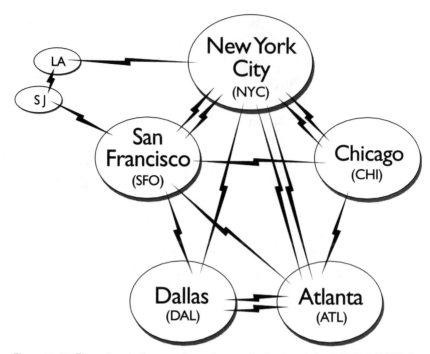

Figure 2-40: The network diagram shown is a meshed network for ACME. A WAN that has been built with redundancy in the links between specific locations or sites is commonly referred to as a meshed network.

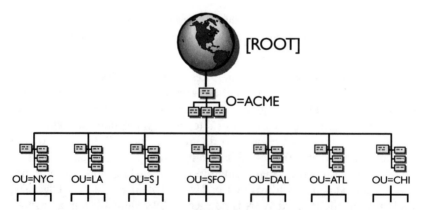

Figure 2-41: Each of the geographic sites or locations on the meshed WAN are connected by redundant hub and spoke links and should be represented as OUs in the top layers of the NDS tree.

If your company has many locations or sites within the meshed WAN infrastructure, you will need to create regional containers to distribute the individual sites. For example, Figure 2-42 shows a larger meshed network with more physical locations throughout the world. Figure 2-43 shows an NDS tree design driven by the information in the meshed network diagram.

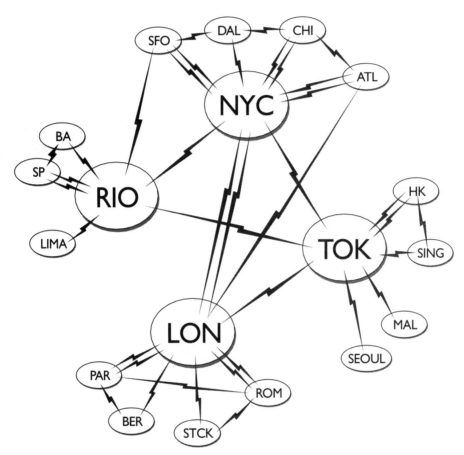

Figure 2-42: A larger meshed network for ACME with more physical locations throughout the world

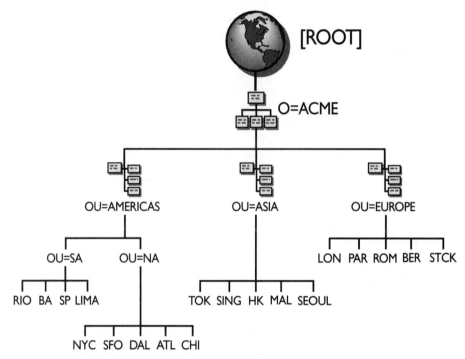

Figure 2-43: An NDS tree design driven by the information in the meshed network diagram

Once you have a design that meets your needs for the top level of the tree, you can move to designing the bottom levels of the tree. Then you can begin the installation or migration to NetWare 4. Keep in mind that while you can always make changes to your tree later, a properly designed tree will almost never need significant changes, and ongoing changes will occur mostly at the bottom of your tree. Modifications may be necessary at some point to meet the needs of your changing organization.

# Chapter 3

# Design the Bottom of the Tree to Represent Network Resources

## IN THIS CHAPTER

- ◆ Designing the bottom of the NDS tree
- ◆ Creating containers at the bottom of the tree
- ◆ Determining the depth of the NDS tree
- ◆ Creating common resource containers
- ◆ Determining your design criteria

AFTER COMPLETING THE DESIGN of the top of the tree based around the network infrastructure, you are ready to start the bottom levels of the NDS design. The bottom of the tree is designed around your LAN using your company's organizational charts or similar documents. If your network infrastructure is LAN only with no WAN, you may not have any network documents to assist you in designing your tree. In that case you should still use the information presented in this chapter to design your tree in the absence of a WAN infrastructure and the other documentation.

# Designing the Bottom of the Tree to Represent Your Company's Organizational Units

All NDS trees regardless of their design must utilize the information presented in this chapter for maximum efficiency of NDS. Figure 3-1 shows an example of a LAN-only tree that has a few departments created for a small NDS tree. In addition to the O=Organization object, another level was created to allow for separate login scripts for each of the two departments.

83

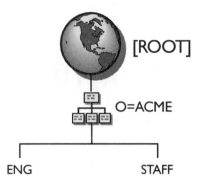

Figure 3-1: A LAN-only NDS tree design
utilizes the bottom of the tree design
information presented in this chapter.

For larger networks such as those utilizing the campus, hub and spoke, or mesh network topologies, the bottom of the tree consists of the remaining levels of OU=Organizational Units based on your company's departments or workgroups. Your company's organizational charts are useful in determining the OU=Organizational Units that need to be defined in your tree. As shown in Figure 3-2 many NDS designs will identify a level of organizational units in the bottom half of the tree to represent the departments or workgroups found on the company's organizational charts.

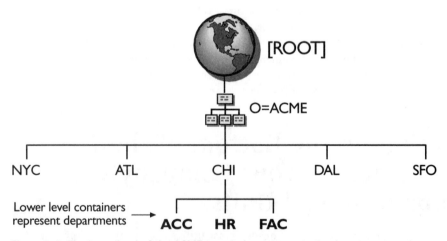

Figure 3-2: The lower level of the ACME tree design represents the departments and workgroups.

The tree design in Figure 3-3 consists of two layers of OU=Organizational Units in the OU=ATL container. Multiple layers representing departments may be necessary in some trees to allow for additional security assignments, login scripts, or placement of resources. For example, as shown in this figure you may want to provide separate login scripts for users in the Accounting and Payroll containers, which are both part of the Finance department.

# Creating Containers at the Bottom of the Tree

Because you have flexibility at the bottom of the tree to create many containers, when should a container be created? Should you try to create a container for every division shown on your organization chart? The simplest answer is that a container should be created when you have users, servers, and printers that need to be represented together for common access at a particular site. Therefore, if you have a group of users that shares the same servers and printers you should group them into the same container if possible. Now, sometimes this approach results in neatly separated divisions having their own servers and printers. However, this is not always the case as some departments may share servers and printers. This situation requires further investigation as to whether separate containers should be created for other reasons in addition to grouping users and resources together. These considerations are discussed in the "Design Criteria" section of this chapter.

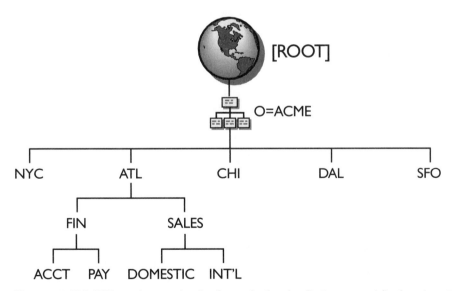

Figure 3-3: This NDS tree has two levels of organizational units to represent its departments.

The following rules can help you determine when to create a container:

1. Create containers for all divisions that have common resources under your geographic locations as shown in Figure 3-4. If there are no separate divisions at a site, do not create an additional organizational unit.

2. Create additional containers in the bottom of the tree as discussed in the "Determine Your Design Criteria" section later in this chapter.

## Determining the Depth of the NDS Tree

Many LAN administrators who design NDS trees are concerned about the depth of the tree and how many levels are appropriate for the best performance. Based on our experience with numerous customer sites, most NDS trees can be designed adequately with four or five levels counting from the O=Organization object downward. These levels would represent the WAN and the LAN with all the network resources.

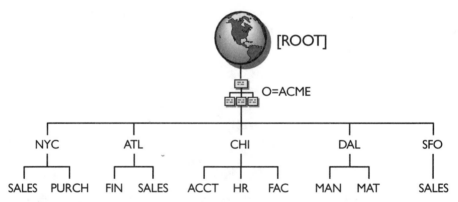

Figure 3-4: Defining a container for each department at each geographic site that has common resources

Some organizations may need more than four or five levels for their NDS trees. For example, some companies with many branch and regional offices will need to design trees with about six levels starting from the O=Organization object downward. If you follow the rules presented in this book, the depth of your tree will not be an issue because the design will reflect the right number of levels based on your network. You will have a tree that is appropriately designed for your environment.

## Consulting Experience

There is an actual limit to the total number of layers in the tree you can access. For instance, NDS has a limit of 256 characters for a distinguished name. Thus, the actual limit for the number of layers is dependent on the number of characters in the names of your objects. If your OU names are long, you will not be able to have as many layers. We recommend that you assign short, descriptive names to the OUs in your tree.

An NDS tree can be properly designed for a network of any size. The tree in Figure 3-5 has four levels and represents an NDS tree that is for a medium-sized company. The top of the tree follows the hub and spoke WAN, and the bottom of the tree represents the company's departments. No additional levels are required to sufficiently represent the WAN and the LAN in this tree. Notice also that not all locations have the same levels of OU=Organizational Units. It is not necessary for the tree to have the same depth across all containers.

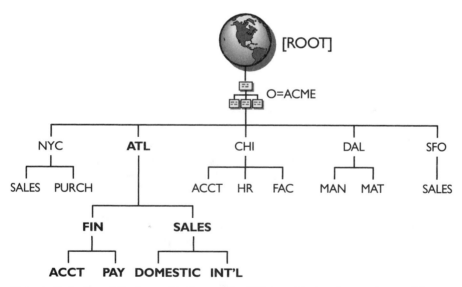

Figure 3-5: A view of the top and bottom of the NDS tree. The tree is a maximum of four levels deep in some places, not counting the [ROOT] object.

## Creating Common Resource Containers

Some NDS designs attempt to group similar resources into the same containers, such as a container for all servers, all printers, and all users. Keep in mind that this approach may work well for smaller companies that do not have a WAN environment. An example of a design approach in a LAN-only network is shown in Figure 3-6. Large companies that have multiple sites, thousands of users, and multiple partitions should not use this design approach if they want to achieve optimal performance.

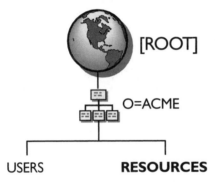

USERS          **RESOURCES**

Figure 3-6: Using the resource container design approach is acceptable for small companies that do not have a lot of users or other objects.

### Consulting Experience

The resource container approach (OU=RESOURCES) is generally not recommended for most large companies because of the high number of external references that are created to track all the objects not physically residing on that server. In addition, the server container has to be available at all locations for login and authentication to occur. For detailed information on external references and backlinks refer to *Novell's Guide to IntranetWare Networks* and *Novell's Guide to NetWare 4.1 Networks* from Novell Press.

In addition to small companies using the resource container approach, universities can also design an NDS tree in their campus environments. Although this topic was discussed in the previous chapter, we discuss it again here in terms of creating containers in the lower portion of your tree. The university NDS design approach always presents a very unique situation in that the logical design of an NDS tree is to create a large container for servers and an extremely large container to store all the students. Usually the network topology is a campus, meaning that the buildings are fiber connected and most likely using FDDI. Therefore, the connections between the buildings are very high speed.

The general approach has been to design the tree with containers such as OU=SERVERS and OU=STUDENTS as shown in Figure 3-7. The problem with this design is the large amount of external reference traffic that can be created if the Student and Server containers are each partitioned and stored on separate servers. In addition, the containers tend to be extremely large and cumbersome, sometimes holding upwards of 5,000 to 10,000 student objects or more in the STUDENT container, and the login/authentication process can be very slow. Each login triggers a synchronization of the entire partition and causes a slowdown for that server holding the partition.

A more suitable approach, from an NDS design standpoint, is to create more containers at the same level in the tree and divide the students into smaller groups. These containers can be arranged in alphabetical order as shown in Figure 3-8. You will still have many backlinks and external references on the servers to track the User objects; however, you'll have smaller, more efficient containers. In addition, this approach will reduce the size of the containers and allow for smaller partitions.

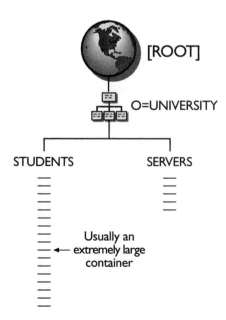

Figure 3-7: A typical university NDS design approach

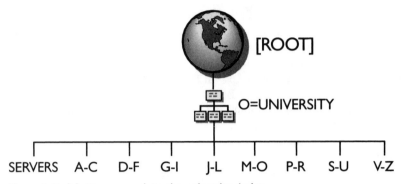

Figure 3-8: A better approach to the university design

For more information on designing an NDS tree for a university, refer to Chapter 2.

# Determining Your Design Criteria

Each company's NDS tree will be slightly different and will be impacted by the different design criteria presented below. For example, one tree will have more containers because of how the tree will be managed and the type of security that will be provided for each of the departments. Another tree may not need as many container levels because a very centralized approach to network management will not need additional containers to define security access.

Many network administrators attempt to design the NDS tree and consider all the design criteria at once. The easiest approach is to design the NDS tree based on Chapters 2 and 3 and then review your design to make changes and adjustments where necessary. Therefore, understanding the design criteria for the bottom of the tree is absolutely necessary regardless of the size and scope of your tree.

Experience has shown that designing the tree is simple if you base the top layers of the tree solely on the WAN infrastructure (if any) and the bottom layers according to your organizational information and the criteria presented here. If your network is LAN only, you should review these criteria to determine if you need to create additional containers.

The design criteria presented here generally impact only the design at the bottom of the tree, not the top of the tree. For this reason, we will focus these design criteria concepts on the bottom of the tree where most of your tree design will be impacted.

The design of the bottom (or LAN) portion of the tree is not dependent on the speed of the network because the LAN supports the largest bandwidth or throughput of information as compared to the WAN. Therefore, the design of the bottom layers is more flexible than the design of the top layers. The design of the bottom, however, does need to consider other criteria that come into play at the LAN level of the tree. The following factors need to be considered for networks of all sizes:

◆ Network Administration

◆ Placement of Network Resources

◆ Login Scripts

◆ Bindery Services

◆ Partitions and Replicas

# Administering the Network

One of the most important design considerations at the bottom level of the tree is how the NDS tree is going to be managed at your company. Will the tree be managed from a single group in a centralized fashion or by multiple groups in a more decentralized fashion? Perhaps you will employ a combination of the two for different types of operations, such as a partition administrator (centralized) and a site administrator (decentralized). Another consideration is the maintenance and repair of your NDS tree. Who will have the responsibility for monitoring and ensuring the health of your network? Your decision on how the tree will be managed may affect the design at the bottom levels of the tree and for that reason you should consider as part of your design the management of the tree.

## CENTRALIZED MANAGEMENT APPROACH

In the centralized management approach the entire NDS tree is controlled by one individual or group in the company. For many small companies, this person may be a part-time network administrator who performs other daily job responsibilities. This person manages all the creations and deletions of the NDS objects as well as partitioning and replication functions, if required, and everything else related to the NDS tree.

The ADMIN user, for example, may be the only user with Supervisor privileges in the entire company. This situation is very similar to a single network administrator on a NetWare 3 file server. Figure 3-9 shows an example of a centralized administrator in an NDS tree for a LAN-only environment.

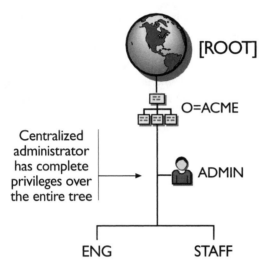

Figure 3-9: A centralized management approach in which an administrative user is granted rights to the entire tree

For the small-network environment there are very few design considerations. A centralized administrator basically has complete control over the entire tree and all its resources. As a precaution you should still create an organizational role for the administrative object (ADMIN or whatever you've named it) and add a second User object to the role in case the first administrator forgets his password, for example. You must grant Supervisor rights at [ROOT] for the organizational role. An example of this rule is shown in Figure 3-10.

For more information on creating organizational roles refer to Chapter 6.

## DECENTRALIZED MANAGEMENT APPROACH

Decentralized management is created when a part of the NDS tree management is delegated to an individual or independent group within the company. These individuals or groups are usually administrators for each department or site and have the responsibility to manage all the network resources in a particular location. Typically, only very large NDS trees and trees that are separated by geographic locations make use of the decentralized approach because each site will probably have its own network administrator.

Figure 3-11 illustrates how decentralized administration can be defined for the lower containers in the tree. Note that either the site container or the individual department containers can be defined for security points where an administrator may be granted privileges to the tree. Again, we recommend that organizational roles be used at the site containers to provide sufficient rights for administrators. See Chapter 6 for more information on using organizational roles.

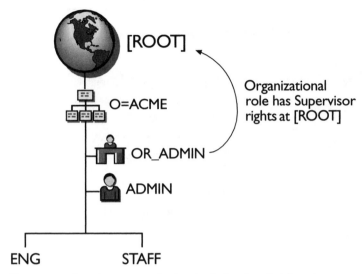

Figure 3-10: Creating an organizational role for the administration: adding the ADMIN user and a second user to occupy the role

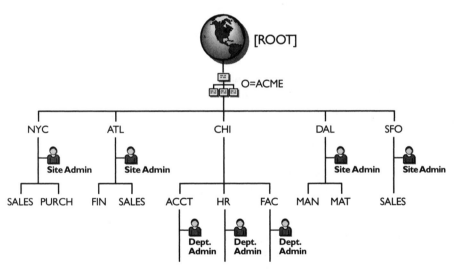

Figure 3-11: Create a distributed administrative approach by creating container administrators at different access points in the tree.

---

## Defining Access for Subadministrators

The following guidelines can be voluntary or enforced by using NDS access controls:

1. Subadministrators will have sufficient security over their containers to create, delete, or change all objects within their subcontainer through the use of organizational roles.

2. Subadministrators should create containers only when absolutely necessary. In addition, subadministrators should place users and resources together for ease of access.

3. Subadministrators will do their part to maintain the naming standards as defined by the corporation and closely control security access at their site.

4. Subadministrators will not attempt to further partition their OU without the assistance of the central IS department.

5. Subadministrators will inform the central IS staff before adding a new server into the corporate tree.

6. Subadministrators will not rename containers in the tree without the permission of the central IS staff.

---

If the tree is going to be decentrally managed, each department administrator or site administrator can decide independently how its area's resources will be organized. The upper-level administrators have full responsibility to create the tree down to the department or site and then relinquish control at that layer to each of the independent LAN administrators.

Top administrators of the tree will still want to give design guidelines and suggestions to the lower-level administrators on organizing the bottom containers and grouping network resources. The rules in the following section govern the rights and responsibilities of the subadministrators.

## COMBINATION OF CENTRALIZED AND DECENTRALIZED MANAGEMENT

Large companies tend to use a combination of centralized and decentralized management approaches to network administration by having some NDS operations performed centrally and being strictly controlled, while other operations are performed by many subadministrators. A large company should control partitioning and replication functions for all parts of the NDS tree, while leaving the day-to-day tasks up to the subadministrators. An example of this approach to managing NDS is shown in Figure 3-12.

The depth of the tree or number of layers in the tree can also be affected by whether your administration is centralized or decentralized. As stated in Chapter 1, you should build the NDS tree like a pyramid (or upside down tree) with fewer layers at the top and more layers at the bottom. A centralized administration approach may imply that a tree designed flat and wide would be easier to administer because you don't need containers to define access for security. If your company has only a few servers and users, you can build a shallow tree that is good for centralized administration as shown in the previous examples.

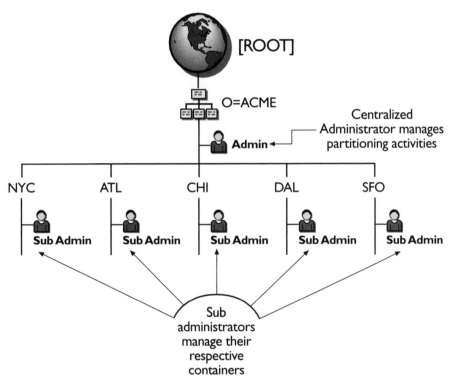

Figure 3-12: A combination of centralized and decentralized administrators

However, if your company is large with many servers, users, and geographic sites you will definitely have to add more layers to the tree. Each layer can be a breakout point for defining network administrators. More layers simply means a longer context for each object's name in the tree. Again, most trees can be adequately represented by using a maximum of four or five levels. Some larger organizations may need a few more layers.

## Placing Network Resources in Your Tree

The placement of resources in your tree is the next important design criteria. It is during this step that you may add or remove containers based on the placement of resources. As you decide where to place the physical network resources in the tree, you should consider the needs of the users who will share those resources. If the network resources are organized according to divisions, departments, and work-groups, they should be placed in the same container with those users. However, if the network resources offer services to multiple departments in one site or location, you should place the resources in the location OU or in the container one level higher in the tree.

For example, in Figure 3-13, the Atlanta office has two departments. The administrator manages an e-mail server at the site, and this server is shared by both the Finance and Sales departments. In order to provide easier access to all the users at the Atlanta location, the easiest solution is to place the resource one level up in the Atlanta container. You can also use an alias in one of the containers. For more information on the use of aliases see Chapter 6.

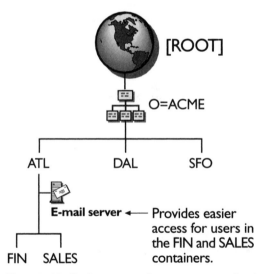

Figure 3-13: Placing a network resource up one level higher in the tree minimizes rights assignments and eases administration for the site administrator.

In addition, the placement of the network resources is a design criteria for the bottom of the tree because containers must be defined before you begin to place resources. If the containers do not exist, they will need to be created to group together the resources from a particular area, location, or department. Remember, one of the primary reasons for designing the NDS tree is to organize your network resources for ease of access as discussed in Chapter 1.

One of the corporate documents that is useful at this point in your NDS design is a list of network resources. A network resource document lists where your current servers are located, such as NT and NetWare 3 servers, and will assist you in placing them in the newly defined tree. For information on the corporate documents refer to Chapter 2.

For small sites, a resource list may not be available. In this case simply include the resources you want to define in your tree on your preliminary design as shown in Figure 3-14. The tree in this example has only two servers, and all resources are simply placed under the O=Organization object.

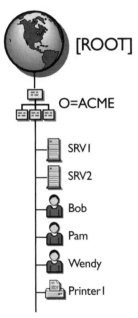

Figure 3-14: A LAN-only tree design showing the resources that are to be defined in the NDS tree

For larger companies a network resource list can be very helpful in the placement of resources at their appropriate locations in the NDS tree. Below are figures of the ACME tree's five main geographic sites. Included with each of these figures are some examples of how objects can be used for the greatest impact and efficiency in the ACME tree. Figure 3-15 shows the New York City (NYC) subtree and and the placement of its resources. Note that for large numbers of users it does not make sense to include them all in the diagram when designing your tree. As shown in this example you can simply state the number of servers and users.

At the NYC site, as well as all other sites, we have placed the e-mail post office server at the top OU=NYC. The same process is repeated at all five sites for a post office.

Your file servers should always be defined by unique names and addresses across the entire tree because of the SAP requirements of NetWare. Printers and print queues, however, can have the same name as long as they reside in different containers, such as HPPRINTER found in both OU=SALES and OU=PURCH containers.

Note also that the Purchasing Department has an NT domain object that contains 50 users.

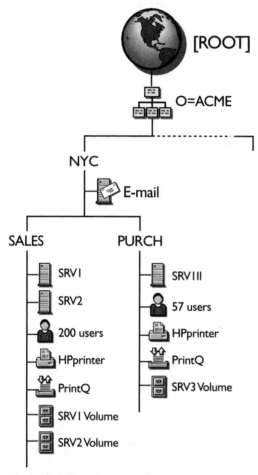

Figure 3-15: The placement of resources as shown in the OU=NYC location

This location shows the placement of resources in each of the departments. It is not necessary to place all users in your tree with drawings such as these. We have included a user in each location merely as an example. The primary purpose in placing objects in this fashion is to determine their placement in the tree.

For the Atlanta location, as well as all other major locations, you should create an organizational role object defined as the site administrator. After creating this object, you should grant Supervisor rights to the role at the site container, such as ATL. For example, you can create a role called ADMIN_ATL. You can then move a user or two in as occupants of the role from the Atlanta container. If you have multiple administrators managing organizations at the same site, you may want to create separate roles for each department as demonstrated in the CHI container. An example of the CHI site is shown in Figure 3-16.

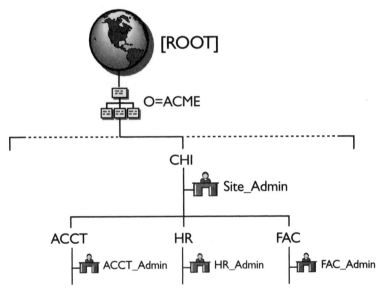

Figure 3-16: ACME Chicago container has multiple administrators for each department defined for that location.

Since OU=NYC is basically the center of activity for the ACME tree, you will want to maintain control over the ADMIN User object from this location. Change the password frequently and limit the number of users who know the password.

The use of the Directory Map object can simplify the administration of your users and can be noted during the placement of resources. For example, the Dallas (DAL) office uses Directory Maps in all their container login scripts. As versions of their specialized software change, the Dallas site administrator changes only the path attribute of the Directory Map object to the new version of the software. This automatically enables all users in Dallas to see the new software version because all container login scripts use the same Directory Map. In addition, using Directory Map objects is more efficient than creating a bindery-based drive mapping because it removes the reliance on SAP and uses instead the addresses stored in NDS.

We will show mobile users on our NDS design as well as a NetWare Connect server that they will dial into for access. The use of a NetWare Connect server makes the login process much easier for users who travel so that they can continue to access their network resources.

## Placing NT Users in the NDS Tree

Another consideration while designing your NDS tree is to take into account the NT users that you plan on placing in the NDS tree. When you install NDS for NT, you will see a domain object created in the container that you have specified. For more information on the installation process please see Chapter 10. This domain object functions similar to an NDS group object and contains members just like a group. Therefore, you should be aware of how many users are in the domain because these users will be stored as objects in NDS as well.

As mentioned in other sections of this book, Novell recommends up to 1,000 objects in an NDS partition and the NDS for NT users must be counted in this recommendation. For example, assume you have a partitioned container with 250 NetWare users, 5 printers, 5 print queues, and 5 print servers. Your object count would be 265 objects. However, if you add 250 NT users to an NT domain stored in NDS, you boost the object count to 515 objects. This is still less than 1,000 total objects, but be aware that you may have to do further partitioning to take into account the additional NT users you have added to NDS.

## Organizing Login Scripts

Another design criteria for the bottom of the tree is how the users will access information in the tree. Do they need the same login script? The users will primarily access NDS through the use of login scripts. Remember, the users need login scripts to map network drives and applications, capture to print devices, and set other variables. NetWare 4 provides login script variables that can assist users with a variety of access needs.

### CONTAINER SCRIPTS

The number of containers with different login scripts can impact the lower levels of your tree design. For example, a small site with one or two servers may not have any other containers defined because all users, regardless of their department, share the same resources. Typically, users needing the same login script will be grouped together in the same OU container. Figure 3-17 shows where a container login script will be used by everyone in the container.

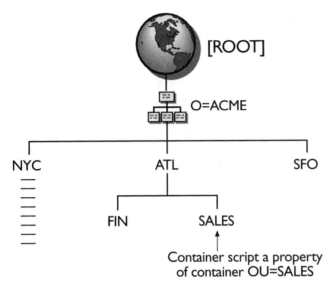

Container script a property
of container OU=SALES

Figure 3-17: Users will execute a login script in their respective containers.

Another strategy for organizing the login scripts is to have the same login script for all users and copy it to multiple containers. In this manner, the user placement in the tree is less affected. Although this strategy may simplify administration, it requires that the network administrator be responsible for keeping all copies of the same script up to date.

Container login scripts replace the functionality of a NetWare 3 system login script, but provide many more variables for customizing a script to meet your users' needs. Knowing how your users will access the information in the tree will help you determine the type of scripts needed as well as the number of containers so that you can organize the bottom layers and containers in your tree.

Your NT users can execute the login script associated with their NT domain as they would normally.

## PROFILE SCRIPTS

Profile login scripts are also useful when you have a group of users in a container that needs additional environment variables defined after executing the container script. The profile login script also enables you to utilize a login script across multiple OU containers by assigning the profile to specific users.

For example, a container in Chicago (OU=CHI) has a profile script created for the ACCT, HR, and FAC containers. All the users need slightly different access to a server placed one level up in the OU=CHI container. The script can reside in any container, and NDS users from any container can execute it.

Spend some time defining your login scripts as explained in Chapters 6 and 7. A well-defined login script not only saves the user time in accessing resources in the tree, but also saves administration time as well. Any process that can enable all users to map their network drives to the appropriate network server and establish access to specific network applications and services in the tree is worth the effort. Most login scripts will still depend on groups and Directory Map objects for these drive mappings. These groups and Directory Map objects must be accessible enough so that any users needing them can find them during the login process.

In order to simplify the mapping to generic network applications (ones needed by all NDS network users), place the applications in the same subdirectory structure on all the servers. To simplify network administration, all servers in the tree should have the same file system directory structure. For example, all applications can be in a directory called APPS. All data can be in a directory called DATA, and so on. When you define NDS naming standards for objects, include a standard for the file system as well.

## USER SCRIPTS

User scripts have no impact on the design of the lower levels of the NDS tree. Generally, user scripts cause more administrative work and should be regarded as a last resort for users whose needs cannot be met by a container or profile script. Small network environments may use this script if necessary. A default script will execute if no other script is available.

# Bindery Services

Bindery services influences how you design the lower levels of your NDS tree in terms of how many containers you create holding objects that utilize the bindery. Bindery services requires a writeable replica to be stored on the server where you are setting the bindery context. NDS provides compatibility with NetWare 2 and NetWare 3 using bindery services. This feature lets bindery-based versions of NetWare applications and other third-party software requiring the bindery to access the NDS database as if it were the bindery. For example, a client can use the NETX shell (NetWare 3 client) to log in to a NetWare 4 server and run any bindery-based application that may exist on the NetWare 4 server.

Bindery services can be enabled through the server SET Server Bindery Context command. The bindery context can be set to one Organizational Unit, Organization, or Locality container. Alternatively, up to 16 containers can be set as the bindery context. All leaf objects in the NDS container(s) that are also objects in the NetWare 3 bindery (that is, users, groups, queues, print servers, and profiles) are seen as objects through the bindery application programming interfaces (APIs). Figure 3-18 shows how you can set a server's bindery context(s) using the SERV-MAN utility. Figure 3-19 shows how you can verify that a server's bindery context has been set.

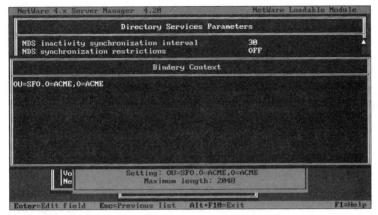

Figure 3-18: Using the SERVMAN utility to set the server's bindery context

SERVMAN parameters are now found in Novell's Monitor utility in NetWare 4.11.

Typing **Set Bindery Context** at a NetWare 4 server shows the string of bindery contexts, both valid and invalid. If you want to see only the valid (effective and active) contexts, you must type **CONFIG** at the server console.

Figure 3-19: Typing SET BINDERY CONTEXT at a NetWare 4 server console will display a server's bindery context(s) if one has been set.

Bindery services in NetWare 4 lets you select up to 16 containers as the server bindery context. The major requirement for bindery services is that the server must store at least a read/write replica of the partition where the bindery context is set. If a server has set a maximum of 16 bindery contexts, the server would have to store 16 separate replicas just to support bindery services on all contexts. Figure 3-20 shows how your design would be impacted at the Chicago container if you had to set multiple containers. Notice that we created additional containers to reduce the total number of replicas for a partition. We wanted to keep the total number of replicas at 7 to 10 as explained in the guidelines in Chapters 4 and 5.

As you can see, placing replicas on servers to support bindery services will increase the total number of replicas for each partition. Bindery services is the main reason you will maintain more than a few replicas of any partition.

You may need to place many of the users requiring bindery services from a particular file server into the container where you have set the server bindery context for access to a particular application. This design consideration can affect the NDS tree design at the bottom level because it may require you to combine users into the same container or use large numbers of groups to provide mappings to these bindery-based applications.

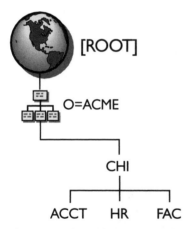

Figure 3-20: Multiple bindery contexts are required at this site, and we have created additional containers to reduce the total number of replicas of the same partition.

For example, some companies have many bindery-based custom legacy applications that cannot readily be converted to use NDS. Therefore, they will have servers with bindery services enabled and may have to use groups to provide access to multiple servers. If possible, try to combine bindery applications on fewer servers so that fewer servers need to enable bindery services, thus reducing the number of replicas of that partition.

Some of the more common applications you may encounter that make bindery calls are listed below. This is a brief list and many of the applications requiring the bindery could have been written internally by your corporation. Review this list as a starting point for applications that require the bindery:

- ◆ NetWare 3 Print Services

- ◆ Menuing systems at the desktop

- ◆ Backup and Restore Utilities (most are now DS aware)

- ◆ Host Connectivity Products

- ◆ Network Management Utilities

- ◆ Other NetWare 3-based applications and utilities

Before you change the bottom of the tree design to accommodate bindery services, determine whether you even need bindery services for all the servers. Remember, bindery services is an optional feature that does not have to be enabled at each server. You should determine if the clients are using NETX or applications that require bindery services. You can also identify the users and key applications and force them to use bindery services on specific servers only.

## Partitions and Replicas

The final design criterion that affects the bottom of the tree is the way in which NDS will be split into partitions. For this discussion, we need to consider the size of the partition (total number of objects), the total number of replicas, and where in the tree the partition is created. A container object is required for the creation of a partition and is designated as the root-most object of the partition. Figure 3-21 shows a partition root called OU=NYC in the New York City site. The partition root is named NYC because that is the starting point of that partition.

When deciding where to create a partition, you should follow the physical network infrastructure. Like the top layer of the tree, the partitions of the tree should represent the WAN, making each site or location its own partition. The benefit of partitioning the NDS database according to the WAN is that the information needed by the local users stays inside that location and is not synchronized across the network. We have partitioned each of the location organizational units by site as illustrated in Figure 3-22.

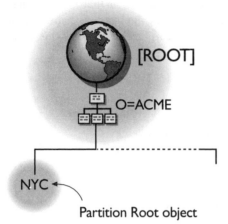

Partition Root object

Figure 3-21: A partition root object is named
NYC at the New York City site in the ACME tree.

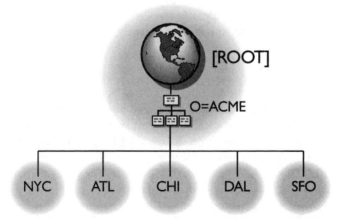

Figure 3-22: Each site is its own partition and maintains its portion
of the NDS database on its own servers within the site. This keeps
NDS traffic localized to the site.

The size of your partitions and the total number of replicas will influence the
design of the bottom of the tree. Typically, partitions range in size from 50 to 1,000
objects depending on your hardware. This would include the NT user object that
you move into NDS as well. For more detailed information refer to Chapters 4 and
5. If the partition has more than 3,500 objects you should split the partition into
two partitions to provide faster NDS synchronization. In order to partition further
at a site you may have to create additional containers as the partition roots.

In Figure 3-23 we have created a new partition called MAT in the DAL container to keep our partition size down around 1,000 objects. More partitions, in the right places, make your tree design more efficient. Remember, a partition contains all the objects in a defined subtree, not just the objects in a single container.

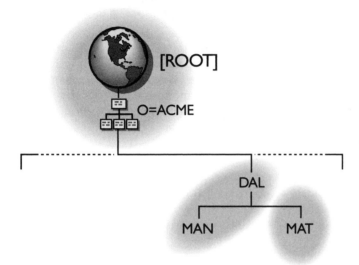

Figure 3-23: A new partition is created in the MAT department. It is now a child partition of its parent named DAL.

NDS partitions larger than 3,500 work less efficiently. Based on our experiences at many customer sites, partitions work most efficiently when they contain up to 1,000 objects. Partitions larger than this size may work more efficiently if you split the partition into two smaller partitions. Check your user's performance and synchronization performance and use that as a guide.

The last consideration is the total number of replicas of a partition. Remember, the ideal range for the number of replicas of a partition is 7 to 10. If the number of replicas is greater than 10 (depending on the speed of your hardware), consider creating additional partitions to reduce the total number of replicas. Novell recommends three replicas for each partition to provide fault tolerance. The primary reason you would need more than three replicas of any partition is for bindery services. Bindery services requires a writeable copy of the replica. Refer to the "Bindery Services" section earlier in this chapter.

Decide which group at your company is responsible for the partitioning of the NDS tree. If you manage the tree centrally, all the partitioning decisions are made by the central staff. If the tree is decentralized then you may turn over the rights of partitioning the tree to each of the local site or facility administrators. Before you install NetWare 4, establish a company policy stating who will handle the partitioning. You can enforce this policy through access controls if needed.

During the design of the bottom of the NDS tree, ensure that there is a place for every user and network resource currently in your company. Remember that the primary goal for designing the NDS tree is to organize your network resources, including the NT users. If you have not defined a place for all the users or network resources then you need to adjust your tree design. The bottom layers are typically the only ones affected. If you have a resource list it will most likely show information on servers and printers and provides you with helpful information for placing these resources in your tree.

As mentioned earlier, the bottom containers or OUs in the tree are typically the divisions, departments, workgroups, and teams of your company. Do not include as containers any individuals that appear as division or department heads in your company's organizational charts. You simply want to identify the functional groups or departments; the individuals become the users in each container.

Remember that a properly designed tree will have the right depth regardless of how many levels it contains.

# Second Step

## Divide NDS into Partitions and Replicas, Which Provide Scalability and Fault Tolerance

**CHAPTER 4**
Divide NDS into Partitions to
Scale NDS Across Network Servers

**CHAPTER 5**
Replicate for Fault Tolerance
and to Reduce Synchronization Traffic

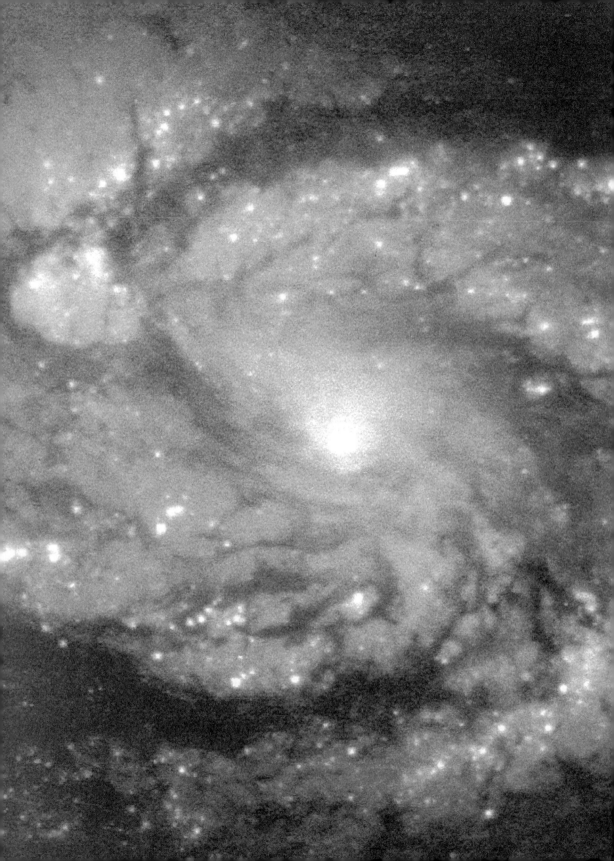

# Chapter 4

# Divide NDS into Partitions to Scale NDS Across Network Servers

## IN THIS CHAPTER

◆ Designing NDS partitions

◆ Managing NDS partitions

THE NDS OBJECT INFORMATION is stored on NetWare 4 servers in the form of data files. These internal data files may be either centralized on a single network server or distributed across many NetWare 4 servers in the tree. Although the NDS tree can be distributed to servers across the network, the users see a consistent, single view of its resources.

Partitioning the NDS database is completely transparent to users, and they can access the entire NDS tree, regardless of the server to which they are connected. For example, a user at a workstation using the Windows 95 Network Neighborhood utility will see the NDS tree as a single logical entity, even though the NDS tree may have been partitioned and distributed across multiple servers.

Although a specific server may not contain all user defined and default NDS data files for the network, users can still get the information they request through background processes that NDS establishes and maintains between the separate partitions.

In order to create the most efficient NDS tree possible, the following partition design rules should be observed:

1. Base partitions on the WAN infrastructure.

2. Do not create a partition that spans your WAN.

3. Partition around the local servers in each geographic area.

4. Keep the partition size small (no larger than 1,000 to 1,500 objects).

5. Limit the number of subordinate partitions from 10 to 15.

# Designing NDS Partitions

Designing partitions for your NDS tree can be very simple if you remember why you create a partition. You create a partition to scale NDS across the network servers for better performance of the NDS tree. If your tree does not need to be partitioned because you have a small network with few users and no WAN links, then simply maintain the default [ROOT] partition. Understanding your network infrastructure is necessary in defining the partitions of your NDS tree.

During the installation of the first NDS server in a tree, the [ROOT] partition for the tree is created automatically and a copy (replica) of [ROOT] is placed on this server. In NetWare 4, the [ROOT] partition is the only partition that the installation program will create. You or other system administrators must create all other partitions of the NDS database. The [ROOT] partition cannot be removed unless you remove NDS from all NetWare 4 servers, in which case you are really removing the entire tree.

After the first server has been installed, you can add more objects based on your NDS design to build the tree structure for your company. As you define objects in the tree, you are adding information to NDS on the server where these objects were created.

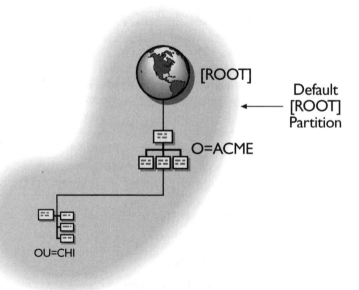

Figure 4-1: The [ROOT] partition holds all the objects in the tree until further partitioning takes place.

All the objects that have been added to the ACME_TREE are held by a single partition called the [ROOT] partition. Figure 4-1 illustrates how the [ROOT] partition is holding all the objects in the NDS tree until further partitioning can take place. After a new NetWare 4 installation, this partition resides only on the first NetWare 4 server installed.

Because there is only one copy of the [ROOT] partition, you should place the partition on other servers as they are installed on the system. The Novell Install (NLM) automatically creates additional copies (up to three) of the partition as you add additional servers. For example, the servers ATL-SRV1 and SFO-SRV1 are additional servers installed into the tree and receive a read/write copy of the [ROOT] partition. Figure 4-2 shows two additional copies of the [ROOT] partition placed on the servers ATL-SRV1 and SFO-SRV1.

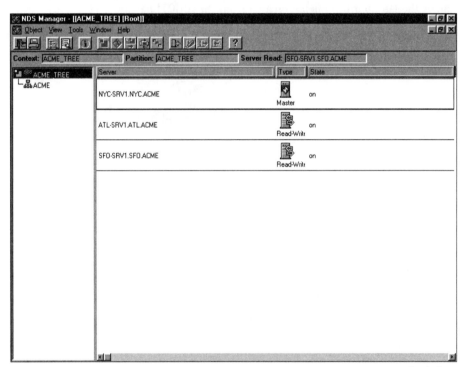

Figure 4-2: Using the NDS Manager utility you can see two additional copies of the [ROOT] partition that have been placed on the servers ATL-SRV1 and SFO-SRV1 for the ACME_TREE.

Child partitions can be created from the [ROOT] partition by selecting a subordinate container object, typically an OU, as the top of the partition. A partition can have only one top-most container object (referred to as the partition root object).

When the partition is created, it takes its name from the partition root object. All the objects in the tree under the partition root object are the contents of the new partition. This is always true until a subordinate partition is encountered lower in the tree. Creating a partition does not affect the child partition boundaries.

You can create a child partition from the parent partition by using the partition split operation or the Create option in the NetWare utilities. The partition split operation is fast and in most cases does not generate large amounts of traffic on your network unless you have large numbers of replicas of the partition. The operation simply divides one partition into two with all the information staying on the same servers that contained the original partition. This split operation will create a new child partition on all the servers that had a copy of the parent partition. Figure 4-3 shows the DAL partition being created from the [ROOT] partition.

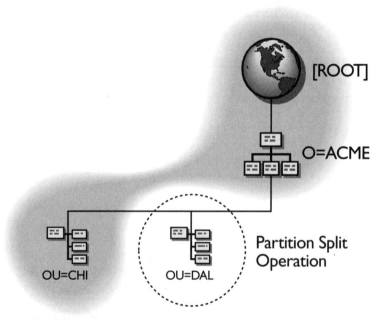

Figure 4-3: A conceptual view of a partition split operation of the [ROOT] to create the DAL partition. This operation affects all copies of the [ROOT] partition, which are currently stored on NYC-SRV1, ATL-SRV1, and SFO-SRV1.

It is recommended that the [ROOT] partition be kept small, with only the [ROOT] object and O=Organization containers and perhaps a few objects if necessary. For example, in order to keep the [ROOT] partition small for ACME, further partitioning needs to take place. As illustrated in Figure 4-4, if more partitions are created directly under the [ROOT] partition, the [ROOT] partition holds only the top-most levels of the tree.

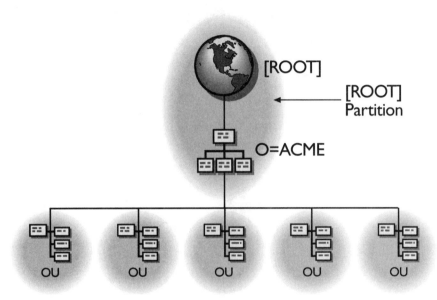

Figure 4-4: The [ROOT] partition for the ACME tree should hold only the top-most portion of the tree — the [ROOT] object and Organization object.

## Basing Your Partitions on the WAN Infrastructure

For networks using a WAN the most important design criteria for partitioning are the physical layout of your network infrastructure, the WAN links, and the network servers. Using these criteria, your main task is to partition the NDS tree to localize the information.

For example, this means that you want to partition the Directory to keep the NYC information in NYC, the ATL information in ATL, and so on. Figure 4-5 illustrates the physical WAN layout for the ACME company. Figure 4-6 shows how the ACME tree has been partitioned to support the physical WAN layout. In this example the [ROOT] partition is very small and includes only the [ROOT] and organization container objects.

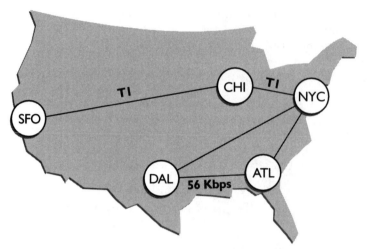

Figure 4-5: The physical WAN network layout for the ACME company

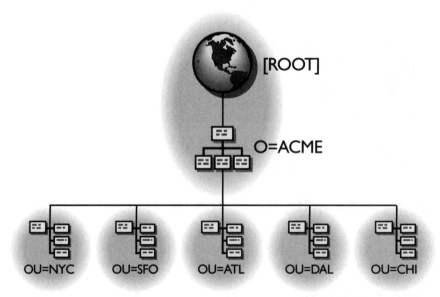

Figure 4-6: The ACME tree has been partitioned according to the WAN infrastructure.

Continuing with this same example, as illustrated in Figure 4-7, you can see that the NYC partition and its object information have been placed on the server in NYC. The same is true for all the locations. By partitioning the NDS tree based on your WAN network layout, you can keep the information local to each location and yet still find and use the resources throughout the entire NDS tree.

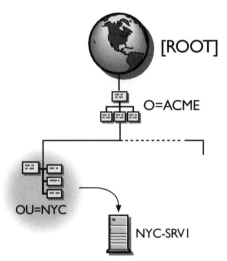

Figure 4-7: NDS distributes information across the network servers for ACME. The NYC partition is stored locally on the NYC server NYC-SRV1. Each of the other partitions is stored on the local server.

When selecting server hardware keep in mind that the slowest server holding the same replica will affect all synchronization activities of even faster servers in the same partition. If you are operating on slower hardware, you should understand this consideration.

## Characteristics of NDS Partitions

All NDS partitions have the same characteristics or are governed by the same set of rules. These characteristics or rules are as follows:

1. The partition must be named by the top-most container object.

2. Two-peer containers need a common parent.

3. Partitions cannot overlap.

4. A partition must represent a logical subtree.

## NAMED BY THE TOP-MOST CONTAINER OBJECT

A partition takes its name from the container object at the top. When a partition is created the container object that is used as the start of the partition is called the partition root object. Only one partition root object exists for each partition and is the top-most container object. Do not confuse a partition root object with the partition [ROOT]. An example of a partition root object is shown in Figure 4-8.

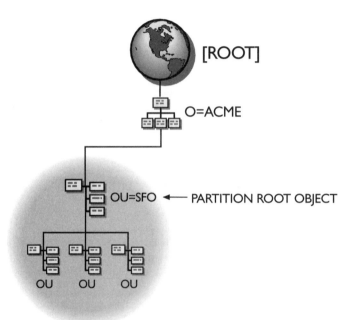

Figure 4-8: An example of a partition root object in the ACME tree.
In this example, the partition root object is OU=SFO and the partition
takes its name from OU=SFO. Thus, the partition is called the SFO partition.

## TWO-PEER CONTAINERS NEED A COMMON PARENT

Peer-level containers cannot exist in the same partition without the same parent container. This partition characteristic is very similar to the first one. Figure 4-9 illustrates how two-peer OUs in the ACME tree must have a common partition root object (parent object) to exist in the tree.

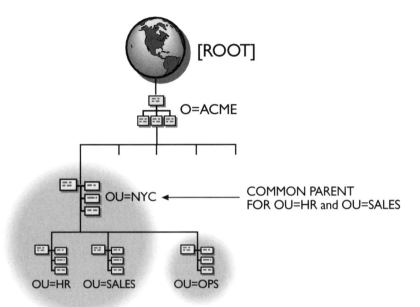

Figure 4-9: An example of how two-peer OUs in the ACME tree must have the same parent container to exist in the same partition. In this example, OU=HR and OU=SALES must have a common parent (OU=NYC) to be in the same partition.

## PARTITIONS CANNOT OVERLAP
NDS partitions cannot overlap with any other part of the NDS tree. This means that one object will never reside in two partitions, as shown in Figure 4-10.

## PARTITIONS ARE LOGICAL SUBTREES
The partition contains all of the information for the connected subtree. Each partition may be thought of as a section or subtree of the entire NDS tree and indirectly communicates with its parent and child partitions.

# Partitioning the Top Layers of the Tree

As discussed earlier, the top layers in the tree should be partitioned according to your WAN infrastructure. Since the top layers of the tree should already be designed according to the WAN links, partitioning will naturally follow these boundaries.

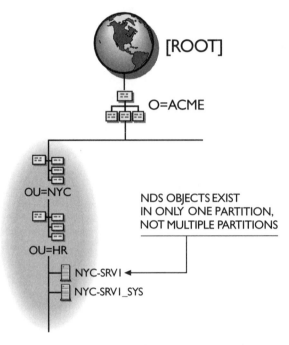

Figure 4-10: Partition information cannot overlap. An object can exist in only one partition.

The NDS database will not scale as well if you try to combine multiple geographical sites into one partition. If you try to span more than one location in a partition the information in the partition will synchronize with the other copies across the slower WAN links. This reduces the efficiency of the network and defeats the purpose of creating a partition in the first place.

If you have implemented regional OU containers in your tree, you should create a partition for each of the regional OUs. After the region partitions are defined in your tree, you will need to partition at the locations under each of the regions and store them on separate servers from their parents. This is necessary in order to distribute the subordinate references to multiple servers as explained in Chapter 5.

## Partitioning the Bottom Layers of the Tree

Since the bottom of the tree design is based on the divisions, departments, and workgroups within each location of the WAN, the tree should already be partitioned at the WAN site or location. Further partitioning may not be necessary. Follow the partitioning guidelines presented in Chapter 1 if you need to add more partitions. The bottom layers of the tree should be partitioned only if there is a special requirement. These special cases are discussed below.

The bottom organizational units should be partitioned based on either the size of the partition (total number of objects is greater than 3,500) or on more than 7 to 10 replicas of the same partition.

The previous partitioning thresholds assume you are operating on high-end server hardware. For many servers the thresholds may be 1,000 to 1,500 objects per partition and 3 to 7 replicas. Read the information discussed below and also refer to Chapter 5 for more specific guidelines.

# Minimizing the Number of Replicas

If the total number of replicas for the same partition goes beyond 7 to 10, you should consider splitting the partition just to reduce the total number of replicas for that partition. You may need more than three replicas of any partition in order to support bindery services at NetWare 4 servers for backup or other utilities that need the bindery.

Also, keep in mind that more replicas may require more management if a partition needs to be repaired. Using Novell's utilities to make repairs becomes a bigger task if you have large numbers of replicas. Each server holding a replica (and the subordinate reference replicas) may need to be repaired if you encounter problems. Obviously, the more replicas you have, the longer the task of repair for you, your administrators, or other outside support personnel. For more information on replication refer to Chapter 5. For in-depth information regarding repair operations refer to *Novell's Guide to IntranetWare Networks*.

# Controlling the Partition Administration

NDS can give several different administrators responsibility for partitioning the NDS tree. If a departmental or site manager wants the responsibility to manage his or her own partitioning, you will need to plan the parent partitions accordingly. For example, the rights needed to perform the split partition operation on the NDS tree are effective write rights to the Access Control List (ACL) of the top container object of the partition. You'll also need Supervisor rights on the server where the new partition will be placed. There are several ways to receive this privilege. One way is to have Supervisor object rights at the container object that defines the partition. You can also grant explicit write rights to its ACL. Also, if there is a need to create a new partition from the parent, then the administrator creating the child also needs full rights to the parent.

In order to perform other partition operations such as Add/Remove replica and Change Type you must have rights to the server object that is being affected. For more information on security and rights see *Novell's Guide to IntranetWare Networks*.

# Partitioning in the Shape of a Pyramid

The pyramid-shaped design for the partitions automatically distributes the subordinate reference replicas. Having a smaller number of partitions at the top of the tree with more at the bottom satisfies the requirement for fewer subordinate reference replicas per server and maximizes the supportability and reparability of your tree if problems should occur. As a general rule you should partition all containers in the top of the tree, except the O=Organization object. You can keep this object together with [ROOT] in a single partition.

The pyramid-shaped design can be accomplished if you always create partitions at the top layers according to the WAN infrastructure and then create the bottom layer partitions as specified in the previous guidelines. For example, as illustrated in Figure 4-11, the ACME tree has been partitioned according to the WAN infrastructure with some further partitioning at the lower layers. The partitioning for the ACME tree is pyramid shaped and occurs very easily.

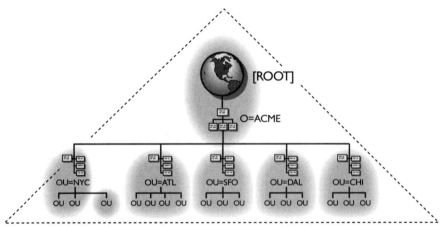

**Figure 4-11: The ACME tree has been partitioned according to the WAN infrastructure, which naturally takes the shape of a pyramid.**

The partitioning should resemble a pyramid with fewer partitions at the top of the tree and more at the bottom. If you have designed the tree based on a pyramid shape, your partition design will naturally follow the tree design.

By following the partitioning guidelines for both the top and bottom layers, the NDS information will always remain close to the user and other leaf objects because the partitions have been based on the locations. An exception would be the [ROOT] partition, which is created automatically during installation of the first NetWare 4 server.

# Not Spanning a WAN Link or Physical Locations with a Partition

This design rule is very important in providing the best performance of NDS. Unnecessary NDS traffic will travel between two locations and across your WAN infrastructure if this rule is broken. The extra traffic will occur during each of the normal synchronization operations. Spanning a partition across the WAN link is shown in Figure 4-12 and should be avoided if you want to achieve the best performance of NDS and minimize traffic across your WAN.

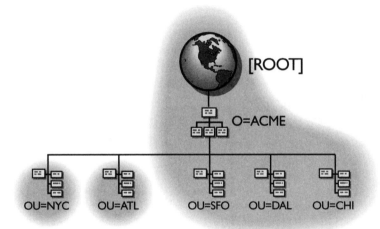

Figure 4-12: Do not span the WAN link of the [ROOT] partition, which in this example includes the SFO, DAL, and CHI sites.

Each geographic location should be its own individual partition. Partition locally wherever possible. These guidelines do not suggest that you partition every Organizational Unit in the bottom level of your tree. Rather, you should do additional partitioning at any geographic site only if the partition has exceeded 1,500 objects, depending on your hardware. See the "Keeping the Partition Size Small" section later in this chapter and also Chapter 5 for more size specifications for partitions and replicas.

# Partitioning around the Local Servers in Each Geographic Area

Partitioning should be done around local servers in each geographic area. For example, the New York City site (OU=NYC) has three servers, and each server should contain a replica of the NYC partition. Do not create a partition for a location if there is no server locally to store it on. This situation is common with small remote offices that do not have servers at their local site. Users would currently access all the network services across the WAN infrastructure. Access to NDS is no different. Figure 4-13 shows how these users at the OU=SALES would still be part of a partition contained on a server in OU=SFO because they do not have their own server.

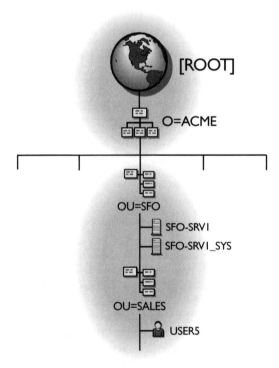

Figure 4-13: Users will be part of a partition stored on another server if they do not have a local server in their office.

You may determine to create a container called SALES for some other reason, such as login scripts. The creation of this container is acceptable; it just doesn't need to be its own partition because no server exists at the site for the storage of that partition.

# Keeping the Partition Size Small

As the partition size grows you should consider creating another partition to help distribute the workload that any one server or set of servers has to handle. A larger partition can have approximately 1,500 objects stored on a Pentium class PC. As the partition grows you should split the partition by creating a new child partition to bring the original partition's size back within the guidelines. Remember, a partition contains all the objects in a defined subtree, not just the objects in a single container.

Figure 4-14 shows the CHI partition being split into two partitions. The OU=ENG container object becomes a new child partition to CHI. This new partition was created because the CHI partition contained more than 1,500 objects. The OU=ENG container and subtree holds a large portion of the objects and was split off as a new partition.

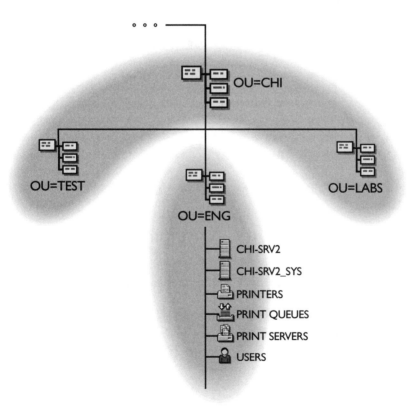

Figure 4-14: The OU=ENG container object is created as a new partition because the CHI partition had over 1,500 objects.

## Keeping the [ROOT] Partition Small

The [ROOT] partition should include only the [ROOT] object and the O=Organization object. As shown in Figure 4-15, do not include additional containers in the [ROOT] partition other than the [ROOT] object and Organization=ACME. This means that you should not include any other subordinate container OUs in the partition with the [ROOT] partition. Avoid including an individual location within the [ROOT] partition because the location information would be distributed unnecessarily to other servers during replication.

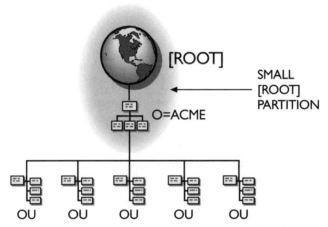

Figure 4-15: Do not include additional containers in the [ROOT] partition other than the [ROOT] object and Organization=ACME.

## Limiting the Number of Subordinate Partitions from 10 to 15

Understanding the purpose of partitions and how to implement them at any site is an important part of any NDS design strategy. NDS is represented as a hierarchical structure called a tree in which all the network resources are placed. Figure 4-16 illustrates the NDS database as a hierarchical tree. The NDS partitions are also hierarchical following the same structure as the tree. A partition can be considered a subtree.

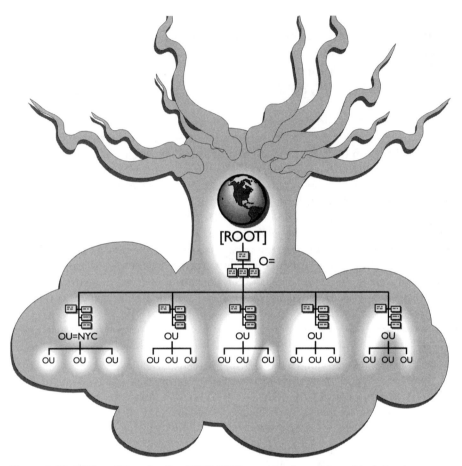

Figure 4-16: NDS partitions for the ACME_TREE are viewed as a hierarchical structure called a tree.

NDS partitions are logical sections of the NDS tree. The NDS partitions are based on the same structure as the NDS tree. Partitioning is the process of splitting the NDS hierarchy or tree into smaller parts or subtrees that can be physically stored on your network servers as replicas of the partition. Partitioning the NDS tree lets you selectively distribute the NDS tree information to the areas in the network that need the information.

Don't confuse NDS partitions with file system partitions. An NDS partition is a portion of the NDS tree and does not contain any file system information. A file system partition, on the other hand, splits a hard drive into logical segments for use by the operating system.

Partitioning gives you the ability to scale the NDS tree across the network servers. Splitting up the NDS tree into partitions and storing them on separate network servers will distribute the workload for each of the servers. In addition, the NetWare utilities enable you to select the servers in the network where you want to store the different NDS partitions.

As mentioned earlier, the layout of the NDS partitions are hierarchical, meaning that one partition is parent to a subordinate or child partition. When all partitions are taken together, they form a hierarchical map back to the [ROOT] object.

The relationship between the individual partitions in the tree is a parent/child relationship. Where the boundaries between the partitions meet, the partition that is closer to the [ROOT] is considered the parent and the one farther away is the child.

The parent/child relationship is also described in terms of subordinate and superior partitions. A subordinate partition (or child) is the partition that is down the tree or farther from the [ROOT]. The superior partition is the parent or partition that is closer to the top of the tree than its subordinate partition.

Figure 4-17 shows the parent/child relationship between the partitions in the ACME partition map. In this example, the OU containers that have been partitioned at NYC, ATL, CHI, DAL, and SFO are child partitions to the partition [ROOT], which is the parent. The CHI partition is also a parent partition, with the three subordinate partitions as the child partitions.

When subordinate partitions are created, the partition root must maintain the location of the subordinate partitions. If the server does not hold both the parent and its child partitions, NDS will create a subordinate reference replica for each of the child partitions and place it on the server with the parent.

NDS requires that the location of the subordinate partitions be linked with its parent to form a common set of information. The users can then traverse the tree. The partition root only needs to know the location of its child partitions if a child partition is not stored on the same server as the parent. The mechanism that maintains this relationship is called a subordinate reference replica. This topic will be discussed in more detail later in this section and also in Chapter 5.

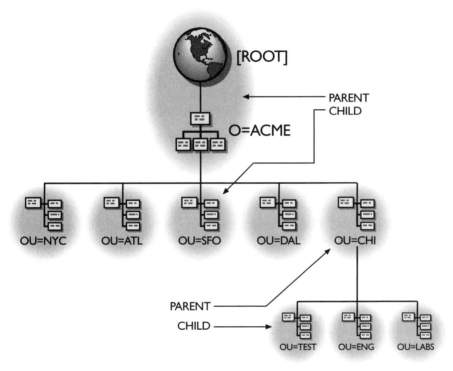

Figure 4-17: An example of the parent/child relationship between the partitions in the ACME tree

If you should create new partitions below the CHI partition, then CHI becomes a parent partition to the newly formed partitions. Although CHI is a new parent, it is still a child partition of [ROOT]. However, there is not a grandparent relationship in which the [ROOT] partition knows about a partition below the CHI partition. Only the parent-child relationship exists in NDS among partitions.

 NDS maintains the relationship between the parent and child partitions. If a server is holding a parent partition but not the child partition, NDS creates a subordinate reference replica pointing to the child partition. This replica links the parent partition to the child partition and vice versa in the NDS tree. Again, the subordinate reference replicas are placed on servers holding the parent partition but not the child partition. Therefore, any server holding a parent partition can end up storing subordinate reference replicas to child partitions.

Servers can also end up holding many subordinate reference replicas, depending on how you design the partitions for your NDS tree. For example, you may create or partition each of the organizational units beneath the [ROOT] partition. If you have too many partitioned organizational units below the [ROOT] and organization object, NDS creates a subordinate reference replica automatically for any server holding a copy of the [ROOT] partition and not the child partitions. For more information and examples on subordinate reference replicas refer to Chapter 5.

# Managing NDS Partitions

In order to properly manage NDS partitions and replicas, there are several NDS partition and replica operations that you need to understand and use: create new partition, merge partition, move partition, add replica, remove replicas, change replica type, and abort partition operation. You can use the NDS Manager utility to perform NDS partition and replica operations on the NDS tree.

The NDS Manager utility is a Windows-based program that system administrators use to manage all partitions and replicas in the NDS tree. This utility also has a set of additional tools that can be selected to help you to determine the health of partitioning and replication. Figure 4-18 shows you the main menu for the NDS Manager.

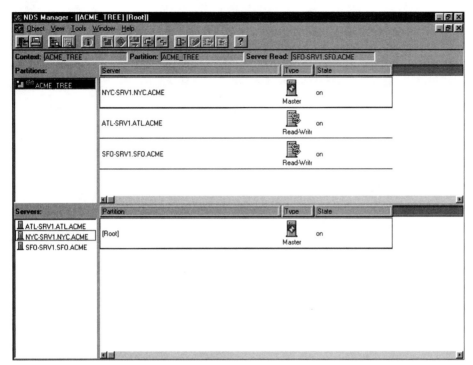

Figure 4-18: The main menu of the NDS Manager utility which controls the partitioning and replication of the NDS database.

In Figure 4-19 you can see that the partitions are denoted with a small box icon to the left of the OU container object. In this example, the OU=NYC and OU=SFO are partitions.

The PARTMGR utility is a DOS-based program that provides functionality to perform partition operations on the NDS database. The partition operations are create, merge, move subtree, add replicas, remove replicas, and change replica type. Figure 4-20 displays the main menu of the PARTMGR utility.

## Understanding NDS Partition Operations

All partition and replica operations require that the master replica for the partition be available. The master replica locks the partition before it starts the partitioning operation. The only partition operations that do not require the master replica to lock the partition are the add replica and remove replica operations.

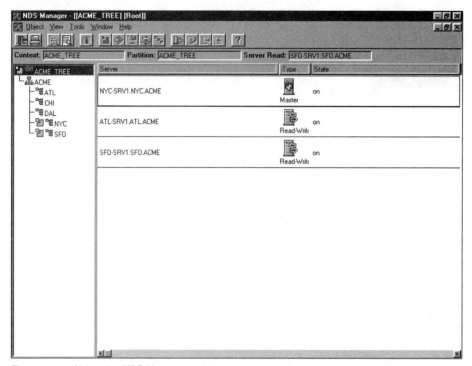

Figure 4-19: Using the NDS Manager utility, you can see the partitions denoted with a small box icon to the left of the OU container. OU=NYC and OU=SFO are shown as partitions.

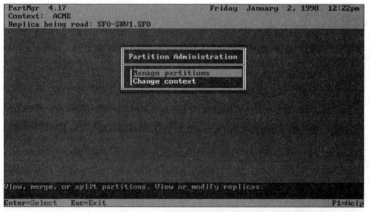

Figure 4-20: The main menu of the PARTMGR utility. This utility can be used to perform partition operations such as create, merge, move subtree, add replicas, remove replicas, and change replica type.

## Consulting Experience

Before you start a partition operation, you should *always* check the status of the partition replicas. You will avoid a lot of problems if you check before you perform any partition operation. You can use DSREPAIR or NDS Manager to check the status of the replicas and synchronization. Make sure the synchronization process is completing without errors before starting a new operation on that partition. Figure 4-21 displays the status check of the replicas in DSREPAIR.

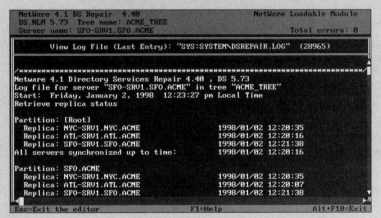

Figure 4-21: Use the DSREPAIR Check Synchronization Status option to check the status of the replicas before starting a partitioning operation.

If your NetWare 4 servers are running the code release of DS.NLM (Version 5.73) or greater, you can use DSREPAIR to read the partition status after the partition operation. It will be more accurate than the Check Synchronization Status option of DSREPAIR, which often generates the "partition busy" error message.

All the replicas for a specific partition must be available in order to perform the complete operation. If a replica is not reachable, NDS will wait until it is available. The partition operation appears to have been completed because the utility returns control to the administrator. However, the operation has not actually completed until all the servers are available.

If you are performing a merge or join partition operation, you need to check the status of both the parent and child partitions involved in the merge. Again, you should check the status of the partitions before you start the merge or join partition operation.

After you have started a partition operation, you should be patient and wait for all the synchronization work to complete. It takes time for the partition changes to be reflected across the network. A partition with many objects and replicas will naturally take longer than one with just a few objects.

You can also use DSTRACE to check the partition status. Figure 4-22 shows when the synchronization process for a partition has been completed.

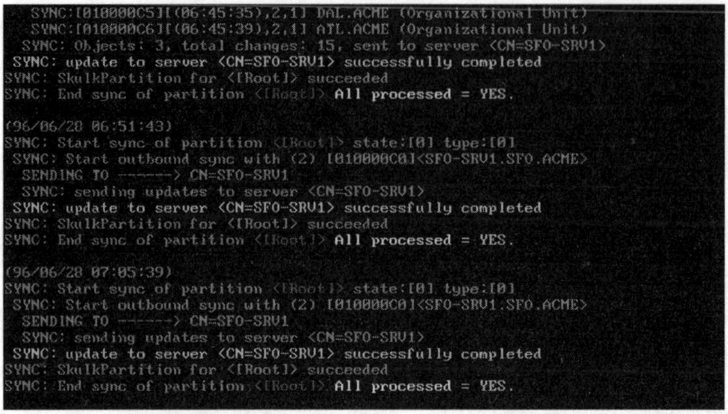

Figure 4-22: The Replica synchronization screen in DSTRACE indicates when the synchronization process has been completed for a partition.

The DSTRACE information can be more difficult to read and interpret because the information is more cryptic than the DSREPAIR information. For example, in Figure 4-23, we see the synchronization process for the [ROOT] partition stored on this server. The state:[0] means the partition is ON, and type:[0] means that this is the master replica. In the example, an outbound synchronization is started with (2), which is the replica number, stored on [020000D7]<NYC-SRV1.NYC.ACME>. The value of [020000D7] indicates the ID of the server (NYC-SRV1) or whatever server you are looking at. All updates are sent and the "All processed = YES" message is displayed, meaning that the synchronization is successful and that there is no further processing needed.

If possible, we recommend that you centralize the partition operations management. Only one person or a small group of people should be responsible for all of the partitioning and replication for your company. You may decide that there is only one workstation on the network that should start the partition operations. This way you can eliminate the possibility that two people or two different workstations are making changes to the partitions simultaneously.

The following sections discuss each of the partition and replica operations that can be performed. These operations include create new partition, merge partition, move partition or subtree, add replica, remove replica, change replica type, rebuild replicas, and abort partition.

```
SENDING TO ------> CN=NYC-SRV1
  SYNC: sending updates to server <CN=NYC-SRV1>
SYNC: update to server <CN=NYC-SRV1> successfully completed
(96/06/28 16:51:56)Purger: Start purge on NON  MASTER partition <NYC.ACME>
Purger: Checking for Root Rename . . . .
Purger: Checking for Expired Expectations . . .
Purger: purged 0 entries and 0 values
Purger: End partition purge succeeded
SYNC: SkulkPartition for <NYC.ACME> succeeded
SYNC: End sync of partition <NYC.ACME> All processed = YES.

(96/06/28 16:51:56)
SYNC: Start sync of partition <SFO.ACME> state:[0] type:[1]
  SYNC: Start outbound sync with (1) [010000BA]<NYC-SRV1.NYC.ACME>
  SENDING TO ------> CN=NYC-SRV1
  SYNC: sending updates to server <CN=NYC-SRV1>
SYNC: update to server <CN=NYC-SRV1> successfully completed
(96/06/28 16:51:56)Purger: Start purge on NON  MASTER partition <SFO.ACME>
Purger: Checking for Root Rename . . . .
Purger: Checking for Expired Expectations . . .
Purger: purged 0 entries and 0 values
Purger: End partition purge succeeded
SYNC: SkulkPartition for <SFO.ACME> succeeded
SYNC: End sync of partition <SFO.ACME> All processed = YES.
```

Figure 4-23: The DSTRACE information regarding the synchronization status of NYC-SRV1 is shown.

## THE CREATE NEW PARTITION OPERATION

Creating a new partition is the same as creating a child partition from the parent partition. This operation is sometimes called a partition split. The terms create and split are used interchangeably. The operation is generally fast because it generates less network traffic than other partition operations. The traffic is limited to changes to the replica pointers and partition control. However, once again, if you have a large number of partition replicas before the split, NDS must contact each server holding a replica to perform the operation there as well.

The operation simply divides the partition into two with all the information staying on the same servers that it originally started. This split operation will create a new child partition on all the servers that had a copy of the parent partition.

When the partition is created, it takes its name from the top-most container object (partition root object). The new partition contains all the objects in the tree that are under the container object. The partition defined previously is not affected.

In the following examples, assume that we have installed another server in the tree called DAL-SRV1. The result of installing the DAL-SRV1 server into the tree is that it will receive a read/write copy of the [ROOT] partition. Figure 4-24 shows how you can use the NDS Manager utility to create a new partition called DAL for the ACME company. All the objects in the subtree under DAL are included in the new partition.

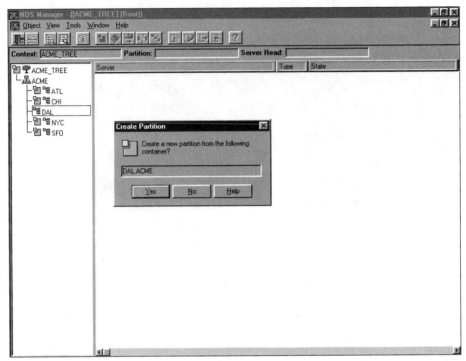

Figure 4–24: The OU=DAL container is created as a new partition in the ACME tree.

In addition, a create partition operation for DAL creates copies of the new DAL partition on all the servers that originally had copies of the parent [ROOT]. You can remove the additional replicas if they are not on the servers you want.

The DAL partition and its information can be placed on the servers in the DAL container. The same is true for all the locations. By partitioning the NDS tree, you can keep the information in each location while still locating and using the resources throughout the entire NDS tree.

In order to perform a create partition operation, you must have rights to the top of the partition or container that defines the partition. The effective rights needed are the write rights to the ACL of the top container object that defines the partition. There are several ways to receive this privilege. You can either be granted the Supervisor object right or the explicit write property right to the ACL property. Having either of these two rights assignments will enable you to perform a create partition operations on the tree.

## THE MERGE PARTITION OPERATION

The operation used to combine a child partition with its parent is called a merge. This operation is sometimes called partition join. The terms merge and join are used interchangeably. This operation takes different amounts of time and could generate network traffic depending on which servers the partitions were originally placed.

The merge operation requires that each server holding a copy of the parent partition must receive a copy of the child partition before the merge can take place. In return, each server holding a copy of the child partition must receive a copy of the parent before the merge can complete. The merge operation will attempt to move copies of either the parent or child partitions to the appropriate servers as needed. After the copies have been moved successfully the merge operation then joins the partitions together.

We recommend that you manually place copies of the parent partition on all the servers with a child partition before you initiate the merge operation. You should also place copies of each of the child partitions on the servers holding the parent partitions before you start the merge operation.

You will have greater control when merging partitions back together if you manually place copies of the parent and child partitions on appropriate servers. In order to accomplish this task, you must know where each of the copies of the partitions is located. Refer to the "Create a Partition and Replica Matrix" section later in this chapter.

If all the servers have copies of both the child and parent partitions before the merge operation is selected, the merge operation is quicker with less likelihood of having a problem and not completing. This also prevents large amounts of data or information moving across the network during the operation. The network traffic occurs when you prepare for the merge by placing the appropriate replicas on the servers.

An example of a merge partition operation is illustrated in Figure 4-25, where the SALES partition is merged back with its parent partition ATL. The NDS Manager utility will ask you to confirm the merge operation before completing it.

## Consulting Experience

Check the synchronization status of all replicas in the partition with DSREPAIR before initiating this partitioning operation or any other partitioning operation. All replicas must be available and functioning properly before you can proceed with the merge partition operation.

In order to perform the merge partition operation, you must have rights to only the child partitions. The effective rights needed are the write rights to the ACL of the child partition. There are several ways to receive this privilege. You can either be granted the Supervisor object right or the explicit write property right to the ACL property.

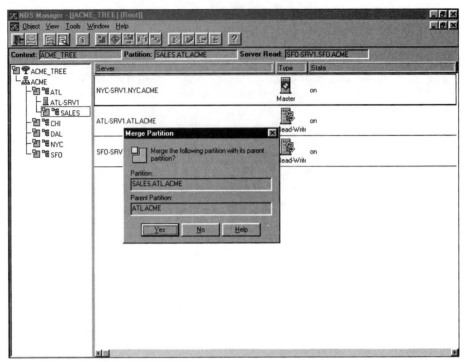

Figure 4-25: The SALES partition is merged back with its parent partition ATL.

## THE MOVE SUBTREE PARTITION OPERATION

The operation used to move a container and its entire contents or subtree from one location in the NDS tree to another is called a move subtree partition operation. This operation is very important when you reorganize the information in your NDS tree because it lets you move the container objects in the NDS tree. In order to move a container two conditions must exist:

- ◆ The OU container object being moved must be a partition. This means that the OU container object must be a partition root object. You may need to create a partition from the OU container before moving it.

- ◆ The partition or subtree you want to move cannot have any child partitions. You may be forced to merge child partitions with its parent in order to move the subtree.

Because this operation essentially moves a partition from one location in the NDS tree to another location, it can generate network traffic depending on which servers the parent partitions were originally placed.

In the following example, we assume that the joint operation in the previous example did not occur or was aborted. A move partition operation is illustrated in Figure 4-26, where the NDS Manager utility is used to move the SALES partition under the ATL location to another location in the NDS tree, in this case under the NYC.ACME container.

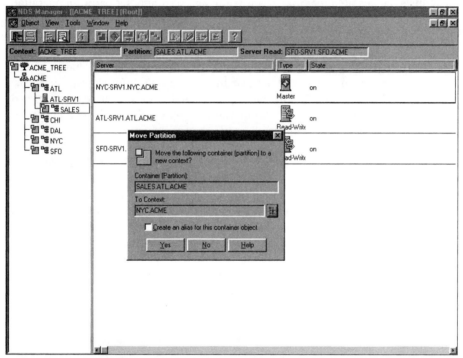

Figure 4-26: The SALES partition is moved to another location in the NDS tree. In this example, the SALES partition under ATL is moved to NYC.

In order to perform the move subtree partition operation, you must have rights to all the partitions involved. The effective rights needed are the write rights to the ACL of the top container object that defines the partition. There are several ways to receive this privilege. You can either be granted the Supervisor object right or the explicit write property right to the ACL property.

## THE ABORT PARTITION OPERATION

You have the ability to abort a partition operation that was previously started. The abort partition operation is valid only for a create or split, merge or join, move subtree, and change replica type. The abort partition operation cannot be used on add replica and remove replica.

This operation enables you to back out of partition operations that do not complete. For example, only one partition operation can take place at a time. So if a partition operation starts and does not complete, no further partition operation can be started. A partition operation will hang if one of the servers in the replica list of the partition becomes unavailable from either a downed server or a downed communication link. This problem is manifested by the "partition busy" message, or the replica is in a state other than ON if you try to start another partition operation.

If you suspect that a partition operation is having difficulty completing, you can either wait until the situation causing the problem is cleared up or you can abort the operation. To abort the partition operation you can use the NDS Manager utility, select the partition, and press the abort key. For example, the change replica type operation has not completed because the replica state information shows each replica with "Change Type 0." This message means that the current change state of the replicas is 0. For more information and a complete list of the change states, refer to the chapters on NDS Internals.

To execute the abort partition operation press the abort key at the bottom of the screen. A confirmation screen will appear, giving you another chance to verify the operation.

You can also abort a partition operation using the DSREPAIR utility as shown in Figure 4-27. From the DSREPAIR main menu select Advanced Options and then select Replica and partition operations. A list of all the partitions and replicas stored on the server is displayed. After you select the partition that is having the problems, the Replica Operations menu is then displayed. Select Cancel partition operation from the menu. When you select this menu item you will be asked to log in to Directory Services as someone who has rights over the partition.

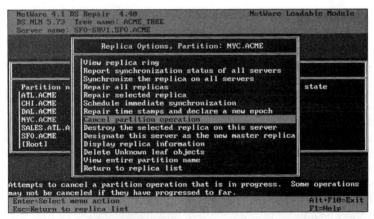

Figure 4-27: You can use DSREPAIR to abort or cancel a partition operation.

## Creating a Partition and Replica Matrix

The best method for keeping track of where partition and replicas are stored in the system is to use a Partition and Replica Matrix. The matrix, shown in Figure 4-28, helps you document the creation of partitions and replicas of the partitions. The matrix also helps you design and implement the partitions and replicas more efficiently. If you need to perform any partition operation, you have a quick and easy tool to refer to.

| SERVER \ PARTITION | [ROOT] | NYC | ATL | SFO | DAL | CHI |
|---|---|---|---|---|---|---|
| NYC-SRV1 | M | M | | | | |
| NYC-SRV2 | | R/W | | | | |
| ATL-SRV1 | R/W | | M | | | |
| ATL-SRV2 | | | R/W | | | |
| SFO-SRV1 | R/W | | | M | | |
| SFO-SRV2 | | | | R/W | | |
| DAL-SRV1 | | | | | M | |
| ○ | ○ | ○ | ○ | ○ | ○ | ○ |
| ○ | ○ | ○ | ○ | ○ | ○ | ○ |
| ○ | ○ | ○ | ○ | ○ | ○ | ○ |
| CHI-SRV2 | | | | | | R/W |

Figure 4-28: You should document your NDS partitions and replicas using a Partition and Replica Matrix.

In addition, the NDS Manager utility provides printing capabilities and can display a replication matrix for you.

With these partitioning rules in place, you can move to the next step in the NDS design process: the placement of the replicas.

# Chapter 5

# Replicate for Fault Tolerance and to Reduce Synchronization Traffic

## IN THIS CHAPTER

- ◆ Using three replicas for fault tolerance

- ◆ Replicating locally

- ◆ Replicating to reduce subordinate references, provide bindery service access, and improve name resolution

- ◆ Replica types and synchronization

- ◆ Managing NDS replicas

NDS IS A GLOBAL distributed name service that can be split into partitions, which are logical sections of the NDS tree or database. The partitions can then be distributed or placed on any number of NetWare 4 servers. An NDS replica is the physical copy of a partition that is stored on a specific NetWare 4 server. Any NDS partition can have multiple replicas or copies. The group of replicas that exists for a particular partition is called a replica list.

The replicas of an NDS partition have several purposes and benefits. The primary purpose for a replica of a partition is to increase the availability of that partition for the users. By placing multiple replicas, any NetWare 4 server can fail without hurting the NDS availability for your users. Thus, the capability of having multiple replicas of a single partition is a major advantage of NDS. The replicas simply provide fault tolerance for the information stored in the partition.

When changes or updates to a partition take place on an individual replica, that replica must in turn pass the changes to all the other replicas of that partition. NDS will automatically distribute these changes among all the replicas for a specific partition. This process of ensuring that all the latest changes or updates to a particular partition are passed along to each of the replicas is called synchronization.

The synchronization process between replicas can have an additional impact on the performance of each NetWare 4 server and the traffic on the network, both local LAN and WAN. You need to decide where to place the replicas so that the impact of the synchronization traffic is reduced.

In fact, one of the most important responsibilities of the network and NDS administrators is to design the placement of the NDS replicas. In order to accomplish the proper distribution and placement of the replicas to the specific NetWare 4 servers, you must use the following design principles or objectives:

◆ Provide fault tolerance

◆ Reduce synchronization traffic

Specific replica design rules have been created to assist you in meeting the design objectives for replicas and in understanding how the replicas should be implemented throughout the NetWare 4 servers on the network. The following are the design rules for replica placement:

◆ Always have three replicas for fault tolerance

◆ Replicate locally

◆ Keep the maximum number of replicas per partition from 7 to 10

◆ Keep the maximum number of replicas per server to 15

◆ Replicate to reduce subordinate references

◆ Replicate to provide bindery service access

◆ Replicate to improve name resolution

The design rules must be considered when organizing the replicas for your network. While we discuss each of the design rules in the following sections, we will stay focused on two replica design principles or objectives: provide fault tolerance and reduce synchronization traffic.

# Using Three Replicas for Fault Tolerance

NDS replicas increase the availability (fault tolerance) of a partition. A replica increases the availability because the partition now has more than one copy of its information. For example, if a server holding a replica of the partition becomes unavailable, then the users can use another copy or replica for authentication and updates.

A primary goal of NDS replicas is to eliminate the single point of failure for an NDS partition. Having multiple replicas of a partition on separate servers increases the availability of object information if one of the servers should become unavailable. In Figure 5-1 the NYC and SFO partitions have been replicated to multiple servers to provide fault tolerance for each partition. If one of the servers in the partition becomes unavailable, the other server will respond to the NDS requests.

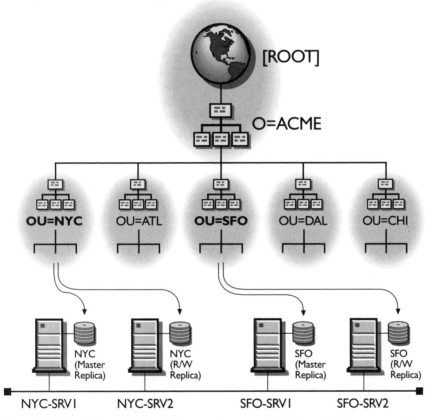

Figure 5-1: The NYC and SFO partitions have been replicated to multiple servers on the network to provide fault tolerance for the respective NDS partitions.

We strongly recommend that you always have *at least three* replicas for each of the NDS partitions in your tree. This means you should always have one master and two read/write replicas for every partition. Three replicas will provide you with adequate fault tolerance and still minimize the synchronization traffic between the servers.

The NetWare 4 installation program will automatically create up to three NDS replicas for fault tolerance. When you are installing additional servers into the tree, the installation program will place a replica of the partition where the server is going to be located in the tree. This will occur until there are three replicas for the partition. If the partition where you are installing the server has fewer than three replicas, the installation program will place a read/write replica on the new server in that partition.

If the server installed is being upgraded or has an existing bindery, such as NetWare 3.12, then the installation program will automatically convert the bindery to an NDS replica of the partition where the server is being installed. A NetWare 3.12 server being migrated or upgraded will receive either a master or read/write replica of the partition even if there are already three other replicas for that partition. For example, in Figure 5-2 the NYC partition has been replicated automatically to the servers NYC-SRV1, NYC-SRV2, and NYC-SRV3 by the installation program. Since NYC-SRV1 was the first server installed into the NDS tree and has the master replica for the [ROOT] partition it will also receive the master replica for the NYC partition. The others will receive read/write replicas until there are at least three replicas for the NYC partition. Notice that a fourth server, NYC-SRV4, has been installed into the partition but did not receive a replica automatically. It is assumed that the NYC-SRV4 is a new server and was not migrated from NetWare 3.12 (meaning there was no bindery to convert to a replica).

These replicas are created automatically only for the partition where the server object is being installed. The other partitions in the tree are not affected. The installation program performs this automatic replication to support fault tolerance of the NDS tree information. If you are comfortable with where the three automatic replicas were placed during installation, you do not need to change any of the replicas for a partition.

# Replicating Locally

You can increase the performance of the NDS access by the physical placement of the replicas. Since replication enables you to have multiple replicas of the partition, it makes sense to place those replicas local to the users who need the information. Placing a replica close to the users will decrease the time needed to authenticate, make changes, do searches, and extract NDS information.

Thus, the best method to guarantee an efficient design is to replicate each of the NDS partitions locally. This means that you would place all the replicas of a partition on the NetWare 4 servers that are in the same location as the partition. You should never place a replica across a WAN link if you have available servers that are local. A local server is defined as a server that is on the same side of your WAN link as each of the other servers holding replicas.

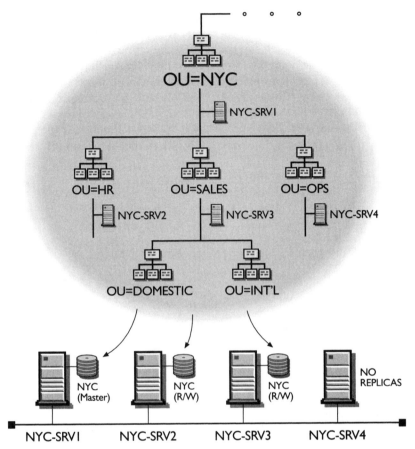

Figure 5-2: The NYC partition is replicated automatically to the first three servers, NYC-SRV1, NYC-SRV2, and NYC-SRV3, by the installation program. A fourth, NYC-SRV4, was installed into the partition but did not receive a replica automatically.

Remember that one of the objectives for proper placement of the replicas is to reduce the synchronization traffic between servers holding copies of a partition. Therefore, if you place a replica on a server that is physically located across a WAN link, you have increased the synchronization traffic. Each server with a copy or replica of the same partition will now have to communicate across the WAN link to keep all of the information in the partition synchronized. This increases both the time and effort for each of the servers.

Another drawback of placing a replica across the WAN link is that most, if not all, partition operations need to communicate with each of the replicas during the operation. For example, if a server is not available during a partition operation because a WAN link is temporarily down, the operation will wait until it can finish communicating before completing the operation. It is highly recommended that you check communication between servers holding the replicas of a partition and for the master replicas of the other partitions involved before starting an operation.

Figure 5-3 shows an example of placing a replica that is not local to the other replicas of the NYC partition. The servers NYC-SRV1, NYC-SRV2, and NYC-SRV3 all have replicas and all are local servers to the partition NYC and to each other. On the other hand, the server ATL-SRV1 should not be holding a replica of the partition because it is physically located across a WAN link in the ATL location.

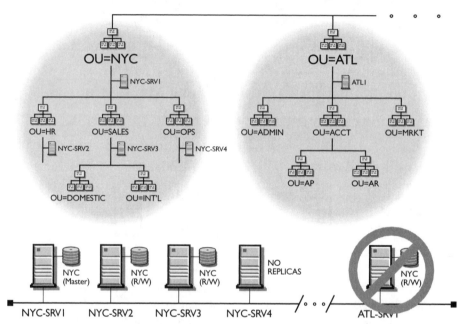

Figure 5-3: You should always try to place replicas on local servers in the partition. This means that the replicas for a partition are placed on the servers that are in the same location or site. Do not place a replica across a WAN link from the original partition.

On the other hand, following the rule of placing replicas locally will guarantee that users will always retrieve their personal information from servers that are physically close to them. Ideally, the replica should be placed so that the users' information is stored on the server that also stores the users' home directory. This may not always be possible, but it does improve the users' access to the NDS objects and properties. For example, during the login process users will map drives to volumes, capture to print queues, and access several of the user properties. NDS will execute each of these requests regardless of where the replicas are stored. However, the login speed for the user will be increased if the user finds the requested information on their preferred server.

# Replicas for Remote Offices with One Server

As stated, one of the primary design rules is that you always have three replicas of a partition and always replicate the partition on local servers. However, meeting these criteria may not always be possible. For example, a partition is created for a small remote office location on your network that has only one server. The master replica is held on the central server, which holds the parent partition. Although it is recommended that you place at least two more read/write replicas for fault tolerance, it is also recommended that you place these replicas on local servers or servers that are in the same physical location as the master replica.

For this type of situation, a small field or remote office with only one server is an exception to the design rules. The following questions are frequently asked:

◆ What happens if the location or site has only one server?

◆ How do I create three replicas for fault tolerance?

◆ Do I still partition and replicate locally?

In the case of a remote site with just one server, you should still partition at that site and place the replica of the partition on the local server. In order to replicate for fault tolerance, a second replica of the partition must be placed on a server that is in the nearest location. Although the design rule states that you should not place replicas across WAN links, it is more important to provide fault tolerance for NDS. It is better to replicate a partition at least twice, even if across a WAN link, than lose the NDS information if the server ever goes down.

Typically, the remote office or site contains a small number of users and objects. Therefore, although we recommend against replicating across your WAN, a small replica across your WAN is your only alternative for fault tolerance. It is better to replicate a small partition across a WAN than lose the NDS information if the server ever goes down. Novell Technical Support has stated that it is easier to recover or restore the NDS information for a partition if the partition has a current replica. Thus, for the remote office or site it is recommended that replicating for fault tolerance is more important than replicating locally.

However, we do not necessarily recommend that you place two replicas on servers across the WAN link making three replicas all together. Although three replicas for fault tolerance is ideal, it is better to reduce the synchronization traffic overhead across the WAN by having only two replicas for the remote office partition.

Figure 5-4 illustrates how a small remote office in the ACME tree should be replicated. For this example only, assume that there is a small remote site in Boston called BOS, which is connected to the NYC hub. There is only one server (BOS-SRV1) in the remote office of Boston. You should create a small partition for BOS and replicate it to the server BOS-SRV1. You should also place a replica on the nearest server, which would be NYC-SRV1 in the New York City hub location.

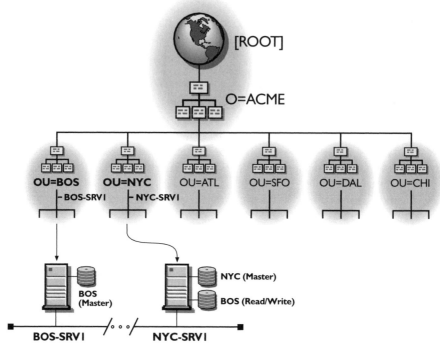

Figure 5-4: There is only one server (BOS-SRV1) in the remote office site of Boston. You should create a small partition called BOS and replicate it to the local server BOS-SRV1 and to the server NYC-SRV1 in the New York City location. It is more important to replicate for fault tolerance than to not replicate across the WAN links.

## Replicas for Other Types of Remote Offices

When you are trying to develop a replica design for your company and there are remote or field offices that have been partitioned, you also need to consider a couple of more situations. The following situations can cause some confusion on how to design replication properly according to the rules for fault tolerance and placing the replicas locally.

## Remote Offices That Have Two NetWare 4 Servers

In this case, the remote office has two NetWare 4 servers. You should create and place a replica for the partition on each of the local servers. This will establish at least two replicas for the partition defined for the remote office. Since there are already two local NetWare 4 servers at the remote office, you may decide that the replication is sufficient for fault tolerance. A third replica placed across a WAN link will cause more WAN traffic that may not be needed. We typically do not recommend that you create the third replica and place it across the WAN link. However, depending on the speed of the links it may be feasible. If the WAN link is T-1 or greater, a third replica may be appropriate.

## Remote Offices That Have No Servers

The case of a remote office that does not have a local server is easier. Since the remote office does not have a server, the users are reaching across the WAN infrastructure in order to log in to servers at the hub location. The remote office location should have an organizational unit (OU) or container defined in the tree to provide better access to resources. However, the container should not be its own partition.

Since the remote office is not a partition, it will be part of the partition defined at the hub location. All the replicas for the partition defined at the hub will be stored on local servers, which are the same servers that the remote office users log in to.

# Not Exceeding 7 to 10 Replicas per Partition

The maximum number of replicas per partition is 7 to 10. This range will minimize the total amount of network traffic that has to be generated by the replica synchronization process between servers. Reducing the replica synchronization traffic meets one of the replica design objectives.

You will create more replicas than you initially planned because you may need to enable bindery services on more NetWare 4 servers. Bindery services require that each server have at least a read/write replica where the server is setting its bindery context. Although the installation program will only try to create up to three replicas per partition for fault tolerance, you may need to create more replicas simply to support bindery services on more servers.

Bindery services are also required during a NetWare 3 to NetWare 4 server upgrade. For example, if you are upgrading a NetWare 3 server, a read/write replica of the partition where the server's object is placed will be held on the upgraded NetWare 4 server. The read/write replica is placed on the server regardless of whether there are already three replicas. (Refer back to the "Always Have Three Replicas for Fault Tolerance" section earlier in this chapter.) The assumption is that since the server is being migrated from NetWare 3 and the bindery, bindery services in NetWare 4 will be needed.

The rule of no more than 7 to 10 replicas per partition implies that the replicas are full NDS replicas. A full replica is considered to be either a master, read/write, or read-only replica. A full replica does not include the subordinate reference replicas. If you have more than 10 replicas, consider splitting the partition just so you can reduce the total number of replicas per partition and decrease the overhead for the replica synchronization process.

If any of the object information for a partition changes in one of the replicas, it needs to change in all the other replicas for that partition. Remember that the NDS database is loosely consistent, which means that all the replicas are not instantaneously updated. For example, each user object's information changes when the user logs in to NDS. The change is written to the replica on the server that logged the user in. These changes are then synchronized to each of the other replicas of the partition. You can see that replica synchronization increases by simply having more objects in the partition and having more replicas per partition.

The replica synchronization process runs in the background and works to maintain consistency across the replicas of a partition and the entire NDS database. Although the information passed between the replicas during the synchronization exchange is limited to just the updates, it could impact the traffic on the network, both local LAN and WAN, depending on where you place the replicas. Also, since the LAN infrastructure is typically faster than the WAN, we recommend placing all the replicas local.

# Not Exceeding 15 Replicas per Server

One of the primary objectives of replica design is to minimize the impact of the synchronization between replicas. The replica synchronization process will execute on an individual NetWare 4 server and manage all the updates to the other replicas. The replica synchronization process will run for each of the individual replicas held by that server. A single server cannot hold more than one replica of the same partition. A server can only store multiple replicas if the replicas are from different partitions in the NDS tree. In order to reduce the overall impact of the replica synchronization process on any one server, you should avoid having more than 15 replicas per server.

The best method to reduce both the synchronization workload of the servers and the network traffic is to maintain only a few replicas per partition and just a few replicas per server. These two factors go hand in hand to reduce the total number of replicas on a single server and to avoid having more than a total of 7 to 10 replicas per partition.

Plan the placement of the file servers into the tree so that a single container does not hold servers that are on different WAN segments. A partition and its replicas should contain only file server objects that are physically close on the network.

We always recommend that you place the NDS replicas on high-end servers that will keep up with the other servers holding the other replicas. The synchronization process between all the replicas is only as fast and efficient as the weakest link. Do not place replicas on a low-performance server because it will affect the entire process.

> ## Consulting Experience
>
> A dedicated NDS replica server is a high-end NetWare 4 server whose sole purpose is to maintain NDS replicas in the tree. If the dedicated NDS replica server is a super server that has extremely fast hardware, then it could be possible to have 100 replicas or more stored on the server. The major dependencies would still be the network infrastructure, the speed of the links between servers, and the speed of the hardware where each of the other replicas is placed. Remember that each of the replicas placed on the server must be from different partitions. This assumes a very large NDS tree that has at least 100 or more separate NDS partitions.

The number of total replicas per server may vary depending on your specific network environment, server hardware, and the application of the server in use. For example, the number of replicas for a main file and print server, which holds the home directory for each user, should not hold more than 7 to 10 replicas. An application or e-mail server can possibly hold a few more, such as 20 to 25 replicas. A NetWare 4 server dedicated as an NDS replica server can possibly hold up to 100 replicas per server. Again, the other network infrastructure and the services that each server is providing will affect the total number of replicas per server.

# Replicating to Reduce Subordinate References

When designing the placement of the NDS replicas, you should consider the distribution of subordinate reference replicas. You should design your replica placement to reduce the number of subordinate reference replicas for a partition. Subordinate partitions that cause subordinate reference replicas should be limited from 10 to 15 per parent. This means that a parent OU or container that is a partition should not have more than 10 to 15 child OUs beneath it that will also be partitions.

It is possible to have more than 10 to 15 child partitions, which create the subordinate references. However, in order to push past 10 to 15 child partitions, you should understand the impact and ramifications of the placement of each of the subordinate references. Most NDS tree and partition designs will be able to meet the recommendation of 10 to 15 child partitions. If you have to have more then it should only be implemented in a small portion of the tree. Although you can have more than 10-15 child partitions, you should never have more than 35 to 40 child partitions for any one partition. Having more child partitions could cause each server holding the parent to store more subordinate reference replicas.

A subordinate reference replica provides the connectivity between the parent partitions and child partitions. A subordinate reference is essentially a pointer from the parent down the tree to the next layer or child partitions.

Subordinate reference replicas are a design issue because they participate in the replica synchronization process for each of the partitions. The major difference between a subordinate reference replica and the other replica types is the amount of information passed during synchronization. The subordinate reference replicas exchange timestamps with the other replicas and update only the top-most object of the partition, as needed. Thus, the amount of information exchanged between servers for the subordinate reference replicas is very little.

Before we discuss the subordinate reference replica issues, it is comforting to know that if you have designed your NDS tree properly the subordinate references will be correctly distributed. A good NDS tree and partition design based on the design rules in this book will automatically distribute the subordinate references appropriately.

This entails that the top of the NDS tree is based on the WAN infrastructure with each of the WAN locations being a partition. In this fashion, the partitions are built hierarchically and in the shape of a pyramid. If you created only a few replicas per partition then the subordinate reference replicas will have been optimized and there is very little else that you can change.

NDS as a system is responsible for creating, removing, and maintaining the subordinate reference replicas for each partition. Each NDS administrator should be aware (not beware) of the subordinate reference replica placement and understand its impact on the synchronization process. This means you should try to understand where the subordinate references are being created and, if possible, try to replicate so that the overall number of subordinate replicas is reduced. Reducing the number of subordinate reference replicas will increase the performance of the synchronization process for each server.

One way to reduce subordinate reference replicas is to reduce the number of replicas of a parent partition. Limiting the number of servers that will store a copy of the parent partition does this. Another way to reduce subordinate reference replicas is to place the child partitions on the same servers as their parents. The second option is not always recommended or feasible.

## Example of Subordinate Reference Replicas

A good example for illustrating subordinate reference replicas is to use the [ROOT] partition, which is at the top of the tree. Figure 5-5 illustrates the ACME tree partitioned with the [ROOT] partition. Directly beneath the [ROOT] partition are 200 partitions for the cities or locations in the tree. This is an extremely bad tree and partition design. However, for this example assume that we have created 200 cities or locations and that each are partitioned under the [ROOT] partition.

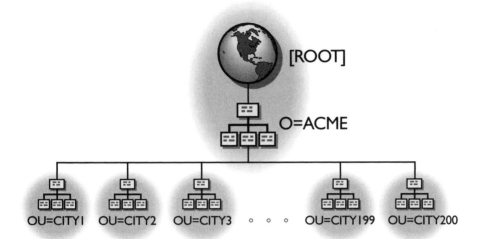

Figure 5-5: Assume for this example that the ACME tree has over 200 cities, each partitioned under the [ROOT] partition.

Consider what would happen each time that you place a replica of the [ROOT] partition on another NetWare 4 server. The NDS system will be forced to create 200 subordinate references on that server, one for each of the child partitions. This assumes that the server holds only a replica for the [ROOT] partition. From the server perspective, it now has to participate in the replica synchronization process for each of the 200 partitions. This amount of work will probably overload the one server. The server will probably not be able to keep up with all the changes in the network. You can see the problem, especially as you add more replicas of the [ROOT] partition to other servers in the network.

In this case of 200 cities being partitioned off the [ROOT], the issue is not just the number of replicas held by one server, but also the amount of traffic between the replicas. Although very little data is passed between a subordinate reference replica and the other replicas, each replica must be contacted. Subordinate reference replicas, by nature, are typically stored across the WAN links and the impact of synchronization to more servers could be an issue.

Another concern is the effect that the large number of subordinate reference replicas has on partition operations. Each replica of a partition must be contacted before a partition operation can complete successfully. See the "Managing NDS Replicas" section later in this chapter.

The simplest way to eliminate all of these problems is to design your tree and partitions like a pyramid based on the WAN infrastructure, which naturally distributes the subordinate references appropriately. The rules for designing the NDS tree and partitions correctly were discussed in previous chapters.

To fix the problem with the ACME tree depicted in Figure 5-5, you simply need to change the design of the tree. The quickest design fix is to add another layer of OUs or containers directly under the [ROOT] partition and then create each of the containers as partitions. By doing this you will distribute the subordinate reference replicas across more NetWare 4 servers. Figure 5-6 illustrates how adding the regional layer OUs and partitions in the ACME tree will help distribute the subordinate reference replicas.

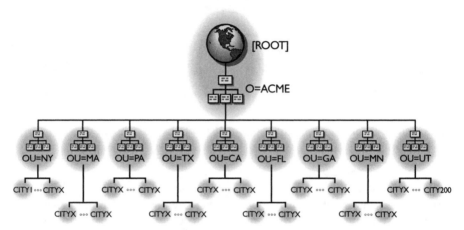

Figure 5-6: Adding a layer of regional OUs and partitions in the ACME tree design will help distribute the subordinate reference replicas.

## Subordinate References' Effect on Partitioning Operations

Partitioning operations is another issue that could affect the placement of the subordinate reference replicas. During any partitioning operation all the replicas in the replica list must be contacted in order to complete the operation. This includes the subordinate reference replicas. If, for any reason, the server with a replica is not available, the partition operation will not complete until that server is available. If any replica is unavailable, the partition operation will continue and try to contact the replica until it can be reached. Thus, the greater the number of subordinate references the greater the possibility they could affect the efficiency of the partitioning operations.

You may be wondering why the subordinate reference replicas are contacted during a partition operation. Even though subordinate references do not contain all the partition information, subordinate references do contain the partition root object and its properties, such as the replica list, which could change during the operation.

# Replicating to Provide Bindery Service Access

The NetWare 4 feature known as bindery services enables the NetWare 4 server to respond to the bindery calls made by the bindery-based utilities and applications. Bindery services let these applications run on NetWare 4 and NDS without modifications.

## Planning Bindery Services

In order for a NetWare 4 server to support bindery services, it must hold either a read/write or master replica of a partition where the server is installed or where the server is setting the bindery context. You will need to place read/write replicas on the NetWare 4 servers to support bindery services. This requirement of bindery services will force you to place more NDS replicas than initially planned.

You will need to plan bindery services requirements and replica placement in order to provide proper access and minimize the total number of replicas per partition and server. Remember that a single partition should not have more than 7 to 10 replicas. Bindery services may force you to exceed these numbers and make you split the partition just to reduce the number of replicas.

Bindery services are also required during a NetWare 3 to NetWare 4 server upgrade. For example, if you are upgrading a NetWare 3 server, a read/write replica of the partition is placed on the upgraded NetWare 4 server. The read/write replica is placed on the server regardless of whether there are already three replicas as described in the "Always Have Three Replicas for Fault Tolerance" section earlier in this chapter. The assumption is that since the server is being migrated from NetWare 3 and the bindery, bindery services in NetWare 4 will be needed.

## Understanding the Server Bindery Context

The bindery context set at the server is officially known as the *server bindery context*. The server bindery context is the name of the container object(s) where bindery services is set for the server. The server bindery context is also referred to as the bindery path. Figure 5-7 illustrates how the server NYC-SRV1 needs to hold a read/write replica of the NYC partition in order for the server bindery context at OU=NYC to be available.

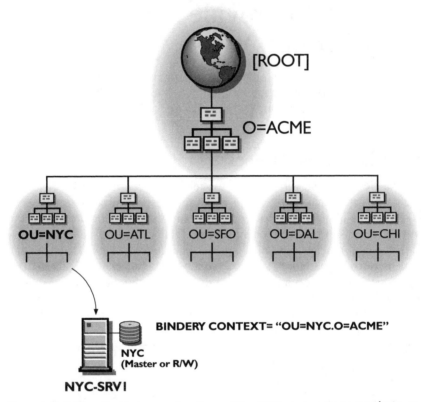

Figure 5-7: Setting the bindery services for partition NYC requires that a read/write or master replica be stored on the server NYC-SRV1. The NetWare 4 server is setting the server bindery context to OU=NYC.

You can set the bindery context using a SET command at the console. In order to set the bindery context for the server NYC-SRV1 in ACME enter the following at the server console prompt:

```
SET SERVER BINDERY CONTEXT = "OU=NYC.O=ACME"
```

In Figure 5-8 all the objects in the container OU=HR.OU=NYC.O=ACME that are NetWare 3 bindery object types are viewed and accessed as if they are in a bindery. The NDS objects that are available through bindery services include the user, group, print queue, print server, and profile. This list is included because these are the only objects that were defined in the NetWare 3 bindery. The new NDS objects, such as directory map, organizational role, computer, and alias, will not show up as bindery objects in your Directory.

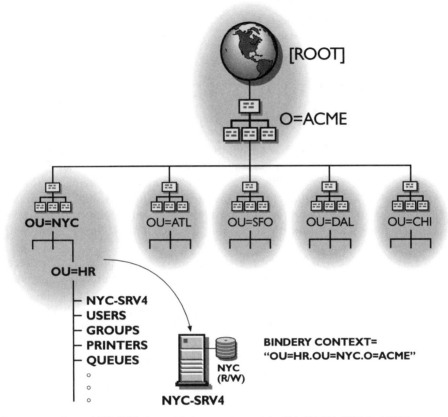

Figure 5-8: Server NYC-SRV4 has a bindery context set to OU=HR.OU=NYC.O=ACME.

Bindery-based clients and servers can access the objects subordinate to the containers where the bindery context is set. Because NetWare 4 now allows you to set multiple bindery contexts for the server, the handling of the invalid context error has changed. NetWare 4 cannot fail the entire SET command because one of the containers specified may be valid.

In order to see or verify the effective bindery path for a server, you should enter the following command at the server console prompt:

```
CONFIG
```

When you check the effective bindery path this way, you will see the distinguished names of each NDS container object listed on separate lines. Each container listed here is a valid bindery path. Objects created through bindery services are created as subordinate to the first effective (or valid) bindery path.

In previous versions of NetWare 4, you were limited to setting the bindery context at only one container object. With NetWare 4, you can now set up to 16 container objects as the bindery context.

# Replicating to Improve Name Resolution

The mechanism NDS uses to find the object location is referred to as name resolution. If the object information is not stored locally, the server must walk the directory tree to find the server that has the correct information. Every replica maintains a set of pointers to all the other replicas in the same partition. Using these pointers NDS can locate the partitions that are above and below in the directory tree. With this detail, NDS can follow these pointers to locate the servers holding the requested data.

To speed the access of locating the appropriate server, replicas can be placed closer to help the user find the requested information. For example, if you are trying to locate information from one side of the tree to the other, the partition and replicas that will naturally help you is the [ROOT] partition. In this case, we recommend that you replicate the [ROOT] partition to the major hub site in your company. This is recommended only if the [ROOT] partition is set up as a small partition. Small means the [ROOT] partition should include just the [ROOT] object and the O=ACME object. See Figure 5-9 for an illustration of a [ROOT] partition that is created as a small partition for replication across a WAN link.

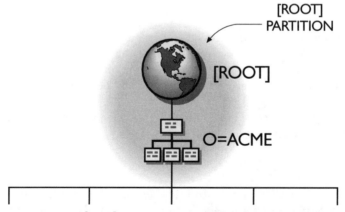

Figure 5-9: The [ROOT] partition can be replicated across the WAN links if it is created as a small partition containing just the [ROOT] object and O=ACME object.

Figure 5-10 illustrates how the [ROOT] partition can be replicated to a few strategic locations in the WAN infrastructure to facilitate improved name resolution. In this case, we have placed a copy of [ROOT] in New York City (NYC) on the NYC-SRV1 server, in Atlanta (ATL) on the ATL-SRV1 server, and in San Francisco (SFO) on the SFO-SRV1.

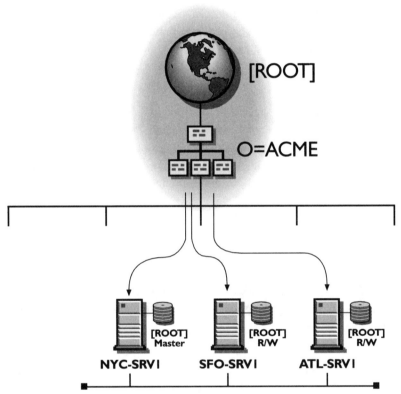

Figure 5-10: NDS replicas for the [ROOT] partition are stored on different servers throughout the network to facilitate improved name resolution. A copy of [ROOT] is placed in New York City (NYC) on the NYC-SRV1, in San Francisco (SFO) on the SFO-SRV1, and in Atlanta (ATL) on the ATL-SRV1 server.

Again, the [ROOT] partition should be kept small to keep NDS synchronization traffic to a minimum. A small [ROOT] partition (containing very few objects) is fairly static. So the replication of [ROOT] across the WAN links is okay. However, do not go overboard on replicating this partition. Three or four replicas of the [ROOT] partition are sufficient.

We do not recommend that you replicate any other partition across the WAN infrastructure for the purpose of name resolution. Because [ROOT] is at the top of your tree and name resolution that traverses the tree from one side to the other must go through the [ROOT] partition, it only makes sense to replicate [ROOT] at key hub locations in your tree.

 NDS replicas do not provide fault tolerance for the file system stored on NetWare 4 servers. Replicas only increase the availability of the NDS object and property information stored in the NDS partition.

# Using a Partition and Replica Matrix

The best method for keeping track of where partition and replicas are stored in the system is to use a Partition and Replica Matrix. This matrix will help you design and implement the partitions and replicas more efficiently and will also help you track the replica type and placement for each partition. The matrix, as shown in Figure 5-11, helps you document the creation of partitions and the placement of each replica. If you need to perform any partition operation, you have a quick and easy tool to refer to.

| PARTITION / SERVER | [ROOT] | NYC | ATL | SFO | DAL | CHI |
|---|---|---|---|---|---|---|
| NYC-SRVI | M | M | | | | |
| NYC-SRV2 | | R/W | | | | |
| ATL-SRVI | R/W | | M | | | |
| ATL-SRV2 | | | R/W | | | |
| SFO-SRVI | R/W | | | M | | |
| SFO-SRV2 | | | | R/W | | |
| DAL-SRVI | | | | | M | |
| ○ | ○ | ○ | ○ | ○ | ○ | ○ |
| ○ | ○ | ○ | ○ | ○ | ○ | ○ |
| ○ | ○ | ○ | ○ | ○ | ○ | ○ |
| CHI-SRV2 | | | | | | R/W |

Figure 5-11: You should document your NDS partitions and replicas using a Partition and Replica Matrix.

# NDS Replicas

NDS is a global name service that can be split into partitions and then distributed to any number of network servers. It is important to remember that a partition is a logical structure, while the replica is a physical copy of the partition. Figure 5-12 illustrates that a replica is the physical copy of a partition. The [ROOT] partition for ACME is placed on servers NYC-SRV1, ATL-SRV1, and SFO-SRV1.

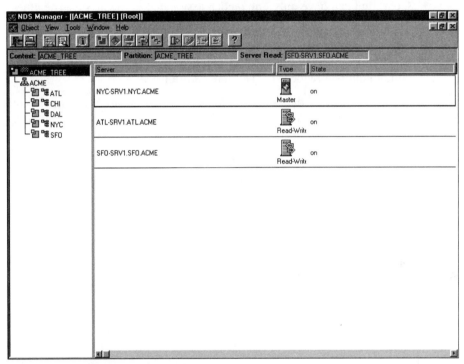

Figure 5-12: NDS replicas for the [ROOT] partition are stored on different servers throughout the network. In this case, the [ROOT] partition for ACME is placed on servers NYC-SRV1, ATL-SRV1, and SFO-SRV1.

The fact that NDS trees can be partitioned and replicated makes NDS a powerful facility for storing, accessing, managing, and using information about the network resources regardless of where they are physically located.

Before you can complete your replication design there are some basic replica characteristics you will need to know. The following characteristics apply to all replicas and will help you understand how they are implemented or placed throughout the servers on the network:

◆ A partition can have multiple replicas. Multiple copies of a partition are known as replicas and can be stored on separate servers across your network as explained in previous sections.

◆ A partition can have only one replica designated as the master. The other partitions will be read/write replicas and in some cases read-only.

◆ Only one replica of a partition can be stored on any given server. A NetWare 4 server can hold multiple replicas from different partitions. It cannot hold two replicas of the same partition.

◆ All replicas will participate in the replica synchronization for a partition. All replicas are part of the partition's synchronization list and therefore participate in synchronization operations. This is true regardless of replica type.

These rules are important because they describe the characteristics of replication. Knowing these rules will help you efficiently design the replica placement during implementation or production of your NetWare 4 network.

# Replica Types

Proper placement of replicas on the network servers is important to ensure proper operation of the Directory. A NetWare 4 server can contain any number of replicas if they are from different partitions in the NDS tree. A NetWare 4 server also does not have to contain any replicas. In order to understand where and when to place the replicas, you must understand the different types of replicas and their characteristics.

As we have already stated, each partition can have multiple replicas. And each replica will be one of the following four replica types: master, read/write, read-only, and subordinate reference.

## Master Replica

The master (M) replica of a partition is created when the partition is first created. Although the first replica is always designated as the master, it can be changed as other replicas are added. There can be only one master replica for each partition. The master replica provides the following features:

◆ Accepts client updates to the NDS object and attributes. This is the capability to add, delete, and modify the objects in the partition.

◆ Controls all partitioning operations. These operations include splitting and joining partitions, moving objects, moving subtrees, adding and removing replicas, and repairing the replicas.

◆ Conforms to the X.500 model, which enables clients to request the use of only the master replica.

NDS permits only one master replica per partition because the master replica controls all the partitioning operations. The master replica essentially locks the partition during the majority of the partition operation. This ensures that there is only one operation being performed at a time. This mechanism provides the NDS database integrity.

For example, in order to change the partition structure of the tree through either a Create or Merge Partition operation, you must be able to contact the master for that partition. The master then controls the operation and works with the other replicas to compete the operation. Each of the partition operations is controlled by a master-slave relationship between the master replica and the other replica types. As the system administrator, you must also have sufficient rights to the partition before NDS will let you do the operation.

The master replica is equal to all other replicas during the replica synchronization process. The replica synchronization is a peer-to-peer mechanism or operation. It is not driven by a master-slave relationship. The master does not control the synchronization of all the replicas for the partitions.

The master replica provides complete access to the object and property information in the partition. This means that the users can log in through this replica and make changes to the information in the replica. The changes include adding, deleting, and renaming the objects with modification to the properties.

Figure 5-13 shows the master replicas for the NYC, ATL, SFO, CHI, DAL, SALES, and [ROOT] partitions of the ACME tree. The master replicas are stored on the server SFO-SRV1.

# Read/Write Replica

The read/write (R/W) replica is the most frequently used because there can be any number of them for any given partition. Although there is no limit to the number of read/write replicas per partition, we do recommend that you keep the number small and create a new read/write replica only when needed.

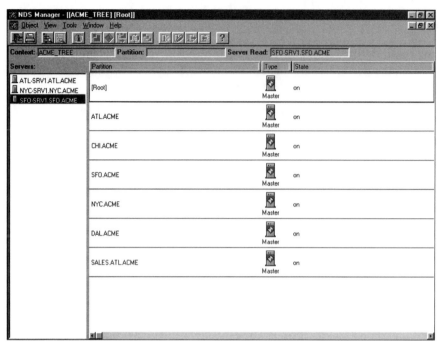

Figure 5-13: The master replicas for the [ROOT], SFO, and NYC partitions of the ACME tree are stored on the server SFO-SRV1.

## Consulting Experience

The placement of the master replica should be determined according to the physical layout of the network and the servers. If possible, you should place the master replica on a server that is in a central location and has reliable connectivity (and speed) to other replicas. For example, the master replica can be placed on a server that is located on the network backbone. Placing the master replica of the partition on the backbone gives the master replica better performance in order to complete the partition operations. The master replica should also be close to the master replicas of parent and child partitions, if possible.

In large networks with many servers the type of replica that is mostly used is the read/write. The purpose of the read/write replica is to distribute the NDS partition information across the servers on the network for fault tolerance and performance. A read/write replica provides the following features:

♦ Accepts client updates to the NDS object and attributes. The read/write replica can add, delete, and modify the objects in the partition.

♦ Provides fault tolerance for the partition. The read/write replicas improve availability of the information stored in the partition.

♦ Increases performance of the NDS access by the physical placement of the read/write replicas. The read/write replica enables you to have multiple replicas of the partition and place those replicas local to the users who need the information.

Like the master replica, the read/write replica provides complete access to the object and property information in the partition. A read/write replica also enables the clients to make modifications. Since updates can be made on a read/write replica, it also can be used for login requests for the users of the network.

In some of the other documentation on NetWare 4 the read/write replica is often referred to as a secondary replica.

The bindery services feature in NetWare 4 requires that at least a read/write or master replica of the partition containing the bindery context exist on the server where the services are needed.

Figure 5-14 shows the read/write replicas for the [ROOT] partition of the ACME tree. Several read/write replicas are stored on the servers ATL-SRV1 and NYC-SRV1.

# Read-Only Replica

The read-only (RO) replica, as its name implies, will not accept changes from users. The only way that a read-only replica discovers changes is through synchronization with the other replicas (read/write and master).

The read-only replica provides:

♦ Access to the NDS objects and attributes in the partition. The read-only replica does not accept client updates but does accept read requests from the clients.

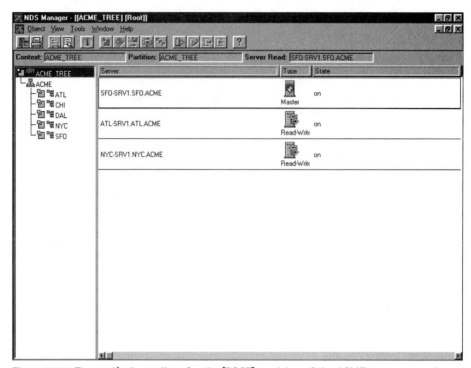

Figure 5-14: The read/write replicas for the [ROOT] partition of the ACME tree are stored on the servers ATL-SRV1 and NYC-SRV1.

◆ Fault tolerance for the partition. The read-only replicas improve availability of the information stored in the partition.

◆ Increased performance of access to NDS by the physical placement of the read-only replicas. The read-only replica enables you to place those replicas local to the users who need the information.

Since the read-only replica cannot be updated, it cannot support login requests from the users. For this reason, the read-only replicas are seldom used or implemented into production. There are currently very few reasons to implement read-only partitions.

Be aware that if you disable login on a NetWare 4 server (in this case a server with a read-only replica), the other NetWare 4 servers will not be able to connect and log in to the server to perform the replica synchronization. Disabling logins on any server with or without replicas should be avoided because it will block the replica synchronization.

---

### Consulting Experience

When a network user logs in to Directory Services, four properties of the user object are updated: Network Address, Login Time, Last Login Time, and Revision. In order for users to change or update these four properties, they must log in to at least a read/write or master replica. The read-only replica cannot accept user logins because these properties cannot be updated.

When a network user logs out of Directory Services, the Network Address and Revision properties for the user object are modified.

---

One possible reason for implementing a read-only replica is that you are trying to provide read access to the NDS information but no client update activity. For example, you may want to build an off-site disaster recovery center for the servers. You could place a read-only replica, which would maintain itself through replica synchronization, but not let any users log in to that server.

## Subordinate Reference Replica

The subordinate reference (SR) replicas provide tree connectivity by linking the parent partition with its child partitions. A subordinate reference replica is essentially a pointer down the tree to the next layer of partitions. NDS depends on the subordinate reference replicas for proper operation and to make it more efficient because it does not have to place a full replica (master, read/write, and read-only) to provide the tree connectivity. The NDS system will place a subordinate reference replica on a server that contains a replica of the parent but does not have the child replica. The subordinate reference replicas are good because the system does not require you to connect the tree manually by placing full replicas.

A subordinate reference replica contains only one object, the top-most container object in the partition (typically an OU). The top-most container object in the partition defines the partition and is called the partition root object. This container object stores partition information that links the partitions in the tree together. One of the pieces of information that the partition root object holds is a list of all the replicas in partition (master, read/write, read-only, and subordinate references). This replica list is used during the replica synchronization process. This means that all subordinate reference replicas of a partition participate during each replica synchronization for that partition. Thus, the greater the number of subordinate reference replicas the larger the impact on the replica synchronization process.

The subordinate reference replicas are created and managed by NDS and the servers. You do not need to manage them. The NDS system will place a subordinate reference replica on a server that contains a replica of the parent but does not have the child replica. NDS places a subordinate reference for each child of the parent on that server. Figure 5-15 illustrates a partitioned tree and its subsequent replica placement on the network servers. Some of the servers have subordinate reference replicas.

Some of the servers in Figure 5-15 are storing subordinate reference replicas because the servers are holding the parent partition but not the corresponding child partition. For example, ATL-SRV1 holds a copy of the [ROOT] and ATL but not NYC, SFO, DAL, and CHI. So subordinate references are established on ATL-SRV1 to link the parent with its children.

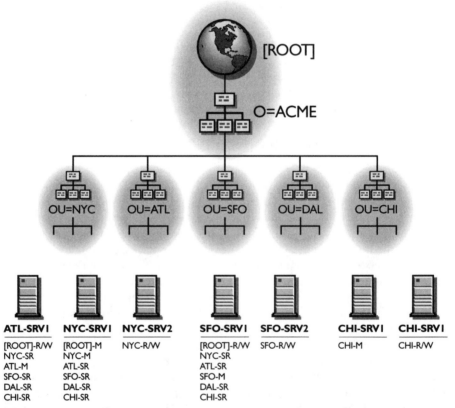

Figure 5-15: An example of the ACME tree being partitioned with subordinate reference replicas created whenever a parent partition exists on a server without a copy of a child partition

The subordinate reference replicas that connect the tree together are visible in Novell's NDS Manager utility and the DSREPAIR utility. They are not visible from the DOS-based NETADMIN or PARTMGR utilities. Figure 5-16 displays all the replicas on the server ATL-SRV1. Notice the subordinate reference replicas.

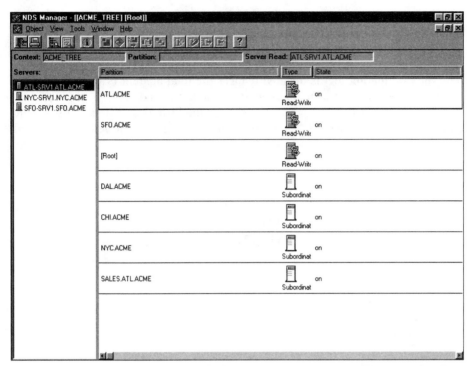

Figure 5-16: NDS Manager displays all of the replicas on the server ATL-SRV1, including the subordinate reference replicas.

Since a subordinate reference replica does not contain all of the information for each of the objects in the partition, it cannot provide the users access to the object and property information. The user cannot log in through this replica because there is no object information except for the partition root object.

# Replica Synchronization

NDS is a loosely consistent database, which means that changes or updates can occur at various replicas and that not all the replicas may have the exact information at the same time. However, since NDS is loosely synchronized, an update made at one replica propagates to other replicas of the partition over time. The replicas exchange information with each other to perform all updates. These changes are automatically sent to the other replicas of that partition by a background process called replica synchronization. Replica synchronization guarantees consistency of the information across all the replicas of a partition over a period of time.

The updates or modifications that affect the NDS data include adding, deleting, moving or renaming an object, as well as changing the properties or attributes of the object. The replica synchronization process only passes the data that has changed for each object or property between the replicas of the partition. Passing only the information that is updated reduces the total amount of information sent and keeps the network traffic for synchronization at a minimum.

Figure 5-17 illustrates how the replicas for the [ROOT] partition will stay synchronized among the servers. The illustration should only be viewed as conceptual.

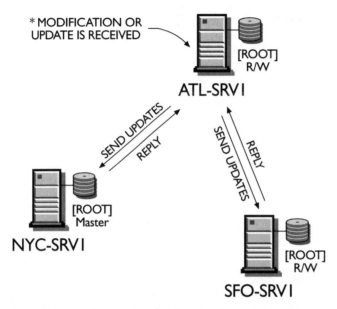

Figure 5-17: The NDS replicas synchronize with each other to maintain consistency of the [ROOT] partition information. The synchronization is loosely consistent because the changes are not passed instantaneously between all replicas.

Replica synchronization is a background process that is event driven. Any modification to the NDS database activates the replica synchronization process. This means that it is scheduled to run on a server after an object or property on that server has been updated. The process is scheduled according to the property or attribute being changed. Each property has a flag that determines if it is high convergence or not. The flag has the following settings:

◆ Fast synchronization

◆ Slow synchronization

# Fast Synchronization

The fast synchronization is the normal synchronization that is scheduled to occur 10 seconds after a client update event occurs on the server. The changes or updates to NDS objects that are made by the client are scheduled using the fast synchronization setting. The synchronization is scheduled for 10 seconds after the first update is received so that several subsequent modifications, if any, can be processed at the same time.

# Slow Synchronization

When a user logs in to the NDS tree, there are four properties or attributes of the user object that are changed. These properties are:

♦ Network Address

♦ Last Login Time

♦ Current Login Time

♦ Revision

The slow synchronization, which is login-related, is scheduled to take place 30 minutes after the login event. The properties or attributes that are used when a user logs in to the network are scheduled using the slow synchronization.

The Network Address property added to the user objects when they log in indicates the physical workstation address that the user is logging in from. The Last Login Time and Current Login Time properties are modified to reflect the current status. The Revision is used to reflect that there has been a change to the object.

# How Replica Synchronization Works

The replica synchronization process involves updating all the replicas for a specific partition with all the changes made to the partition since the last synchronization cycle. The process takes the replica pointer table (replica list or replica ring) and synchronizes each of the replicas one at a time with the most recent changes. The process must contact each server in the replica ring one at a time to complete a synchronization cycle for the partition.

The subordinate reference replicas are included in the synchronization process for a partition because they are found in the replica pointer table for a partition. This means that each of the replicas, including the subordinate reference replicas, is contacted during the synchronization cycle. The subordinate reference replica contains only one object, which is the partition root object, and changes to that object are synchronized.

After a server successfully sends all pending updates to a replica on another server, it proceeds to the next replica until all replicas have been updated. If the operation fails for any reason and is not able to update one or more replicas during the cycle, it reschedules them for a later synchronization cycle.

## Scheduling the Replica Synchronization Process

Every object and property that exists in Directory Services has an associated time-stamp. There is a creation timestamp and last modification timestamp for the objects. The properties have a timestamp that indicates when it was last changed. The modification to a property or attribute value consists of deleting the old value and creating the new one. Thus, the timestamp associated with the property could be called a creation timestamp.

Each replica of a partition on a server maintains a property or attribute called the synchronized up to vector. The synchronized up to vector is a list of time-stamps, one for each replica in the partition plus one for every replica where a modification has occurred. The synchronization process will examine the time-stamp held in the synchronized up to attribute for each replica and determine if the information needs to be updated. The synchronized up to values for each replica of a partition can be viewed using either the NWADMIN or DSREPAIR utilities. Figure 5-18 shows the replica information for the SFO partition.

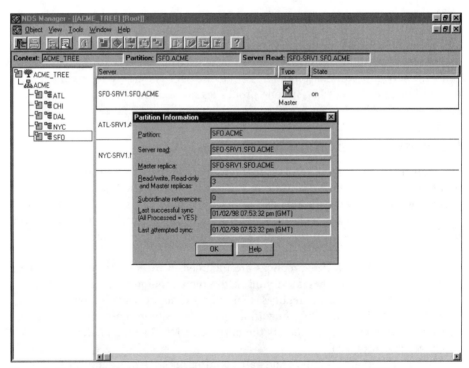

Figure 5-18: The replica information for the SFO partition as shown in the NDS Manager utility

Before starting the replica synchronization process and the first replica update, the server takes a snapshot of its own synchronized up to vector. The server saves the snapshot of these values in memory until all replicas have been contacted and updated successfully.

## Performing the Replica Synchronization

The purpose of the replica synchronization process is to send any changes to the other servers that have a replica for a given partition. One factor that determines whether synchronization is necessary is a modification or change occurring with an associated timestamp. The synchronized up to vector from the other servers in the replica pointer table of a partition is compared to the local synchronized up to vector. If there are differences, the appropriate updates are made.

Directory Services examines the replica pointer table (replica ring) for the local partition to locate the replicas of the partition. The timestamps in the synchronized up to vector are compared to determine the need to synchronize changes. Figure 5-19 gives you a logical representation of the dialog that occurs each time the local server contacts one of the other servers in the replica pointer table.

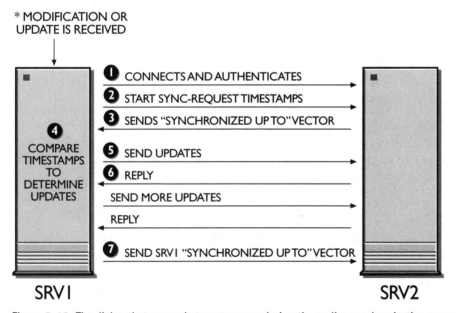

Figure 5-19: The dialog that occurs between servers during the replica synchronization process

By default the replica synchronization process is scheduled to execute only when changes are received to the object or properties in the NDS tree. However, by using a DSTRACE command you can force the process to start (even if there are no changes to be propagated). To manually start the replica synchronization process enter the following DSTRACE command at the server console:

```
SET DSTRACE = *S
```

This setting checks to see if the partition has been marked as changed; if not, it will not do anything. To force the replica synchronization process to exchange the timestamp (synchronization up to), enter the DSTRACE command at the server console as follows:

```
SET DSTRACE = *H
```

## The Replica Synchronization Heartbeat

NDS provides a trigger, or heartbeat, every 30 minutes to schedule replica synchronization. The purpose of the heartbeat is so that each NetWare 4 server will contact all of the other NetWare 4 servers that it has in its replica pointer tables. This is checked in case the server has become disconnected from the network. The heartbeat starts the replica synchronization process for each partition that it holds.

The network administrator can adjust the heartbeat time interval using the SET command called the NDS inactivity synchronization interval. The default value for this parameter is 30 minutes, but you can set this parameter by entering the following command at the server console:

```
SET NDS INACTIVITY SYNCHRONIZATION INTERVAL = 60
```

A SET DSTRACE command may be used to initiate the heartbeat synchronization immediately. This command is entered as follows:

```
SET DSTRACE = *H
```

The SET DSTRACE command SET DSTRACE = !H [time in minutes] may be used to change the default time interval parameter.

## Replica Synchronization Cycle on a Server

Each NetWare 4 server can store replicas for more than one partition. The replicas held by the server have to be from different or separate NDS partitions. As mentioned previously, the purpose of the replica synchronization process is to maintain consistency across all the replicas for a partition. All changes received by one replica for a partition will be sent to the other replicas on the other NetWare 4 servers.

The replica synchronization cycle is the name given to the process of synchronizing the replicas it stores to every other server in the replica lists of these partition operations. Figure 5-20 gives you a conceptual illustration of how one NetWare 4 server synchronizes each partition for each of the replicas it holds. Notice that each partition will perform a replica synchronization process for each of the replicas stored on the server. In this case, SRV1 is the server performing the cycle.

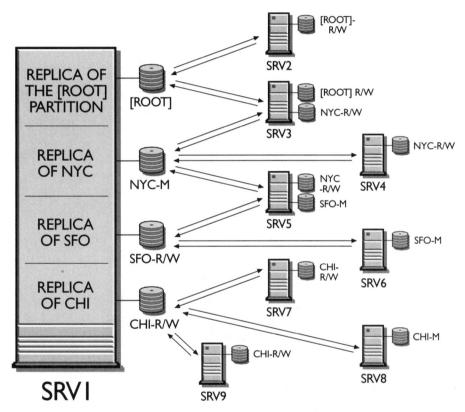

Figure 5-20: The NetWare 4 server called SVR1 synchronizes each partition for each of the replicas it holds. This method of synchronizing all replicas held by the server is called the replica synchronization cycle.

This replication synchronization cycle for an individual server should complete within 30 minutes. In some specific situations servers that are highly utilized and storing too many NDS replicas will not complete the cycle in 30 minutes. If the cycle does not complete in 30 minutes, the replica heartbeat will start the cycle again. This means that the last replicas that did not finish will get synchronized, but the server cannot process immediate synchronization requests because it is always synchronizing. It may take more than 30 minutes to synchronize a change.

# Managing NDS Replicas

The NDS replica operations are add replica, remove replica, change replica type, and rebuild replicas. The NetWare 4 utility you should use to perform NDS replica operations is NDS Manager.

The replica operations require that the master replica for the partition be available. As mentioned earlier, the master replica locks the partition before it starts the operation. The only partition operations that do not require the master replica to lock the partition are the add replica and remove replica operations.

All the replicas for a specific partition must be available in order to perform the complete operation. If there is a replica that is not reachable, the NDS system will wait until it is available before it can finish.

Before you start a partition operation, you should check the status of the replicas of the partition. You will save yourself a lot of problems if you check before you perform any partition operation. You can use DSREPAIR to check the status of the replicas and synchronization. Make sure that the synchronization process is complete before starting a new operation on that partition. Figure 5-21 displays the status check of the replicas in DSREPAIR. For more information on specific interpretation of each of the items shown you can refer to the chapter about the NetWare Utilities, which includes DSREPAIR.

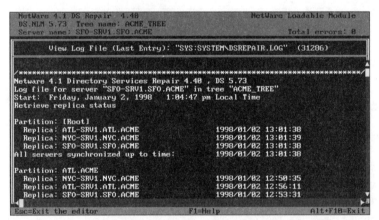

Figure 5-21: Use DSREPAIR to check the status of the replicas before starting a partitioning operation.

If you are performing a merge or join partition operation, you need to check the status of both the parent and child partitions involved in the merge. Again, you should check the status of the partitions before you start the merge or join operation.

Another operational guideline to follow is that after you have started a partition operation, you should be very patient and wait for all the synchronization work to complete. We mentioned that because NDS is loosely consistent it takes time for the partition changes to be reflected across the network. A partition with many objects and replicas will naturally take longer than one with just a few objects.

As an alternative to checking the partition status using the DSREPAIR utility, you can check and see when the synchronization process completes using DSTRACE. Figure 5-22 shows you the screen in DSTRACE to check when the synchronization process is completed.

```
SYNC: Start outbound sync with (1) [010000BB]<SFO-SRV1.SFO.ACME>
   SYNC: sending updates to server <CN=SFO-SRV1>
SYNC: update to server <CN=SFO-SRV1> successfully completed
SYNC: End sync of partition <CHI.ACME> All processed = YES.

(96/06/10 01:21:31)
SYNC: Start sync of partition <DAL.ACME> state:[0] type:[0]
SYNC: Start outbound sync with (2) [010000D0]<ATL-SRV1.ATL.ACME>
   SYNC: sending updates to server <CN=ATL-SRV1>
SYNC: update to server <CN=ATL-SRV1> successfully completed
SYNC: Start outbound sync with (1) [010000BB]<SFO-SRV1.SFO.ACME>
   SYNC: sending updates to server <CN=SFO-SRV1>
SYNC: update to server <CN=SFO-SRV1> successfully completed
SYNC: End sync of partition <DAL.ACME> All processed = YES.

(96/06/10 01:21:31)
SYNC: Start sync of partition <SALES.ATL.ACME> state:[0] type:[0]
SYNC: Start outbound sync with (2) [010000D0]<ATL-SRV1.ATL.ACME>
   SYNC: sending updates to server <CN=ATL-SRV1>
SYNC: update to server <CN=ATL-SRV1> successfully completed
SYNC: Start outbound sync with (1) [010000BB]<SFO-SRV1.SFO.ACME>
   SYNC: sending updates to server <CN=SFO-SRV1>
SYNC: update to server <CN=SFO-SRV1> successfully completed
SYNC: End sync of partition <SALES.ATL.ACME> All processed = YES.
```

Figure 5-22: The Replica screen in DSTRACE can show you when the synchronization process has been completed for a partition.

The DSTRACE information can be more difficult to read and interpret because the information is more cryptic than DSREPAIR. For example, in Figure 5-22, we see the synchronization process for the [ROOT] partition stored on NYC-SRV1, which is this server. The state:[0] means the partition is ON; type:[0] means that this is the master replica. In the example, an outbound synchronization is started with (2), which is the replica number, stored on [010000D0]<ATL-SRV1.ATL.ACME>. The value of [010000D0] indicates the local server's ID of the server ATL-SRV1. All updates are sent and the "All processed = YES" message is displayed meaning that the synchronization is successful and that no further processing is needed.

If possible, we recommend that you centralize the partition operations management. This means that only one person or a small group of people be responsible for all of the partitioning and replication for your company. You might decide that there is only one workstation on the network that should start the partition operations. This way you can eliminate the possibility that two people or two different workstations are making changes to the partitions simultaneously.

The following sections discuss each of the partition and replica operations that can be performed. These operations include Add Replica, Remove Replica, Change Replica Type, and Rebuild Replicas.

## Add Replica Operation

The add replica operation is used to create a new copy of the partition information and store it on another server. Adding replicas to other network servers requires that all the data in the partition be copied to the new servers across the network. This operation will cause network traffic, but the amount of traffic is dependent on the number and size of the objects in the partition. It is a good idea to schedule this operation during a low time in the network.

Figure 5-23 shows the NDS Manager screen used to perform an add replica operation. You first select a partition to which you want to add a replica. In this case the [ROOT] partition is selected. You then select a server on which to place the new replica.

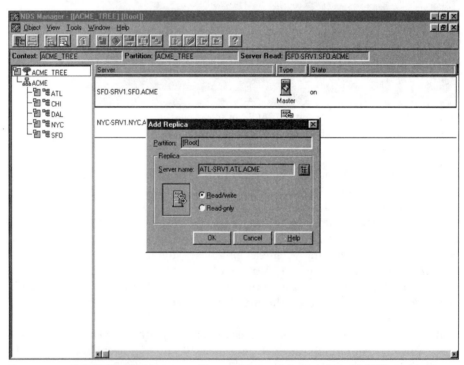

Figure 5-23: Using the NDS Manager utility to add a new replica of the [ROOT] partition to the NetWare 4 server ATL-SRV1

# Remove Replica Operation

The remove replica partition operation is used to delete a copy of the partition information from a specific server. You might think this operation to delete the replica happens very quickly because it simply marks the information to be removed from the server. However, every object in the replica must now be set up as an external reference, which is essentially a pointer to the real object in another replica on another server. With the creation of the external references, backlinks (which are pointers back to the external references) are established. Even though the backlinks are checked in the background process, the initial setup will take time.

Figure 5-24 illustrates removing a replica from a partition. You first select a partition. In this case the [ROOT] partition is selected. You then select a server. In this example, we have selected the server ATL-SRV1 from which to remove the replica. The result after this operation is that there will be only two replicas left on the servers SFO-SRV1 and NYC-SRV1.

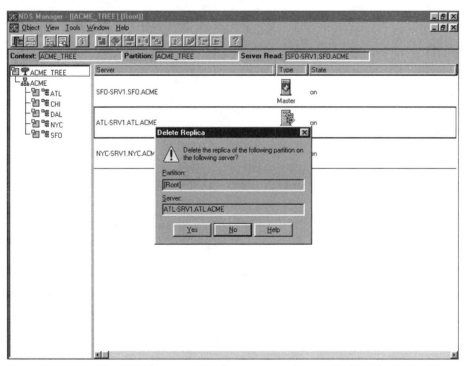

Figure 5-24: Using the NDS Manager utility to remove a replica of the [ROOT] partition. The [ROOT] replica on the server ATL-SRV1 will be removed. After the remove operation, the replicas left will be stored on SFO-SRV1 and NYC-SRV1.

# Change Replica Type Operation

This operation can be performed when the type of replica needs to be changed. For example, if you want a different replica to be the master replica for the partition, you highlight which replica you want to be the new master and NDS will change the type and propagate the change to the other replicas. In order for you to change to the master, the target server must have a read/write or read-only replica.

Figure 5-25 shows the NDS Manager screen used to change the replica type for a partition. You first select a partition to perform the change replica type operation. In this case the [ROOT] partition is selected. You then select a server. We have selected the read/write replica on NYC-SRV1. We can now change its type to master. The result is that the master replica on SFO-SRV1 will change to a read/write.

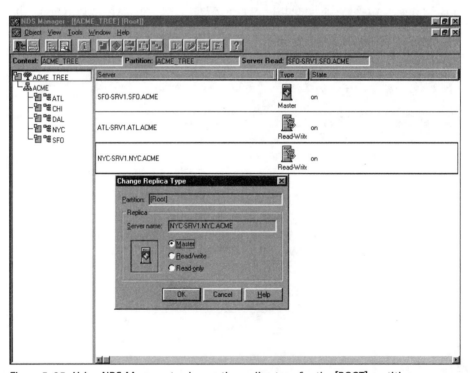

Figure 5-25: Using NDS Manager to change the replica type for the [ROOT] partition

You are not allowed to change a master replica to a read/write or read-only by selecting the server holding the master replica. The utility requires you to select either a read/write or read-only replica and then change it to the master replica.

# Rebuild Replicas Operation

There are a couple of ways you can rebuild the replica information for each of the partitions. These operations are used when you feel that the information on the current server is not completely accurate or has become corrupt.

The most current rebuild replica type operations in NetWare 4 are called Send Updates and Receive Updates. These operations should not be confused with the older Rebuild Replicas from previous versions of NetWare 4 (specifically NetWare 4.01 and 4.02). The Send Updates and Receive Updates replica operations are nondestructive to the partition information. Instead, they simply send and receive all information between all the other replicas.

The previous versions of NetWare 4 used the rebuild replica operation to rebuild the timestamps for each object in the partition. The operation to rebuild timestamps is a very aggressive troubleshooting technique and is not the purpose of this discussion.

From the NDS Manager utility there are two ways to update the replica information. These two operations are called Send Updates and Receive Updates. Both these functions are network intensive because they move all the partition data across the network to the servers. The Send Updates operation tries to send all the object information to all the other replicas in the ring.

The Send Updates operation synchronizes all the other replicas for the partition with the replica you have selected. You would perform this operation when the partition information on some of the servers is not complete or has become corrupted. By selecting the most current replica or the replica that has the best information, you can send its information to all the other replicas in the partition. You can use either NDS Manager (Send Updates) or DSREPAIR (Send all objects to every replica in the ring).

Figure 5-26 shows an example of using DSREPAIR to perform the Send Updates operation. In this example, the server named SFO-SRV1, which is the master replica of the [ROOT] partition, is selected as the sending replica. This operation will send the contents of the selected replica to all the other replicas in the partition.

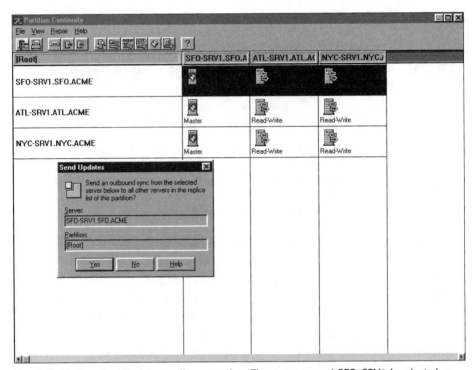

Figure 5-26: The Send Updates replica operation. The server named SFO–SRV1 is selected as the sending replica. This operation will send the contents of the selected replica to all the other replicas in the partition.

The Receive Updates operation synchronizes a selected replica with the information from the master replica. You would perform this operation when the partition information on one of the servers is not as complete as the master replica. This operation can be done using both NDS Manager and the DSREPAIR utilities.

The Receive Updates operation essentially marks the affected replica as a new replica. The operation begins the process of adding the partition information to the replica again.

Figure 5-27 shows an example of the Receive Updates operation using DSREPAIR. In this example, the server named ATL-SRV1 receives the replica information from the master replica of the [ROOT] partition stored on server SFO-SRV1. Notice that "Send all objects to every replica in the ring" is the Send Updates mentioned earlier.

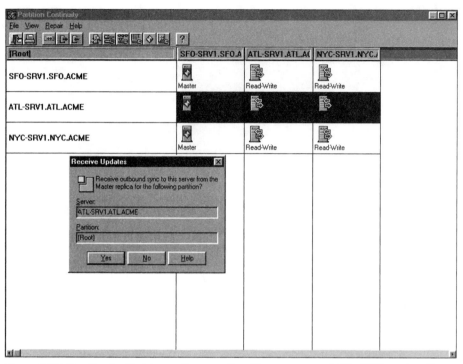

Figure 5-27: The Receive Updates replica operation. The server named ATL–SRV1 receives the replica information from the master replica of the [ROOT] partition from SFO–SRV1. This operation will send the contents of the master replica to the server holding the selected replica.

# Third Step

## Use NDS Objects to Establish the Organization, Administration, and User Access for NT and intraNetWare

**CHAPTER 6**
Use NDS Objects to Define Organization, Administration, and User Access

**CHAPTER 7**
Apply NDS Access Methods

# Chapter 6

# Use NDS Objects to Define Organization, Administration, and User Access

IN THIS CHAPTER

♦ Using a naming standard for NDS objects

♦ Goals for creating naming standards

♦ Producing a naming standard document

♦ Using container objects to organize network resources

♦ Using leaf objects to provide user access and place physical network resources in NDS

NDS OBJECTS ARE THE mechanism by which all activities are performed in the tree. Objects represent resources and are used to manipulate and control these network resources.

NDS is a collection of objects that follows a set of rules regarding their creation and use. Becoming familiar with NDS objects and properties and how they are used will assist you in designing the most efficient NDS tree possible. The following rules support this principle:

♦ Use a naming standard for NDS objects.

♦ Produce a naming standards document.

♦ Use container objects to organize network resources.

♦ Use leaf objects to provide user access.

♦ Use leaf objects to place the physical network resources in NDS.

# Using a Naming Standard for NDS Objects

Create a naming standard before installing your first NetWare 4 server. Once an installation has begun it becomes more difficult to implement a naming standard because you'll have more object names to change. At a minimum, you should determine how your organizational units, servers, and user objects will be defined. These will be the most widely created objects along with your printing objects.

If you have already implemented some existing naming standard, that's the place to start your review. Many companies already have some standard in place for defining their users. This is usually based on an e-mail standard. Review the standard and make modifications where necessary to add or modify your current standard. If your company's network is small, you should still create naming guidelines because the network will most likely grow to include more users and resources where naming becomes more important. Supporting a network with consistent naming is made easier as well.

Your naming guidelines need to be global in nature. You should strive to implement your naming guidelines consistently across the entire network so that all users and all departments can readily and easily access resources anywhere on the LAN. Global naming guidelines can also help your administrators, enabling them to understand the purpose and use of all objects in the tree.

Most likely you will need the input from others in your company in order to create some naming guidelines. You should gather information from the organizations within your company that must participate to form the standard. These individuals may include input from e-mail administrators, network administrators, and mainframe personnel.

Usually an established host environment will have user naming standards in place. Review these standards as a basis for your NetWare 4 user naming guidelines. Some customers prefer to maintain their host user IDs on the LAN rather than create a new standard at the network level. Others can't wait to change their host user IDs.

Consider all other naming guidelines that you may have in place from a NetWare 3 or NT environment to determine how well they might fit into the NetWare 4 environment. Your NetWare 3 printers and servers may already have names defined that will work just fine after migration to a NetWare 4 tree. If you have sufficient or acceptable guidelines for your organization, there is no need to change them.

The purpose of producing naming guidelines is to provide consistency across your network. If you already have consistency, you can move on to the next phase of designing your NDS tree. If you do not have an existing naming standard, you should consider making naming guidelines that meet the following goals.

# Goals for Creating Naming Standards

The objectives for creating naming guidelines for NDS are as follows:

♦ Make browsing and navigation of the NDS tree easier for the users.

♦ Make maintenance of the NDS tree easier for the administration staff.

♦ Make merging separate NDS trees easier.

♦ Keep the NDS object names unique as required by certain services.

♦ Avoid special characters reserved by the operating systems.

## Help NDS Browsing and Navigation

Your primary objective for creating the naming guidelines is to provide the network user a simple view of the network resources contained in the tree. You may not see the immediate need for good naming guidelines, which enable the user to navigate the tree easily. But, as more applications are written to take advantage of NDS and its searching capabilities, an uncomplicated naming standard will be needed.

Objects named with purpose and consistency will provide you a solid foundation that benefits your administrators as well as your users. Other benefits recognized as applications make more use of the Directory and its services. You will see that the system is much more efficient if the users can quickly identify the network resources available to them and minimize the impact on searching NDS.

You should keep the names of all the objects short and simple, yet descriptive enough that the user knows by the names what the object is and the services it provides. For example, the object name HP4SI-P1 is short yet descriptive and it lets the user know that this object is an HP 4si laser printer. The object name HP4SI-PQ1 is another example of a short name. The PQ1 suffix lets the user know that the object is the print queue that supports the printer (P1).

As you can see, there are many instances throughout the book where we have benefited by using the names of containers and network resources from the ACME tree. It has been helpful to have clear and simple names. Some examples of the naming guidelines for ACME are shown in Table 6-1.

TABLE 6-1  Examples of Naming Guidelines for ACME

| Object | Entity | Standard |
|---|---|---|
| [ROOT] | Tree Name | ACME_TREE |
| O=Organization | ACME | ACME |
| OU=Organizational Unit | New York City | NYC |
| | Atlanta | ATL |
| | Chicago | CHI |
| | Human Resources | HR |
| | Finance | FIN |
| | Facilities | FAC |
| NDS and NT Users | Amy Isaacson | AISAACSO |
| | Craig Banyard | CBANYARD |
| | Pam Thomas | PTHOMAS |
| Servers | Server in NYC | NYC-SRV1 |
| | Server in MAN | MAN-SRV1 |
| Printers | HP 4si in DAL | HP4SI-P1 |
| Print Queues | Queue in DAL | HP4SI-PQ1 |

# Help Maintain the Network and NDS

Consistent naming provides a framework for the network administrators to monitor and maintain the network and NDS. The administrators will be installing file servers, creating users and printers, modifying existing objects, and moving objects within the tree. The administrators will also set up all the user configuration files at the workstation to connect to NDS in the predetermined fashion. The administrator's job is going to be much easier if there are naming guidelines in place.

**TIP**  If possible you should maintain the same naming standard for your NT and NDS users and not duplicate users with the same name. In other words, user "DSMITH" in NT should be the same "DSMITH" in the NDS as well.

# Help Merge NDS Trees

The capability to merge multiple NDS trees together is a feature of NetWare 4. However, two trees being merged within the company will be made much easier if the trees being merged are based on the same naming standards for container and leaf objects. The tree merge will be more seamless to the users because they will know where to locate resources in the tree.

# Help Keep NDS Object Names Unique

It is a requirement that some of the NDS objects have unique object names in order for the network to work properly. For instance, the file server and print server objects stored in NDS broadcast their services using different SAP types. While it is not a requirement that the file server and print server object have unique names on the network, it is highly recommended in order to avoid confusion.

Establishing and dictating the naming guidelines to all the network administrators in the network will help keep the NDS objects unique. As stated previously, it is recommended that the user objects have unique names throughout the network. This way the users can be moved or new users added without conflict.

Not all the objects in the NDS tree will need unique names throughout the network. You decide which NDS objects you want unique names for. The SAP requires that file server object names be unique on the network.

Keep in mind that all network devices on the network that communicate using the SAP should have unique object names in the entire network. Therefore, all file servers and print servers should have unique names on the network. The maximum length of the names of the objects that use SAP is 47 characters. The space character is illegal for server names.

# Avoid Special or Reserved Characters

NDS requires the use of the escape character with some characters and therefore we recommend you avoid the use of them in your naming guidelines. The characters are:

◆ **Period (.)** – The period is used by NDS to separate the name segments of distinguished names. For example, the distinguished name for the user Pam Thomas is:

```
CN=PTHOMAS.OU=MAN.OU=DAL.O=ACME
```

- **Comma (,)** – The comma is allowed by NDS naming rules. However, it is very confusing and generally should be avoided.

- **Plus (+)** – The plus sign is used by NDS to represent objects with multiple naming attributes, such as the bindery objects. A common use of the plus sign is for the bindery objects placed in the NDS database. For example, a bindery object with the plus sign in the name is seen as CN=BinderyObject+Name. In the case of an AppleTalk print server it might appear as:

```
CN=AtpsQuser+83
```

- **Equal (=)** – The equal sign is used by NDS to tie name types and object names together. For example the object type O=Organization would appear as:

```
O=ACME
```

- **Backslash (\)** – The backslash character precedes the special characters described above if they are used as part of an object name. For example, you may want to use the name "ACME Inc.," which has a period at the end. In order to make it a legal NDS name, you would need to enter:

```
"ACME Inc\."
```

Understand the following guidelines if you use spaces in any of the object names. You may want to use the underscore character instead. Spaces are used as delimiters for all the command line parameters. If you use spaces in the NDS object names and need to use the name with a command line utility, you will need to enclose the name in quotes.

For example, the user Pam Thomas is named "Pam Thomas" in NDS with a space separating the first and last name. In order to use the relative distinguished name with the LOGIN.EXE program you would enter:

```
LOGIN "PAM THOMAS"
```

Notice the quotes around the name. It would be incorrect to enter the user name as

```
LOGIN PAM THOMAS
```

If you were required to provide the full distinguished name during login, the name would then appear as:

```
LOGIN "PAM THOMAS.MAN.DAL.ACME"
```

You can also use the underscore character as a replacement for the space character as NDS interprets the space and underscore characters the same. In the example of the user PAM THOMAS, her name would appear as:

```
PAM_THOMAS
```

When the name is used during login, you would enter it without the quotes as follows:

```
LOGIN PAM_THOMAS
```

You should also avoid the use of the forward slash (/) in your names of any container or leaf objects. Novell's Windows-based NWUSER utility will fail if you map permanent drives or capture a print queue. This is a Windows issue that does not allow for the use of the forward slash in any name.

# Producing a Naming Standards Document

The following are the steps you can take to produce your naming standards document as quickly and efficiently as possible:

◆ Document the naming standard for each object used in the NDS tree.

◆ Provide a brief example for each object used.

◆ Specify properties for each of the objects selected.

## Determining the Naming Standard for Each Object Used in the Tree

In order to create the naming guidelines, review which NDS objects you will use in your NDS tree. Typically, these objects include organizational units, servers, users, printers, print queues, groups, organizational roles, directory maps, and profiles.

Other possible areas for naming consistency include the attributes associated with each object you define in the NDS tree. In short, any information that you plan on using to search the NDS database needs a naming standard for consistency.

## Providing an Example for Each Object Used

Be sure to show some examples of how to name the objects in your naming document. As shown below in Table 6-2, you can convey your meaning more quickly and easily by providing an example. The naming standard for each of the objects used for the ACME tree, with examples, is included in Table 6-2.

---

**TABLE 6-2  NDS Object Naming Standard for ACME Tree**

| NDS Objects | Standard |
| --- | --- |
| Users | First character of first name plus entire last name; all titles spelled out |
| | Examples: BTHOMAS, CBANYARD |
| NT Domain Object | Example: SJS_Domain |
| Organization | Example: ACME |
| Organizational Unit | Location, division, or department name; abbreviate names if over eight characters long |
| | Examples: NYC, DAL, SFO |
| NetWare Server | Department-SRV# |
| | Examples: DAL-SRV1, CHI-SRV1 |
| Volumes | ServerName_VolumeName |
| | Examples: NYC-SRV1_SYS, ATL-SRV1_SYS |
| Print Server | Department-PS# |
| | Examples: FAC-PS1, MAN-PR-PS1 |
| Printer | PrinterType-P# |
| | Examples: HP4SI-P1, CANONBJ-P2 |
| Print Queue | PrinterType-PQ# |
| | Examples: HP4SI-PQ1, CANONBJ-PQ2 |

# Specifying Properties for Each Object Class Selected

For some installations it may be necessary to determine which properties will be required for the selected objects. Some properties are mandated by NDS when you create the object. This means that if the mandatory properties are not filled in then NDS will not create the object. For example, during the creation of a user object, NDS requires you to specify the Login Name and Last Name properties.

You may have additional attributes that you would like your administrators to include when they create a new object. This type of information might include addresses, fax number, department, and so on. Table 6-3 illustrates the naming standards for a user object with additional properties you want filled in when the users are created. Some properties are required and a value must be entered when the properties are created, while other properties are optional and it is left up to you to determine if they should be used. System properties are those properties that NDS automatically populates during the creation of the object.

---

**TABLE 6-3  NDS Property Naming Standard for User Object in ACME Tree**

| Property | Req/Opt/System | Standards |
|---|---|---|
| Login Name | Required | First character of first name plus entire last name; add middle initial to resolve name conflicts |
| Given Name | Required | First name of user |
| Last Name | Required | Last name of user |
| Full Name | Required | First and last name of user |
| Generational Qual. | Optional | |
| Middle Initial | Required | Middle initial of the user, if known |
| Other Name | Optional | |
| Title | Required | Job title |
| Description | Optional | |
| Location | Required | City or site location (NYC, SFO, etc.) |
| Department | Optional | |
| Telephone | Required | Business phone number with area code |

*continued*

---

**TABLE 6-3** *(Continued)*

| Property | Req/Opt/System | Standards |
|----------|----------------|-----------|
| Fax Number | Required | Fax phone number with area code |
| Language | Optional | Preferred language of user |
| Network Address | System | |
| Default Server | Optional | Enter same server as home directory |
| Home Directory | Required | Enter volume/subdirectory/user path |
| Require Password | Required | Force user to have a password |
| Account Balance | Optional | |
| Login Script | Optional | Determined by site administrators |
| Print Job Config. | Optional | Determined by site administrators |
| Post Office Box | Optional | |
| Street | Optional | |
| City | Optional | |
| State or Province | Optional | |
| Zip Code | Optional | |
| See Also | Optional | |

# More Ideas for Naming Standards

Some of the more common objects that you will want to have a standard for are user names, organization and organizational unit names, servers, and printers. Since these objects are very common in your NDS tree, you should give special attention to their naming standards.

## USER ACCOUNTS

When creating a naming standard, one of the first steps is to decide how to standardize your user names. NetWare 4 allows user names to be up to 64 characters long. However, a 64-character user name is very long and not easy to use.

In the example of ACME, the user name was limited to the first character of the first name plus the entire last name. If there are duplicate names within a single container, the middle initial is added to resolve the name conflict. This type of user name may not be used globally because of the number of user name conflicts.

Some companies have limited the length of the user name to eight characters. This naming convention for the user accounts matches the name of the user's DOS home directory. Since DOS is limited to just eight characters for subdirectory names, limiting the user names to eight characters will automatically match the name of the DOS subdirectory assigned to the user.

## ORGANIZATION AND ORGANIZATIONAL UNIT NAMES

Your organization name should reflect your company name. In our tree example the O=Organization is called O=ACME. For the Organizational Units, the locations and departments with short but descriptive names are used. For instance, OU=NYC and OU=DAL are examples of the location OUs. Examples of the division and department Organizational Units are OU=FAC for the Facilities department and OU=FIN for the Finance department.

## NETWARE SERVER NAMES

NetWare Server names must be unique on the entire network because each server name is broadcast through the use of the SAP. You may wish to consider a server name that signifies a location and department. For ACME, a NetWare server in the Accounting department of CHI is called CHI-ACCT-SRV1 and a print server in the same location is called CHI-ACCT-PS1.

## PRINTER AND PRINT QUEUE NAMES

Printers and print queue names do not have to be unique on the network. The department and location information is obtained by where the printer and print queue is placed in the tree. The distinguished name of the printer or print queue object is used to discover the location and department where the printer is placed. Thus, the individual object name for the printer and print queue should show the functionality of the printer.

For example, in the ACME tree an HP 4si printer is named HP4SI-P1 and the print queue that supports the printer is called HP4SI-PQ1. A Canon Bubble Jet printer is named CANONBJ-P2 and the print queue is named CANONBJ-PQ2. This type of naming provides the users fundamental information about the printer they will be using.

The user can obtain the location and department where the printer has been placed from the distinguished name or location in the ACME tree. For example, a Canon Bubble Jet printer (CANONBJ-P1) in the Manufacturing (MAN) department in Dallas (DAL) has a distinguished name of CANONBJ-P1.MAN.DAL.ACME.

The difference between the printer object and the print queue object is defined by the object suffix. For instance, the "P" is for the printer object and the "PQ" is for print queue object.

# Using Container Objects to Organize Network Resources

Your primary responsibility as a network administrator is to maintain the servers, volumes, users, groups, printers, and other resources in the network. In order to help with this task, NDS lets you view all the network resources as objects within a distributed or network-wide naming service or NDS tree. You decide which network resources are created and placed as objects in NDS. These objects will include NT and NDS users, groups, printers, servers, volumes, computers, and so on. Each of the entries in the NDS tree consists of the object and the properties or data stored as a property. For example, the User object has up to 75 properties, and some of the properties have multiple values.

The NDS objects are the entities that store the information or data about a network resource. The NDS objects represent both physical and logical entities on the network. Since there can be many NDS objects in the network, the objects are organized into a hierarchical structure called the NDS tree. This structure is actually an inverted tree. A good analogy here is the file system. The file system is a hierarchy of subdirectories and files. The reason for the hierarchy is that the files are more manageable with this structure than storing them at the same level. The same is true with the Directory.

NDS classifies all objects as either container or leaf objects (non-container objects). The container objects are analogous to subdirectories in the file system and leaf objects are analogous to files.

The container objects are those objects that are allowed subordinate objects. The container objects form the hierarchy of the NDS tree and are typically named after the locations, divisions, departments, and workgroups in your company. The container objects enable you to group the other NDS objects together in the tree. A branch or subtree of the NDS tree consists of a container object and all the objects it holds, which can include other container objects.

There are several types of container objects defined for your use. The container object base classes are as follows:

- ◆ TOP [ROOT] – a special object at the top of the tree

- ◆ **Organization (O=)** – typically represents the name of your company

- ◆ **Organizational Unit (OU=)** – represents locations, departments, divisions, or workgroups

- ◆ **Country (C=)** – represents a two-letter country designator

- ◆ **Locality (L=)** – is named by "L" or "S" for state or both (currently not enabled by the Novell utilities)

Although the NetWare 4 Directory defines five container objects, the current utilities support only the O=Organization, OU=Organizational Unit, and C=Country. The TOP ([ROOT]) class is supported but only the NetWare system can create it. Future releases of the NetWare utilities as well as third-party products may implement the L=Locality and S=State containers. Both the Locality and State can be represented currently by using the OU=Organizational Unit, which serves the same purpose.

# Using Leaf Objects to Provide User Access

The leaf objects are located at the ends of the NDS tree branches and do not contain any other objects. These are the objects that are used to represent the network resources. In the NDS tree, you can place container objects and leaf objects in different arrangements, according to your company's needs.

The properties (also referred to as attributes) of the objects specify the type of information that the object can store. The terms *property* and *attribute* have the same definition. We have tried to use the term property throughout this book. Different types of objects have different types of properties. Thus, it can be said that the properties define or describe the object. For example, a User object has the following properties: Login Name, Last Name, Group Membership, Telephone, Fax Number, and so on. On the other hand, a Printer object has the properties: Name, Network Address, Location, Print Server, and so on. The NT user object in NDS follows the same properties found in the actual NT object in the domain such as First Name, Last Name, and so on.

There are two categories of properties for the object: the mandatory and optional properties. The mandatory properties are required during the object creation and cannot be deleted. The Novell utilities determine which properties are mandatory. Typically, these are properties that name the object necessary for operation. Many properties are mandatory in order to comply with the X.500 standard. For instance, the surname (or last name) of a User object is mandatory. The host server property is mandatory when creating a Volume object. An object's optional properties (such as fax number, job title, etc.) can be entered as the network administrator deems appropriate.

The value of the property is the data information stored in each property. This is the object information that the users can read and write in many cases, although some properties are not readable or writeable by the client. One property type can have a single value, while another can have multiple values. For example, the Telephone property of the user can hold several different telephone numbers. This is known as a multi valued property.

There is a specific syntax for the value or data type of each property. One use of the syntax is to define the acceptable characters for the value field(s). More details on the syntax for each property are found in the next section of this chapter.

# Using Leaf Objects to Place Physical Network Resources in NDS

You will discover if you haven't already that some NDS objects will be used much more than others. Obviously, the User object will be the most commonly used object in your tree. Some other leaf objects may never be used in your tree. That's okay. There are probably no NetWare 4 networks that will need all the objects defined in NDS. But, they are in the schema for a general audience that may need them at some point. The following are the NDS object types:

- ◆ **Required objects.** These are the objects that either you must define or are defined for you during the installation of NetWare 4.

- ◆ **Commonly used objects.** These objects include both the container and non-container objects with their defined uses and, where applicable, examples of how these objects are used. These examples are based on actual consulting experiences. You benefit from the short synopsis of how the object can be used.

- ◆ **Less commonly used objects.** These are the objects that may have less importance for you. Where appropriate, we have listed consulting recommendations with these objects as well.

# Required Objects

The following objects are required in your NDS tree. When you install your first NetWare 4 server, these objects will be present in your NDS tree. All of these objects will require you to name them at some point in the NetWare 4 installation. When you install NDS for NT onto a NetWare 4 server you will be prompted to name an NDS for NT domain object in a container that you specify during installation.

## TOP AND [ROOT]

The Top object class is the super class for all other object classes in the schema. This object is also the container object for all other objects in the Directory hierarchy. The Top class is an effective class object in which the only instance of the object class is the [ROOT] object in the tree. The [ROOT] object is at the top of your inverted tree structure. The [ROOT], from a visual standpoint in the utilities, is the starting point of your tree and branches downward. The name of the [ROOT] object is your tree name, although this is not indicated or displayed in the utilities. When you install the first NetWare 4 server in your tree, you are prompted for a tree name, which is actually the name of the [ROOT] object. Each tree will contain one and only one [ROOT] object.

The [ROOT] object's name, which is the tree name, is broadcast on your network using the Service Advertising Protocol. If you have multiple trees running on the same network infrastructure, you must ensure that the names are unique. Choose a name for [ROOT] that will clearly identify the organization or company for the tree. Keep in mind that renaming the [ROOT] object or tree name can only be done with the DSMERGE.

Most companies simply use the same name as their company or Organization object and add a _TREE to the name. For example, our tree name for ACME is ACME_TREE. The organization name is O=ACME. You want to choose a name that you can recognize as the tree name if you are using software analysis tools on your network and looking at server-to-server communications.

## ORGANIZATION

This object class is used to define organization objects in the tree. An organization is located directly under the [ROOT] object or C=Country object. This object is used to define the name of a company, and you are required to define at least one organization in your NDS tree. The ACME tree has defined O=ACME as the name of its organization. The organization represents the name of our company or organization and should be an overall descriptor of the business. The name of your Organization object if you are a non-profit group or university can be the name of the university or group.

Most companies typically define only one Organization object in their NDS tree. If all businesses are connected with the same network, then a single Organization object more accurately represents your network. Our guideline for using multiple Organization objects is based on the network infrastructure in which you operate. For example, if you are a large conglomerate with varied businesses that have decided to communicate information together using NetWare 4 for the exchange of information, you can use multiple Organization objects. If each company is separately managed with a separate network infrastructure, you can create multiple Organization objects for each business unit under the [ROOT] object. You can also use the Organizational Unit objects to represent your business units.

## USER

 The User object is obviously the most common object in your tree, and it represents every user that is part of your NetWare 4 network. The User object is similar to the User object found in NetWare 3 environments but contains more attributes. During the installation of your first NetWare 4 server, you will be prompted to assign a password for the first user ADMIN created on the network. This user, named ADMIN, has object Supervisor rights assigned to the [ROOT] object of your tree. The ADMIN user has all rights (NDS and File System) initially to the entire tree. At this point in your installation, it is the only object with such complete and extensive access to your network. The importance of maintaining the ADMIN user or another object with the same rights at [ROOT] is well known. If you should delete this object without making other rights assignments, say to an organizational role, your access to the tree is lost. Your options in this situation would be to reinstall NDS or call Novell Technical Support to help you re-enter your tree.

After you have installed the first couple of NetWare 4 servers, make sure that the ADMIN password is protected. Following the steps below will diminish the likelihood of losing access to your tree:

1. Your first NetWare 4 server installation will prompt you for a password for the ADMIN user. Remember that the first password you assign to the NDS for ADMIN is also assigned to the bindery Supervisor object that is created by the install utility. If you are doing a bindery upgrade, the supervisor's password is taken from the bindery unless it does not exist, then the NDS ADMIN password is used. If you later change the ADMIN user's password, the bindery Supervisor password does not change. Choose a password that will not easily be guessed. Change your passwords periodically for greater security. The ADMIN user password is changed through the NWADMIN or NETADMIN utilities. The bindery Supervisor password can be changed through the NetWare 3 SYSCON utility.

2. Create an organizational role in the O=Organization level of your tree and assign this role object Supervisor rights at the [ROOT] object of your tree.

3. Do not make this organizational role object a security equivalent to the original ADMIN user. If the original ADMIN were to be deleted, your organizational role would have no access to the tree because the security equivalency would be lost.

## NCP SERVER

A NetWare Core Protocol (NCP) server object will automatically be created for any server being installed or upgraded to NetWare 4. This server object holds key information such as the network address and the version of NetWare you are running on that machine. This object type is used to represent any server that provides NCP transport and session services and can represent either bindery or NDS-based NCP servers. This subclass of the Server object provides further definition of NCP services available on a particular server.

The supported Services attribute can be used to list NCP-based features and services available for this network address. As part of an NDS search engine, you can search for available NCP services.

Another useful feature is the Operator attribute, which is used by an NCP server as an access control list. If a particular object is part of this access control list, that object can perform remote console operations. This is not RCONSOLE; this is the capability to exercise the console APIs, which RCONSOLE does not use. The server object is basically managed by NDS and requires little attention from the administrator.

## VOLUME

The Volume object is automatically created when you install a NetWare 4 server into the tree. A file server must have at least one volume called the SYS volume. The server may have additional volumes that are defined during the installation of NetWare 4. A Volume object will be created for each mounted volume during the installation. The naming convention is <file server name> _ <volume name>. This object type exists primarily to differentiate it from other types of resource objects and to allow greater flexibility for volume management if needed. It is also used in MAP commands and is required by the FILER utility to grant file system rights.

NetWare 4 gives you flexibility to place print queues on any NetWare 4 volume. We recommend that you always create at least one other volume in addition to the SYS volume so that your print queue will not fill up the SYS volume and cause NDS to become disabled.

Use the volume restrictions to limit the size of your volumes before they fill up completely. You can also limit the disk space used on the Home Directory if you are short on space or want to limit each user on the volume.

## NT DOMAIN OBJECT

 The NT Domain Object is similar to an NDS group object in that it holds members (users) of an NT domain. During the installation of NDS for NT the installation wizard will prompt you to specify a name for your NT Domain object in NDS. We suggest that you use the same naming standards you would for any NDS object. You'll want to name the Domain Object similar to your NT domain.

# Commonly Used Objects

Here is a list of the most commonly used NDS objects. Most, if not all, of these objects will be used in your NDS tree. Small sites with perhaps one server may not use all of these objects. In fact, it is only necessary to make use of the objects that can best serve the purposes of your network environment.

## BINDERY OBJECT

 This leaf object represents any object other than user, group, queue, profile, and print server created through bindery services. The bindery object has the format of Common Name + Object Type and is used to provide backward compatibility for bindery-oriented applications or utilities. You will see bindery objects appear after a migration from NetWare 3 to NetWare 4 if an object is not identifiable by NDS. Some applications will create bindery objects as well to suit their particular purposes. For applications that still require the bindery services, a bindery object could exist in the tree. Although these objects appear in utilities such as NWADMIN, they are not manageable from NWADMIN or NETADMIN and are present for information purposes.

Do not delete any bindery object until you verify its purpose in the Directory. Some installation utilities will create a bindery object and if that object is removed problems with the application will occur. Always check first before deleting bindery objects that appear in your containers.

## ORGANIZATIONAL UNIT

 Nearly all NDS trees, except environments with a single NetWare 4 server, will use Organizational Units. They are, however, optional. Organizational Units subdivide the tree into either locations or organizations, which can be departments, divisions, or workgroups. The Organizational Unit is also referred to as a container that contains the login script property, also known as the container login script. All users in a container will execute that container's script if it is available. The ACME tree uses containers to make logical divisions in the tree. Notice that the first level of OUs represents geographic sites based on the network infrastructure and that the subsequent levels represent the departments of ACME. Many trees will be designed in this fashion with several levels of nested organizational units. Most companies use the Organizational Unit to represent geographic locations, divisions, and workgroups. You generally use an Organizational Unit to group common users and resources in the same container. Organizational Units should not be created to represent a single person or a single resource. They are used to provide network access to a group of users in a particular part of the tree. NetWare 4 does provide the capability to move containers to new locations in the tree should your needs change.

## ORGANIZATIONAL ROLE

 An Organizational Role object is typically used to define a role or position within an organization object or container object. The role is extremely useful because the object or file rights are granted to the role itself and not to the occupants who may belong to the role. However, this rule is different for object creation. For example, an object is created by a user assigned to the organizational role. The object create rights on the new object go to the user creating the object, not to the organizational role.

Organizational Roles are especially useful in the maintenance of subadministrators. The occupant can be moved in and out of the role quickly to facilitate short-term assignments. For example, if the regular administrator is absent for any length of time, another user can be moved into the role temporarily to manage the network. The implementation of this object is just like a group. The organizational role occupants derive their rights through security equivalence to the role object.

The use of an organizational role is highly recommended as a way to administer rights in your network to various administrators in your network. You can more easily track who has received rights as administrators in your tree by checking who has been made an occupant of a role. Assigning rights to individuals other than through the use of roles is not recommended because it is more difficult to track which individuals have been granted rights in your tree. After a few months or even weeks, you'll forget who you've assigned rights to.

## GROUP

 This class is used to represent a set of names (users) from any part of the NDS tree. The membership of the group is static and is modified only by administrative action. Groups function the same way they did in NetWare 3. There is very little difference between using group objects and organizational unit (OU) objects. Both have the same function, which is to place common users close together. It is true that users as members of both objects receive rights by security equivalence, but there are some differences. Because of security equivalency, any member of an OU will receive whatever rights the OU possesses. Users inside groups also receive whatever rights the group possesses, and just like a container there is no IRF provision.

Groups are used to differentiate rights within a particular Organizational Unit. Rather than create multiple subcontainers you can simply use groups within a container for users that need a specific environment created.

Within the container or OU login script (known as the system login script in NetWare 3) the "IF MEMBER OF GROUP" statements are used to determine which group a user belongs to for rights assignments. When each user logs in to the network, the login script determines if a user is a member of a group and sets the appropriate environment variables.

Groups are great to use in a container to provide further differentiation of rights to a subset of users. We recommend that groups be used in a container instead of creating more containers. Additional containers would require the use of additional container login scripts. Limit the number of groups to fewer than 15 in a container login script, if possible. The more groups, the longer the container login script will be and a slower login will occur. You'll get the best performance with 15 groups or fewer.

## DIRECTORY MAP

 The Directory Map object is a pointer that refers to a file system directory on a NetWare volume. It is used in login scripts or by the MAP command to point to a directory that contains a particular application. Let's assume you have WordPerfect installed into a directory called WP60. If you were to upgrade your software to WordPerfect 6.1, you could choose to rename the subdirectory to WP61. You would also have to change every login script to reflect this change for the new subdirectory. Through the use of a directory map you can eliminate making changes to your login scripts. Your Directory Map object is used in your login scripts and points to a subdirectory on a NetWare volume. Your only change is to have the directory map point to WP61. All container login scripts are left intact.

Directory Map objects are useful for providing a standard container login script on multiple servers. We recommend that you have standard file structures for all your NetWare 4 file servers so that you can facilitate easier use of directory maps. If you maintain a directory map for an application, you can make a change to the directory map pointer and have it be effective for many servers. The directory map requires the administrator to make each user security equivalent to the map object and for containers with large numbers of users. This can be a drawback from an administration standpoint. You can, however, grant rights on the directory pointed to by the directory map to the container to simplify this situation.

## ALIAS

An alias is another name for an object. An alias is an object that points to another object you specify in the Directory tree. An alias can point to either a container object (an object that holds other containers) or to a non-container object (one that does not have any other containers). Why not just say that an alias can point to a container object or to a leaf object?

An alias is a name containing at least one Relative Distinguished Name. As a network administrator you may grant users access to a particular resource contained in another OU, such as a printer. You can create an alias to reference that printer, for example. The alias can be considered a relay to another object in a different part of the tree.

You can also alias one OU to another OU, giving one OU to the other OU's resources. It appears as if the alias places the alias's container inside of the other container.

The Alias object is very useful in moving subtrees or renaming containers so that you can easily make the transition. The alias can assist you in this migration path. In addition, the alias can be useful for some companies wishing to create mobile users who do not want to remember their user context. The alias can be created at the top of the tree below the Organization object, for example, to shorten the user's context. If user David wants to log in to the network he only has to remember that his context is David.Acme because that alias points to his actual context in the tree.

## PRINT SERVER

The Print Server leaf object represents a server that takes print jobs out of a print queue and sends them to a network printer. This object is used in conjunction with the Printer and Print Queue objects. A Print Server object must be created for every actual print server that exists on the NetWare 4 network.

All NetWare 4 networks using printers will have at least one Print Server object. You can use this object to define which printers to print to and a specific group of users based on a context. You can also define the print server operators.

## PRINTER

Used in conjunction with the Print Server object, you use the Printer object to manage a printer. The assignment for a print queue can be made within the object. You can attach printers in several different ways to the network – directly to the network, to a printer port of a NetWare server, or to a printer port of a PC.

Place the Printer object along with the Print Queue object as high as possible in your NDS tree so that you can support many users needing to print. If your printer is for your container only, then place the printer in your container. If more containers need access to the printer, place the object in the next level in your tree. Keep in mind that the placement of printers higher in the tree also adds overhead to NDS in terms of name resolution. We also recommend that you configure printers as network-direct printers in queue server mode.

## QUEUE

 This object represents a print queue defined on a NetWare 4 server. The queue actually represents the directories where the print jobs are sent to be serviced by a printer. Place the Print Queue object along with the Print object at the highest level possible in your tree to service the most users.

All NetWare 4 print queues should be placed on a volume other than the SYS volume for greater fault tolerance of the server. A queue object must be created for NetWare 4 printing. A Print Queue object is assigned to a printer.

## PROFILE

 The Profile object is used as a special purpose scripting object that is executed by LOGIN.EXE and is a shared login script after the execution of your container login script. The profile script can contain special drive mappings or environment settings you want a select group of people to receive. One of the properties of a User object is the profile. When a user is first created using the NWADMIN utility, you can specify that the user be part of a profile. You can also add a user to a profile any time after by going back and adding the profile to a user object's properties. Profiles can be used in any of the following cases:

♦ Creating a global login script

♦ Creating a location login script

♦ Creating a special function login script

**GLOBAL LOGIN SCRIPTS**    NetWare 4 does not use a global system login script. Each Organizational Unit created will have its own login script referred to as the OU login script. The order of execution of login scripts is:

1. OU login script

2. Profile login script, if used

3. User login script, or

4. Default login script if no other script is available

Therefore, if you want to create a more global login script and include multiple Organizational Units, you could employ the Profile object to set up a specific environment for a group of users. Keep in mind that this type of solution is expensive in terms of NDS overhead that will be created on your network.

LOCATION LOGIN SCRIPTS    A profile can also be used for determining resource allocation based on location. For example, each department of a company may have three printers and three print queues. With a profile you can assign a particular group of users to a specific print queue. You can use a profile login script to capture to a particular print queue and the users will automatically capture to that print queue.

SPECIAL FUNCTION LOGIN SCRIPTS    A profile can be used for a special function script to assign access for applications and so on. For example, you can create a profile script that will be used by administrators only. This script may give these users a specific drive assignment to a help desk utility. In this scenario, you would move the help desk utility out of the SYS:Public directory into a new subdirectory you create called HELPDESK. When users log in to the network, the admin Profile executes and assigns them a drive mapping to the HELPDESK directory. Only the users executing the profile script will be assigned rights to access the help desk utility.

Typically, the profile is used as a global login script for a workgroup or organization. Keep in mind that the Profile object will execute from one container, although users may be participating from other containers and may see some performance issues if the script is executing over a wide area connection. In addition, you will notice increased overhead of NDS traffic as NDS walks the tree to locate a particular object.

## UNKNOWN

 This class represents any object created by the server to restore any object whose base class is currently undefined in the schema. Objects of this class type are created only by the server and not the client and usually occur when a mandatory property of an object has been lost.

Unknown objects are created for the following reasons:

◆ As place holders during synchronization of objects

◆ Because of the loss of a mandatory attribute of an object

◆ An object class was deleted and the server had an object of that class

This object is automatically created by NDS. If an unknown object appears in your tree, check to see if some other object has been deleted. In the case of a deleted server object, the server's volume objects will appear as unknown objects and must be deleted by an administrator. In other circumstances an unknown object may appear temporarily as the NDS background processes work through a synchronization process.

Check before deleting an unknown object as the object may resolve itself. If you have verified that the object is not needed, then remove it from your tree. There is no point in maintaining unknown and unused objects.

# Less Commonly Used Objects

Here is a list of less commonly used NDS objects. These objects are not required, but you may use them in your NDS design.

### AFP SERVER

The AFP Server object represents an AppleTalk Filing Protocol based server that is part of your NetWare 4 network. This object serves only as a descriptor object and does not provide any management capability for your AFP server in a NetWare 4 environment. You can use this object for informational purposes about AppleTalk in your NetWare 4 environment.

### BINDERY QUEUE

The Bindery Queue object represents a leaf object queue that has been placed in the Directory through an upgrade or migration to NetWare 4. A bindery queue is used to support other queues upgraded from NetWare 3.1.

### COUNTRY

This object is used to define country entries in your NDS tree. The Country Name attribute is restricted to two characters as defined by the ISO3166 standard. Directory Services does not check to see if characters are correctly defined, just if there are two. For companies desiring to use the Country object, there are several considerations. First, the object must be placed directly below the [ROOT] object. Specifying this option can be done during installation of NetWare 4. Second, consider the ramifications of adding the Country object to your tree in terms of adding another layer to your tree and lengthening your user's context. Also, carefully plan your tree design so that your user's context will be logical and make sense. For example, let's assume we added the Country object to the ACME tree under [ROOT]. Since our company is global in nature, which country do we choose? If we say that C=UK notice what the context would be for users not reporting under the UK region.

Our recommendation is to avoid using the Country object in your tree. Even with emerging gateway technology to interconnect disparate directory databases, the gateway will handle the distinction between a database using and not using the Country object.

## COMMEXEC

 This object is used to manage Novell's NetWare for SAA NetWare Loadable Module on a NetWare 4 Server. This object is used only with NetWare SAA and provides management capabilities for and rights privileges at the [ROOT] level of your NDS tree.

## LOCALITY

 This object is used to define geographic locations in the NDS tree such as states or regions or counties. The Locality object is currently not enabled by Novell's NWADMIN or NETADMIN utilities and therefore is not visible through the current utilities. Programs are available to define and view this object class. The object must be named by one or both of its attributes L=Locality Name or S=State or Province Name. Most companies will not need to use this object. Some Directory Service providers that are providing connection services using NDS will use the Locality object.

The Locality Object exists in the NDS schema and can be defined by using Novell's latest NWADMIN utility.

## COMPUTER

 This object class can represent both computers used as NetWare servers and computers used as client workstations. A key attribute of this object is the Operator, which can be used to identify individuals or groups that handle the day-to-day maintenance of this computer typically from a hardware standpoint.

## DEVICE

 This object subclass is used to represent a physical device such as a modem or printer that you want to have defined in your tree. One attribute contained in this object is the Locality Name, which can be used to identify the physical location of a device. In addition, as more devices become NDS enabled, the Device object will possibly come into greater use for managing those objects.

## EXTERNAL ENTITY

This object is used to store information about non-native NDS objects in the Directory tree. Some situations may require that an NDS object have information about an object that does not exist on the Directory Tree. A messaging service, for example, can use the External Entity class to store information about e-mail users that exist on other systems outside of the NetWare 4 tree.

## LIST

This object is used to represent an unordered set of object names in the Directory. It can be a list of leaf objects or other objects that you want to logically group together based on some type of search criteria.

The Member attribute is used to define the objects that are members of the list. The members can be any individual objects, even including Group objects. However, the key difference between this object and a Group object is that membership in a list does not imply security equivalence as it does in a group. This object can be used to logically list objects for NDS searches.

## MESSAGE ROUTING GROUP

Closely related to the Messaging Server object, this object is used to represent a group of messaging servers that communicate with each other for transferring messages. The Member attribute is used to define the messaging servers that belong to the Message Routing Group.

## MESSAGING SERVER

This object is used to represent messaging servers such as Novell's MHS servers that may exist in the Directory tree. If you are using Novell's MHS services for NetWare 4 you will use this object. Important attributes such as the Message Routing Group, Messaging Server Type, and Supported Gateway will be configured to define the types of services that will be provided for e-mail communications on your network.

## ORGANIZATIONAL PERSON

This object defines anyone who represents a particular organization, either as an employee or in some other way associated with the organization. This object is part of two subclasses defined in the X.500 standard: Organizational Person and Residential Person.

The User object is a subclass of the organizational person. The user class inherits from the organizational person.

## PERSON

 This object contains the more common attributes of the Organizational Person and Residential Person objects. The X.500 specification defines two subclasses of Person: the Organizational Person and Residential Person. The current NetWare 4 schema does not include Residential Person. The separation of Person from Organizational Person has been done for future compatibility with x.500.

## RESOURCE

This object class is used to identify the logical resources available on your network. The resource class is similar to the device class in that a device is a physical unit, and a resource is a nonphysical or logical unit.

A very useful attribute in this object is the Host Resource Name, which can be used if a host's local identification differs from a more global resource identification. If a resource is being used by multiple localities you can define a Locality name, Organization name, and Organization Unit name as separate identifiers. If you define appropriate values, you can initiate NDS searches for a particular resource name, locality, or organization.

# Chapter 7

# Apply NDS Access Methods

## IN THIS CHAPTER

- ◆ Using client software to provide network connections

- ◆ Establishing bindery services

- ◆ Setting up user environments using login scripts

- ◆ Setting up mobile user access

- ◆ Supplying network applications using NetWare Application Launcher

- ◆ Distributing software using NetWare Application Launcher

ONE OF THE FUNDAMENTAL goals of NDS is to simplify the access to the network resources. These resources include NT users. NDS accomplishes this goal by providing several key features, such as a logical view of the network resources in a hierarchical tree, a single login to the network, and a single point of administration using GUI utilities such as NWADMIN. This chapter gives you more specific information you can use to take complete advantage of NDS and its capabilities in a mixed NetWare and NT environment.

Providing access to the NDS tree and NetWare 4 servers can be accomplished through several different kinds of client software components available in conjunction with NetWare login scripts. The client software provides the first level of access to NetWare 4, and the login script then creates the environment for the NDS user. After the users are logged in, NDS will then automatically manage the users' physical connections to the servers and enable them to access files, applications, and NDS information.

Each of the various access methods should help you provide specific access to both the NDS tree and the NetWare 4 servers to meet the following design principles:

- ◆ Centrally manage the user's working environment

- ◆ Simplify management of the applications and services

There are specific design rules or access methods that you need apply to your overall NDS design in order to accomplish these design principles. The access design rules outlined below will assist you in providing the most complete implementation of NDS and network resource access. The design rules for applying the access methods include the following:

♦ Use client software to provide network connections.

♦ Establish bindery services.

♦ Set up user environments using login scripts.

♦ Set up mobile user access.

♦ Supply network applications using NetWare Application Launcher.

♦ Distribute software using NetWare Application Launcher.

# Using Client Software to Provide Network Connections

The client software provides an extension to each network user and provides access to the corporate network resources. The client software is tasked to communicate with the desktop operating system and the network operating system and serves as a liaison between the two. If a desktop application requires the use of network services, the client redirects the output to a server. If a server application needs to communicate with a client, it directs that communication to the network client in response to the client's request.

Because of the many types of clients that may exist in your network, your responsibility as a LAN administrator will be to determine the type of client access needed for a connection to NetWare 4 and to create the appropriate accessibility to meet those needs.

The NetWare 4 client software is designed to support connectivity for workstations including DOS/Windows, Windows 95, OS/2, Macintosh, NT, and UNIX operating systems. The newest client software is Novell's Client 32 architecture, which provides full connectivity to NetWare 4 services from both DOS/Windows and Windows 95 users.

# DOS/Windows Requester (Virtual Loadable Modules)

One of the common types of client software in use for connecting to NetWare 4 is the NetWare DOS Requester, which supports both DOS and Windows clients. The DOS Requester is actually a group of Virtual Loadable Modules (VLMs) that work together to provide client connectivity to a NetWare 4 server. The great advantage of this type of software is that you can install only the VLM modules that are required for your user environment. You can create a standard configuration for the majority of your users.

An important difference between the NetWare 3 NETX shell and the NetWare DOS Requester (VLM) is how each architecture handles network requests. Because NETX.EXE is a shell, all calls from an application to the operating system are intercepted by the shell and then directed to either the network or to DOS.

On the other hand, the NetWare DOS requester receives all calls from DOS through the DOS Redirector Interface known as Int2Fh. Therefore, any calls sent to this interrupt are always intended for the network. Each of these approaches has advantages and disadvantages in terms of memory usage and performance.

An example of how the NETX shell works is found in Figure 7-1. An example of how the NetWare DOS Requester receives network requests from DOS is shown in Figure 7-2.

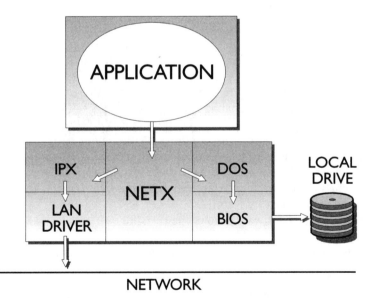

Figure 7-1: A view of how NETX routes the operating system requests from the application

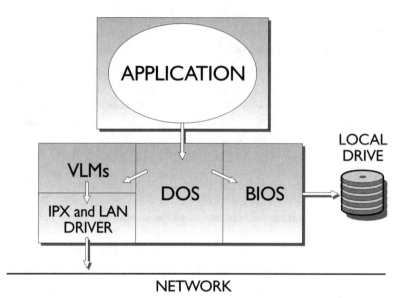

Figure 7-2: A view of how VLMs route the operating system requests from the application

## NetWare Client 32

NetWare Client 32 for DOS/Windows and the NetWare Client 32 for Windows 95 represent the next generation of the client software from Novell. It combines the best elements of the previous client software (the NETX shell and the NetWare DOS/Requester) and adds some significant enhancements. The most notable improvement is the fact the NetWare Client 32 offers 16-bit desktop users full 32-bit access to NetWare services, including NDS.

The NetWare Client 32 for both DOS/Windows and Window 95 leverages the Window interfaces. For example, in Windows 95 the client software provides tighter integration for the users while easing installation and delivering comprehensive NDS access and support. You, as the administrator or the user, can customize the client's configuration through the Windows 95 Registry to optimize performance and enable security features.

The NetWare Client 32 software enables the users to:

♦ Operate the workstation with a smaller footprint in conventional memory

♦ Access network services globally through native Windows 95 Network Neighborhood and Explorer interfaces

♦ View NDS network-wide resources, including NetWare servers, printers, and other services, using the Windows 95 Provider interface

♦ Use a Windows-based login with full login scripts

♦ Connect and authenticate to multiple NDS trees, all with NDS connections

♦ Automatically reconnect, including opening files and locks

♦ Support long file naming conventions

# Client for Windows NT

The Novell Client for Windows NT provides the necessary capability for you to use NDS for NT. This client provides features such as single sign-on to NetWare and NT servers and password synchronization.

## USER AUTHENTICATION AND SINGLE SIGN-ON

To effectively integrate Windows NT networks and NDS into a single heterogeneous network solution, you need to provide users with single sign-on capability. Single sign-on means that when a user needs to access network resources from NetWare or Windows NT, the user enters a single username and password and is granted access to the appropriate resources on either a NetWare or NT server. Using NDS for NT and the NetWare Client for Windows NT, IS managers have a reliable authentication solution that will provide the desired single sign-on capability.

## USER PASSWORDS

Windows NT uses the MD4 password encryption algorithm while NDS uses the RSA encryption. When user passwords are created, they are hashed (encrypted or scrambled) by the respective algorithms. The hashed values are stored on the respective servers. When a user logs in, the password is passed through the RSA encryption algorithm at the workstation and the encrypted value is sent to NDS for verification. If the hashed value of the entered password matches the value stored in NDS, the user is authenticated to NDS.

At the same time, the same password is also hashed with the MD4 algorithm and sent to the Windows NT domain controller. This hashed value is compared to that stored in the domain User object; if they match, the user is authenticated to the NT Server. This authentication process is secure because the encryption process that is performed on each password is non-reversible. This means that even though the hashed value is sent on the wire, there is no way to reverse the encryption process and determine the clear text password from the encrypted value.

When you migrate a domain to NDS, the hashed user passwords from the NT server are also migrated. This allows a user to log in to a recently migrated domain using the same password that was defined before the migration took place. NDS holds both hashed passwords for the user, one encrypted using the MD4 algorithm for NT and one encrypted using RSA for NetWare.

Because there is no modification to the workstation, the login process used to authenticate to NDS and the NT Server does not change. The login process hashes the user password with RSA and sends that directly to a Novell server for authentication to NDS. The login process also hashes the password using MD4 and sends that to the Windows NT domain controller. The redirected domain controller retrieves the hashed user password from NDS and compares it to that sent from the workstation. If they match, the user is authenticated to the Windows NT domain. All of this information is sent using multiple encryption techniques. The clear text and hashed password values are not sent natively on the wire.

Novell does not jeopardize any Microsoft security that is a part of domains. For this reason, it is necessary to store both the Microsoft and NDS passwords in NDS. This way when the workstation sends an MD4 encrypted password to the domain controller, the NT Server is able to retrieve the encrypted password from NDS and authenticate the user to the NT Server.

## MAINTAINING PASSWORD SYNCHRONIZATION

Because Novell maintains Microsoft's security, it is necessary to keep the NDS and NT passwords synchronized. Most users will change their password when prompted or when they have forgotten and have to call their network administrator. In either case, the passwords are easily changed and synchronized. The methods used to maintain this synchronization are identical to those used when authenticating users to standard NT domains.

The best way to maintain synchronized passwords involves setting up the client workstation to authenticate to both NDS and Windows NT simultaneously. The following methods and utilities will help you maintain password synchronization:

1.  Use the NetWare Client for Windows NT (also known as the intraNetWare Client for Windows NT) and check the Automatically Synchronize Passwords check box at login if the passwords are not currently synchronized. The intraNetWare Client change password feature is made through the NWGINA module. You can also use Novell Clients for Windows NT, Windows 95, and Windows 3.1x, which also provide password change utilities that will simultaneously change the password for all servers currently attached. For Client 32, this is the Change Password utility.

2.  Use NWAdmin and the snap-in provided with NDS for NT to change user passwords. This snap-in provides a change password option that will change both the NDS and NT passwords. Using the snap-in for NWAdmin instead of the User Manager, NETADMIN, and SETPASS utilities to ensure password synchronization.

3.  Set the passwords to expire through NDS and not through NT. This ensures that an NT password will not be changed without changing the corresponding NDS password.

NDS for NT provides significant administrative savings for networks using both NetWare and Windows NT. Making sure users, who need both NDS and NT resources, authenticate to both NDS and NT simultaneously is the best way to avoid any password synchronization issues

# Client Software Connection States

There are several different connection states that each client software supports to a NetWare 4 server. The connection states can also be referred to as connection types and are identified as follows:

♦ Connected but no identity established

♦ Authenticated

♦ Licensed/Authenticated

### CONNECTED BUT NO IDENTITY ESTABLISHED

This state is a user who has attached to a NetWare 4 server either through the NETX shell, VLM client, or the NetWare Client 32 software. A connected but no identity established state can exist for either NetWare 3 or NetWare 4 users to the first attached server or, if a connection is made after walking the tree, after the first attached server. This means that workstation has exchanged the login protocol with the server but it was not authenticated.

### AUTHENTICATED

Authentication is a process of proving identity to a server. The authentication process occurs for both NetWare 3 and NetWare 4 users, with NetWare 4 adding more security to this process. In NetWare 3 this simply means logging in to the server. In NetWare 4, this type of connection indicates that the server has established a user's identity after the user has initially entered a correct name and password. After the user has entered the name and password once, connections to additional NetWare 4 servers will happen as a "behind-the-scenes task" at the client. Thus, authentication is invisible to the user. During the login sequence, the user will enter a password when prompted and the remaining process occurs behind the scenes. All sensitive data is never transmitted across the wire for security purposes. Authentication relies on encryption algorithms based on a public/private key system.

After successful authentication has occurred, a process known as background authentication may occur if the user's login script specifies connections to other servers. A connection to another NetWare 4 server, for example, does not require the user to re-enter his password. However, all connections are authenticated in the same way and no distinction is made between the first and subsequent server authentication in terms of the process.

## LICENSED

A connection is said to be licensed when a user has made a request of the server, such as mapping a drive or capturing to a printer. Each user will cause the user license to decrement by one after the connection has been licensed. Only an authenticated connection can be licensed.

A combination of these states determines what level a user currently has in a NetWare 4 environment. For example, when a connection is neither authenticated nor licensed, users can navigate the NDS tree through the use of the CX (Change conteXt) command. They have attached to a server, but have not yet authenticated. The users can see all the objects in the tree that the trustee [PUBLIC] has rights to.

Once the user is licensed and authenticated, he can then access the NDS object, property, and file system information to the extent allowed by his rights.

## ADDITIVE LICENSING

Additive licensing gives administrators the ability to increase the total number of licenses on any given NetWare 4 server. This enhancement enables administrators to more closely match the number of licensed users to their actual needs. A company that currently has a 100-user license can add a 25-user license to the NetWare 4 server to accommodate increased growth. NetWare 4 supports 5, 10, 25, 50, 100, 250, 500, and 1000 user versions together in any combination.

# Types of Client Connections: NDS and Bindery Services

The client software running at the workstation provides two types of NetWare 4 services: NDS connection and bindery services connection. The major difference between these types of connections is the fact that a bindery services connection is server centric. This means that multiple connections require a user name and password at each server, and the login process is repeated at every server. Using multiple user names and passwords to connect different servers will most likely appear as drive mapping in login scripts or other automated menuing software.

On the other hand, the NDS connection enables you to have a single login to multiple NetWare 4 servers. NetWare 4 and Directory Services provide the network user with a single login to access any network resources as needed. The user does not have to log in to each server to gain access to the resources on that server. Instead, Directory Services automatically authenticates the user to the server. The authentication process is completed seamlessly for the user.

The single login simply enables the users to enter their name and password once. Any additional drive mappings to other NetWare 4 servers will be handled in the background by NDS. The great benefit is that administrators only need to manage a single user account if they are operating completely on NetWare 4 servers.

However, in order for Directory Services to support backward compatibility for the bindery application and users, it provides the object information to these users through bindery services. These services are on a server-by-server basis. Bindery services enables the objects in a container to be accessed by both the NDS workstations or clients and bindery-based clients.

Unlike the NDS tree, which is hierarchical, objects in the bindery have no hierarchical relationship (a flat structure) and these objects are specific to one server. To provide access for bindery users and clients, NDS imitates a flat structure for leaf objects within one or more container objects.

An NDS connection requires the use of the VLM client or NetWare Client 32 software for authentication to a NetWare 4 server. An NDS connection provides a security mechanism known as RSA encryption between the client and server to provide background authentication for a single sign-on to multiple NetWare 4 servers.

# Establishing Bindery Services

The NetWare client software provides compatibility with previous versions of NetWare through the use of bindery services. In previous versions of NetWare, information was not available from a distributed directory. Instead, each server in the network stored information that contained the name, object ID, and password of every user or object that had access to the services provided by that server. These services are on a server-by-server basis. Bindery services allows the objects in a container to be accessed by both the NDS workstations or clients and bindery-based clients.

Because the NetWare 3 servers in the network did not share or communicate the bindery information, the user or object's information was stored separately on every server to which it had rights. For example, if user BTHOMAS had rights to NetWare 3 servers NCS, ENG1, and MKTG1, his information was stored on each of the three NetWare 3 servers. Each time BTHOMAS wanted to access services on a different server, he would have to establish a connection and log in to that server.

This type of connection does not provide the capability of a single login to the network. For example, a client using the NETX shell or the LOGIN /b option to log in to a NetWare 4 server must enter a username and password for that server. Additional connections to other NetWare 4 servers would require the user to enter another username and password.

Bindery services can be enabled on any NetWare 4 server through the Set Bindery Context command. The server can select one container or multiple containers in the NDS tree to set as the bindery context. All the leaf objects in the NDS container(s) that are also objects in the NetWare 3 bindery (that is, users, groups, queues, print servers, profiles, and other user-defined objects) are seen as the bindery.

## Multiple Bindery Contexts

In NetWare 4, you can actually set more than one server bindery context for each user. When a client searches for a bindery object using bindery calls, it looks through the containers in the order they appear in the list. Bindery services in NetWare 4 lets you select up to 16 containers as the server bindery context. The requirement for bindery services is that the server stores at least a read/write replica of the partition where the bindery context is set.

Multiple bindery contexts can create one potential problem, which is known as eclipsing. In NDS, two objects can have the same relative distinguished name, but the objects must be in different container objects. For example, in Figure 7-3 there are two user objects created in the ACME tree with the relative distinguished name of JOHN, which exist in the OU=HR and OU=OPS containers. This example assumes that there is a server with the server bindery context set to both the OU=HR and OU=OPS containers in that order.

NDS distinguishes between the two objects because their distinguished names are different. However, the bindery client sees only the object's relative distinguished name. If a bindery client searches for the object JOHN, it finds the object in OU=HR first and stops searching, whether that is the object the client is looking for or not. In this situation, the client is unable to access the object JOHN in the OU=OPS container. This effect is called eclipsing and happens only in bindery services, not in NDS.

You can solve this problem by making sure that no two objects in the NDS tree have the same relative distinguished name. A good naming standard is important and should be enforced.

Eclipsing also occurs when a dynamic bindery object has the same name as a static bindery object, although this situation is rare. In such cases, the dynamic object always eclipses the static object.

## Objects in the Bindery

The bindery used in previous versions of NetWare allowed two categories of objects. These objects classes are:

♦ Static bindery objects

♦ Dynamic bindery objects

These object categories are specified by a flag on the object itself. The difference between the two categories (static and dynamic) is the longevity expected for each of the objects rather than a specific type of object.

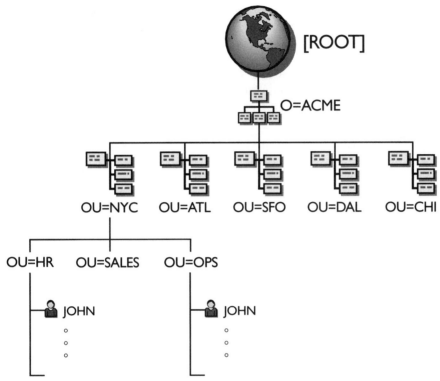

Figure 7-3: There are two user objects created in the ACME tree with the relative distinguished name of JOHN, which exist in the OU=HR.OU=NYC.O=ACME and OU=OPS.OU=NYC.O=ACME containers.

## Static Bindery Objects

The static bindery objects are the normal user, group, print queues, print server, and profile objects that are defined in the bindery of NetWare 3. These objects are created permanently in the bindery until someone manually deletes them.

When static bindery objects are migrated, they are stored in NDS container objects specified in the bindery context of the NetWare 4 server. If multiple containers are specified, the objects are migrated or placed in the first valid container in the bindery path.

The NDS schema defines what attributes each object class has, thus regulating the makeup or creation of each object class. The NetWare 3 bindery is not hierarchical and does not need to distinguish objects by classes in order to build a hierarchical structure or tree. Therefore, the bindery does not have formal schema definitions. However, the bindery does allow for specific object types. These object types are used to identify the object within the bindery. For example, objects of type 1 are user objects, and group objects are type 2.

Some of the well-known object types have direct counterparts in the NDS schema and can be converted or mutated during installation, migration, or creation. The mutation occurs for object types from the bindery to the appropriate NDS object class. For each bindery object type to be mutated, it must have all the mandatory attributes of the targeted NDS object class and cannot have the same name as another object in the container.

The bindery object types that are mutated by NDS are as follows:

♦ User

♦ Group

♦ Print Queue

♦ Print Server

♦ Profile

For example, a client using a bindery-based application wants to create a user object called JOE on a NetWare 4 server in the NDS tree. The application makes a bindery API call to create a user object. The request is made as follows:

```
ADD OBJECT "JOE" TYPE=1
```

The data is immediately converted to an NDS object class of user and the name becomes:

```
CN=JOE
```

Not all the NDS objects in the tree are available or visible to the bindery APIs. Bindery services applies only to leaf objects that are in the NetWare 3 bindery definitions. This includes the objects for user, group, print queue, print server, and profile. Also included is the bindery object base class CN=XXXX+Bindery Type=643.

# Dynamic Bindery Objects

The dynamic bindery objects are used for SAP object names and information. This enables the advertising servers or services to have their objects added to the bindery as dynamic objects. For example, these objects are the file server and print server names that use SAP to become known on the network. In NetWare 4 additional services use SAP to become known, such as the NDS tree and time synchronization.

If the bindery is closed and reopened, these objects and their properties are automatically deleted. Figure 7-4 illustrates how the information from the network would be directed logically to the appropriate section of the bindery according to the type of information.

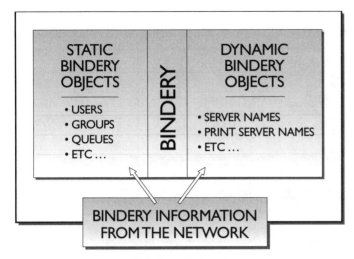

Figure 7-4: NetWare 3 bindery information from the network is directed to the appropriate section of the bindery according to the type of information.

Figure 7-4 is a logical representation of the bindery services. In reality, the bindery does not have separate sections for the dynamic and static information. All bindery information is stored in the bindery files. The properties of the dynamic objects are mostly network addresses.

In order for NetWare 4 to provide complete compatibility with previous versions of NetWare, the dynamic bindery objects need to be supported. Since the bindery is no longer the mechanism to store objects in NetWare 4, NDS must provide this functionality.

The parent objects of dynamic bindery objects are not in the NDS hierarchy. They are not associated with a specific parent container in the tree. Instead, the dynamic bindery objects are stored in the NDS system partition called the Bindery Partition. These objects can be accessed by a bindery client or server and are not dependent upon a set bindery context for the server.

Figure 7-5 illustrates logically how the information from the network would be directed to the appropriate section of NDS to provide the same function as the bindery.

Again, Figure 7-5 is a logical representation of NDS. In reality, the Directory does not have separate sections for the dynamic bindery object information. All the dynamic bindery objects are located adjacent to the other NDS objects in the NDS data files. See Figure 7-6 for an illustration of the object data file in NDS. The properties of the dynamic objects are mostly network addresses.

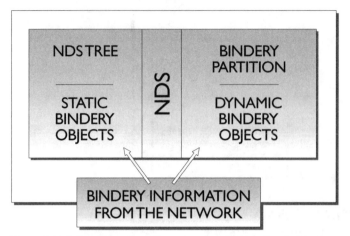

Figure 7-5: Information from the network would be directed to the appropriate section of NDS to provide the same function as the bindery.

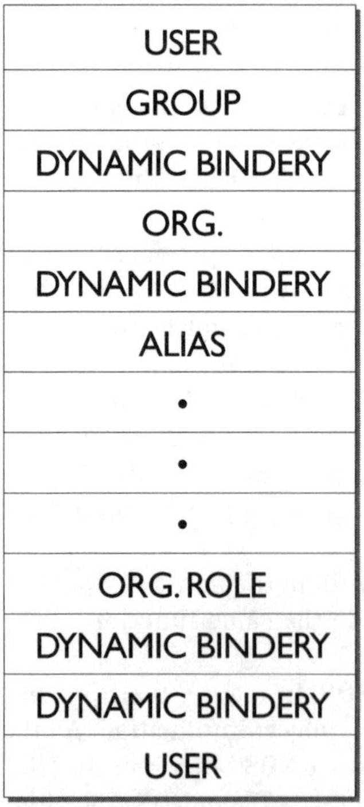

| USER |
|---|
| GROUP |
| DYNAMIC BINDERY |
| ORG. |
| DYNAMIC BINDERY |
| ALIAS |
| • |
| • |
| • |
| ORG. ROLE |
| DYNAMIC BINDERY |
| DYNAMIC BINDERY |
| USER |

Figure 7-6: An example of the object structure in NDS. The dynamic bindery objects are stored adjacent to all the other NDS objects.

# SafeGuard the Bindery Supervisor Account

The bindery Supervisor account or user is created during installation of the NetWare 4 server. The Supervisor is a server-centric account created on every NetWare 4 server. The Supervisor account is created even if you don't install NDS replicas on that server or if a bindery services context is not set on the server. This account is created whether you install NDS replicas on that server or not. The Supervisor account is created and exists whether a Bindery Services context is set on the server. However, the Supervisor user is accessible only if a valid bindery context is set for the server. This is true with the exception of the Server Console Lock and Unlock operation, which can be performed using the Supervisor password.

The Supervisor account is not seen as an object of the NDS tree because it is server centric. The Supervisor user is stored in the bindery partition, which is one of the four partitions that exists even if an NDS replica is not installed on the server.

The Supervisor account has all rights to the individual server, which includes the file system and objects at the effective server bindery context. If there is a valid bindery services context(s) set on the server, the Supervisor user will automatically have all rights to the bindery objects in the context(s). The Supervisor account has rights only to the NDS objects that are also bindery objects. For example, these objects are users, groups, queues, print servers, and profiles. The profile object was first made available in the bindery by the NetWare Name Service (NNS) product.

Since the Supervisor user does not show up in the NDS tree, you cannot log in as Supervisor using an NDS connection. This means that the NWADMIN and NETADMIN utilities cannot be used by someone logged in as Supervisor. The Supervisor account can only access the objects using SYSCON or other bindery-based utilities.

Although it is possible to create an object in the NDS tree called SUPERVISOR using the administrative utilities — such as NWADMIN — the new user is not the same Supervisor user seen in the bindery. Any modifications made to the bindery Supervisor account are limited to bindery-based modifications. The individual logging in as the Supervisor user has to have a bindery connection to the server and use the bindery-based utilities.

The Supervisor account will always be assigned a password during creation. This was not the case in NetWare 4.01 because the individual installing the server, typically the ADMIN user, was not required to have a password. The Supervisor user receives its password during creation according to the following conditions:

♦ The server is a new NetWare 4 server. This means that the server is not migrated from NetWare 3. The Supervisor is assigned the password of the user that logs in to the tree to perform the installation of the server. This is typically the ADMIN user.

♦ The server is being migrated from NetWare 3 to NetWare 4 using the INSTALL.NLM program. The Supervisor account information remains the same as before the upgrade. If the Supervisor account in NetWare 3 does not have a password, the password of the user that logged in to the tree to do the install (usually ADMIN) is assigned to the Supervisor in NetWare 4; otherwise, the user uses the Supervisor password from NetWare 3.

♦ The server is being migrated from NetWare 3 to NetWare 4 using the MIGRATE.EXE or the Across-the-Wire Migration utility. When you migrate using the Across-the-Wire Migration utility, the NetWare 4 server is already installed and running. This means that the Supervisor account on the new NetWare 4 server is already created and has a password. The password is created according to option number 1. The Across-the-Wire Migration utility does not change the password with the password from the NetWare 3 server.

It is very important that you safeguard the password for the Supervisor. The password that the Supervisor is assigned is not synchronized with the user that installs the new NetWare 4 server in to the tree. For example, the ADMIN user installs the server and the Supervisor user is assigned the password for ADMIN. If the ADMIN user ever changes its password, the password for the Supervisor account is not changed. The two accounts are completely separate after the initial installation.

# Setting Up User Environments Using Login Scripts

Network users will execute login scripts as the primary access to the NetWare 4 servers and other network resources. Traditionally, the login scripts are used to establish the user's network environment. The login scripts for NetWare 4 are used to map network drives, map to applications, capture to printers and print queues, and set other important environment variables. The login scripts become the standard mechanism for user access and may require careful consideration.

When a user logs in to the NetWare 4 network or server, the login scripts associated with the user are executed. There are two categories of login scripts available to the user of the NetWare 4 network: the NDS login scripts and the bindery-based login scripts. The NDS login scripts support the Directory connections and the bindery-based login scripts support the bindery services connections.

The focus on login scripts in this chapter is to provide information on designing access to NetWare 4 and not to encompass every login script variable and command. However, well-designed login scripts will help you create effective working environments for your users.

 We recommend that you execute the login scripts before launching Windows 3.1. If there are users who go into Windows immediately after they boot their workstation, you need to have them log in to the network that runs the login scripts before launching Windows 3.1. The exception to this tip is if you are running the new NetWare Client 32 software that provides a Windows login utility.

Login scripts execute in the following order:

1. User logs in to a server.

2. User executes the OU or container login script if it exists.

3. User executes Profile login script if the user is associated with one.

4. User executes User login script if it exists.

5. If the user login script does not exist, the default login script will be executed.

# Bindery-Based Login Scripts

The bindery-based login scripts that you may place in NetWare 4 are the same bindery login scripts found in NetWare 2 and NetWare 3. These login scripts can be copied onto the NetWare 4 servers to provide bindery services scripts to your NETX clients. For example, a user attaching to a NetWare 4 server with the NETX workstation software will look for the system and user login scripts on the server. The user script would be in the SYS:MAIL directory, and the system login script would be placed in the SYS:PUBLIC directory. Even if the user is using the VLM workstation software and selects the LOGIN /B option, that user will be attached as a bindery connection.

The NetWare 3 system login script is used for commands that affect all the bindery-based users on that server. Commands that might be placed in the system login script include the commands for displaying messages, mapping network drives, mapping search drives, and setting environment variables. The system login script is the best place to manage the mapping and capture statements for all the bindery users that may still exist on your NetWare 4 network.

After a user successfully attaches to the server with a bindery connection, the system login script will execute SYS:PUBLIC\NET$LOG.DAT if it exists. If the user login script is present it will execute from the SYS:MAIL\USERID subdirectory. If the user login script does not exist, the default login script is executed. The default login script is hard coded into the LOGIN.EXE program.

Figure 7-7 shows the order of execution for the bindery-based login scripts. If you are familiar with NetWare 3, notice that the bindery-based login scripts for NetWare 4 are executed in the same order.

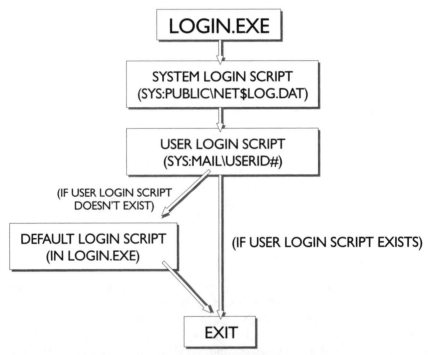

Figure 7-7: The bindery-based login scripts in NetWare 4 are executed in the same order as NetWare 3 login scripts.

The individual user login scripts are stored in each of the user's mail subdirectories on the SYS volume of any server where a bindery account exists. For example, user BTHOMAS (with server ID of 19000023) stores the bindery-based user login scripts in the subdirectory:

```
SYS:MAIL\19000023
```

The individual user login script serves to customize the user environment to the specific needs of the user. The same type of commands placed in the system login scripts can also be placed in the individual user login scripts. It is recommended that the user login scripts be used only in situations where the system login script will not suffice.

The bindery-based login scripts are server centric, meaning that they are used only if a bindery user logs in to the server that is holding them. Because the login scripts are server centric there are not a lot of design issues. However, you should try to move all the users to the NDS login scripts as soon as possible.

You can make changes to both the system and user login scripts using the NetWare 3 SYSCON.EXE utility. You can also edit the NET$LOG.DAT file (or any script) directly with any text editing program. Although the bindery-based login scripts can be edited, any changes made are not automatically synchronized to the corresponding NDS login scripts. You can use Novell's NETSYNC utility to synchronize login scripts if you need to maintain consistency.

# NDS Login Scripts

The login scripts used in NDS are different than those used by bindery services. The NDS login scripts are a property of an object and are accessible only through a Directory Services connection. The only NDS objects that have the login script property are the container (O=Organization and OU=Organizational Unit) objects, profile objects, and user objects.

The users that obtain a Directory Services connection to the network will enable LOGIN to execute the container login script in which they reside. The container script is roughly equivalent to the NetWare 3 system login script. After the container login script, a profile login script can be executed if the user is associated with one. The user may also have a user script, which is executed after a container and profile script. If no scripts are available, the user will execute a default script. Again, the default login script is hard coded into the LOGIN.EXE program.

Figure 7-8 shows the order of execution for the NDS login scripts. Notice the profile login script, which falls between the container and user login scripts.

In order to manage the NDS login scripts, you can use either the NWADMIN or NETADMIN utilities that ship with NetWare 4. With these utilities, you can create and edit all the login scripts, except for the default login script. You can also add a profile login script for execution by selected users. An example of editing a login script using NWADMIN shown in Figure 7-9. In this example, the administrator is editing a container login script for the NORAD container.

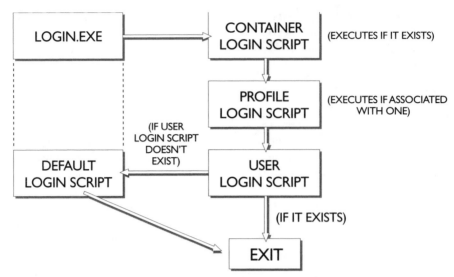

Figure 7-8: The order of execution for the NDS login scripts in NetWare 4

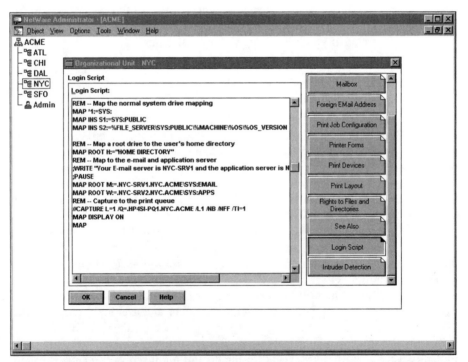

Figure 7-9: Adding or modifying an NDS login script can be done by using the NWADMIN utility as shown here.

# NDS Container Login Scripts

Typically, the NDS users needing the same network resources will be grouped together in the same NDS container. These users will probably need similar drive mappings and capture statements to establish access to the network resources they are grouped with. You can then use the container login script to provide access to the NDS tree in this fashion.

---

 We recommend that you use the NDS container login script to replace the functionality of the NetWare 3 system login script. The container login script is stored as a property of the O=Organization, the OU=Organizational Unit objects, or any other container objects.

---

After the LOGIN utility has authenticated a user to the NetWare 4 network, the program checks the container login script in which the user resides. If the container login script exists it will then be executed. NDS will only search the immediate container (O or OU) where the user is a member. If the container login script is not defined, the system will not search up the tree for another container login script.

For example, Figure 7-10 shows the user JHUGHES in the ACME tree named under the container OU=AP.OU=ACCT.OU=ATL.O=ACME. The container OU=AP does not have a login script. There is, however, a container login script defined higher in the tree at OU=ACCT. The user JHUGHES is an occupant of OU=AP and will not execute a container login script because there is not one currently in OU=AP. LOGIN.EXE will not search for a container login script up the tree. In other words, no other container login scripts above the user will be executed.

The NDS container login script can be used like the NetWare 3 system login script. Container login script commands should establish the network environment of the users. These commands include the network drive mappings, printer and print queue captures, and other environment settings. The users in the container are best managed by using this login script.

The following is an example of a container login script that we have just added for the OU=AP container in the ATL location of the ACME tree:

```
;*********************************************************
; CONTAINER LOGIN SCRIPT EXAMPLE
; for OU=AP.OU=ACCT.OU=ATL.O=ACME
; Creation Date: 7/4/96
; Revisions:
;*********************************************************
COMSPEC=C:\DOS\COMMAND.COM
REM - No default user login script
NO_DEFAULT
WRITE "Good %GREETING_TIME, %LOGIN_NAME."
MAP DISPLAY OFF
```

```
REM - Map the root drive to SYS:PUBLIC and another drive to
  the home directory
MAP ROOT INSERT S1:=SYS:\PUBLIC
MAP ROOT H:="HOME DIRECTORY"
REM - Map to the e-mail and application server
;WRITE "Your E-mail server is ATL-SRV1 and the application
  server is AP-SRV1"
;PAUSE
MAP ROOT M:=.ATL-SRV1.ATL.ACME\SYS:EMAIL
MAP ROOT W:=.AP-SRV1.ACCT.ATL.ACME\SYS:APPS
REM - Capture to the print queue
#CAPTURE L=1 /Q=.HP4SI-PQ1.AP.ACCT.ATL.ACME /L1 /NB /NFF /TI=1
```

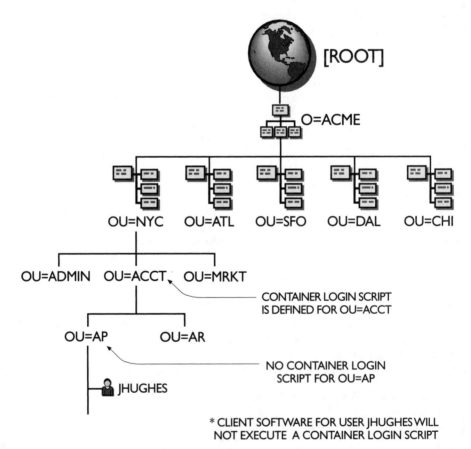

Figure 7-10: Container login scripts are executed only for the immediate occupants of the container. In this example, the user JHUGHES will not have a container login script.

# NDS Profile Login Scripts

If a user has a profile script assigned, it will be executed immediately after the container login script. The profile login script is optional and is used for special cases or for groups with special needs. The profile has the unique capability to include users that are in different containers in the tree. Its purpose is to assign additional environment settings that you may not want to assign to everyone in the container. The scripting and the commands used in the profile login script are identical to the NDS container login scripts.

Since the profile login script is a special-purpose login script it can provide you with greater flexibility than any other login mechanism. Any number of users can be associated with the profile login script, and they can reside in different containers in your tree. Figure 7-11 shows the creation of a profile login script through the NWADMIN utility.

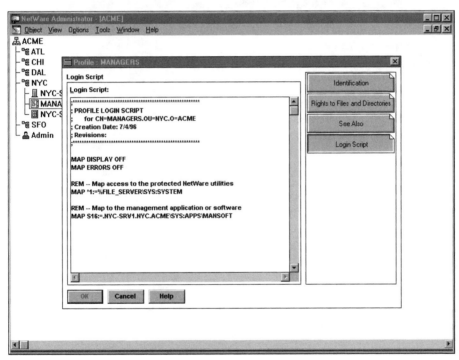

Figure 7-11: Creation of a profile login script through NWADMIN

You can enable users to execute the profile script by assigning individual users to the script by making the assignment to the user object at creation. This method can be accomplished through the NWADMIN or NETADMIN utilities as shown in Figure 7-12.

Typically, the profile login script has been used in several different ways:

◆ For an entire company (if the company and tree are small)

◆ To create an environment based on location

◆ For a special group of users

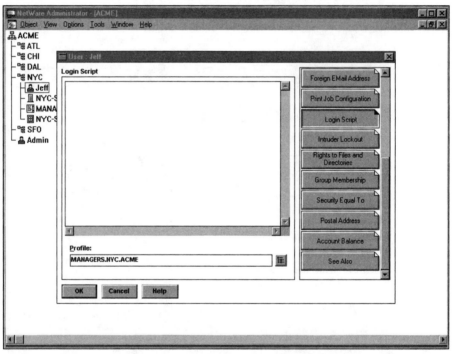

Figure 7-12: Assigning an individual user to execute a profile login script

## PROFILE LOGIN SCRIPT FOR THE ENTIRE COMPANY

The profile script is represented by the profile object that can be placed anywhere in the Directory tree. Using the profile login script to span all the users in the entire company is recommended only for networks where the number of servers is small and there is only one partition. In this case, a small number of servers is fewer than 10 with no wide area links. The reason for this recommendation is that this method is expensive in terms of NDS traffic that will be generated to locate or resolve this object in the tree.

## PROFILE LOGIN SCRIPT FOR ONE LOCATION

Another purpose for the profile login script that is more widely used is to make it a login script to create an environment for a location. This is similar to simply using a container script, except that you may want to create an environment for specific users within the container. This means the users that are organized around a particular site, building, or floor can have specific environment settings based on their particular needs. This eliminates the need to build building or floor containers in your tree just to have a common login script.

For example, you have a specific set of users in a building and you want them to always map to the same e-mail and applications servers. You may also have users on one floor that want to capture to the same printers. You can accomplish these tasks using the profile login script. Using the profile login script in this fashion is considered to be locational.

Figure 7-13 illustrates a profile login script being used as a locational login script that includes the containers in the ACME tree below the OU=ACCT container in the ATL location. Specifically, the OU=AP and OU=AR are in the same building and need similar environment settings.

## PROFILE LOGIN SCRIPT FOR A SPECIAL GROUP OF USERS

The profile login script can also serve as a special-purpose login script for a group of users. The group members can all be in the same NDS container or they can span across a number of OUs. If the profile login script makes assignments for users within a single OU, the profile login script is similar to a group object with its sole purpose of executing a script.

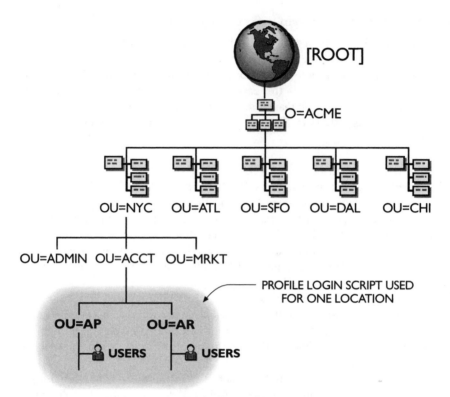

Figure 7-13: The users in both the OU=AP and OU=AR are using the same profile login script.

A more powerful use of the profile login script is to span more than one NDS container. For example, in Figure 7-14, you will see three users each in a different NDS container. These users are members of a special group of administrators who need specialized access to resources in the NDS tree. When each user logs in to the network, they receive the additional drive mapping to perform their job functions. Users BTHOMAS, JHUGHES, CSEAVER, and KNAY are each associated with the same profile login script that gives them the extra drive mappings.

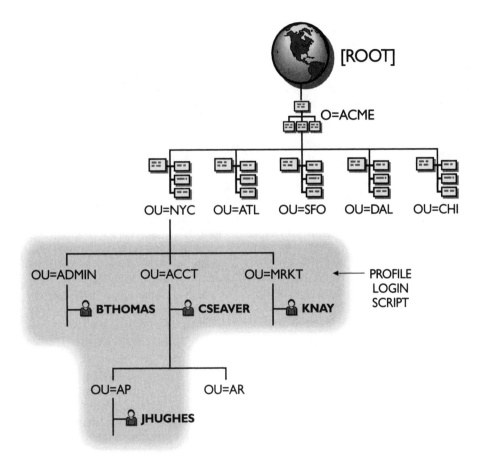

Figure 7-14: The users BTHOMAS, JHUGHES, CSEAVER, and KNAY are each associated with the same profile login script.

## NDS USER LOGIN SCRIPT

The NDS user login scripts are stored as a property in each of the user objects. Like the bindery-based user login script, the NDS user login script serves to customize the user environment to the specific needs of that user. All the login script commands and variables can be used in the individual user login scripts. However, we strongly recommend that user login scripts be used only when the commands in the container login script are not adequate.

## Consulting Experience

Most, if not all, scripting can be accomplished through the use of container login scripts. For most large NetWare environments it is generally not feasible to implement user scripts because of the difficulty in maintaining them. As a network administrator you don't need the extra work.

If you decide to let the users have personal login scripts, keep in mind that maintaining all the users' login scripts can be a difficult and time-consuming task.

The following is an example of a user login script for JHUGHES in the OU=AP container in the ATL location of the ACME tree. These users ideally should support their own user login scripts and not request the assistance of a network administrator.

```
MAP DISPLAY OFF
MAP ERROR OFF
MAP F:=.ATL-SRV1.ATL.ACME\SYS:USERS\JHUGHES
;***** EMAIL *****
SET EMAILUSER = "JHUGHES"
MAP M:=.ATL-SRV1.ATL.ACME\SYS:POSTOFF
;***** PRINTERS *****
#CAPTURE L=1 Q=.HP4SI-PQ1.AP.ACCT.ATL.ACME NB NFF TI=1
;***** WINDOWS *****
MAP ROOT W:=.ATL-SRV1.AP.ACCT.ATL.ACME\SYS:APPS\WINDOWS
;***** BRIEF EDITOR FLAGS *****
MAP S16:=.ATL-SRV1.AP.ACCT.ATL.ACME\SYS:APPS\BRIEF
SET BPACKAGES = "c:t;h:t,r"
SET BPATH ="z:\\apps\\brief\\macros"
SET BHELP = "z:\\apps\\brief\\help"
SET BBACKUP = "c:\\backup"
SET BFLAGS = "-i70 -u300 -l200 -Dega -k1 M"
SET BFILE = ""
SET BTMP = "c:\\tmp"
SET BCC = "\"cl /c %s.c\""
SET BCH = "\"cl -c -Tc %s.h\""
;***** WP *****
MAP S16:=.ATL-SRV1.ATL.ACME\SYS:APPS\WP\6.1
SET WP = "/U=JFH"
;***** Misc. *****
MAP S16:=.ATL-SRV1.ATL.ACME\SYS:APPS\PROGRAMS\BIN
MAP
```

## DEFAULT LOGIN SCRIPT

The default login script is executed only when the user login script does not exist. The default login script is hard coded into the LOGIN.EXE program and tries to create enough drive mappings to the server so that the user can function properly. The purpose of the default login script is only to back up the user login script. The default login script will continue to execute even if you have a container or profile login script.

If you do not want the default script to run, you need to place the NO_DEFAULT command in the container login script or in a profile script. The container login script can also have an EXIT command at the bottom of the script to prevent any other login script from running. This includes the default login script.

The following built-in commands are executed as the default login script:

```
WRITE "Good %GREETING_TIME, %LOGIN_NAME."
MAP DISPLAY OFF
MAP ERRORS OFF
MAP *1:=%FILE_SERVER\SYS:
MAP *1:=%FILE_SERVER\SYS:%LOGIN_NAME
IF "%1" = "SUPERVISOR" || "%1" = "ADMIN" THEN MAP
 *1:=%FILE_SERVER\SYS:SYSTEM
MAP INS S1:=%FILE_SERVER\SYS:PUBLIC
MAP INS
S2:=%FILE_SERVER\SYS:PUBLIC\%MACHINE\%OS\%OS_VERSION
MAP DISPLAY ON
MAP
```

# Setting Up Mobile User Access

NetWare 4 lets the user log in and access resources from anywhere in the network. This feature helps you to manage the mobile or traveling user more easily. In order to completely support traveling users and their specific computing requirements each user will need to answer the following question during login to the network. Are users acting as remote or mobile users?

As users move around from one location to another, they access the network and its resources differently. Knowing how each user wants access to the network will help you set up the user environments. For example, some users just want dial in access to the network from remote locations. These locations can range from their home, hotel rooms, and even airplanes. This type of user, typically, dials into the network from a laptop or home computer.

Some users may travel from one office to another and need full access to all the local network resources of the office they are visiting. Although the users need full access to the local resources, they still want the data from the home directory and server. Essentially, the definition of a traveling user is broken into two types, remote users and mobile users.

> **TIP** Your approach to designing access for NetWare 4 should be first to design for the majority of users and then design for traveling users. In order to design the access properly, you need to know how many users in the network are traveling users. Then determine from the total number of traveling users how many are remote users and how many are true mobile users.

## Remote Users

The remote users are the individuals who travel or carry a laptop computer and simply access the network resources through dial-in. The remote user that takes a laptop on the road is usually self-contained, meaning that the laptop computer is configured with all the necessary applications software. The user can continue to work when on the road and merely dials into the network to transfer e-mail messages, download files, or get other resources.

Remote users require fewer design considerations for access because they will access the NDS tree only as needed for connection to the network. Supporting remote users will not impact the design of the Directory tree or require you to create any special NDS objects. Users simply dial into specific predetermined access points in the network and use their normal NDS context or location. After the normal login to the network, the users can download files and get other necessary resources.

Some remote users dial in just to transfer their e-mail messages. Typically, there are special phones lines dedicated for just the remote e-mail users. These lines may have their own security and access method, which would not currently affect the Directory tree access.

If a remote user travels to another office and plugs his or her laptop computer into the network and wants access to all the local resources, he or she has really become a mobile user. The considerations for the mobile users are addressed in the following section.

## Mobile Users

The mobile users are individuals that travel from one office to another or, more exactly, from one computer to another. They expect full access to all the local network resources of the office they are visiting while maintaining the ability to get data from their home server. The mobile user may not carry a computer (laptop) with him, but he expects to have a computer available at the other site. Some mobile users decide to carry laptop computers and plug them into the network when they arrive. Thus, the best definition of a mobile user is an individual that uses a computer on the network from a location that is away from their home office.

Whether the user travels thousands of miles or across the building, the issues are the same. The user wants access to the network applications, such as word processing, spreadsheets, e-mail, and printing from the local servers, but to retrieve data off their home server. They want these abilities to be as seamless as possible.

 Users who carry laptop computers to a new location are not considered mobile users if they do not need access to the local network resources. If users are content to access their home resources across the network, they are simply remote users. There are no special considerations for remote users. Remember, NetWare 4 will let the users log in from anywhere on the network. The only issue here is speed of access.

In order to support the needs of the mobile user, you need to be able to answer two questions, previously mentioned. Again, these questions are:

♦ Where is the user geographically located?

♦ What is the user's home office?

Several mechanisms exist in NetWare 4 to help you answer each of these questions. These mechanisms include the NDS name context, alias objects, configuration files, login scripts, login script variables, and environment variables.

## NDS NAME CONTEXT

The name context in NDS helps you determine where in the NDS tree the user belongs. The name context is important because NDS requires it for every user logging into the network. The context can be set by typing the user's full name during login as well. While a mobile user's physical location may change, that user's context will remain constant.

If the mobile user has traveled without a laptop computer, he expects to use any available computer in the office he is visiting and log into the network. The main issue with this scenario is how to determine the user's name context for login purposes. There are several ways to work around this problem:

♦ The mobile user can manually enter the context at the computer console before login.

♦ You can create alias objects that point to the user in his normal context.

♦ The name context can be set in the workstation configuration file.

MANUALLY CHANGING THE NDS NAME CONTEXT    The first option mentioned is where the mobile users manually enter their name contexts into the computer they are using. This implies that they understand how to use the proper utilities and know their complete context in the NDS tree. The CX (Change conteXt) utility is used to set the users' context before login. For example, the user JHUGHES in the ACME tree as shown in Figure 7-15 would need to set his name context by typing:

```
CX .AP.ACCT.NYC.ACME
```

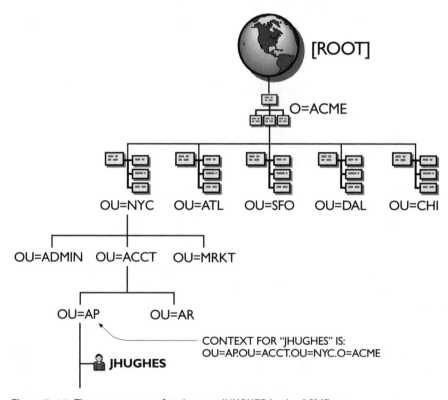

Figure 7-15: The name context for the user JHUGHES in the ACME tree

Notice the leading period in the CX command line. The leading period tells the utility that this is a full name and to start at the [ROOT] object when setting the name context. This is a little easier than trying to figure out where you are in the tree.

The CX utility is stored in the LOGIN subdirectory on the server. The user must have a connection to a server and be in the directory (typically the F: drive) or type the path before running this utility.

USING AN ALIAS OBJECT TO HELP SET THE NAME CONTEXT   The second option that could more easily help set the name context is through the use of alias objects. If you have a small number of mobile users you can create an alias object below the O=Organization for each mobile user. The alias would point to the user's primary object in the appropriate container.

The value of this strategy is that it creates a simple context for each of the mobile users. The users do not need to know what their context is or even how to set it. The user would simply enter the name of the alias during the login process.

For example, there has been an alias object created for the user JHUGHES in the ACME tree. In Figure 7-16 the alias object JHUGHES was created directly in the O=ACME container. The alias object points to the real object in the OU=AP in the ATL location. When the user JHUGHES wants to log into the network from any site, he uses the name of the alias object as follows:

```
LOGIN .JHUGHES.ACME.
```

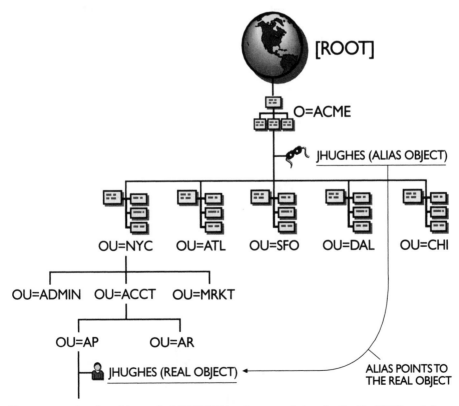

Figure 7-16: An alias object called JHUGHES has been created under the O=ACME container.

Notice the leading period in the LOGIN command line before the name of the alias object. The leading period instructs the utility to start at the [ROOT] object when looking for the alias object.

This method of using the alias object to support the mobile users works well if you have a small number of mobile users at your site. Setting up an alias object for each individual mobile users is feasible if the total number of mobile users is small from a performance standpoint. This method may not work as well if your mobile user population is high. You will need to determine how many alias objects you can manage.

## USING THE CONFIGURATION FILES TO SET THE NAME CONTEXT

The name context for the user can be set using the standard workstation configuration file called NET.CFG. The NET.CFG file is read during the loading of the workstation client. Within the file NET.CFG there is a section called the NetWare DOS Requester where:

```
NAME CONTEXT ="OU=AP.OU=ACCT.OU=NYC.O=ACME"
```

Users that travel to different locations with their own notebook or laptop will typically have the NET.CFG file set already. When they arrive on site and connect to the network, their name context is resolved from the setting in the NET.CFG file on the laptop.

The following is an example of the setting the name context for the user JHUGHES in the ACME tree:

```
Link Support
 MemPool 6192
 Buffers 10 1580
 MAX STACKS 8

Link Driver NE2000
 INT 5
 PORT 300
 MEM D0000
 FRAME Ethernet_802.2

NetWare DOS Requester
 NAME CONTEXT = "OU=AP.OU=ACCT.OU=NYC.O=ACME"
 PREFERRED SERVER = NYC-SRV1
 FIRST NETWORK DRIVE = F
 NETWARE PROTOCOL = NDS,BIND
 SHOW DOTS = ON
 USE DEFAULTS = ON
 PB BUFFERS = 10
```

You can use the PREFERRED SERVER variable in the NET.CFG file (in the NetWare DOS Requester section) to connect the mobile user to the server that has his context. In the example given above, the variable PREFERRED SERVER = NYC-SRV1 enables the user JHUGHES to log in and access the server using bindery services.

If you force the user to connect to the proper server using the PREFERRED SERVER variable, the user can log in using bindery services. This enables users running the older NETX.EXE workstation client to participate in mobile computing. However, this also means that the workstation or client must be able to see the preferred server through SAP. If your network is filtering SAP, this option may not be feasible.

 You can also use third-party utilities that search NDS for a specific user and set his context once he has been discovered.

## LOGIN SCRIPTS FOR MOBILE USERS

The two mechanisms for creating a mobile login script are the login script variables and an environment variable that can be called NW_SITE.

As shown in the following example, we have defined a mobile script that will enable the user to easily log into the network from any of the five major sites shown in the ACME tree. The script demonstrates how a user is mapped to the local e-mail server and to the local application server. This login script would be used as a container login script and also requires the NW_SITE DOS environment variable set on the user's workstation in the CONFIG.SYS file.

```
;*********************************************************
; MOBILE CONTAINER LOGIN SCRIPT
; for OU=AP.OU=ACCT.OU=NYC.O=ACME
; Creation Date: 12/30/97
; Revisions:
;*********************************************************
;
REM Do not execute default script
NO_DEFAULT
Write "Good %GREETING_TIME, %LOGIN_NAME"
REM Map public drive to local server
MAP S16:=SYS:\PUBLIC
REM Map F drive to the user's home server
MAP F:="HOME_DIRECTORY"
REM Map NetWare Drives according to the NW_SITE variable

IF <NW_SITE> == "NEW_YORK_CITY" THEN BEGIN
  MAP ROOT M:= .NYC-SRV1.NYC.ACME\SYS:MAIL
  MAP ROOT W:= .NYC-SRV1.NYC.ACME\SYS:APPS\WP
  MAP ROOT Q:= .NYC-SRV1.NYC.ACME\SYS:APPS\QPRO
```

```
END

IF <NW_SITE> == "SAN_FRANCISCO" THEN BEGIN
 MAP ROOT M:= .SFO-SRV1.SFO.ACME\SYS:MAIL
 MAP ROOT W:= .SFO-SRV1.SFO.ACME\SYS:APPS\WP
 MAP ROOT Q:= .SFO-SRV1.SFO.ACME\SYS:APPS\QPRO
 END

IF <NW_SITE> == "ATLANTA" THEN BEGIN
 MAP ROOT M:= .ATL-SRV1.ATL.ACME\SYS:MAIL
 MAP ROOT W:= .ATL-SRV1.ATL.ACME\SYS:APPS\WP
 MAP ROOT Q:= .ATL-SRV1.ATL.ACME\SYS:APPS\QPRO
 END

IF <NW_SITE> == "DALLAS" THEN BEGIN
 MAP ROOT M:= .DAL-SRV1.DAL.ACME\SYS:MAIL
 MAP ROOT W:= .DAL-SRV1.DAL.ACME\SYS:APPS\WP
 MAP ROOT Q:= .DAL-SRV1.DAL.ACME\SYS:APPS\QPRO
 END

IF <NW_SITE> == "CHICAGO" THEN BEGIN
 MAP ROOT M:= .CHI-SRV1.CHI.ACME\SYS:MAIL
 MAP ROOT W:= .CHI-SRV1.CHI.ACME \SYS:APPS\WP
 MAP ROOT Q:= .CHI-SRV1.CHI.ACME\SYS:APPS\QPRO
 END
EXIT
```

 In the previous script you can specify the actual volume object names instead of the server names for mapping drives. The drives M and W in our example default to searching the bindery, which relies on SAP because we do not specify the NDS volume object names.

# Supplying Network Applications Using NetWare Application Launcher

NetWare Application Launcher (NAL) works with NDS to enable administrators to centrally control the access to network applications and to each of the user's Windows desktops. NAL enables the administrators to manage and access desktop and applications across the network. This significantly reduces the time and costs of administering network applications.

In conjunction with NDS, the NetWare Application Launcher offers:

◆ Central administration of user applications

◆ Filtering of the applications that are available to the user

◆ Automation of user application updates

◆ Login script integration for easy launch

◆ NDS as a central information repository

◆ Machine-independent configuration

The Novell Application Launcher is included in Novell's most current release of the NetWare client, NetWare Client 32, and will be included in all future releases of NetWare. NetWare Client 32 is available electronically via CompuServe in the NetWare Operating System Files forum (NWOSFILES) and through Novell's Web site at http://netware.novell.com.

Using new "snap-in" capabilities in the NDS administrative utility NetWare Administrator (NWADMIN), an administrator creates application objects in NDS for any application to make it available through NAL. Access to files and directories is handled through NDS and the file system to ensure network security. Specific rights to these application objects can then be assigned to containers, groups, and users.

When a user running NAL logs in through NDS, NAL looks at the groups and containers the user belongs to and recognizes any applications that the user is authorized to access. In the background, NetWare Application Launcher locates all the user's applications on the network and accesses them transparently when the user selects the program icon in Windows. A NAL program group displays all the appropriate application icons that the user can select to launch the application. Available applications are scanned and updated automatically for the user.

Since the network applications are delivered through NDS, administrators can deploy these applications to user desktops across the network without leaving their workstations. The effort is the same whether the application is deployed to 10 or 10,000 workstations. This eliminates time-consuming effort and significantly reduces installation costs of new network applications. Network administrators no longer have to travel to each user's desktop to create a standard Windows program item for each application on the network. They can centrally administer and deploy network applications from the convenience of their own workstations.

In addition to NAL, there is a new NetWare GUI Login utility that enables users to log in through Windows, execute a user or system login script, update search drive mappings, and update the environment variables. This is accomplished from within the Windows environment. This service has never been possible before. Both NDS and bindery services connections are supported.

# Minimizing the Need for Login Scripts

Because the NDS application objects store pointers to the actual location of network applications, users no longer need to have drive mappings established through login scripts. Each NDS application object can also store login script-like subroutines that can map additional drives and capture printers as users launch applications. This saves considerable administration time and cost, since administrators are no longer required to create and manage drive mappings for each application in network login scripts. In addition, the number of licensed server connections is reduced since drives are mapped and printers are captured only when users access applications. The connections are released when the user exits the application, eliminating unused but connected licenses that commonly occur when mappings and captures take place through login scripts.

# Setting Up Network Applications

Users access applications by running the application launcher from their Windows Startup group or other Windows program group. This gives users a set of network applications the administrator has assigned to them through NDS. To launch an application, a user simply double-clicks the appropriate icon in the group. The application launcher does the rest, taking care of drive mappings and paths automatically.

Standard Windows program items that represent network applications are no longer required and can be deleted from Windows desktops. And administrators no longer have to worry about users deleting or changing the properties of network application icons on their individual desktops.

The NDS-delivered network applications are associated with a user's network login ID, so they "follow" the user around the network. Regardless of the login location, the user always sees the same set of network applications. This ensures that people who work from multiple locations or physical workstations always have a consistent set of network applications.

For each NDS-delivered network application, the administrator can include a support number and e-mail address to use if help is required. This information is displayed in the properties of each application icon on the users' desktops. The help information can be tailored so each user is directed to the support group for his or her location. The administrator can also specify that some network applications are to be launched automatically when the user runs the application launcher.

# Distributing Software Using NetWare Application Launcher

The NetWare Application Launcher offers network administrators easy distribution, updating, version control, and license management for applications stored on the network. This means that using NAL you can easily install new applications and migrate users to the new versions of the network applications without requiring the administrator to travel to and change each user's workstation.

With the NAL, network applications delivered to users' Windows desktops are dynamic and can be refreshed automatically. This ensures that any changes the administrator makes are quickly reflected on users' desktops. For example, if a new version of a network application is installed, the administrator can quickly move the appropriate users to that new version using the NAL configuration. The administrator simply modifies the properties in the application object defined in NDS to point to the new version of the application. The NAL then updates that network application on the appropriate user desktops. The next time a user double-clicks the icon for that application, the updated version is launched automatically.

The NAL consists of both an administrator component and a user component. The administrator component is a Windows DLL that snaps into the NetWare Administrator (NWADMIN) utility and adds new property buttons to the Details listing of the appropriate NDS objects. This enables administrators to work from a familiar and consistent interface. The user component is an executable file, NAL.EXE, that is run in each user's Windows Startup or other program group as desired. For more information on using and installing NAL see Chapters 10 and 11.

# Fourth Step

## Configure Time Synchronization to Support NDS Operations

**CHAPTER 8**

Design and Configure Time Synchronization

**CHAPTER 9**

Manage Time Synchronization
through SET Parameters

# Chapter 8

# Design and Configure Time Synchronization

## IN THIS CHAPTER

- ◆ Time synchronization design, communication, and purpose

- ◆ Time server types

- ◆ Time synchronization design options

- ◆ Time synchronization communication methods

AN IMPORTANT STEP IN your NDS design is to design and configure time synchronization for your NetWare 4 servers. Time synchronization is the capability of the NetWare 4 servers to coordinate and maintain consistent time across the entire network and NDS tree. Time synchronization ensures that each NDS modification or event receives an accurate timestamp.

The design and configuration of time synchronization can be easy and quickly established for a NetWare 4 network of any size. As part of your overall NDS design, you should evaluate the specific time synchronization design options and choose the one that best meets the needs of your network and company. Each time synchronization design option has specific requirements associated with it. These requirements must be met in order for time synchronization to be effective and efficient. Along with the design options there are a couple of different communication methods that are also discussed.

## Time Synchronization Design

Only two time synchronization design options or configurations should be used for your NetWare 4 network. These options are the single reference time synchronization configuration and the time provider group configuration. Two factors determine which time synchronization option you should choose:

♦ Is your network a local area network (LAN) and does it have fewer than 30 NetWare 4 servers? If so, then you should use the default option or single reference option. Using this configuration, the LAN environment can easily contact a single reference server without having to cross a wide area network (WAN) link. In addition, your servers can easily contact the single reference without burdening the server designated as the single reference.

♦ Is your network connected by a WAN or is your network a LAN with more than 30 NetWare 4 servers? If so, then you should always use the time provider group option. A time provider group gives your network greater fault tolerance in a WAN configuration by distributing the time sources to the geographical locations or sites in your network.

Before deciding which option to use, you should consider the following requirements for each of the time synchronization design options.

## Single Reference Configuration

♦ The single reference time synchronization option is used for small networks that have fewer than 30 servers on a LAN and a network that is only a LAN.

♦ Regardless of the size of network, you can initially accept the single reference or default option until your installation grows beyond 30 servers or unless you immediately begin with NetWare 4 servers on both sides of a WAN.

♦ Do not use any other time provider such as a primary or a reference sever with the single reference configuration. A single reference is the only time source required on the entire network with this configuration.

## Time Provider Group Configuration

♦ The time provider group configuration is used for larger networks with wide area networks connecting the NetWare 4 servers. This configuration is also used for networks that have more than 30 NetWare 4 servers on a single LAN.

- ◆ The time provider group requires one reference time server and a minimum of two other primary time servers that will participate in the synchronization process to coordinate the network time.

- ◆ The time provider group should never have more than one reference time server and never more than seven primary servers.

- ◆ The time provider group has multiple time providers and protects against failures in any of the time providers. If any single time provider within the group fails there are others that can communicate the network time.

- ◆ The time provider group lets you place time servers across the WAN links in your network and distribute the time locally to the other secondary time servers in the network.

- ◆ Do not use a single reference time server on the network with a time provider group. The time provider group is the only time source required on the entire network with this configuration.

# Time Synchronization Communication

In addition to the two time synchronization design options, two methods enable the time servers to find and communicate with each other. These communications options are Service Advertising Protocol (SAP) and configured lists.

Before selecting the time communication method that best meets your needs, you should consider the following requirements for each method.

## Service Advertising Protocol Communication

- ◆ The SAP method is the default and requires no administrative intervention.

- ◆ If no configuration changes are wanted as new NetWare 4 servers are added to the network, you should use the SAP method for communication. SAP does not require custom configuration changes to the existing time servers to establish communication for time synchronization.

◆ Time providers such as primary, reference, or single reference servers advertise their presence by default on the network using SAP.

◆ Do not use this method if your network requires a reduction in SAPs. The SAP from the time servers can cause a small amount of additional traffic on your network.

◆ Since SAP is self-configuring, a new time server that is incorrectly configured in the same tree could disrupt your current time synchronization.

◆ The SAP type for time synchronization is 0x026B. If you use SAP for your time synchronization communication you must not filter this packet type on any routers that connect your NetWare 4 servers. If you are using the time provider group configuration, you should not filter SAP type 0x0004 (file server) because each of the time providers will use this SAP type to locate each other.

## Configured Lists Communication

◆ The configured list communication method requires administrators to provide a special configuration for every server.

◆ If you are implementing a time provider group you should use configured lists instead of SAP. The configured list method enables you to specify exactly which servers should be contacted for a time provider group.

◆ If all time providers are not sending out the time synchronization SAP, every server in the tree must have a configured list if it is to participate in network time.

◆ Configured lists also reduce the SAP traffic for SAP type 0x26B on your network, as SAP broadcasts are not used. Instead, the configured list specifies the time providers by name.

◆ The configured list method prohibits anyone from placing other time servers on your network that may cause problems with the network time.

◆ Configured lists give you complete control of the time synchronization hierarchy.

◆ You must use configured lists if you want to specify one secondary time server as the time source for another secondary time server in the network.

# Purpose of Time Synchronization

Time synchronization services provided in NetWare 4 is the mechanism by which the same network time is maintained on all NetWare 4 servers. Currently, time is only synchronized on NetWare 4 servers and not on any other operating system. NetWare 4 uses the TIMESYNC NetWare Loadable Module (NLM) to coordinate the time between servers on the network. TIMESYNC.NLM maintains each server's local time which, in turn, calculates the Universal Coordinated Time (UTC), which is the world time standard. The local time is used as a reference from which all servers can calculate the UTC. Local time will be either ahead or behind UTC time depending on your geographic location. Each time zone has an offset (+ or –) in relation to the UTC. For example, the United States time zones are behind UTC time and most of Europe's time zones are ahead of UTC.

For example, the local time in the Mountain Standard Time zone in the United States is seven hours behind UTC. By applying the time zone offset and daylight saving offset to the server's local time you calculate UTC. Time synchronization tries to maintain consistency of the UTC time on the servers by adjusting (slowing down or speeding up) the local clock but never setting the clock backwards.

The TIMESYNC.NLM is automatically loaded each time the server is started. Time synchronization is active only when the TIMESYNC.NLM is loaded. Do not unload this module because you will create problems with resolutions of duplicate event collisions for NDS timestamps, and some NDS partition and replica operations will not be able to finish.

A strict relationship exists between local time and UTC. Each server uses this relationship to maintain both a UTC and a local time counter. The TIMESYNC.NLM attempts to force the local time counters with the appropriate offsets on all servers to be identical. This in turn affects the UTC time on each server. If the time on a specific server is ahead, then the local clock will adjust its tick rate to slow down and wait for the other time servers to catch up. If the server time is behind the network time, then the local clock's tick rate accelerates in order to catch up with the other time servers on the network.

Figure 8-1 illustrates how the time server to the right (time consumer) is five minutes ahead of the other time servers on the network (time providers). The time consumer will need to adjust or slow down the internal clock tick rate to wait for the other time provider servers to catch up.

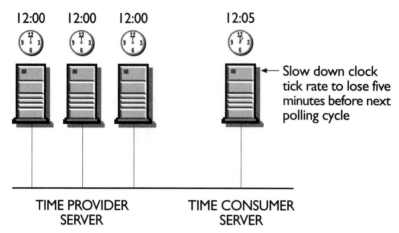

Figure 8-1: The time consumer server's internal clock tick rate slows down so that the other network time servers can catch up.

To the extent that an accurate time signal is available both UTC and local time will be accurate, but TIMESYNC.NLM does not guarantee accuracy, only consistency. The difference between UTC time and local time is dependent on the time zone and daylight saving time (DST) status of the server as illustrated in the following equation.

```
UTC = LOCAL TIME + (timezone offset) - (current daylight adjustment)
```

For example, consider a server located in Mountain Standard Time in the United States that is seven hours behind UTC. The server is located in Provo, Utah, which uses Mountain Standard Time during part of the year and Mountain Daylight Time the rest of the year. Since Mountain Standard Time is seven hours behind UTC, during Mountain Daylight Time the local time moves forward by one hour from Mountain Standard Time. So, local time for the server in Provo is behind UTC by seven hours when daylight saving time is not in effect and six hours when it is. The equations for calculating UTC during Standard Time and Daylight Saving Time are illustrated below.

```
UTC = LOCAL TIME - (7 hours) + (0 hours) [when MST is in effect]
UTC = LOCAL TIME - (7 hours) + (1 hour) [when MDT is in effect]
```

## Checking Time Synchronization

If you want to view the current status for time and time synchronization at the server, type TIME on the console. Figure 8-2 shows how you can see the time information from the server, which displays the current status of time synchronization, status of daylight saving time (including when it starts and ends), the server's local time, and the UTC time value. Using this information you can easily detect whether the server is synchronized to the network time.

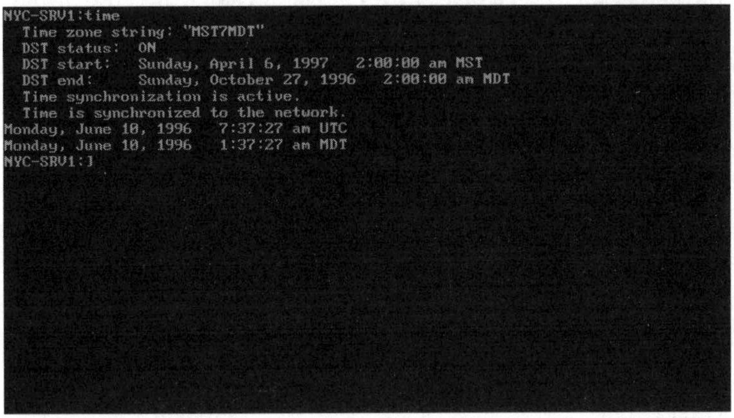

```
NYC-SRV1:time
  Time zone string: "MST7MDT"
  DST status:  ON
  DST start:    Sunday, April 6, 1997   2:00:00 am MST
  DST end:      Sunday, October 27, 1996   2:00:00 am MDT
  Time synchronization is active.
  Time is synchronized to the network.
Monday, June 10, 1996   7:37:27 am UTC
Monday, June 10, 1996   1:37:27 am MDT
NYC-SRV1:]
```

Figure 8-2: Time information is displayed on the server console by entering TIME. The current status of time synchronization, daylight saving time, local time, and UTC time values is displayed.

## Assigning Timestamps

Because the NDS object hierarchy can be distributed or replicated across the NetWare 4 servers in the network the information in each of the replicas can change without the other replicas immediately knowing about it. This form of synchronization is known as being loosely consistent.

The sequence of events that occurs within NDS can produce unexpected results unless a mechanism is provided to ensure that the events are updated to each replica as they really happened. The term "event" refers to a creation of or modification to the NDS objects or properties.

Once time is synchronized on all NetWare 4 servers, the Directory can accurately timestamp the many NDS events. An NDS event could be adding a new user or assigning rights to a new administrator, for example. The mechanism that ensures that the events are applied in sequence are the timestamps for each of the objects and properties.

When an event occurs, NDS issues a new timestamp and associates the timestamp with that event. Each event that occurs in NDS is marked with a unique timestamp. The timestamp is a unique value within an individual NDS partition. The timestamps are used to order the events or changes that occur on multiple servers. These timestamps keep all NDS changes in their proper order.

Synchronization between replicas of a partition uses the timestamps associated with every NDS object, property, or attribute to indicate when the modification was made. For example, if the same object (or same property) is modified by two different administrators at approximately the same time, both updates will take place. However, one of the updates may be replaced with the later change because the last timestamp wins the update. Figure 8-3 illustrates how the login script property for the user JOE.SFO.ACME is modified on two different servers by two different administrators at approximately the same time. The login script property for JOE.SFO.ACME on SRV1 was last modified at 02:03:15 PM, and the same login script property for JOE.SFO.ACME on SRV2 was last modified at 02:03:18 PM.

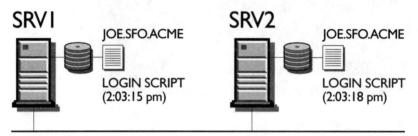

Figure 8-3: The login script property for JOE.SFO.ACME is modified on two different servers by two different administrators at approximately the same time.

Timestamps ensure that information stored in NDS will converge across all NetWare 4 servers over time. The object creation timestamp and the last modification timestamp exist for each object or property when it is created or modified. A timestamp is also issued for every change to a property value.

Remember, the timestamp value for the objects and properties is unique within an NDS partition because the timestamps are assigned by the replica where the objects exist. This provides an ordering of the events that occur across all the servers holding replicas of a partition. Figure 8-4 illustrates the timestamp structure, which has three parts or fields. Each of the fields for the timestamp value is described in Table 8-1.

The timestamp is a critical component in the replica synchronization process. When NDS updates a replica, it requests the timestamps from that replica to identify the data. The timestamp provides a unique value for the object and property that identifies when and where the event originated. If the same object or property is updated on different replicas (or servers) at exactly the same second and event ID, the replica number between the servers will be different. NDS will make the updates using the greater or latest timestamp. When timestamps are compared, they are treated as 32-bit, 16-bit, and 16-bit unsigned (with seconds as the most significant).

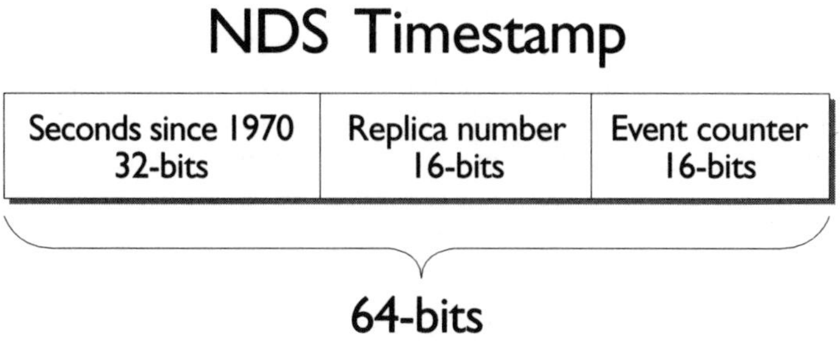

# NDS Timestamp

| Seconds since 1970<br>32-bits | Replica number<br>16-bits | Event counter<br>16-bits |
|---|---|---|

## 64-bits

Figure 8-4: The components of an NDS timestamp

**TABLE 8-1  Three Parts of the NDS Timestamp Value**

| Field | Description |
|---|---|
| Seconds | A 4-byte (32-bit) value that stores UTC time in whole seconds since midnight January 1, 1970. The whole seconds represent the actual time that the NDS event (creation or modification) took place. This value ensures that there is a unique timestamp for any changes that are at least one second apart. |
| Replica Number | A 2-byte (16-bit) field that stores the replica number where the event occurred and the timestamp was issued. Every replica of a partition held on a NetWare 4 server is assigned a unique number when it is created. The master replica is responsible for assigning a new number to the replica. The replica number ensures a unique timestamp within any given partition. |
| Event ID | A 2-byte (16-bit) field that stores the number of events that occur during one second. Many events can occur within any one second. The event ID issues a timestamp for events that occur in one second. This counter further enables a unique timestamp for events occurring in rapid succession on the same replica within the same second. The event ID is a sequence number starting at 1 and can increment up to 64K. The event ID value is reset every second. |

In general terms whenever a client or workstation deletes an object or property from a replica on a server, the server does not immediately purge it from its local database. Instead, it issues a timestamp for the object or property and marks the object or property value as "not present" or deleted. After the replica synchronization process propagates the change to all other replicas, the Janitor process purges the object or property.

 This explanation of an object being deleted is valid only as an example. The actual procedures and processes are more complex. However, for the purposes of understanding timestamps in this chapter, a deeper or more complete step-by-step process for deleting objects is not needed.

To support accurate timestamps, the servers must maintain accurate time and that time must be synchronized between the servers. Time synchronization ensures that each server is synchronized to the network time. You want accurate timestamps so that the order of modification is accurate. This means that the last modification timestamp is the winner.

## Setting the Network Time

Time synchronization does not require that network time be the actual time of day. Time synchronization cares only that all the NetWare 4 servers are reporting the same time (in UTC), regardless of the real time of day. However, if accurate time of day is important to your users, and it typically is, then you will need to feed the accurate time of day into the network at the appropriate time server (or time provider).

You can accomplish this task by setting the local time on the main time provider and having all the other time servers acquire the time from it. You can also provide a more automated solution for providing time of day to the network by attaching your NetWare 4 time provider (reference or single reference) to an external time source service such as a radio clock, an atomic clock, or the Internet (a time source provided by connecting to the Internet).

Although an external time source is not mandatory for the operation of a NetWare 4 network, its use in larger network installations is highly recommended because it eliminates the need for network administrators to manually verify time. In addition, the external source provides accurate time of day for your network, which is required by some NLMs or backup devices. The use of an external time source is shown in Figure 8-5.

In order to completely design and configure time synchronization you must first understand how each type of time server works and its purpose. It is also important to know which time servers work together and which time servers are best used independently.

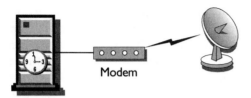

## Time Server
(Time Provider)

Figure 8-5: You can attach your time server (typically the reference time server) to an external source to automatically update the time of day.

Once NetWare time synchronization has been properly configured, very little additional activity is required to maintain it. Time synchronization is both stable and dependable once it is configured. Details of both design options for time synchronization – the single reference and the time provider group – are explained later in this chapter along with background information about how each time server communicates and functions in a NetWare environment.

# Time Server Types

Each NetWare 4 server is configured as a specific type of time server during the installation process. Because all NetWare 4 servers will be some type of time servers, they all perform the same basic time functions, including:

◆ Providing UTC time to any client or other time server making the request

◆ Providing status information on time synchronization

◆ Making adjustments to local clocks in order to correct discrepancies between time servers

A NetWare 4 server will provide time to any client or NLM making a request for network time. For example, your backup or archival software may require accurate network time to know when to initiate a particular process or function. Client utilities may also query time from a NetWare 4 server of any type.

Regardless of the configuration, all NetWare 4 servers will provide time status information. Through time synchronization each NetWare 4 server knows the status of its clock with respect to the network.

All NetWare 4 servers are time servers that participate as either providers of time or consumers of time. The internal mechanism for querying the time is the same for all types of servers. Three types of time providers – primary server, reference server, and single reference server – coordinate time among themselves to determine network time. Time consumers are known as secondary servers and can request time from any of the three time providers. The majority of your NetWare 4 servers will be time consumers. Table 8-2 shows the categories of time servers.

**TABLE 8-2  Time Server Classes**

| Time Providers | Time Consumers |
|----------------|----------------|
| Primary | Secondary |
| Reference | |
| Single reference | |

There are four types of time servers: secondary, primary, reference, and single reference. The rules for each type of time server dictate the server's purpose and how it works. These rules also include recommendations on which time servers work together best and which time servers are best used independently.

Functionally, all NetWare 4 servers are very similar in terms of how they are configured for time. In fact, the reference and single reference time servers are just special cases of the primary time servers. Each NetWare 4 server on the network is responsible for its own synchronization and status. This means that each server will, at periodic intervals, poll other servers for time, calculate network time based on a weighted average, make any necessary adjustments to the internal clock, and wait for the next interval to repeat the process.

Since time synchronization is a server-centric operation, each server determines if its time is within an acceptable limit as compared to the network time. The acceptance limit is known as the synchronization radius. A server is synchronized to the network time when its UTC time is within the synchronization radius.

Figure 8-6 illustrates how the time server SRV4 received time from SRV1, SRV2, and SRV3 and then calculated the network time. If the server SRV4 determines that its UTC time is within the synchronization radius, it raises a time synchronization flag. This synchronization flag indicates that this server has a UTC time that can be used by NDS to accurately timestamp events on the network.

# Secondary Time Servers

The following are some common characteristics of secondary time servers:

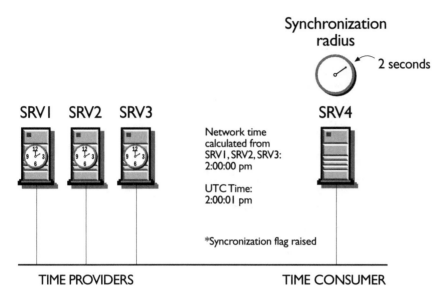

Figure 8-6: Time server SRV4 receives time from SRV1, SRV2, and SRV3 and then calculates the network time.

◆ Secondary time servers are time consumers.

◆ Secondary time servers set their network time according to the time they received from another time server.

◆ A secondary time server can set its network time from any time provider, such as primary, reference, or single reference. Using configured lists, a secondary time server can even get its network time from other secondary time servers. This is not typically recommended.

Secondary servers are the most common type of time server. The majority of the time servers on your network will be secondary servers. These secondary time servers synchronize to the time providers or even another secondary server.

Secondary time servers are time consumers that rely on other time providers to calculate network time. A secondary server can query another secondary, single reference, reference, or primary time server for the network time.

The secondary server will be the most prevalent type of server on your network because most of your time servers do not need to influence the network time. During the installation of your file servers, all servers, except the first server, are designated as secondary servers. The first server is automatically designated as a single reference time server. This is the default configuration. Figure 8-7 illustrates how each of the secondary time servers installed into the NDS tree will attempt to get their network time from the single reference time provider (which was the first server installed).

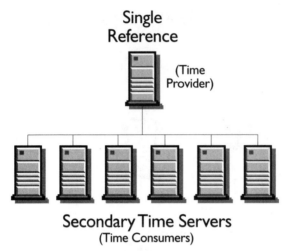

**Single Reference**

(Time Provider)

**Secondary Time Servers**
(Time Consumers)

Figure 8-7: The secondary time servers will attempt to get their network time from the time providers. In this case, all the secondary servers are communicating with a single time provider called a single reference time server.

The secondary server adjusts its internal clock tick rate to make up any difference between its clock and the time it receives from the network. The network time will be provided from another server or servers during each polling interval. Therefore, any discrepancies in the secondary server's time will be resolved during each polling interval. The secondary servers can and do provide time to requesting client or server applications.

Secondary time servers do not determine network time. These servers do not negotiate time with any other time servers. They simply get the network time from another source on the network and make the appropriate adjustments to their own clock during each polling interval. If the UTC time value on the secondary time server is within the synchronization radius, the synchronization flag can be raised. This means that the secondary server will raise its synchronization flag only after the time discrepancy between the UTC time and the network time is less than the synchronization radius set for that server.

## Primary Time Servers

The following are some common characteristics of primary time servers:

◆ Primary time servers are time providers.

◆ Primary time servers need to contact at least one other time provider (primary or reference) to set their network time and raise their time synchronization flag.

◆ Primary servers should be used only with other primary time servers or a reference time server to determine the network time. However, their main purpose is to distribute time to the secondary time servers.

◆ The primary time servers should be placed in separate geographical locations to help distribute network time to the local sites.

The primary time servers are known as time providers because they distribute the network time to other requesting time servers. The secondary servers will be the majority of the requesting servers needing network time. The primary time servers are responsible for determining and setting the network time.

In order to determine the network time, a primary server will poll other primary and reference servers from its list of time servers. This process determines the "official time" for the network as each primary server polls the other time providers and calculates the network time by performing a weighted average.

During the polling process, each primary time server has a weighting factor of one. This weighting factor means that all other primary time servers will be given equal consideration during the polling interval. Each primary time server will "wake up" on its polling interval and begin getting network time from the other time providers on the network. Figure 8-8 illustrates how a primary time server polls the other time providers. In this example, the other time providers are primary time servers. Notice that the configuration shown is not a good example of a time provider group because there is not a reference time server.

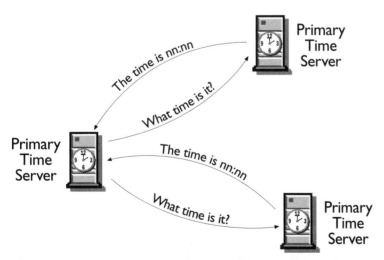

Figure 8-8: Each primary time server wakes up (at ten minute intervals by default) and begins polling the other time providers on the network during its polling process.

After an individual primary time server has received the time from each of the other time providers, it then calculates the network time using a weighted average. The individual primary time server will then adjust its internal clock in order to resolve any discrepancies. This adjustment will be only 50 percent of the difference. Like all time servers, a primary server will determine if its time is within its synchronization radius. If the server is within the radius, it raises its synchronization flag to indicate that time synchronization has occurred.

For example, suppose you have three primary servers on your network. Figure 8-9 shows a primary time server SRV1 with a current time of 10:00:00 AM. The primary time server SRV2 has a current network time of 10:10:00 AM. The last primary time server on the network has a time of 10:20:00 AM.

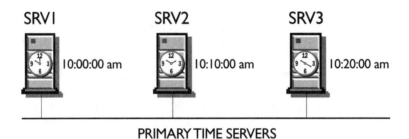

PRIMARY TIME SERVERS

Figure 8-9: Three primary time servers SRV1, SRV2, and SRV3 with current times of 10:00:00 AM, 10:10:00 AM, and 10:20:00 AM, respectively

During the polling process for server SRV1, the time and weight for each of the other two primary time servers are received. The server SRV1 then performs a weighted average calculation. Again, each primary time server has a weight of one. Thus, the values for each primary server are as follows:

- ◆ SRV1 primary time server: (10:00:00 AM) multiply by 1

- ◆ SRV2 primary time server: (10:10:00 AM) multiply by 1

- ◆ SRV3 primary time server: (10:20:00 AM) multiply by 1

Because each primary time server has a weighting factor of one, all of the primary time servers are treated equally, and the weighted average time calculation for all the servers would equal 10:10:00 AM.

In our example, the server SRV1 will then try to adjust its internal clock tick rate to speed up and recover 50 percent of the difference. This means that SRV1 will adjust its clock to match 10:05:00 AM (50 percent of the difference between 10:00 AM and 10:10 AM). The primary servers will try to adjust their local clocks only 50 percent of the difference between network time and their local time so that the several primary time servers will converge over a period of time.

The polling process functions as an independent server-based activity for all time providers. Each time server is responsible for calculating and setting its own network time. The default polling interval for each server is 10 minutes. Although your servers may have the default polling interval of every 10 minutes, each server will most likely be polling at different 10-minute intervals as each primary server checks its time against the other time providers in the tree.

While primary servers alone can achieve network time, they may need the help of a consistent time provider that never makes adjustments to its hardware clock after polling. A special case of the primary server is the reference server. The reference server acts as a special time server, whereas other time providers can only converge or set their own time. The reference server essentially sets the time for the entire network.

# Reference Time Server

The following are some common characteristics of reference time servers:

◆ The reference time server is a time provider.

◆ The reference time server needs to contact a primary time server in order to raise its time synchronization flag.

◆ The reference time server should be the definitive time source on the network.

◆ Never have two reference servers on the same network. They will not synchronize their time.

◆ The reference server should be used only with primary time servers to determine the network time. However, they do distribute time to secondary time servers.

◆ Reference time servers exist mainly so that all the other time servers can converge local time to the reference server's time. The reference server is the place through which the time of day is fed into the network.

◆ The best configuration using a reference time server is to have one reference server with a few primary servers to provide accurate time. This configuration is called a time provider group.

A reference server is a time provider that has more capabilities than a primary time server. Like the primary time server, the reference time server participates with the other time providers, specifically the primary time servers, to determine the "official" network time. One difference between a primary and reference time server is that after the polling process that determines network time, the reference time server will not adjust its internal or hardware clock.

Another difference between a primary and reference time server is that the reference server has a higher weight during the polling process. The reference server carries a weight of 16. This means that the reference server has a weight of 16, and that the primary time servers each has a weight of one during the polling process that establishes the network time. This also means that over a period of time the primary time servers will converge their internal clocks to the reference server's time. On the other hand, the reference time server will never adjust its clock or be influenced by the other time providers. This naturally makes the reference time server the point of reference for convergence in the network. Figure 8-10 illustrates the polling process with a reference time server and multiple primary time servers on the network. In the figure, SRV1 is the reference time server with a current time of 12:00:00 PM. The other time servers SRV2, SRV3, and SRV4 are primary servers with times of 12:05:00 PM, 11:55:00 AM, and 12:02:00 PM, respectively. The primary time server SRV2 performs the polling process.

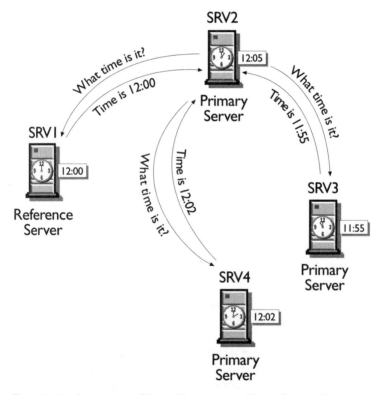

Figure 8-10: An example of the polling process with a reference time server and multiple primary time servers

During the polling process for server SRV2 (a primary server), the time and weight for each of the other time servers are received. SRV2 then performs a weighted average calculation in order to determine its time. The reference time server has a weight of 16, and each primary time server has a weight of one. Thus, the values for the weighted average calculation for SRV2 are the following:

♦ SRV1 reference time server: (12:00:00 PM) multiple by 16

♦ SRV2 primary time server: (12:05:00 PM) multiple by 1

♦ SRV3 primary time server: (11:55:00 AM) multiple by 1

♦ SRV4 primary time server: (12:02:00 PM) multiple by 1

The net result for SRV2 is that all the primary servers will converge their time to that of the reference server because the reference server has a weight of 16 and each of the primary time servers has a weight of one.

As mentioned earlier, the reference server also participates in the polling process just like the primary servers, but does not adjust its clock. Figure 8-11 illustrates the polling process for the reference time server with the other primary time servers on the network. In the figure, SRV1 is the reference time server with a current time of 12:00:00 PM. The primary time servers are SRV2, SRV3, and SRV4 with times of 12:05:00 PM, 11:55:00 AM, and 12:02:00 PM, respectively.

During the polling process for the reference server SRV1, the time and weight for each of the other time servers are received. SRV1 then performs a weighted average calculation. Even though the reference time server performs the weighted average calculation using the following values, it throws the results away and does not adjust its internal or hardware clock. If the polling process for the reference server executed at the same time as the previous example, then the values would be the same:

♦ SRV1 reference time server: (12:00:00 PM) multiple by 16

♦ SRV2 primary time server: (12:05:00 PM) multiple by 1

♦ SRV3 primary time server: (11:55:00 AM) multiple by 1

♦ SRV4 primary time server: (12:02:00 PM) multiple by 1

Because the reference server never adjusts its clock and all the primary servers do adjust their clocks to converge their time to the reference server's time, you will typically want to have only one reference server on your network. The reference server should be the definitive time source on the network. The best configuration is to have one reference server with a few primary servers to provide accurate time. Figure 8-12 illustrates a configuration of one reference server and multiple primary time servers on the network.

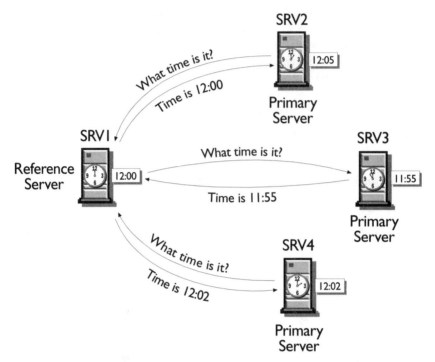

Figure 8-11: The polling process for the reference time server with the primary time servers

The purpose in having multiple primary time servers working with the reference server is primarily to provide fault tolerance and to distribute time sources on the network. The reference server must, like other primary servers, contact another time source during the polling process in order to raise its synchronization flag. In addition, if the reference server should fail, multiple primary servers can still provide consistent network time to requesting servers and clients. Therefore, the reference server is the supreme authority of time, except when it is not accessible. If your reference time server fails and will be down for a long period of time, you should configure or promote another server to be the reference time server.

Having a reference time server on the network gives you a place through which to feed time of day into the network. The reference server then forces all other time servers to converge their time to it. Because the reference server does not make an adjustment to its internal clock you can connect it to an external source. Figure 8-13 illustrates the configuration of connecting the reference server to an external time source. An external time source could be an atomic clock, a radio clock, the Internet, or a UNIX host.

Having an external clock accomplishes several important things. First, it provides an accurate and automated mechanism to provide time of day. Some of your applications may require accurate time of day if they initiate a process, such as a backup, in the middle of the night. Second, an automated time source will help ensure that the reference server's clock is not drifting and consequently is keeping all other servers in your network on accurate time.

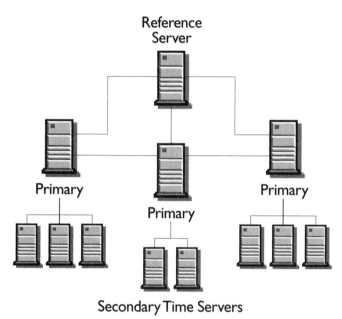

Figure 8-12: An example of a configuration with one reference server and multiple primary time servers on the network

The server's own internal clock can be used as the time source for the network. However, the time must be verified manually by an administrator to make sure that it stays accurate and does not drift. Ideally, the reference server should be connected to an external clock source to provide highly accurate time.

For more information on external clock solutions you can contact Novell's NetWire (CompuServe Forum) to download the TIMESG.TXT file. This file contains companies and their product names that support the external time source solution.

Like all other time servers, a reference server will determine if its current time is within the synchronization radius of network time. If the server is within the radius, it raises its time synchronization flag indicating that time synchronization has been established and that the current time is acceptable for issuing timestamps for NDS events.

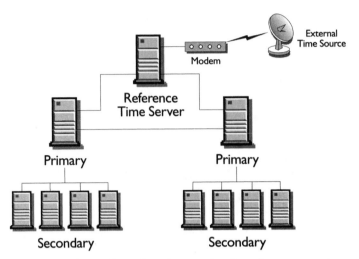

Figure 8-13: The configuration of connecting the reference server to an external time source

Only one reference time server is usually needed on the network. If multiple reference servers are placed on the network they will not synchronize with each other. Some companies with large, worldwide networks prefer to use multiple time provider groups, which means that there will be multiple reference servers on the network. If you use multiple time provider groups on the same network you need to configure them so that they do not contact each other. Thus, using two time provider groups on the same network requires you to connect each group to an external time source. The external time source becomes the common time source for the network.

## Single Reference Time Server

The following are some common characteristics of single reference time servers:

◆ The single reference time server is a time provider.

◆ The single reference time server does not need to contact any other time server in order to raise its time synchronization flag.

◆ The single reference time server is a "stand-alone" or "all knowing" time server, and the time for the network is set to whatever the single reference's current local time is.

◆ The single reference time server is the definitive time source on the network.

◆ The best configuration using a single reference time server is to have one single reference time server on the network. The rest of the network servers can be secondary time servers. This configuration is called the single reference configuration or default configuration.

The single reference time server is a stand-alone time provider for the entire network. The single reference is the default configuration, which requires no intervention during installation. The main difference between a reference server and a single reference server is that the single reference server can raise its synchronization flag without confirming its time with any other time sources. It does, however, go through the polling process like all NetWare 4 servers. In this case, the polling does not expect a response from any server. A response from another server would indicate that another time source has been erroneously placed on the network. This condition would cause the single reference server to report an error.

A single reference time server will enable you to have all the other servers on the network configured as secondary time servers. The secondary time servers in turn adjust their times to the single reference time during each polling cycle. A single reference time server can be connected to an external source to feed the network accurate time of day into the network as well.

In addition, the single reference server's own clock can be used as the time source instead of an external source. Occasionally, it may be necessary to check the server's time against a reliable source because some of your applications may require accurate network time, such as backup or archiving software programs.

# Details About Time Synchronization Design Options

In order to establish the proper time synchronization design, you must become familiar with the SERVMAN utility. The SERVMAN utility is a server-based utility that will help you make the changes necessary to establish a particular design option. This utility is run from a NetWare 4 server console by typing LOAD SERVMAN. From the available Options menu select Server Parameters and then select the option Time as shown in Figure 8-14.

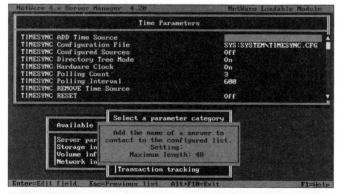

Figure 8-14: The main screen of the SERVMAN utility with the Time option selected.

## Single Reference Configuration

The single reference configuration is the default configuration that is set up automatically by the NetWare 4 installation program. This is a good configuration for small network environments. To establish this configuration you accept the defaults provided by NetWare 4's installation utility. This configuration is commonly referred to as the single reference configuration or default configuration. No steps are required for the LAN administrator because the setup is handled completely by the installation utility.

In the single reference configuration, you choose one server to be a single reference time server, and all the other servers become secondary time servers. The secondary time servers simply contact the single reference to get the network time. Figure 8-15 illustrates the single reference configuration with only one time server providing time to the other secondary servers on the network.

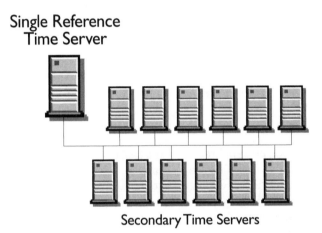

**Single Reference Time Server**

**Secondary Time Servers**

Figure 8-15: In the single reference time synchronization configuration one server provides time to the entire network. This configuration is suitable for a network that has fewer than 30 servers and is located on a single LAN network.

When a NetWare 4 server is installed as the first server in the NDS tree it is automatically configured as a single reference server. All additional NetWare 4 servers installed in the same tree are automatically configured as secondary time servers. The NetWare 4 installation utility assumes this type of configuration and is commonly referred to as the default option. With this option your installation consists of two levels of time servers: a single reference time server at the first level and secondary time servers as the second level. The secondary servers then poll the single reference time server to synchronize their clocks. Figure 8-16 shows a logical view of the two levels of time servers with the first level being the single reference time server and the second level being the secondary time servers.

The advantages of the single reference configuration are that it is easy to understand and requires little or no advanced planning. In addition, use of the configuration files are not needed, and the possibility of errors during time synchronization is considerably minimized.

In order to set up the single reference option, you should select a central file server to be the single reference time server. This server should be easily contacted by all the other NetWare 4 servers in your network. A centralized single reference server means that you place it where there is the lowest number of router hops or closest to the fastest WAN links.

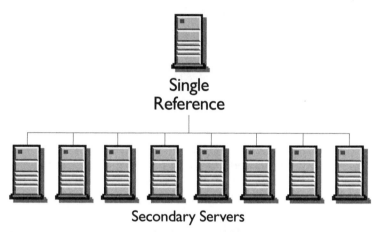

**Single Reference**

**Secondary Servers**

Figure 8-16: A logical view of the two levels of time servers with the first level being the single reference time server and the second level being the secondary time servers. The secondary servers then poll the single reference time server to synchronize their clocks.

Remember, the first NetWare 4 server you install is automatically configured as the single reference server. You can always designate another server as the single reference by using the SERVMAN utility. Figure 8-17 shows an example of the SERVMAN utility setting a server to be a single reference time server.

A potential drawback to this type of configuration is that if the single reference time server should fail, the network has lost its only updated source of network time. However, even if this happens for a short period of time (a day or less), NDS can still timestamp the events. The other NetWare 4 servers should continue to use their internal clocks for the timestamping of NDS events. If your single reference is down for prolonged periods, we recommend that you designate a new server as the single reference to ensure that there is one source of network time on the network.

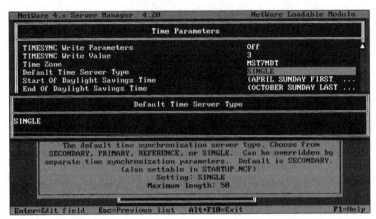

Figure 8-17: Using the SERVMAN utility to designate another server as your single reference time server or to make other time configuration changes. SERVMAN utility functions are now part of the MONITOR utility.

When you try to uninstall Directory Services from the server that is configured as the single reference, you get a warning message. The message states that you should make another server in the network the single reference before continuing.

To overcome the single point of failure in the network that is possible with the single reference configuration, you should use the time provider group configuration.

## Time Provider Group Configuration

For larger networks with more than 30 servers or a network with multiple sites connected by a WAN, the time provider group configuration is recommended. The time provider group is designed to provide greater fault tolerance and efficiency for communication across a wide area network.

The time provider group requires one reference time server and a minimum of two other primary time servers that will participate in the synchronization process to coordinate the network time. This group of time source servers forms a time provider group that in turn provides time to the rest of the NetWare 4 servers, typically the secondary time servers.

Figure 8-18 illustrates the time provider group configuration, which contains only one reference time server and several primary time servers that determine the official network time. This time provider group then distributes the network time to the other secondary time servers in the network.

The time provider group enables you to place time servers across the WAN links in your network so that local time is distributed to the other secondary time servers on the network. Each of the time providers in the group will distribute the network time to the other time servers on the network. The other time servers should be secondary servers. In a large network environment a majority (85 percent to 95 percent) of the time servers will be defined as secondary time servers. Figure 8-19 illustrates the placement of the time providers in the time provider group across the WAN in the different hub locations. In this example the hub locations are San Francisco, Dallas, Atlanta, and Chicago. Notice that the Salt Lake City location has only one server. This server is a secondary time server that receives its time from the reference server in New York City.

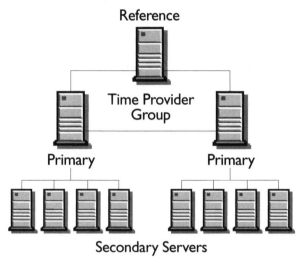

Figure 8-18: The time provider group configuration contains only one reference time server and several primary time servers that determine the official network time. This time provider group then distributes the network time to the other secondary time servers in the network.

In order to set up the time provider group, you must make a few simple changes to the servers that you want to designate as participants in the time provider group. First, you should select a centrally located server and make it the reference server. One server will be designated as the reference and a recommended two to seven servers may be designated as primary time servers. The primary servers may be designated by using the SERVMAN utility's Time parameters screen as shown in Figure 8-20.

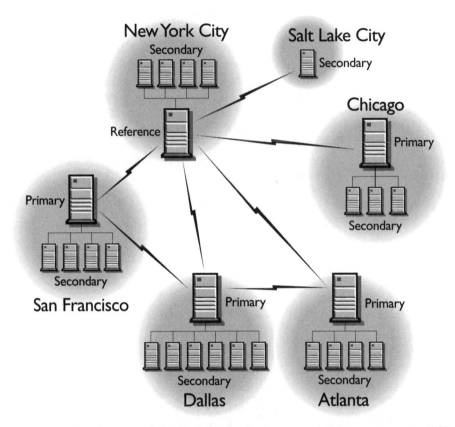

Figure 8-19: The placement of the time providers in the time provider group across the WAN in the major hub locations of the ACME tree. Each time provider distributes the network time to the secondary servers.

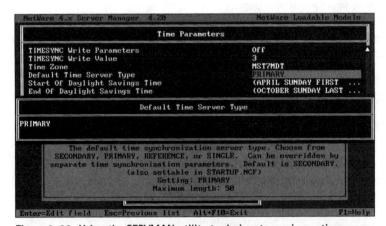

Figure 8-20: Using the SERVMAN utility to designate a primary time server

The selection of your reference server should be based on a centralized location for your network infrastructure. For example, if your WAN is designed in a hub and spoke fashion (like the ACME WAN), your reference server should be centrally placed at the major hub location. The primary servers can then be placed at the regional hub locations to distribute time across your wide area links at the local sites. If your network is a large WAN, place a few extra primary servers in strategic locations. The rest of the time servers installed will be secondary servers. They become secondary servers by default during installation. Figure 8-21 shows you where the reference server and primary servers should be placed to distribute time effectively and efficiently for the ACME network. The figure shows one ACME time provider group, which contains one reference server located in New York City with four other primary time servers located in San Francisco, Dallas, Atlanta, and Chicago. All of the other servers are secondary time servers.

It is highly recommended that you connect the reference server to an external time source to provide accurate time of day. In Figure 8-22, we have connected the reference server to an external time source.

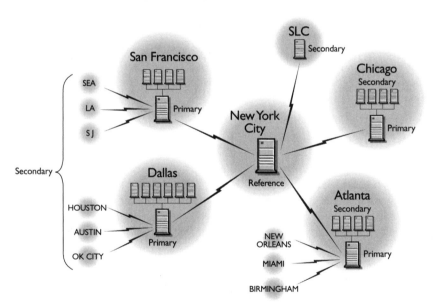

Figure 8-21: The placement of the reference time server, primary time servers, and secondary time servers for the ACME network in a hub and spoke infrastructure

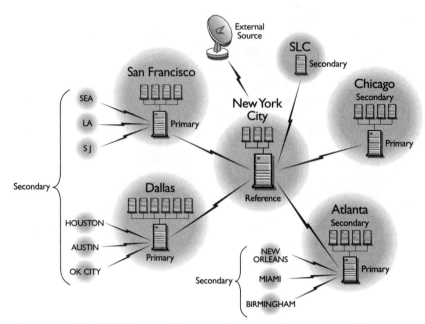

Figure 8-22: The ACME time provider group is connected to an external time source for accurate time of day. This time provider group consists of one reference and four primary time servers. You have redundancy with the five time servers that balance the requests for time.

## Multiple Time Provider Groups

Some companies may feel the need to use multiple time provider groups because they have very large wide area networks within multiple regions of the world. This type of configuration is extremely rare and should be considered only in unique situations.

For example, a company has two very large WANs, one in Asia Pacific and another in Europe. We could create a time provider group in Asia Pacific and another in Europe so that time is distributed from each region or area. Figure 8-23 illustrates multiple time provider groups for one company.

The two time provider groups should be filtered so that they do not communicate with each other. Thus, having multiple time provider groups requires that your reference servers be connected to the same external source clocks because if they communicate together they will not converge their times. In Figure 8-24, each of the reference time servers in each time provider group is connected to an external time source to provide accurate and automated time. Connecting your reference servers to external source clocks ensures that both groups are distributing the same time for the entire NDS tree.

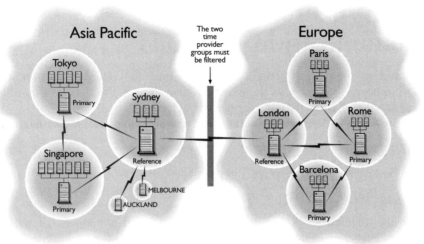

Figure 8-23: Two time provider groups defined for one company that has a large regional WAN in Asia Pacific and another in Europe

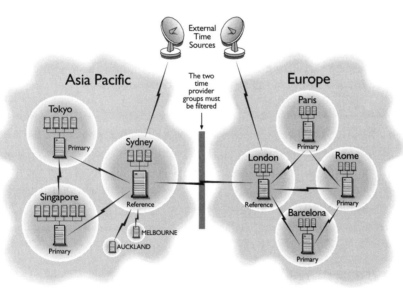

Figure 8-24: Each of the reference time servers in the multiple time provider groups has been connected to an external time source to provide accurate and automated time.

# Time Synchronization Communication Methods

Secondary time servers will periodically request time and will need to communicate with other time sources on the network. Time sources also need to find other time sources in order to determine the correct UTC time.

NetWare 4 servers communicate time information using one of two methods: SAP or configured lists. The following sections discuss these two methods.

## Time Synchronization Using Service Advertising Protocol

The Service Advertising Protocol (SAP) communication method is the default method at installation. If you choose this method, no administrative intervention is required. As new NetWare 4 time servers are installed, the time servers are able to find and communicate with the other time servers. No custom configurations to the existing time servers are needed for the new servers to communicate to establish time synchronization.

By default, time servers such as primary, reference, or single reference servers advertise their presence on the network using SAP. The additional SAPs can cause a small amount of additional traffic on your network. Also, since SAP is self-configuring, a new time server that is unintentionally configured as a wrong type in the same tree could disrupt your current time synchronization.

TIP

Time synchronization SAP type is 0x026B. If you have decided to use SAP for your time communication you must not filter this packet type on any routers that connect your NetWare 4 servers together. You should also not filter SAP type 0x0004 (file server) because each of the time providers will use this SAP type to locate each other.

## Time Synchronization Using Configured Lists Method

The use of a configured list enables you to specify exactly which servers should be contacted for a time provider group and to make requests for time consumers as well. For all implementations using time provider groups, we highly recommend that you use a configured list as your communication option instead of SAP. The configured list option will keep time synchronization traffic to a minimum and will also prohibit anyone from placing other time sources on your network that might cause problems with the network time. Servers must have the configured list if they are to participate in network time for your tree. For the ACME_TREE we have chosen to use a time provider group along with a configured list that specifies the time servers in the time provider group. After the configured list is created, it is then distributed to all time servers in the network through the file called TIMESYNC.CFG.

The configured list is created by using the Time option in the SERVMAN utility and making the entries for each server name that you want to contact in your time provider group. The first step is to enable the configured list option as shown in Figure 8-25. Once the configured list option is set to ON you can begin to create your configured list.

The configured list entries use the NetWare 3 server naming convention for each of the server names as shown in Figure 8-26 for the ACME tree. We have designated NYC1 as the reference server location. All other major sites in our tree will contain one primary server to communicate with the reference server in New York City.

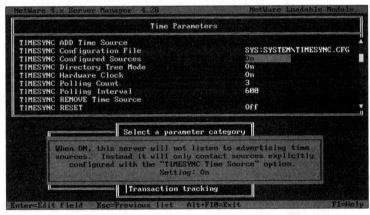

Figure 8-25: Using the SERVMAN utility to enable the configured list option for time synchronization communication

Configured lists give you complete control of the time synchronization hierarchy. Configured lists also reduce the SAP traffic on your network, as SAP broadcasts are not used. Instead, the configured list specifies the source server by name to contact.

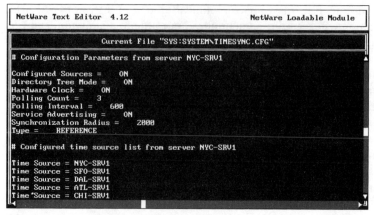

Figure 8-26: A configured list for the ACME time provider group. This list is stored on each file server in the tree.

A proposed time synchronization configuration file is found in the example below. The corporate office is located in New York City. The reference server in New York City (NYC1) is linked to an external time source. The external time source sets both the NetWare server clock and the hardware clock to the most current time of day. The primary time servers are located in San Francisco (SFO1), Dallas (DAL1), Atlanta (ATL1), and Chicago (CHI1). These time providers will work together to determine the official network time during each polling interval. The ACME tree is using the configured sources list so that the primary time servers can contact each other to determine the network time. In the example below, the TIMESYNC.CFG file is shown with its configured list.

## TIMESYNC.CFG FOR REFERENCE SERVER NYC1
# Configuration parameters for a reference time server in New York City:

- ◆ Configured Sources = ON
- ◆ Directory Tree Mode = ON
- ◆ Hardware Clock = ON
- ◆ Polling Count = 3
- ◆ Polling Interval = 10
- ◆ Service Advertising = OFF
- ◆ Synchronization Radius = 2000
- ◆ Type = REFERENCE

# Configured time source list for server NYC1:

- ◆ Time Source = NYC1
- ◆ Time Source = SFO1
- ◆ Time Source = DAL1
- ◆ Time Source = ATL1
- ◆ Time Source = CHI1

## TIMESYNC.CFG FOR REFERENCE SERVER SFO1
# Configuration parameters for a primary time server in San Francisco:

- ◆ Configured Sources = ON
- ◆ Directory Tree Mode = ON
- ◆ Hardware Clock = ON
- ◆ Polling Count = 3
- ◆ Polling Interval = 10
- ◆ Service Advertising = OFF
- ◆ Synchronization Radius = 2000
- ◆ Type = PRIMARY

# Configured time source list for server SFO1:

- ◆ Time Source = NYC1
- ◆ Time Source = SFO1
- ◆ Time Source = DAL1
- ◆ Time Source = ATL1
- ◆ Time Source = CHI1

## TIMESYNC.CFG FOR REFERENCE SERVER DAL1
# Configuration parameters for a primary time server in Dallas:

- ◆ Configured Sources = ON
- ◆ Directory Tree Mode = ON
- ◆ Hardware Clock = ON

- ◆ Polling Count = 3
- ◆ Polling Interval = 10
- ◆ Service Advertising = OFF
- ◆ Synchronization Radius = 2000
- ◆ Type = PRIMARY

# Configured time source list for server DAL1:

- ◆ Time Source = NYC1
- ◆ Time Source = SFO1
- ◆ Time Source = DAL1
- ◆ Time Source = ATL1
- ◆ Time Source = CHI1

## TIMESYNC.CFG FOR REFERENCE SERVER ATL1
# Configuration parameters for a primary time server in Atlanta:

- ◆ Configured Sources = ON
- ◆ Directory Tree Mode = ON
- ◆ Hardware Clock = ON
- ◆ Polling Count = 3
- ◆ Polling Interval = 10
- ◆ Service Advertising = OFF
- ◆ Synchronization Radius = 2000
- ◆ Type = PRIMARY

# Configured time source list for server ATL1:

- ◆ Time Source = NYC1
- ◆ Time Source = SFO1
- ◆ Time Source = DAL1
- ◆ Time Source = ATL1
- ◆ Time Source = CHI1

## TIMESYNC.CFG FOR REFERENCE SERVER CHI1

# Configuration parameters for a primary time server in Chicago:

- ◆ Configured Sources = ON
- ◆ Directory Tree Mode = ON
- ◆ Hardware Clock = ON
- ◆ Polling Count = 3
- ◆ Polling Interval = 10
- ◆ Service Advertising = OFF
- ◆ Synchronization Radius = 2000
- ◆ Type = PRIMARY

# Configured time source list for server CHI1:

- ◆ Time Source = NYC1
- ◆ Time Source = SFO1
- ◆ Time Source = DAL1
- ◆ Time Source = ATL1
- ◆ Time Source = CHI1

The secondary time servers located in each geographical region would use the TIMESYNC.CFG file in the example given below. The server XXXXX indicates any secondary time server located in the ACME tree.

## TIMESYNC.CFG FOR SECONDARY SERVERS XXXXX

# Configuration parameters for server XXXXX:

- ◆ Configured Sources = ON
- ◆ Directory Tree Mode = ON
- ◆ Hardware Clock = ON
- ◆ Polling Count = 3
- ◆ Polling Interval = 10
- ◆ Service Advertising = OFF
- ◆ Synchronization Radius = 2000
- ◆ Type = SECONDARY

# Configured time source list for server XXXXX:

- ◆ Time Source = NYC1
- ◆ Time Source = SFO1
- ◆ Time Source = DAL1
- ◆ Time Source = ATL1
- ◆ Time Source = CHI1

In each geographical region, the time source list should be reordered to place the closest time provider first in the list. Next, place the lowest-cost providers (time and hops) followed by the rest of the providers. This reordering lets the secondary servers initially contact the closest available server to obtain the correct network time. In the case of a secondary time server, it stops looking for time providers after it successfully contacts one.

# Other Time Synchronization Design Rules and Considerations

In some cases it may be necessary to have secondary servers receive their time from other secondary servers. For large companies this may occur as you try to limit the number of primary servers spread across your network as source providers.

## Configuring Secondary Servers to Follow Other Secondary Servers

You can use the configured list option to configure secondary servers to obtain their time from other secondary servers who are obtaining their time from a primary server elsewhere. Figure 8-27 illustrates how a secondary time server can receive its network time from other secondary time servers on the network. This type of configuration is only possible if you use configured lists as the communication method. The synchronization error increases as you make the synchronization hierarchy deeper.

In the configured list for each secondary time server, you must specifically state the other secondary time server as the time source. You must also have the flag for using configured lists turned on.

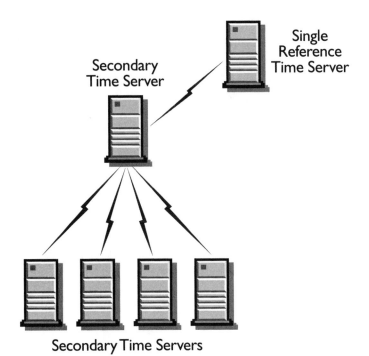

Single
Reference
Time Server

Secondary
Time Server

Secondary Time Servers

Figure 8-27: Secondary time servers can be configured to follow other secondary time servers.

Keep in mind that the depth of the hierarchy will determine the maximum synchronization error between the top provider and the lowest secondary time server. Remember, each time server only has to be within two seconds (2,000 milliseconds) of the synchronization radius and still be able to raise the synchronization flag. As the depth of the hierarchy grows the total error can increase.

Although this configuration is possible, we do not recommend using it to build your long-term time synchronization design. One of the main reasons is that time providers such as primary servers will not follow a secondary server. You can only configure a secondary server to follow another secondary server. For companies with many sites, you can avoid using this configuration by simply placing a primary server at the hub locations. The secondary time servers in the area will then contact the primary time server at the hub.

The secondary servers following other secondary servers may be valid only if your remote locations have multiple servers. In this case, you may want to designate a secondary server to follow another secondary server at the site instead of always crossing the WAN link to contact the primary server. This reduces the number of secondary time servers that have to contact the primary server over the WAN link. Figure 8-28 illustrates how this configuration may look.

**Consulting Experience**

The total allowable time radius for the entire system is 10 seconds. Therefore, you should be sure to keep the number of secondary servers following other secondary servers to a depth of only two to three servers. Any depth greater than two to three servers may lead to errors that are unacceptable for NDS.

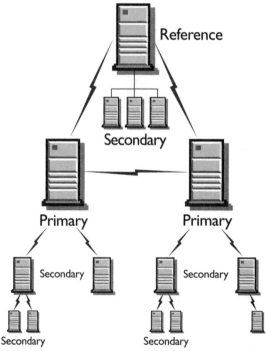

Figure 8-28: Hub and spoke arrangement with primary and secondary servers

# Having More Than One Reference Server

Some organizations with dispersed locations may require more than one reference server. For example, you may want to have a time provider group in two different countries, rather than having time traffic crossing over expensive or extremely busy wide area connections. As shown in Figure 8-29, you can have multiple reference servers as long as they are each connected to an external time source. The external source is needed so that these reference servers will maintain the same time and not drift.

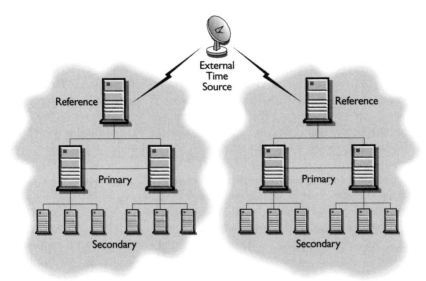

Figure 8-29: Multiple time provider groups with multiple reference time servers can be used as long as they are connected to external time sources.

# Time Synchronization Traffic Considerations

Although the amount of time traffic is generally small, it might be useful to know what kind of a network load is generated by time synchronization. The actual workload is controlled by the number of time exchanges during each polling loop. You can take steps to further minimize the workload if you have bandwidth constraints on your network. The actual traffic load is determined by how many time exchanges you have configured for each polling loop.

The default is to make three time exchanges, each of which involves an NCP send/receive pair, totaling 332 bytes of data. Thus, the default three exchanges involve six packets, totaling 996 bytes of data. You can calculate the amount of traffic for each server during a specific polling interval with the following equation:

```
NDS Traffic = (N-1) * (Polling Count) * 332 where N = the number of
  providers to contact
```

For example, let's assume that a network has five time providers in its group (one reference and four primary servers) and is using the default intervals of three send/receive exchanges every 10 minutes for each server. The amount of traffic generated will be as follows:

```
(5-1) * (3) * (332) = 3984 bytes/10 minutes/per time source server
```

Each time source server would, at its own 10-minute interval, generate 3,984 bytes of traffic on your network. Obviously, the more primary servers you have, the more traffic will be generated on your network.

When time synchronization first begins, polling occurs every 10 seconds, but then slowly backs off to every 10 minutes. So the workload of about 1K every 10 seconds eventually stabilizes to 1K every 10 minutes. If these loads are too high, they can be adjusted by changing the polling count and polling interval parameters as long as those adjustments don't cause problems in maintaining synchronization.

There is nothing wrong with changing the polling interval to cut down on network traffic. The default polling interval is 10 minutes. As long as the server clock is not drifting and synchronization is maintained, that polling interval may be extended.

In situations where perhaps dozens of secondary servers would poll a single primary server across a slow LAN or WAN segment, it may be helpful to increase the polling period to even one or two hours. This would cut back on the network traffic and probably have little or no effect on synchronization, unless the server clocks drifted by several seconds a day.

In actual fact, once a server has reached a stable state, the amount of network traffic attributed to time synchronization will probably be minuscule compared to the normal background traffic.

## Adding or Booting Time Servers

When adding a new server or booting an existing time server to an already synchronized network, time synchronization acts on two basic premises:

♦ Adding a server or booting an existing time server should not disrupt the network's time synchronization (even if the time server being booted is the reference time server). Time synchronization makes no assumptions that the server being added or rebooted has the current time.

♦ If the new server's time doesn't agree with network time, the network time is more likely to be correct. The new server or rebooted server then sets its time immediately to match the network time that has already been established.

Therefore, the first act of time synchronization (for a server of any type) is to set the time on the server to the time reported by the other time servers. This is true even for reference and single reference servers that do not normally adjust their hardware clocks.

When you bring up a server, make sure that time synchronizes properly, and, if necessary, reset the time on reference and single reference servers manually. It is always a good idea to check the time after bringing up a server just to make sure that all the time parameters are set correctly and that time is synchronized.

# Changing the Type of Time Server

If you are currently using the default option of a single reference server and all other servers as secondary, you may not need to read this section because the server type is set automatically during installation. However, it may be necessary for you to occasionally change the single reference server if it fails.

In this section, we want to set up or establish a time provider group. This configuration requires you to change the time server type on the server you want to designate as a reference by using the SERVMAN utility. As shown in Figure 8-30, only one server will be designated as the reference time server.

The next step is to change some time servers to become the primary time servers. Using the SERVMAN utility again you will change your selected time server type to primary. Repeat this step for at least two servers, but never for more than seven. Remember, the number of primary time servers is limited to seven for one time provider group. It is possible to have more than seven primary time servers, but keep in mind that the more primary servers, the greater the amount of traffic on your network during each polling interval for all the time servers.

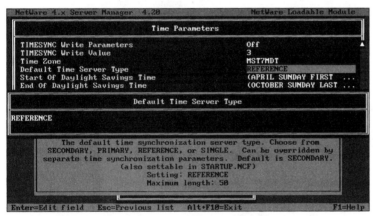

Figure 8-30: An example of a server being designated as the reference time server

## Consulting Experience

Experience has shown us that most companies can have very stable time by using only three or four primary servers in the entire network. Only a few servers need to work with the reference server to determine time for the entire network.

After you have made configuration changes for both the reference server and the primary servers, save the changes when prompted before exiting the utility. An example of how this screen appears is shown in Figure 8-31.

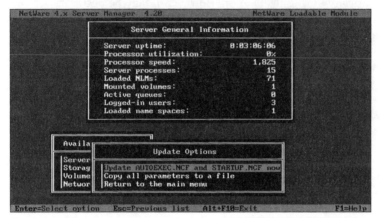

Figure 8-31: Be sure to save your changes to the TIMESYNC.CFG file before exiting the SERVMAN utility.

# Chapter 9

# Manage Time Synchronization Through SET Parameters

IN THIS CHAPTER

- ◆ Periodically viewing time on servers

- ◆ TIMESYNC debug commands

- ◆ SET parameters

- ◆ Troubleshooting time-related problems

NETWARE 4 INCLUDES SEVERAL new time-related features of time synchronization. Time synchronization is the method in which all the NetWare 4 servers maintain the same UTC time across the network. Although it is not directly part of NDS, time synchronization is used primarily by the Directory to maintain the order of NDS events. Because the computer hardware inherently does not maintain consistent time, time synchronization continually attempts to correct time variance. Many other NDS operations including partitioning are dependent on consistent time as well.

There are many time synchronization parameters that you can set on a NetWare 4 server. Altering these parameters can enhance the system performance for time on the network if they are properly understood and implemented. Once configured, time synchronization is stable and dependable, and it almost never needs changing unless your network changes in size or location or your time provider servers should happen to change.

Time synchronization for NDS can be managed and optimized through the use of SET parameters on your NetWare 4 servers. It is important to understand how these parameters can affect the performance of time synchronization. The first step is to check the status of time synchronization through the various tools provided by Novell. Then you can make minor adjustments as necessary. Follow the guidelines presented in this chapter to monitor and achieve optimum time configuration.

# Periodically Viewing Time on All NetWare 4 Servers

Time synchronization is vital to the correct operation and performance of NDS. Therefore, it is important to periodically check that your NetWare 4 servers are properly synchronizing. Checking time on a single NetWare 4 server can be done by typing TIME at the server console. You will see a message stating that time is synchronized or not synchronized to the network. Keep in mind that time synchronization is a server-centric operation, meaning that each server is responsible for synchronizing its time with the network.

To gain a status of time on all NetWare 4 servers load the DSREPAIR utility at a NetWare 4 server console. Select the option Time Synchronization to view the time synchronization status information as shown in Figure 9-1. This option immediately contacts the NetWare 4 servers in your tree for their time status.

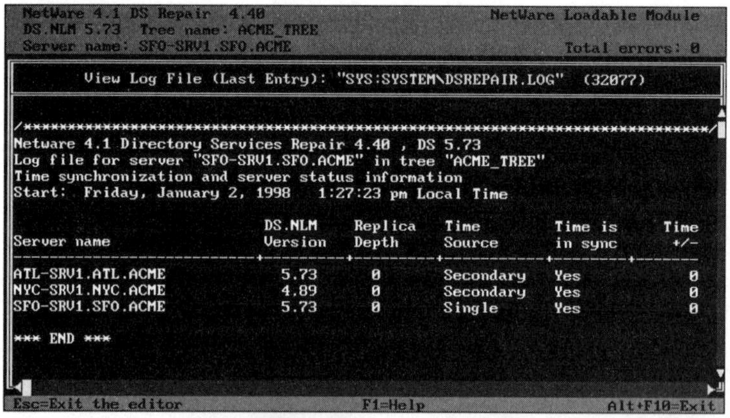

```
NetWare 4.1 DS Repair  4.40                    NetWare Loadable Module
DS.NLM 5.73   Tree name: ACME_TREE
Server name: SFO-SRV1.SFO.ACME                      Total errors: 0

        View Log File (Last Entry): "SYS:SYSTEM\DSREPAIR.LOG"  (32077)


/***********************************************************************/
Netware 4.1 Directory Services Repair 4.40 , DS 5.73
Log file for server "SFO-SRV1.SFO.ACME" in tree "ACME_TREE"
Time synchronization and server status information
Start:  Friday, January 2, 1998   1:27:23 pm Local Time

                        DS.NLM   Replica   Time        Time is   Time
Server name             Version  Depth     Source      in sync   +/-
-----------------------+--------+--------+-----------+---------+------
ATL-SRV1.ATL.ACME        5.73      0       Secondary   Yes        0
NYC-SRV1.NYC.ACME        4.89      0       Secondary   Yes        0
SFO-SRV1.SFO.ACME        5.73      0       Single      Yes        0

*** END ***



Esc=Exit the editor              F1=Help              Alt+F10=Exit
```

Figure 9-1: Time synchronization status information can be viewed for all servers by using DSREPAIR and selecting the Time Synchronization option.

The time synchronization screen shows the following information:

♦ **DS.NLM version:** The current version of DS.NLM that is running on that server. Make sure that all your NetWare 4 servers are running the same version of DS.NLM.

♦ **Replica Depth:** The replica level where this server exists in the tree in relation to the [ROOT].

♦ **Time source:** Type of time source such as secondary, primary, reference, or single reference. Make sure that you do not have two single reference or reference servers defined in your tree.

◆ **Time is in sync:** Yes or no. If any server shows a NO response, check that server to determine why it is not synchronized to the network.

◆ **Time +/- :** The time this server is ahead or behind as compared to network time and is listed in hours and minutes.

If you are running DSREPAIR's Time Synchronization option on a server that has a replica of [ROOT], the utility will search all NetWare 4 servers after making a list of all NCP server objects, servers in the replica rings, and remote/local ID list, which may include the entire tree beginning at [ROOT]. Running the DSREPAIR utility on a server without a replica of [ROOT] will search that server's container downward.

# TIMESYNC Debug Commands

NetWare 4 provides time synchronization debug commands to monitor the synchronization status of a particular server. (However, note that as undocumented commands they may or may not work in future versions of NetWare 4.) When these commands are executed, they start a separate time synchronization screen on the file server console. After the debug screen is started, information about the time synchronization function will be written to the console. This information may be helpful if you are trying to determine if the servers are contacting each other correctly. The debug messages can also provide valuable information about the way in which the system changes the time on each server to synchronize with the network time. Enter **SET TIMESYNC DEBUG = 7** to turn on the time synchronization debug screen. Enter **SET TIMESYNC DEBUG = 0** to turn off the debug screen. Figure 9-2 illustrates the time synchronization debug screen.

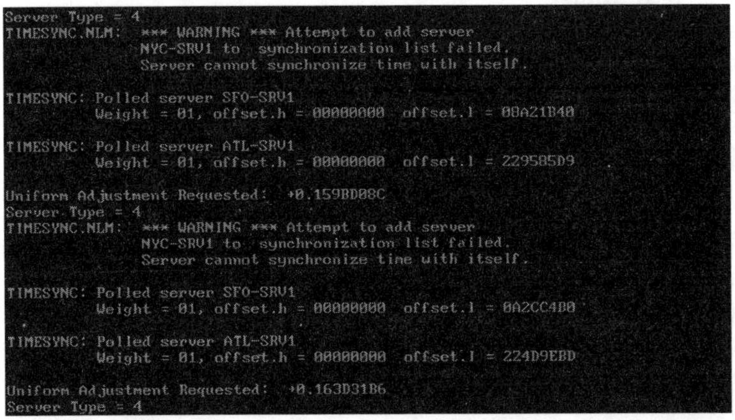

**Figure 9–2:** The time synchronization debug screen provides useful information on how well time is being synchronized on a given server.

You can set the debug flag to values other than 7, but the results are not very useful since each bit in the value controls a group of messages or disables output altogether. The debug information that appears on the screen is not particularly well formatted. Some portions are language enabled and may be translated.

The following messages are examples of the type of information provided by the debug screen:

```
TIMESYNC: Polled server ENG-SRV1
Weight = 16, OFFSET.H = FFFFFFFF OFFSET.L = F1F06723
```

The most useful pieces of information are the name of the server (ENG-SRV1) and the weight (normally 0, 1, or 16). If time synchronization cannot actually exchange information with the other time server or if out-of-range data is detected, the weight will be zero. Generally that means that the server is not up or is not reachable across the network.

The values for OFFSET.H and OFFSET.L are the calculated deviation of this server's time from the target server's time. The values form a 64-bit signed number with an implied hexadecimal point separating the whole and fractional parts:

```
FFFFFFFF.F1F06723
```

This number means that this server is a fraction of a second ahead of ENG-SRV1. Another possibility that may occur is a weight of zero with nonzero offset values, which indicates that the synchronization data is out of range (one server is more than 10 years ahead of the other).

If this message does not appear at all, there are no time providers or sources on this server's list. Either the configured time source list is empty, or no SAP time sources can be found, or both. Of course, if you have disabled the use of SAP, the only possible cause is that the configured time source list is empty. You can check the state of the list by entering

```
SET TIMESYNC Time Source =
```

at the system console screen. Notice that the equal sign with no parameter following is required to return the list of time sources.

The next message is:

```
Uniform Adjustment Requested = -0.0E0F98DD
Server type = 4
```

This message shows the actual time adjustment that needs to be applied to the clock during the next polling interval. The message also shows the time server types, which are 2 = Secondary, 3 = Primary, 4 = Reference, and 5 = Single.

The adjustment value is hexadecimal, but the sign is displayed so that the magnitude of the adjustment is easier to understand. In this case, the value 0.0E0F98DD (one tick) is significant to time synchronization. This server is ahead of ENG-SRV1 by one tick. It is very common to see one tick or one-half tick errors that are caused by randomness between the two machines.

When the adjustment is +0.00000000, the servers are in exact synchronization, which really means that no error can be detected by the algorithm. It is also common to see this value stabilize at a very small negative value, such as –0.00000094, because of a small round-off error in the synchronization algorithm when slowing the clock. The error of 0.00000094 is 34 nanoseconds, much smaller than the resolution of the clock. It is nothing to worry about.

The next message is:

```
Adjustment smaller than Correction Floor was ignored.
```

This message is quite common. It means that the clock adjustment is so small that it is being ignored. Actually, the parameter that determines the cutoff point is called TIMESYNC Correction Floor and is set to one millisecond by default.

# SET Parameters to Adjust Time Configurations

After viewing your time synchronization status as explained in the previous sections, you may find it necessary to make slight adjustments to your time configuration. For example, if you have decided to use a configured list rather than SAP to communicate time, you will need to make adjustments to some of the time parameters. Although few changes to the time parameters are usually necessary, some network environments may require adjustments for the best performance.

NetWare 4 provides adjustable parameters that govern time synchronization. The time synchronization parameters can be set from the server console using the SET commands or through the menu-driven SERVMAN utility. In addition, your current time synchronization SET parameters can be viewed from the server console by typing SET and then selecting option 9 as shown in Figure 9-3 and Figure 9-4. The settings for time synchronization are stored in a special configuration file called TIMESYNC.CFG. This file is located in the SYS:SYSTEM subdirectory on the NetWare 4 server. After making changes to any time synchronization parameters you are prompted to save this information to the TIMESYNC.CFG file before exiting the utility. You may not have a TIMESYNC.CFG file if only the defaults are being used.

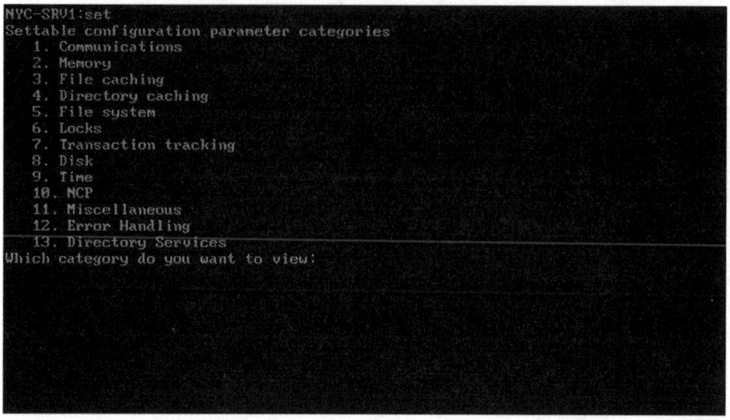

Figure 9-3: To view the SET parameters at the server console enter "SET."

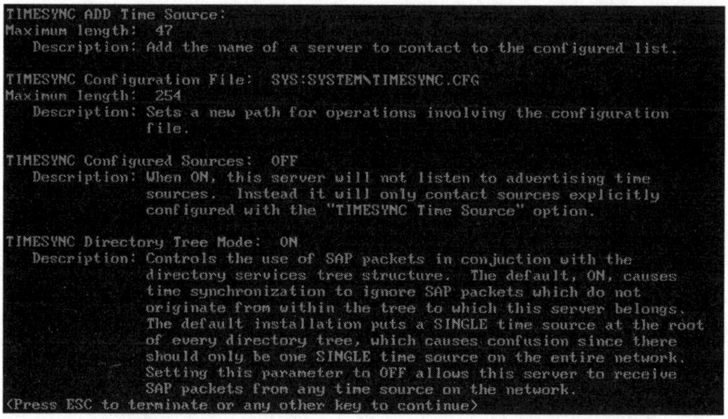

Figure 9-4: To view the current settings for time synchronization select
option 9. This figure is only a partial view of the time SET parameters,
as you can page down through the list.

The easiest way to modify the time synchronization parameters is to use the
SERVMAN utility. After you load SERVMAN from the server console select Server
Parameters. Select the Time option. The screen for the time synchronization para-
meters is shown in Figure 9-5. Note that all the time parameters found by typing
SET are also accessible from this menu selection in the SERVMAN utility and are
easier to use.

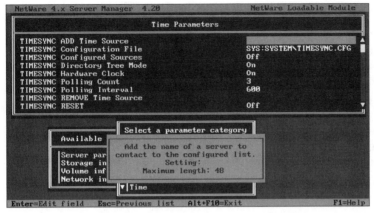

Figure 9-5: The NetWare 4 Server Manager (SERVMAN), after selecting the
option Time from the Server Parameters. The time synchronization parameters
screen lets you modify many aspects of time.

Each of the adjustable time synchronization parameters is discussed below as to
its function and rules. These settings can be modified through the server SET commands or through the SERVMAN utility now found in the MONITOR utility.

### TIMESYNC Add Time Source = server name

### Default: Empty

This parameter enables you to add the name of a particular NetWare 4 server or
servers as potential time providers to your configured list. The server name(s) you
enter here will be stored in the TIMESYNC.CFG configuration file. The TIME-
SYNC.CFG configuration file is updated if you choose the update TIMESYNC.CFG
option after exiting the time parameter screen. Duplicate entries are not accepted
in the time sources list and will be ignored.

Take note:

- Use the least significant segment of the server name, not the distinguished
  name. For example, a NetWare 4 server in the ACME tree has a
  distinguished name of CN=ENG-SRV1.OU=PHL.O=ACME. The name
  entered in the time configuration field is ENG-SRV1.

- To add multiple servers to the list such as ENG-SRV1, ENG-SRV2, and
  ENG-SRV3 in the TIMESYNC.CFG file enter the following:

```
SET TIMESYNC Add Time Source = ENG-SRV1
SET TIMESYNC Add Time Source = ENG-SRV2
SET TIMESYNC Add Time Source = ENG-SRV3
```

- Small network environments can simply rely on SAP for communicating
  time. They do not need to use a configured list.

### TIMESYNC Configuration File = volume:subdirectory\file
### Default: SYS:SYSTEM\TIMESYNC.CFG

This option defines the path or location of the configuration file used by time synchronization. The TIMESYNC.CFG configuration file is the default name that stores all the settings for time on your NetWare 4 server.

Take note:

◆ There is little if any need to change the name of this file, and we recommend that you accept the default TIMESYNC.CFG. This file can easily be copied to multiple NetWare 4 servers if needed.

◆ If you want to store the TIMESYNC.CFG file in another directory such as SYS:SYSTEM\TIME subdirectory, you would issue the following command:

```
SET TIMESYNC Configuration File = SYS:SYSTEM\TIME
```

### TIMESYNC Configured Sources = ON/OFF
### Default: OFF

This parameter determines whether the NetWare 4 server finds the time providers on the network using SAP or an existing configured list. A setting of OFF tells the server to listen to any time providers that are sending out the SAP. A setting of ON tells the server to ignore SAP and to rely only on the configured list set up in the TIMESYNC.CFG file. The server will try to contact only the time providers that are in its configured list.

Take note:

◆ This parameter must be set to ON in order to support custom configured lists.

◆ When using configured lists we recommend that each of the secondary time servers have a primary or reference time server as the first member of its list.

◆ Secondary time servers may also be entered in the configured lists. This option enables a secondary time server to get its time from other secondary time servers if a primary and reference time provider do not respond.

◆ To view the list of servers that have been established as the time providers in the configured list on a particular server, enter the following command from that server's console:

```
SET TIMESYNC TIME SOURCE =
```

Notice the equal sign is required with no additional parameters. An example of the configured source information is shown in Figure 9-6.

```
┌─────────────────────────────────────────────────────────────────────┐
│ NetWare Text Editor  4.12                      NetWare Loadable Module │
├─────────────────────────────────────────────────────────────────────┤
│              Current File "SYS:\SYSTEM\TIMESYNC.CFG"                   │
│                                                                        │
│ # Configuration Parameters from server NYC-SRU1                        │
│                                                                        │
│ Configured Sources =     OFF                                           │
│ Directory Tree Mode =    ON                                            │
│ Hardware Clock =    ON                                                 │
│ Polling Count =    3                                                   │
│ Polling Interval =     600                                             │
│ Service Advertising =    ON                                            │
│ Synchronization Radius =    5000                                       │
│ Type =    REFERENCE                                                    │
│                                                                        │
│ # Configured time source list from server NYC-SRU1                     │
│                                                                        │
│ Time Source = SFO-SRU1                                                 │
│ Time Source = ATL-SRU1                                                 │
└─────────────────────────────────────────────────────────────────────┘
```

Figure 9-6: An example of a TIMESYNC configured server list

## TIMESYNC Directory Tree Mode = ON/OFF

### Default: ON

This parameter controls the use of SAP in the NDS tree. A setting of ON, which is the default, tells the time server to ignore the SAP packets from servers that are not part of your tree. A value of OFF enables the server to listen to all time SAP packets from any time provider on the network even if the time provider is outside the server's tree.

Take note:

◆ Leave this setting to ON to maintain tighter control over the NDS tree of this server so that other SAPs will not interfere with this tree.

◆ Enable this parameter if you want to use a time provider for multiple trees.

## TIMESYNC Hardware Clock = ON/OFF

### Default: ON

This parameter synchronizes the hardware clock to the software clock, which is maintained by NetWare 4 servers. A value of ON, which is the default, has a different meaning depending on the type of time server that is being used. For example, the value of ON for the single and reference time servers enables them to read their hardware clock at the beginning of each polling loop and to set the software clock accordingly. The capability of the single and reference time servers to read their hardware clock and reset the software clock provides a basic external clock synchronization for the entire network. In this case the hardware clock acts as an external time source.

Take note:

◆ Set this parameter to OFF only if the single or reference time servers use an external time source, such as an atomic or radio clock.

◆ Leave the value set to ON for primary and secondary time servers. The hardware clock will be set after each polling process to the time of the software clock. This is useful because the corrections made to the software clock during the polling process can be written to the hardware clock. Thus, the network time is reflected the next time the server is brought down and back up. Each time the server is booted it reads the hardware clock.

◆ All primary and secondary servers in the same Directory tree should use the same setting for this parameter.

### TIMESYNC Polling Count = number (1–1,000)

### Default: 3

This parameter determines how many time packets to exchange during the polling process. Increasing the number of packets adds more traffic to the network.

Take note:

◆ Leave the default at 3, which works well in most cases.

◆ Change this value when you have unreliable or erratic network communication links between the time servers.

◆ If you set the value at higher than 3, the amount of network traffic will increase. Any value lower than 3 will result in a less accurate exchange of time information. For these reasons, we highly recommend the default value of 3.

### TIMESYNC Polling Interval = number (10–2,678,400)

### Default:  600 seconds (or 10 minutes)

This parameter determines the length of time between each polling process. In the case of the default, every 600 seconds (or 10 minutes) the server will poll the other time servers in the tree.

Take note:

◆ After the initial installation of your NetWare 4 servers, you may want to increase this value to reduce the total amount of polling traffic on the network. Remember that the time polling process does not generate an inordinate amount of traffic on your network.

◆ Leave the default setting if you keep the total number of time providers under 10. All the time servers in the same Directory Services tree should have the same setting for this parameter.

◆ If you decrease this parameter the amount of network traffic will increase, but time synchronization will be more accurate.

◆ We recommend that you increase this interval when the time servers have to cross a WAN link to get time.

### TIMESYNC Remove Time Source = server name
### Default: Empty

This parameter enables you to specify a server or servers to be removed from the time source list. The server name you enter in this field will be removed from the configuration file if you exit and choose YES to update TIMESYNC.CFG after updating and exiting the time parameter screen. This field will return a blank screen after you have specified a value in this field. If you try to delete an entry that does not exist in the time sources list, the request will be ignored.

This option is the reverse of the TIMESYNC Add Time Source. Like the Add Time Source the name of the NetWare 4 server is not the distinguished name. Instead, it is the least significant segment of its name. For example, a NetWare 4 server in the ACME tree has a distinguished name of CN=ENG-SRV1.OU=PHL.O=ACME. The name you enter in this field is simply ENG-SRV1.

Take note:

◆ Use this parameter primarily at the server console to remove a time provider that has gone down or become unavailable for any reason.

◆ If you are trying to add or remove a time source permanently, the TIMESYNC Add Time Source and the TIMESYNC Remove Time Server parameters will not tell you whether the instructions were successful. An alternative to using these fields is to edit the configuration file TIMESYNC.CFG directly using any text editor.

### TIMESYNC Reset = ON/OFF
### Default: OFF

This parameter resets all time synchronization parameters to the default values and clears the configured lists. A value of ON resets the TIMESYNC parameters and writes the configuration file after exiting from the SERVMAN screen. Be careful, any changes you have made previously to the TIMESYNC.CFG file will be lost. For example, all the configured server lists are cleared and set back to the internal defaults.
Take note:

◆ If you reset the parameter to ON and then press Enter, the values will be reset and the parameter will automatically default to OFF. Be careful when you use this parameter.

◆ You should never have to reset the TIMESYNC parameters on a production server. This option is most valuable as a method to restore the parameters as you experiment with them in a lab situation.

### TIMESYNC Restart Flag = ON/OFF
### Default: OFF

This parameter controls the restart of time synchronization.
Take note:

◆ Use this feature to restart time synchronization after you have created or changed the configuration parameters in the file.

◆ After this command is issued from the file server console, the parameter automatically resets to OFF.

### TIMESYNC Service Advertising = ON/OFF
### Default: ON

This parameter controls the time servers that are time providers advertising using the SAP. When this parameter is set to ON, the single reference and primary time servers send out or advertise using the SAP. Setting this value to OFF means that the time provider servers will not send out the SAP.
Take note:

◆ Set this parameter to OFF when you use configured lists.

◆ Turn SAP off to reduce the amount of traffic on your network.

**TIMESYNC Synchronization Radius = milliseconds (0 to 2,147,483,647)**

**Default: 2,000 (or 2 seconds)**

This parameter controls the maximum time a server's clock is allowed to vary from network time and still be considered synchronized. The default of 2,000 milliseconds works well for most installations. This time parameter can be adjusted or increased to enable a wider margin for error for time synchronization between servers. By setting this parameter to a higher value, you reduce the collision resolution that occurs in NDS. A lower value causes the server to maintain tighter time synchronization. A tighter synchronization radius may be difficult or impossible to achieve, causing the time servers to lose time synchronization.

Take note:

◆ Never set the synchronization radius under the 2,000 millisecond value.

◆ Only change this parameter when you have a slow response across a WAN or satellite link. If you need to change this parameter use the SERVMAN utility as shown in Figure 9-7.

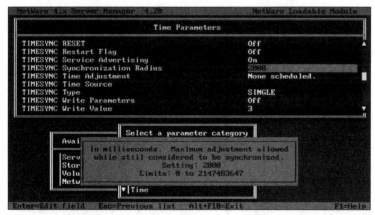

Figure 9–7: Changes to the synchronization radius can be made through the SERVMAN utility.

**TIMESYNC Time Adjustment = [+ | –] hour:minute:second [AT month/day/year hour:minute:second [AM | PM] | [CANCEL]]**

**Default: One hour from the current time or six polling intervals, whichever is longer.**

This parameter allows time adjustments to be made to the network time. The misuse of this parameter will affect the servers networkwide and could change the order of NDS events.

Take note:

◆ Use this parameter at a time during the day that will not be excessively disruptive to network operations.

◆ Use the optional AT parameters to schedule the time adjustment to take place in the future. For example, the command for a time adjustment scheduled in the future might look as follows:

```
SET TIMESYNC TIME ADJUSTMENT = +00:01:30 AT 4/6/99
11:00:00 PM
```

The command will adjust network time ahead one minute and thirty seconds on April 6, 1999, at eleven o'clock PM. Use the CANCEL command to remove a previously scheduled time adjustment from taking place. For example, to cancel the time adjustment of +00:01:30 enter the following:

```
SET TIMESYNC TIME ADJUSTMENT = +00:01:30 CANCEL
```

◆ If you do not use the optional AM or PM parameters, NetWare 4 assumes a 24-hour (military time) clock. Use a plus sign (+) to indicate a time adjustment forward and a minus sign (–) to indicate a time adjustment backward.

◆ This command would not normally be used in a time server configuration that is receiving its time from an external source. Use this option only when a significant one-time correction must be made to the network time.

◆ You should perform the time adjustment operation on either the reference or single reference time servers.

◆ The TIMESYNC Time Adjustment parameter can modify only the network time on time providers (primary, reference, and single reference) because they can affect the network time. Do not use this parameter with a secondary time server.

### TIMESYNC Time Source = server name

### Default: None

This parameter is the same as the TIMESYNC Add Time Source parameter described earlier. You can specify a server to be added to the configuration list. You may be wondering why there are two parameters that perform the same function. The TIMESYNC Time Source option makes more sense and is easier to enter at the server console command line. For example, you simply enter:

```
SET TIMESYNC Time Source = server name
```

By entering this command at the server console you are adding the server to your configuration list. Use the TIMESYNC Remove Time Server parameter to remove the servers out of the configured list.

Take note:

◆ Use this parameter only at the server console and use the TIMESYNC Add Time Source parameter in the SERVMAN utility.

◆ You can display the current list of time servers that have been established in the configuration list by entering TIMESYNC Time Source = at the server console. Notice that there is no server name entered as shown in Figure 9-8.

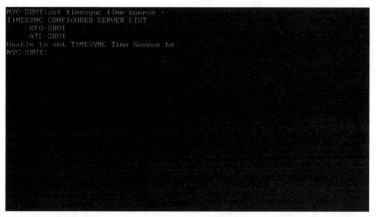

Figure 9-8: A current list of time servers established in the configured list

### TIMESYNC Type = time server type

### Default: Single (during the first installation of NetWare 4); Secondary (during all subsequent installations)

This parameter sets the time server type for the NetWare 4 server. The possible values are: SECONDARY, PRIMARY, REFERENCE, SINGLE (for single reference).

Take note:

◆ Use this parameter to change the time server type for the NetWare 4 server on the fly. This value is placed in the TIMESYNC.CFG configuration file and is used when TIMESYNC.NLM is initialized as the server is booted or when the restart flag is used.

### TIMESYNC Write Parameters = ON/OFF

#### Default: OFF

Writes all the current time synchronization parameters to the TIMESYNC.CFG configuration file. The value of ON writes the parameters; the value of OFF does not write the parameters. This SET parameter is a trigger and automatically resets to OFF.
   Take note:

- ◆ Use this parameter after making changes to time synchronization that you want written to the TIMESYNC.CFG file.

### TIMESYNC Write Value = number

#### Default: 3

This parameter controls which parameters are written to the TIMESYNC.CFG configuration file by the Write Parameter ON/OFF action. The possible values are:

- ◆ Write only the internal parameters.

- ◆ Write only the parameters for TIMESYNC Add Time Source.

- ◆ Write both internal and time source server parameters.

Take note:

- ◆ Accept the default of 3 to write all parameters unless you make a specific change to time source parameters.

### Default Time Server Type = time server type

#### Default: Secondary

This parameter is used when the server first initializes because it is placed in the AUTOEXEC.NCF file. The value of this parameter is overridden by the TIMESYNC type parameter found in the configuration file. The default server type is used if the TIMESYNC configuration file is not present or is invalid.
   Take note:

- ◆ Set the default time server type to the same value as the TIMESYNC Type value indicated above. This will reduce confusion and the potential for problems if the configuration file is lost for some reason.

### Time ZONE = time zone string
### Default: NO TIME ZONE

This parameter specifies the time zone where the server is located. The value is a time zone string indicating the abbreviated time zone name, the offset from UTC, and the alternate abbreviated name for daylight saving time. This parameter causes UTC time to be recalculated to local time.

Take note:

♦ To avoid confusion, set this parameter correctly for the actual physical server location.

The format for the time zone string is *xxxN[yyy]* where *xxx* is the time zone (MST = U.S. Mountain Standard Time and EST = U.S. Eastern Standard Time). The *N* is the number of hours offset from UTC (7 = U.S. Mountain or 5 = U.S. East Coast). The *yyy*, which is optional, indicates that daylight saving time is in effect (MDT = U.S. Mountain Daylight Saving Time or EDT = U.S. Eastern Daylight Saving Time). Thus, the time zone string for the U.S. Mountain Time Zone is:

```
MST7MDT
```

and the U.S. Eastern Time Zone is:

```
EST5EDT
```

### Daylight Savings Time Status = ON/OFF
### Default: OFF

Indicates whether daylight saving time is in effect. Possible values are ON and OFF. The status of this parameter may be changed at any time. However, changing the status does not change the local time, but it does cause UTC to be recalculated.

Take note:

♦ When set to ON, use the DST (Daylight Standard Time) parameter.

### Daylight Savings Time Offset = [+ | –]hour:minute:second
### Default: +1:00:00

This parameter controls the offset applied to time calculations when daylight saving time is in effect. The offset, in seconds, is added to local time at the beginning of daylight saving time. A change causes UTC to be recalculated from local time.

Take note:

◆ Do not modify this parameter.

### Start of Daylight Savings Time = Month [Day | Day of Week] [Condition] hour:minute:second

### Default: April Sunday First 2:00:00 AM

This parameter enables you to set up the local date and time when the change from standard time to daylight saving time occurs. The following example sets the start of daylight saving time at 2:00 AM on the first Sunday of April (which is also the default):

```
SET Start of Daylight Savings Time = (April Sunday First 2:00:00 AM)
```

Take note:

◆ Do not modify this parameter except in the rare instance in which daylight saving time does not begin on the date already specified by NetWare.

### End of Daylight Savings Time = Month [Day | Day of Week] [Condition] hour:minute:seconds

### Default: October Sunday Last 2:00:00 AM

This parameter enables you to set up the local date and time when daylight saving time ends. The following example sets the end of daylight saving time at 2:00 AM on the last Sunday of October (which is also the default):

```
SET End of Daylight Savings Time = (October Sunday Last 2:00:00 AM)
```

Take note:

◆ These parameters almost never need adjusting.

◆ The preferred method of setting the daylight saving time (DST) status is through the use of the SET Start of Daylight Savings Time and SET End of Daylight Savings Time commands placed in the AUTOEXEC.NCF file during system initialization.

◆ There are two ways to indicate when DST should start or end: Specify an exact date when the change to daylight saving time occurs; and specify a rule for calculating the dates. The operating system recalculates the next change and automatically schedules it for the following year.

◆ Both the start and the end date and time for daylight standard time (DST) must be set before either date is actually scheduled.

### New Time with Daylight Savings Time Status = ON/OFF
### Default: OFF

This parameter controls the adjustment of local time when DST is in effect. This command is similar to the TIMESYNC Daylight Savings Time Status parameter, but when this value is set to ON it adjusts the local time by adding or subtracting the DST time offset but does not change UTC for the server. This is accomplished by not only changing the daylight saving time status but also adjusting the local time by the daylight saving time offset. This effectively leaves UTC unchanged. This is designed to correct a DST error. If a supervisor arrives and sees that DST did not change when it should have, this command will change it.

Take note:

◆ When changing daylight saving time information manually on a server, be aware that you may cause UTC time to be recalculated from local time. The SET New Time with Daylight Saving Time Status command is expressly intended to avoid the recalculation of UTC time and to force local time to be recalculated instead.

◆ Use this command to change the daylight saving time status on a system that is otherwise correct and in time synchronization with the network. Attempting to accomplish the same thing by changing local time and then changing the daylight saving time status will result in loss of time synchronization.

# Additional TIMESYNC SET Commands

The following NetWare 4 SET commands for time synchronization are not documented in Novell manuals. These SET commands can assist you in fine-tuning your environment even more. However, these parameters may or may not work in future versions of NetWare 4. We have documented them here simply to provide you with all of the time synchronization options for NetWare 4. We recommend that you do not adjust these parameters unless you are solving a specific problem and understand the use of each parameter with your support provider.

### TIMESYNC Immediate Synchronization = ON/OFF

**Default: OFF**

This parameter triggers the synchronization process to start immediately, which means that it will start a polling process. After the value has been set to ON, it automatically resets to OFF, which is the default. This trigger is sometimes useful after the debug flag has been set to cause some screen output, rather than waiting for the process to awaken normally.

Note that using this SET parameter does not speed up synchronization in any way; it simply wakes up the synchronization process. Normally, the synchronization process will respond within two seconds. Occasionally there may be a delay of several seconds (10 or fewer) due to normal network overhead while attempting to reach the target server.

Take note:

♦ Use this parameter only when troubleshooting a time synchronization problem.

### TIMESYNC Short Interval = number (10–600 seconds)

**Default: 10**

This parameter determines the shortest interval between polling processes. This parameter is used when the server falls out of time synchronization. If the server falls out of time synchronization it immediately polls the network more frequently to try and establish time synchronization more quickly. The default interval is very 10 seconds.

Take note:

♦ Increase this value for very expensive WAN links that you don't want to monopolize all the bandwidth just to support time synchronization when it has been lost.

### TIMESYNC Maximum Offset = number (10–16,777,215 seconds)

**Default: 600**

This parameter specifies the maximum adjustment that the server will try to gain between polling processes. The default is 600 seconds or 10 minutes. The greater the value, the faster the time server will adjust itself toward the network time.

Take note:

♦ Leave this parameter set to the default.

## TIMESYNC Correction Floor = number (in milliseconds)

### Default: 1

This parameter sets the minimum value in milliseconds that the clock's time must differ from network time before the correction is applied. Any adjustment must be larger than this value or the correction is ignored. This value must always be less than the synchronization radius. If it is not less than the synchronization radius then time synchronization will not be possible.

Take note:

♦ This parameter is undocumented or hidden so that system administrators will not change it without knowing the consequences.

♦ Leave the default setting of one millisecond to support NDS.

♦ Change this parameter only to eliminate the correction for the one-tick jitters that sometimes occur. This may be an issue if there are other applications that depend on time being synchronized and are extremely sensitive to larger numbers of error corrections over a 10-minute period.

## SET TIMESYNC Offset Ceiling = number (0–315,532,800)

### Default: 10 years

A time provider whose clock is so far behind it won't be able to participate in the voting process. This parameter sets the value to determine if a server's clock is too far behind the network time. If the time on a server is farther away than this value from the network time, it will be ignored and the time on the network will not be adjusted based on that server. If two time sources differ by more than this amount, time will not synchronize, and the network may "split" into separate time synchronization trees.

Take note:

♦ Leave this parameter set to the default.

♦ You should manually reset a server's time if it is this far from true network time.

# Troubleshooting Time-Related Problems

Most time synchronization issues are easily resolved by inspecting your time configuration and the server that's having the problem synchronizing. Failure to synchronize server time to the network time is usually the result of no reachable time sources or providers. The following guidelines can assist you in troubleshooting time-related problems:

- Check the configuration information to be sure it is correct by using the SERVMAN utility as explained earlier in this chapter.

- Make sure that the time sources (single reference, reference, and primary) are running and are synchronized themselves.

- Remember that a secondary server will not be synchronized until its time providers are synchronized.

- If necessary, turn on the debug option to verify that the server is actually contacting a time source.

- If the time on the file server has been set far ahead, time synchronization may take a long time to catch up. Remember that the server should not move time backwards. For example, it takes at least two hours of real time to lose two hours when a server's time is set backwards.

Do not set time backwards on a NetWare 4 server, especially for servers that run applications that require synchronized timestamps. If you set the time backwards on a server that is participating in NDS, the system will generate synthetic time to account for the timestamps that are not synchronized. You should always set the DOS time before booting the server just to make sure that the hardware clock has the correct time. (Refer to the "Synthetic Time" section towards the end of this chapter.)

- Time synchronization requires routing information to make contact with the time source. Sometimes it takes awhile for routing information to get to a server, especially when the server has just been booted. Even though time synchronization normally happens quickly, wait a minute or two before jumping to conclusions.

- Use the DISPLAY SERVERS console command to see if the target server is known to the router.

# Booting Time Servers

Always set the DOS time before booting a server to make sure that the hardware clock is correct and to minimize any possible time adjustment.

A rare condition exists when the only two time sources on a network are booted for the first time. Since the first action of any server is to find a time source and set its own clock, it is problematic which server will first set its clock from the other server (the first server polled sets the time). Once servers have synchronized, and as long as one time source remains active, other time sources can be shut down and rebooted. The booting server will set its time to the network time. Since one server remains in operation, that server is not attempting to set its clock, and the rare condition does not exist.

# NDS Time Not Synchronized

This error occurs mostly on small networks that use the default time synchronization configuration. Note that the following is an NDS error, not a TIMESYNC.NLM error:

```
Time_Not_Synchronized - Error -659 (FD6D)
```

When users check the server's status with the TIME command, it reports that time is not synchronized. What this error actually means is that Directory Services has received a timestamp that is older than information already in the Directory or NDS has issued a timestamp and time has then been set backwards. The server time may have been set backwards because of a dead CMOS battery or the time being set incorrectly when the server was booted. Check your server hardware's battery when troubleshooting this problem.

# Correcting Local Time on a Server

Fortunately, once time information is correctly configured, there is little need to change it. When time synchronization is active, you need to be extremely cautious about changing local time information. If local time information is not configured correctly and time synchronization is active, UTC time will also be incorrect. Time synchronization will attempt to adjust UTC time to correspond to network time, which will, in turn, control local time. Time synchronization may therefore fight efforts to correct poorly configured local parameters.

To avoid this problem, you have to unload the TIMESYNC.NLM, configure the local time information correctly, and then reload the NLM.

 The TIMESYNC.NLM is automatically loaded when the NetWare server is booted.

As an alternative to unloading TIMESYNC, use the following command after correctly setting the server time and creating a TIMESYNC.CFG configuration file:

```
SET TIMESYNC Restart = On
```

# Synthetic Time

When time synchronization is lost because the server time is set backwards, NetWare 4 will continue to issue timestamps on the servers using synthetic time. When this situation occurs the synthetic time message will appear on your server console as shown in Figure 9-9 indicating that synthetic time is being used to create timestamps for this server. Synthetic time is also issued when DS loads and time synchronization have not yet been established.

Synthetic time is the process of creating timestamps from the most recent timestamp available in NDS. Synthetic time will take the most recent timestamp and modify just the event counter to create a new time timestamp. This means that the time is not incremented, only the event counter. The event counter is a 2-byte value that will hold up to 65,535 events. Once the event counter rolls over, the time in the timestamp is incremented by one second. Synthetic time will continue until the real time of day catches up with the synthetic timestamps being used.

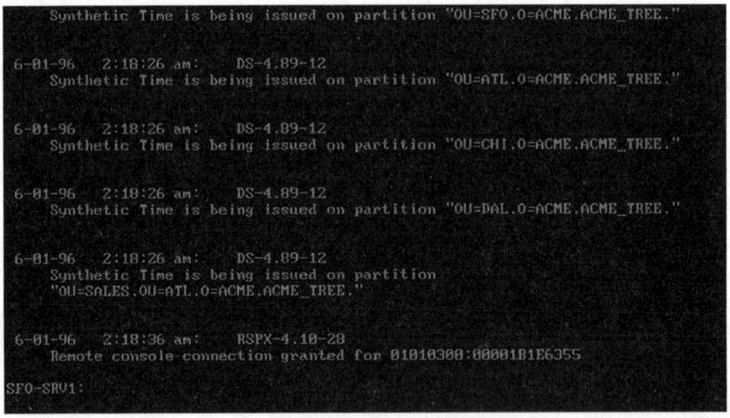

Figure 9-9: Synthetic time is created when your Reference or Single Reference is no longer determining time properly. You will be notified with a server console message when synthetic time is being created.

# Synchronizing Time for NDS Operations

In order for NDS operations to come to completion, time must be synchronized on a server. For example, the Change Replica Type operation must have time synchronized for this operation to finish. The Change Replica Type operation changes the type of any replica. The type of replica that must be defined is either a master, read/write, or read only. You cannot change a replica to be of the type subordinate reference. The subordinate reference replicas are maintained by NDS.

The Change Replica Type operation differs when the operation assigns a new master replica. This section discusses changing a replica to a master replica. In order to change a replica to a master replica, the target server must hold a read/write or read-only replica of the partition.

The important point to keep in mind here is when NDS operations do not complete, one of the first and easiest things to check is the status of time on your NetWare 4 servers. You should also check for communication and data errors, which account for many NDS-related problems as well.

# Fifth Step

## Install and Design NDS for NT

**CHAPTER 10**
Install NDS for NT

**CHAPTER 11**
Design and Manage NDS for NT

# Chapter 10

# Install NDS for NT

## IN THIS CHAPTER

- ◆ NDS for NT core components
- ◆ Bundled administration utilities
- ◆ NDS for NT installation
- ◆ Novell Workstation Manager configuration
- ◆ Novell Application Launcher installation
- ◆ Mail Box Manager for Exchange installation
- ◆ Novell Administrator for Windows NT installation

NOVELL'S NDS FOR NT product provides you with the tools you need to manage your mixed NetWare 4 and Windows NT networks. Installing NDS for NT relocates NT domains that you specify to the NDS tree. This relocation is transparent to your users, but enables NT domains as NDS Domain objects and makes them manageable through Novell's NWADMIN utility. You can also continue to use Microsoft utilities to manage Microsoft domains.

In this chapter we explain the components of NDS for NT and how to install them on your network. See Chapter 11 for information on how to design NDS for NT domains, manage your network environment, and configure the utilities discussed in this chapter.

The Windows NT Security Accounts Manager (SAM) is the database where the NT domain namebase is stored. The NT domain is identified by a unique number. This number, called the Security Identifier (SID), uniquely identifies an NT domain across a network. Objects within the domain are also identified by a SID created by combining the domain SID with a Relative Identifier (RID). This object SID is used throughout the Microsoft network to identify the object and its access to various system resources.

When using NDS for NT, each Windows NT domain is represented by a Domain object in NDS. This object behaves similarly to a Group object in that it not only holds information about the domain and users that are members of the domain, but also contains Member objects such as computers and groups, just like an actual domain. One significant difference, however, is that NDS for NT stores each user's RID in the NT Domain object and not as part of the User object. This means that one NDS User object can be a member of more than one NT Domain object. This provides a way for a single NDS user to access resources in multiple domains without having to set up complicated trust relationships.

# NDS for NT Core Components

NDS for NT core product components include the following:

- ◆ **NDS for NT Domain Object Wizard** is a network administrative tool that relocates NT domains to the NDS tree. Once inside the NDS tree, you can manage an NT domain as you would an NDS group object. NT users are members of the NDS Domain object.

- ◆ **Domain Object Snap-In** is an administrative snap-in to NWADMIN for NT that allows Domain objects to be viewed and managed within NDS. With the use of this tool, you can perform network administrative tasks, such as create a local group, create a new global group, create a new workstation, and so on. You can also continue to use User Manager for your NT users. Any updates made to your NT users will be stored in the NDS Domain object if they are part of that domain.

- ◆ **intraNetWare Client for Windows** NT allows users of NT Workstations to access and use all the services available on NetWare 3 and NetWare 4 servers. The intraNetWare Client for Windows NT brings the full power, ease of use, manageability, and security of intraNetWare to Windows NT Workstations. The intraNetWare Client is installed with NDS for NT. It is a required component in using the Domain Object Utilities.

# Bundled Administration Utilities

Along with the previously discussed core components, NDS for NT bundles some administrative utilities that will assist you in the management of your network. These utilities are discussed here, and their installation procedures are detailed in subsequent sections.

- ◆ **Novell Application Launcher (NAL)** lets network administrators distribute network applications to users' workstations and manage those applications as objects in the NDS tree on their mixed NetWare and Windows NT network. With the Novell Application Launcher you can deliver applications to Windows 3.1, Windows 95, and Windows NT desktops. NAL also gives network administrators powerful, unparalleled control over applications after they have been distributed to workstations.

Network users will not need to worry about workstation configurations, drives, ports, command-line parameters, application source directories, or the latest software upgrades. NAL is installed separately from the NDS for NT product. The installation utilities for NAL are located in the i386\GOODIES\NAL directory on the NDS for NT CD. We explain the installation of this utility in the next section of this chapter.

◆ **NAL Snap-In** is an administrative snap-in to NWADMIN that lets you manage the NAL software. Installing NAL installs this snap-in and provides NWADMIN with the additional capability to create and configure NAL objects.

◆ **NDS Manager** is an administrative tool that allows network administrators to manage partitions, replicas, servers, repair operations, printing, and preferences. This utility is installed automatically with the NWADMIN utility. See Chapters 4 and 5 of this book for examples on partitioning and replication using NDS Manager.

◆ **Schema Manager** is a utility installed with NDSManager that allows you to view and make changes to your NDS schema.

◆ **Workstation Manager** is included with the Novell NetWare (intraNetWare) Client and is a software component that enables administrators to manage both Windows NT Workstation user accounts and NetWare 4 user accounts from within NDS. With this utility, administrators can manage NT Workstations without having to use NT domains. This is installed automatically at the workstation (NetWare Client for NT) and requires some switches to enable it. It also requires a snap-in to be installed on NWADMIN for NT.

◆ **NWADMIN for NT (32-bit version)** is a graphical network administrative tool that allows a single point of administration for your mixed NetWare 4 and Windows NT network. **NWADMIN** for NT helps network administrators manage network resources from a single interface. All peripheral products that work with **NWADMIN** for NT require snap-ins (new DLLs) to provide additional functionality.

◆ **Mail Box Manager for Exchange Snap-In** is an administrative snap-in to NWADMIN for NT that lets you manage Microsoft Exchange Mail accounts in NDS.

◆ **Novell Administrator for Windows NT** provides a solution to the problem of dual administration between intraNetWare and NT Servers. The Novell Administrator for Windows NT integrates the intraNetWare and Windows NT networks so they can be administered from a central point of administration using NWADMIN. You can download a copy of Novell Administrator for Windows NT from the Novell Web site at http://www.novell.com/lead_stories/97/oct6/software.htm.

# NDS for NT Installation

In this section, we discuss how to install the core components of NDS for NT. In order to run the NDS for NT installation programs, you need the following:

- ◆ NDS for NT CD-ROM containing the WINSETUP.EXE file; or, if available, download the trial version of NDS4NTT.EXE from Novell's Web site: http://www.novell.com/download.

- ◆ Windows NT 3.51 with Service Pack 5.0 or Windows NT 4.0 server with Service Pack 3.0

- ◆ Windows NT 4.0 workstation

- ◆ At least one NetWare 4.11 or intraNetWare server

- ◆ Administrator (Supervisor) rights to the NetWare server and [Root] of the Directory tree

- ◆ Administrator rights to the Windows NT domain you want to move over to NDS

## Installation Files

The installation of NDS for NT requires you to run the following two programs, which can be run from a single installation menu known as WINSETUP.EXE. When you run WINSETUP.EXE, you select to install either NDS for NT files on the NT Server or NDS for NT Administrative Utilities, which causes either NDSSETUP.EXE or ADMSETUP.EXE to run, respectively.

## Running the WINSETUP.EXE Utility

Before beginning your installation of NDS for NT, be sure you know the NT Server name, the NT Domain name, and the NT domain administrator password. You also need to know the NetWare 4/intraNetWare server name, NDS tree name, and administrator password for the NDS tree. You then perform the following steps to install NDS for NT.

STEP 1:   If you are using the NDS for NT CD-ROM, insert the CD into the NT Server CD-ROM drive. When the auto-start installation screen appears (WINSETUP.EXE), select the option Install NDS for NT. If you downloaded NDS for NT from the Novell Web site, run the WINSETUP.EXE file located at the root of the NDS for NT directory you created. The installation screen then appears. Select the option Install NDS for NT. The main menu for WINSETUP is shown in Figure 10-1.

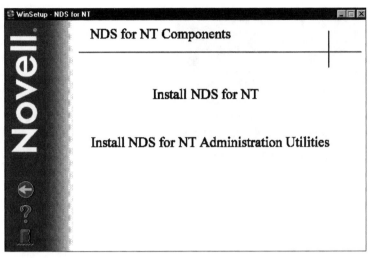

Figure 10-1: The main installation screen for WINSETUP

 The setup program can also be run by using the NDSSETUP.EXE file located in the I386 directory of the NDS for NT CD-ROM or the NDS for NT directory you created.

In any case, selecting Install NDS for NT does the following:

◆ Copies the NDS for NT files to your NT Server

◆ Installs the latest version of NetWare (intraNetWare) Client for Windows NT on your NT Server

◆ Launches the Domain Object Wizard, which creates the Domain object(s) for your NDS Directory tree

The main installation screen is shown in Figure 10-2. An example of the file copy process is shown in Figure 10-3.

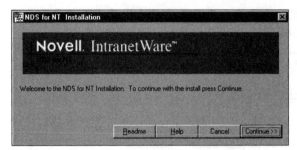

Figure 10-2: Main screen for NDS for NT installation

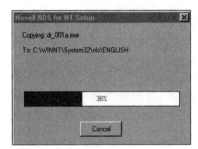

Figure 10-3: File copy process of NDS
for NT installation

STEP 2:    When the software installation is complete, you are prompted to reboot
your machine. Log in as Admin or its equivalent to the NDS tree that will hold the
NT Domain objects. An example of this login is shown in Figure 10-4. You may
also need to log in to your NT Workstation if prompted.

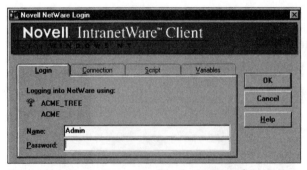

Figure 10-4: The login screen using the NetWare (intraNetWare)
Client for Windows NT

STEP 3:   After you log in, the Domain Object Wizard launches automatically. The wizard allows you to migrate an NT domain to NDS and remove NDS for NT if needed. (You must run this on the Primary Domain Controller.)

STEP 4:   Follow the on-screen instructions. If you need additional information while using the Domain Object Wizard, click the Help button. Once you have completed the domain migration, reboot the Windows NT Server. Follow the on-screen instructions as shown in the next steps.

After clicking NEXT on the main screen, you are asked to select the NDS tree to which you want to migrate NT users, groups, and workstations. The example shown in Figure 10-5 shows that we have selected the ACME_TREE. Notice that the domain is also shown.

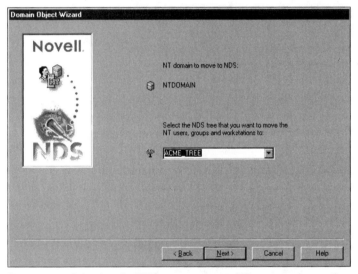

Figure 10-5: Selecting the NDS tree to migrate NT users, groups, and workstations

The next step is to extend the NDS schema to add the new NT Domain object to NDS. The screen that appears confirms that you are allowing the NDS schema to be extended for this purpose.

To move your NT Domain to NDS, the wizard must extend the schema on the NDS tree you just selected. To be able to extend the schema, you must be logged in as a user with supervisory rights at the root of the tree. Press Next to authenticate to the NDS tree and to extend the schema.

The extension of the NDS schema also needs to know the context (location) of the NT Domain object for this migration. As shown in Figure 10-6, you are prompted to specify where in the NDS tree you want to create the Domain object. You are also prompted to specify a default context for the creation of the new NDS users from the NT domain.

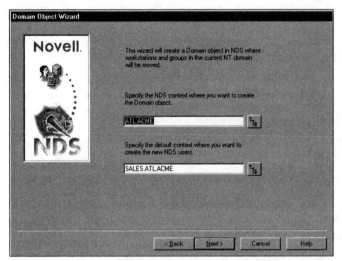

Figure 10-6: Specifying the context for the creation of the NDS Domain
object and a default context for the creation of new NDS users

Next, you are prompted to see if you want to search your NDS tree for users
already in NDS that correspond to your NT users. Skip this step if you have no
users already in NDS that are also NT users. The reason for this search is to avoid
duplicate names in NDS.

You are then presented with a screen to select the containers you want to search
for existing NT users. Select each container by clicking the box next to it, as shown
in Figure 10-7.

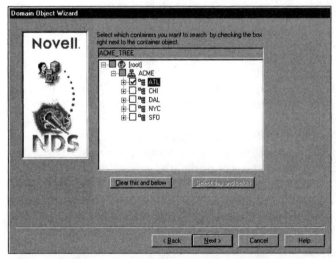

Figure 10-7: Selecting the containers you want to search for existing NT users

The length of time for the search depends on how large your NDS tree is. The search is performed on the selected contexts and the results displayed on screen.

As shown in Figure 10-8, the wizard displays the results of its search. With this information you can see that some NT users have already been created in NDS. You can now move these users or make other modifications to them if you wish.

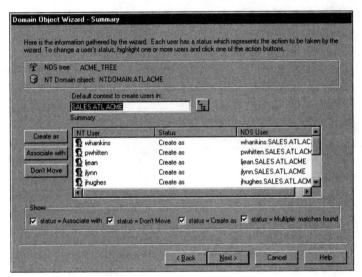

Figure 10-8: The summary screen shows the results of a search for NT users and any users previously created as NDS users.

If you wish to move users from one location in the tree to another, you can do so by selecting the Move button. Doing so causes the Move Object screen to appear. You can select one or all users on the list to be moved.

Figure 10-9 shows an example of the move process; the domain, users, workstations, and groups are being moved to NDS.

Once the process has completed the move from NT to NDS, a screen appears, indicating that the move is complete. A log file is created, and you can view this file by selecting View Log File. You can also view the log file at a later time. An example of the contents of a log file are shown in Figure 10-10. Clicking on Finish reboots the machine.

For assistance during the migration you can check the help screens at any time.

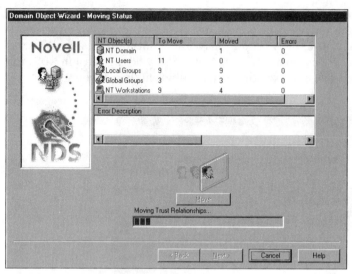

Figure 10-9: The move process in action

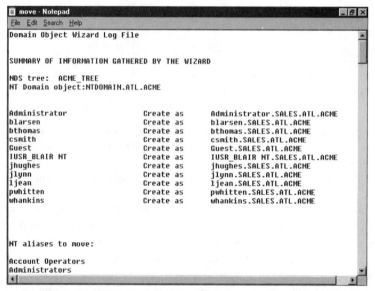

Figure 10-10: The contents of the log file for the migration of an NT domain to NDS

# Installing the NDS for NT Administration Utilities

If you are using the NDS for NT CD-ROM, insert the CD into the NT Server CD-ROM drive. When the auto-start installation screen appears (WINSETUP.EXE), select the option Install NDS for NT Administration Utilities.

If you downloaded NDS for NT, run the WINSETUP.EXE file located at the root of the NDS for NT directory you created. The installation screen appears. Select the option Install NDS for NT Administration Utilities.

The setup program can also be run by using the ADMSETUP.EXE file located in the I386 directory of the NDS for NT CD-ROM or the NDS for NT directory you created.

In either case, running WINSETUP.EXE and selecting Install NDS for NT Administration Utilities installs the following Novell administration utilities:

- NetWare Administrator for NT (includes NDS Manager and Schema Manager installations)
- Novell Workstation Manager

The following prerequisites are necessary before you install the NDS for NT Administration Utilities:

- You must have Administrator (Supervisor) rights on the NetWare 4.11/intraNetWare server and in the container or tree where you are installing the administration utilities.
- The Directory tree that contains the NetWare server where you want to install the utilities must be set as your current tree before you run ADMSETUP.EXE.

Use the following steps to install the NDS for NT Administration Utilities:

**STEP 1:** From the Windows NT Workstation, run WINSETUP.EXE and select Install NDS for NT Administration Utilities.

**STEP 2:** Choose Yes to accept Novell's terms and conditions. If you choose No, you will automatically exit the utility without being able to install the administration utilities.

**STEP 3:** Choose Continue after reading the Administrator Utility title screen. If you choose Cancel, you will automatically exit the utility without completing the installation.

STEP 4: Choose the utilities you want to install by selecting the check box next to the utility's name. You are presented with two choices: the NetWare Administrator and the Novell Workstation Manager. If you select the NetWare Administrator, the installation program will also install NDS Manager and Schema Manager.

STEP 5: Choose a NetWare 4 server from the To Server list. You must have sufficient rights to write files to the server. You should choose a server for which you have Administrator rights. The dialog box in which to make your setup selections is shown in Figure 10-11.

Figure 10-11: Choosing a server in the Setup Selections dialog box

STEP 6: Choose OK. A progress screen with two progress bars appears. The top bar shows which application is being installed. The bottom bar shows the percentage of files that have been installed. When the files are installed, the Installation Complete dialog box appears, as shown in Figure 10-12.

STEP 7: Choose Run NWADMIN to start NetWare Administrator, or choose Close to exit the installer without starting NetWare Administrator.

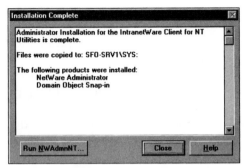

Figure 10-12: This screen indicates the installation
is complete.

# Novell Workstation Manager Configuration

If you chose to have the Novell Workstation Manager utility installed during the installation of the NT Administration Utilities, you have a few more steps to follow to enable the use of this product. This section covers those steps.

## Workstation Manager Components

The Workstation Manager consists of two components:

♦ The NT Workstation Component is included as part of the NetWare (intraNetWare) Client for Windows NT and runs at the workstation. You can use this client to create and delete NT user accounts, as the Novell Client runs with administrator privileges. Novell uses its own implementation of the Graphical Identification and Authentication module for Windows NT (NWGINA). NWGINA gathers the username and password and then authenticates the user to NDS and the NT Workstation. Because NWGINA runs on the NT Workstation with administrative privileges, you can dynamically create and delete NT user accounts, provided NWGINA can obtain the necessary user information from the NT Configuration object.

◆ The Novell Administrator Component is a snap-in DLL to Novell Administrator (NWADMIN). From this utility the administrator can enter workstation configuration information into NDS and associate it with users and groups. This snap-in stores the NT user information in an NT Configuration object that is placed into NDS. The snap-in consists of two DLLs that provide functionality for the NT version of the NWADMIN utility (NWADMNNT.EXE). A network supervisor can create NT Configuration objects within NDS containers. These NT Configuration objects store all the information necessary for NWGINA to dynamically create a user account on the NT Workstation and grant a user access to NT.

# Workstation Manager Installation

The installation of Workstation Manager is accomplished by loading the NetWare Client for NT at the workstation and enabling some parameters to use the utility at that desktop. You also need to install the **NWADMIN** for NT snap-in modules to extend the schema and manage your desktops from this utility. Therefore, we first discuss how to install the NetWare Client for NT software and enable the Workstation Manager at the desktop. The next section discusses the installation of the snap-in for **NWADMIN** for NT.

The installation program for the intraNetWare Client for Windows NT, known as SETUPNW.EXE, installs the default client configuration. SETUPNW.EXE makes the following changes to a user's computer:

◆ Removes any existing NetWare client software, such as the Microsoft Client for NetWare Networks and Microsoft Service for Novell Directory Services

◆ Installs Novell's intraNetWare Client for Windows NT

◆ Copies the Novell intraNetWare Client for Windows NT files to the local hard disk

◆ Creates the folder for the Novell intraNetWare Client for Windows NT under the WINNT\SYSTEM32\NETWARE directory on the workstation's Windows drive

SETUPNW.EXE has the following switches to assist you in the installation:

/U     Uses a text file to specify the default functionality. The default text file, UNATTEND.TXT, is used if no alternative is presented with the /U:<unattended file path> option.

/ACU     Specifies that the program is to check the version stamp and proceed to install using the defaults if an older version of the client software is detected. If not all the values can be defaulted, the user will be prompted only if absolutely necessary. If used in conjunction with the /U option, the defaults will be taken from the Unattended file.

/W        Installs the Workstation Manager utility

/?        Displays help information about using SETUPNW.EXE.

To install the Workstation Manager, run I386/SETUPNW.EXE /W:Tree1,.... You can specify the names of the NDS trees to look for NT Configuration objects. If you only have one NDS tree, select that tree name.

## ENABLING THE NWADMIN SNAP-IN SETTINGS
Included with the intraNetWare Client for Windows NT is a file called WORK-MAN.REG, where the NT client configuration settings are stored. This file must be run for the client to view and manage an NT Configuration object. If this file is not run, you will not be able to administer NT Configuration objects, and a ? (denoting an unknown object) will appear in the NDS tree for this object.

Simply double-click on the I386\WORKMAN.REG file to enable these settings. Failing to double-click on this file will cause the updates not to be made, and you will be unable to create or manage any NT Configuration objects.

## ENABLING THE WORKSTATION MANAGER SETTINGS
If Workstation Manager has not been enabled on a workstation, the Novell intraNetWare Client for Windows NT was not installed using the SETUPNW /W or SETUPNW /U option. You can enable the NT Workstation Manager without rein-stalling the client: enable Workstation Manager on the Novell Workstation Manager property page in the Novell intraNetWare Client Services Configuration dialog box, accessible from the Network Control Panel.

Once Workstation Manager is activated, you need to add at least one tree to the Trusted Trees list on the property page. The Trusted Trees list contains the names of the NDS trees that Workstation Manager searches to find NT Configuration objects.

Therefore, there are four ways to enable the NT Workstation Manager:

1. Run SETUPNW.EXE /W:TreeName1,TreeName2,TreeName3.

2. Update the information in the UNATTEND.TXT file to include Workstation Manager settings and run SETUPNW.EXE /U.

3. Enable a trusted tree from START → Settings → Control Panel → Network → Services → Properties → Novell NDS for NT intraNetWare → Novell Workstation Manager → Enable Workstation Manager on These Trusted Trees. Type in the tree name(s) and click Add.

4. Manually edit the registry (not recommended).

# Novell Application Launcher Installation

In this section we describe how you can install the Novell Application Launcher. A Novell NetWare 4.10 or later (NDS) server is required to support Application objects.

The applications you wish to distribute can reside on either NetWare 4 or Windows NT servers.

 You can distribute applications off of Windows NT servers if the workstation is running both the Novell and Microsoft network client software. Distribution of applications off NetWare 3 servers is not supported.

Your workstation must have the following:

♦ Windows 3.1x, Windows 95, or Windows NT

♦ The latest version of Novell's Client 32 for DOS/Windows, Windows 95, or Windows NT; or Virtual Loadable Module (VLM) client software 1.2.1

♦ A Directory Services connection with the server; no Bindery connection

An administrator's workstation must be configured with the following in order to perform NAL administration:

♦ Windows 95 or Windows NT

♦ Latest version of Client 32 for Windows 95 or Windows NT, or Workstation Manager 1.0

♦ NetWare Administrator (NWADMIN) 4.11 or later

## Product Components

The Novell Application Launcher consists of four product components: two administrator functions and two user functions.

### ADMINISTRATOR COMPONENTS
The two administrator components are the NAL Snap-In and snAppShot.

NAL SNAP-IN   NAL Snap-In is a Windows DLL that extends NWADMIN, making it possible to create and properly display Application objects. NAL Snap-In adds an Application object to the NDS tree, which supports Windows 3.1x, Windows 95, and Windows NT. Earlier versions of NAL added three separate Application objects for each of these three operating systems. This version adds a three-in-one configurable object.

Two new NWADMIN property pages are added for Container and User objects:

◆ Applications page

◆ Launcher Configuration page

One new NWADMIN property page is added for the Group object:

◆ Applications (the same property as for Container and User objects)

The majority of the settings in both these Property pages are discussed in Chapter 11. By applying various settings at the container or group level, they apply to all users in that container or group. By setting them at the user level, they apply only for that user.

Table 10-1 lists the default settings for the Launcher Configuration property. To modify any of these settings, simply select Use Current Settings and modify the properties, as appropriate. A user's default Launcher Configuration property is Use Parent Container Settings, which uses the values in Table 10-1 by default.

TABLE 10-1  **Launcher Configuration Property Default Settings**

| Item | Setting |
| --- | --- |
| Exit the Launcher | On |
| Log In | On |
| Refresh Icons | On |
| View Folders | On |
| Create Personal Folders | Off |
| Save Window Size and Position on Local Drive | On |
| Enable Timed Refresh | Off |
| Enabled Timed Refresh | 3,600 seconds (if Enable Timed Refresh is on) |
| Inherit Container Applications | 1 level |

The NAL snap-in also adds the following selections to the Tools menu:

◆ Export Application Object

◆ Show All Inherited Applications

◆ Migrate Application Objects

**SNAPPSHOT**   snAppShot (when used with the NAL Snap-In) provides for advanced server-to-client software distribution capabilities. snAppShot is discussed later in a separate section.

## USER COMPONENTS
The two user components are the NAL Window and the NAL Explorer.

**NAL WINDOW**   NAL Window is the workstation component that displays the icons of NAL-delivered applications set up for the user. The NAL Window can be run on Windows 3.1x, Windows 95, or Windows NT Workstations.

SYS:PUBLIC\NAL.EXE is the executable file for the NAL Window. It is a wrapper technology, meaning that NAL.EXE takes care of several initialization functions and then runs the correct executable: either NALW31.EXE or NALWIN32.EXE. Once the correct executable is started, NAL.EXE terminates. One of the main functions of the wrapper (NAL.EXE) is to determine the proper launcher executable based on the operating system of the client.

> We recommend that the workstation always start NAL.EXE rather than going directly to one of the launching executables. Additionally, if you run NAL.EXE from a login script (which is generally the way to do it), you don't have to anticipate the operating system of the attaching client.

**NAL EXPLORER**   NAL Explorer is an option to using the NAL Window. It lets network administrators deliver applications not only into the NAL Explorer Window, but also into the Windows Explorer, the Start Menu, the System Tray, the Desktop, or any combination of these. NAL Explorer can only run on Windows 95 or Windows NT 4.0 workstations. NAL Explorer requires a newer version of SHELL32.DLL for Windows 95, which is part of the Microsoft Windows 95 Service Pack 1 Update.

SYS:PUBLIC\NALEXPLD.EXE is the executable file for the NAL Explorer. When installed, it adds a NAL Explorer folder on the desktop. To uninstall the NAL Explorer (the only way to remove the NAL Explorer folder from the desktop), execute NALEXPLD /U. You may have to reboot your workstation for this process to finish. This removes NAL Explorer from the desktop, removes the DLLs installed, and cleans the registry settings from this program.

# Rights Requirements

Supervisor Object rights to the [ROOT] of the NDS tree are needed when the network administrator installs NAL, as NAL extends the NDS base schema to support Application objects and adds new properties to existing objects (as discussed previously). As always, an NDS "health check" should be performed before installing any application that extends the schema to ensure NDS is properly synchronized among all servers in the tree.

No manual assignment of NDS rights is necessary for users to access Application objects. Read and Compare All Property rights will automatically be assigned to any container, group, or user a network administrator associates with an Application object.

Users need Read and Write property rights to their User object's NRD: Registry Data and NRD: Registry Index properties to create personal folders. This assignment is not automatically given. Personal folders allow users to create their own folders and move NAL-delivered applications into these folders. The Create Personal Folders option must be turned on (remember, the default is Off) in either the container's or user's Launcher Configuration property to support this feature.

Users accessing NAL need file system rights to the following:

◆ The directory in which NAL is installed (default is SYS:PUBLIC)

◆ The directories where the applications to be distributed reside

 A future release of NAL will support automatic assignment of file system rights when a user launches a NAL-delivered application and will remove these rights when the NAL-delivered application is exited.

# NAL Installation Files

The NAL installation software consists of two executable files:

◆ SETUPNAL.EXE, which installs three of the four NAL product components mentioned earlier (NAL Snap-In, NAL Window, and NAL Explorer) in a default directory named SYS:PUBLIC. The steps for installing NAL are discussed below.

◆ SETUPSNP.EXE, which installs the fourth NAL product component mentioned earlier (snAppShot) in a default directory named C:\SNAPSHOT. Remember that snAppShot is an administrator utility and does not need to be installed on user workstations. The steps involved for installing snAppShot are not discussed here, as they are straightforward.

Here's how you run SETUPNAL.EXE:

1. Log into a server in the NDS tree where NAL is to be installed. Remember to log in as a user with Supervisor Object rights to the [Root] of the Tree to be able to extend the schema.

2. Close all applications on the workstation you are using. If NAL 1.1 has previously been installed in this tree, make sure no users are running it, as NAL 2.01 will replace NAL 1.1 Application objects during the installation process.

 NAL 1.0*x* Application objects are not automatically upgraded to 2.01. However, NAL 2.01 offers a migration utility that creates NAL 2.01 Application objects based on existing NAL 1.0*x* Application objects. The migration utility is available from the Tools menu in NWADMIN, and this selection will only be active if you select a NAL 1.0*x* object in the tree to migrate. Refer to the online help (within NWADMIN) topic "Migrating Application Objects from 1.0*x* to 2.0*x*" for more information.

3. Run SETUPNAL.EXE and respond to the prompts described below. Notice that the screens show Novell Application Launcher 2.0, even though you are installing NAL 2.01. This was intentional, as NAL 2.01 was primarily a maintenance release from NAL 2.0.

## CHOOSE THE DESTINATION LOCATION

We recommend you install to the default SYS:PUBLIC directory. Make sure that your mapping to SYS:PUBLIC is not a Root mapping. The selection screen is shown in Figure 10-13.

Figure 10-13: Select the directory
where you want to install NAL.

SETUPNAL.EXE installs product files in the following directory structure:

SYS:PUBLIC

SYS:PUBLIC\NLS\ENGLISH

SYS:PUBLIC\WIN95

SYS:PUBLIC\WIN95\NLS\ENGLISH

SYS:PUBLIC\WINNT

SYS:PUBLIC\WINNT\NLS\ENGLISH

Additionally, a NALLIB directory structure is created under the directory in which you installed NAL:

SYS:PUBLIC\NALLIB\WIN31\NLS\ENGLISH

SYS:PUBLIC\NALLIB\WIN95\NLS\ENGLISH

SYS:PUBLIC\NALLIB\WINNT\NLS\ENGLISH

This directory contains login files that get updated by NAL prior to activating the Launcher on the client.

A progress screen shows the progress of the file copy during the installation.

### DO YOU WANT TO EXTEND THE NDS SCHEMA?

You must extend the schema to use NAL (it is a one-time process per NDS tree). It can be done now or after the NAL installation is complete. If you select Yes, Setup extends the schema in the NDS tree that contains the directory in which you are installing the NAL software. If you select No, the first time you open NWADMIN after NAL is installed, a prompt will ask you on which NDS tree you want to extend the schema. Select the appropriate NDS tree and click Modify.

 If you have NAL 2.0 installed in your Tree, you will not be asked to extend the schema, as the schema does not change from NAL 2.0 to NAL 2.01.

### DO YOU WANT SETUP TO CREATE SAMPLE APPLICATION OBJECTS?

We recommend you select Yes so that after installation you can explore Application object properties. The context-sensitive Help available on each of these properties is very helpful in learning about NAL's features. These sample Application objects (that is, NWADMIN95, NWADMINNT, and snAppShot) will be placed in the server context on which you are installing the NAL software and can safely be deleted at any time.

 If you have NAL 2.0 installed in your tree, you will not be asked to create sample Application objects.

### DO YOU WANT TO VIEW THE README?

We recommend you select Yes to view READNAL.TXT, which contains caveats, limitations, and known problems of which network administrators should be aware.

# Mail Box Manager for Exchange Installation

Mail Box Manager for Exchange synchronizes NDS and existing Exchange Sites, Mailboxes, and Distribution Lists to dramatically simplify management of Exchange user accounts. Mail Box Manager for Exchange lets the administrator create and maintain all Exchange mailbox information using the NWADMIN utility, eliminating the need to use Microsoft Exchange Administrator for creating, editing, and deleting mailbox information (including site information).

# Components of the Mail Box Manager

The following sections describe the components of Mail Box Manager.

## NWADMIN SNAP-IN

During installation, a component of Mail Box Manager for Exchange snaps in to NWADMIN, allowing administrators to use NWADMIN to centrally manage Exchange sites, mailboxes, recipient containers, distribution lists, and servers. These Exchange objects are represented in NWADMIN as native NDS objects. The NDS User object is also extended to include an attribute that identifies the user's Exchange mailbox attributes.

Because all Exchange mailbox information is synchronized to NDS, you don't need to use Microsoft Exchange Administrator for managing user mailbox accounts. In fact, changes made using Exchange Administrator are forwarded to NDS. Only changes made using NWADMIN are synchronized with the Exchange system.

## NDS SCHEMA EXTENSIONS

The NDS schema defines the types of NDS objects allowed and the properties associated with each object type. Additional types of NDS objects and additional properties for existing objects can be defined by users with Administrator or equivalent rights. To manage Exchange objects from NDS, Mail Box Manager for Exchange extends the standard NDS schema to accommodate the new objects. New Exchange-related objects include:

- ◆ Recipient Container
- ◆ Distribution List
- ◆ Exchange server

The schema extensions are performed during the installation of Mail Box Manager for Exchange. Once the schema extensions are in place, NWADMIN must be able to manage the new objects. The Mail Box Manager for Exchange snap-in extends the capabilities of NWADMIN to include this feature.

## IMPORT UTILITY

Mail Box Manager for Exchange includes a utility (IMPORT.EXE) to import existing Exchange mailbox information into your NDS directory tree. NDS then becomes the master repository for all Exchange mailbox account information. The Import utility can be launched from the Tools menu of NWADMIN or run as a standalone utility.

This version of Mail Box Manager does not include automatic synchronization from Microsoft's Exchange Administrator to NDS. However, it does include the ability to manually synchronize Exchange data with NDS at any time. To do this, an administrator simply chooses Upload Exchange Mailboxes from the Tools menu in NWADMIN. Mail Box Manager requires NDS for NT and uses the domain association NDS for NT creates to simplify and automate its installation.

### BACKEND.DLL

When you make a change to an Exchange-related object in NWADMIN, BACK-END.DLL makes the corresponding change on the Exchange server, keeping records in NDS and Exchange in sync. For example, if you use NWADMIN to add an NDS user to a recipient container, the BACKEND.DLL makes the corresponding update in the Exchange database on the Exchange server.

The BACKEND.DLL also sends appropriate changes to an Exchange server that has been down. Once the system comes back online, it is brought up-to-date with the current Exchange mailbox information in the NDS database.

## Installation Prerequisites

To install and use Mail Box Manager for Exchange successfully, you must have the following:

◆ Exchange server 5.0 with Service Pack 1

◆ Administrator rights to the NT domain

◆ NetWare server using DS.NLM version 5.95 or higher

◆ intraNetWare/NetWare 4.11 with DS.NLM version 5.95 and Support Pack 4 or higher (you can download these files from Novell's Web site at http://www.novell.com).

 If you're installing Mail Box Manager to a workstation that is not an Exchange server, the Mail Box Manager Installation Wizard will prompt you to log in to your nearest Exchange server so Mail Box Manager can copy five required DLLs to your local System32 directory. To run this import utility successfully, you must have Administrator or equivalent rights to the Exchange directory from where you want to upload Exchange mailbox information.

The installation is a very simple two-step process:

1. Run the Mail Box Manager for Exchange setup program (SETUP.EXE).

2. Run the Import Exchange Mailboxes utility.

The Mail Box Manager for Exchange installation program (SETUP.EXE) is located in the i386\GOODIES\MAILMGR directory on the NDS for NT CD. The setup program is a wizard that walks you through the installation step by step. Simply follow the instructions as they appear in the installation screens.

The installation program modifies the schema and adds a snap-in interface to NWADMIN so you can manage the Exchange mailbox information once it is imported, and it copies the Import utility (IMPORT.EXE) to SYS\PUBIC\WINNT on the NetWare server. Also, the install utility allows you to specify which components you want to install (see Figure 10-14).

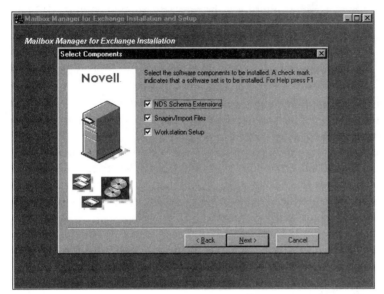

Figure 10–14: The Select Components dialog box allows you to select which components you want to install.

Once you have installed Mail Box Manager, you need to import your Exchange mailbox information. To do so, in NWADMIN choose Tools → Import Exchange Mailboxes, or run IMPORT.EXE from SYS\PUBLIC\WINNT on the NetWare server. The Import utility is a wizard that walks you through the process of importing your Exchange sites into NDS.

The Import utility does the following:

◆ Searches the NDS tree for NT domains

◆ Recreates the Exchange hierarchy in the NDS container you specify

◆ Uses the Domains found in Step 1 and the NT information in each mailbox to match mailboxes to NDS users

◆ Imports mailbox attributes into NDS users

Once your Exchange information is imported, you can manage the Exchange mailboxes with NWADMIN.

# Novell Administrator for Windows NT Installation

Novell Administrator for Windows NT gives network managers a single, centralized point of administration for users and groups in a mixed NetWare and Windows NT environment. It allows user information to be created and managed in NDS and synchronized to the NT domain. This product differs from NDS for NT in that it synchronizes with an NT domain but does not migrate the domain to NDS.

## Installation Prerequisites

Several prerequisites must be met before beginning the installation.

Each NetWare 4.1*x* or intraNetWare server must have the NetWare Administrator utility (NWADMIN for NT) installed.

As an administrator, you need Supervisor rights at the root of the NDS tree and administrative rights to all NT domains or NT workgroups to be brought under NDS administration.

Each NetWare server must run SAP. To check for SAP, complete the following procedure:

1. From the server console, type **LOAD INETCFG**.

2. Select Bindings.

3. For SAP, select IPX External Net.

4. Select Expert Bind Options.

5. Select SAP Bind Options

6. Set SAP State to ON.

The INETCFG screen is shown in Figure 10-15.

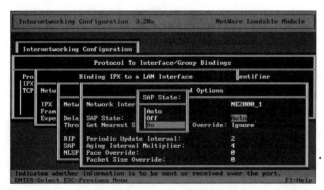

Figure 10-15: Checking the SAP configuration with the INETCFG utility

Make sure each NetWare server has NetWare 4.1.x CLIB Update Kit installed. You can download the update – LIBUPF.EXE – from Novell's Web site at http://support.novell.com/cgi-bin/search/download?/pub/updates/nwos/nw410/libupf.exe&sr. To install the CLIB Update Kit, download LIBUPB.EXE onto your workstation and execute LIBUPF.EXE (it is a self-extracting executable). See the LIBUPF.TXT file for the rest of the installation instructions.

Each NT System must have the Novell NT Client installed. You can download the intraNetWare Client for Windows from Novell's Web site at http://www.novell.com/download. Ensure you have the TCPIP.NLM loaded on the NetWare server.

Check that the NT Event Log Viewer is not open on the systems where you're installing the NDS Object Replication Service.

During the installation process, make sure the system from which you are running the installation program has no NT connections or drive mappings to any NT systems upon which you are going to install the NT agent.

## Easy Installation Wizard

The NAdminNT installation program is a wizard that walks you through each step. If you have questions at any point of the installation process, press F1 or choose the Help button.

The first time you install NAdminNT, you should not receive any warning messages in the Event Log. If you do, remove the program and reinstall, troubleshoot the error, or get technical support.

After installing NAdminNT, make sure the NDS Object Replication Service (ORS) is started on the NT machine. To do so, open Control Panel, launch the Services applet, and locate the ORS service. If it is not started, start it manually.

## Integrating and Synchronizing Users

You can run the Integration Utility (IGRATE.EXE) either from the Tools menu of NWADMIN or as a standalone utility. This utility lets you integrate NDS users to NT, NT users to NDS, or synchronize an existing NDS user with an existing NT user.

Before performing any integration or synchronization operation, you must upload NT domain information into NDS using the Integration Utility's Update feature.

If you experience any kind of failure during an upload from NT to NDS with the Integration Utility, you should NOT delete the users that were uploaded to NDS before the failure and start over. Simply recover from the failure, and then rerun the Update operation.

If you should want to delete the users, clean things up, and start completely over, you should unload NDSDM.NLM before deleting the objects from NDS with NWADMIN. If the .NLM file is loaded when you delete the objects, it will keep track of the delete operations – and when the ORS comes back on line, the objects will be deleted from the NT domain.

For procedures and overview information, choose Help once you are in the Integration Utility.

## Compatibility Issues

For an explanation of compatibility issues, see "Compatibility Issues" under the "Troubleshooting and Reference" section of the help file (MWA.HLP). The following issues are *not* documented in the help file:

◆ When large numbers of events are being placed in the application event log, the log settings for the Application log in the Event Viewer should be set to Overwrite Events as Needed.

◆ Large multiserver trees take longer to propagate the schema extensions. Installation to such environments should run the schema extension during the first install of this product. Be sure to wait some time for the schema extension to propagate to all NetWare 4 servers, and then install NetWare and NT systems. If the NDSDM event monitor NLM fails to load, complaining that the schema is not up-to-date, the most likely reason is that the schema extensions have not yet propagated to that NetWare server.

◆ If you have a large domain, and you are uploading the domain into a partition that already has a large number of objects, you should make sure that the server has sufficient memory and the tree is partitioned properly. The help file (MWA.HLP) gives recommendations on how many objects should be uploaded into a particular partition. See Chapters 4 and 5 for more information on partitioning.

◆ In order to run the NWADMIN snap-in on a Windows 95 workstation, you must have Microsoft's Internet Explorer version 3.01.

# Chapter 11

# Design and Manage NDS for NT

## IN THIS CHAPTER

♦ Designing and managing NDS for NT

♦ Managing NDS users with other Novell utilities

♦ Managing NT Workstation objects in NDS


BECAUSE NDS FOR NT is an add-on software product to NetWare 4, it makes it easier to manage the resources in both your NetWare and Windows NT network. NDS for NT alleviates the dual administration necessary in managing NT domains plus an NDS tree. With NDS for NT, all administration is done from a single point using the NWAdmin utility. NWAdmin stores and manages all information necessary for NT users and domains in the NDS tree, and all NT requests to the domain are redirected to NDS.

This provides a single point of administration for both worlds. The result is that you can manage all aspects of the NT Server domain through NDS. Additionally, you have the inherent ability to provide a single login, which reduces user confusion and provides a single point of administration for the entire network. Thus, if changes are made using MS User Manager, they will automatically be changed in the NDS tree. If the changes are made in NDS using NWAdmin, they are represented in the NT Server domain on NDS. Therefore, you can use either User Manager or NWAdmin to manage your network, and NDS will remain consistent. This is significant if some system administrators primarily use the User Manager to administer objects.

In this chapter, we discuss how to manage all aspects of the NT domain as a part of your NDS tree. But first, we need to discuss how to design your NDS tree to include the domain and all of its users and groups.

# Designing NDS for NT

Because NDS for NT gives you the ability to integrate Windows NT domains directly into your NDS tree, it requires you to design your NDS tree to accommodate these new objects. New topics we need to cover are:

◆ Designing NDS trees with NT domains

◆ Examining the best approach to designing domains

Before we introduce the additional design requirements of NDS for NT, let's quickly summarize the Novell Directory Services (NDS) design guidelines you have learned from the previous chapters. We strongly recommend you learn and follow these design principles before you attempt to integrate the NT domains.

## Summary of NDS Design Guidelines

The basic NDS tree design can be done very quickly once a few design concepts are understood. An NDS design for companies large and small can be mapped out in literally hours. In addition, having a plan before beginning an installation saves you time in the long run. Your design can even serve as your installation guide. No two trees are exactly alike, yet all trees have common characteristics that can be summarized in the following guidelines.

### NDS TREE GUIDELINES

◆ Design the top of tree based on WAN infrastructure.

◆ Design the bottom of the tree based on the organization of network resources.

◆ Do not include global groups or groups that have users from multiple partitions.

### NDS PARTITION GUIDELINES

◆ Partition the top of the tree based on the WAN infrastructure.

◆ Do not create a partition that spans your WAN.

◆ Partition around the local servers in each geographic area.

◆ Partition the top of the tree based on size (1,000–1,500 objects).

## NDS REPLICA GUIDELINES

◆ Maintain three replicas for fault tolerance.

◆ Replicate locally (if possible).

◆ Replicate to provide bindery service access, if needed.

◆ Place the master replica on servers at hub sites, not remote sites.

A balance of replication for fault tolerance and performance can be achieved if the above rules for partitioning and replication are followed as closely as possible. NDS was built scalable to meet the growth needs of your network environment. Partitioning and replication are the methods by which NDS can be logically segmented for greater efficiency across multiple NetWare 4 servers.

## QUICK AND ADVANCED DESIGN OPTIONS

The specific design rules for partitioning and replication of Directory Services can be separated into two different categories, depending on your specific implementation requirements, hardware, and knowledge level of your staff. The two categories defined for the partition and replica design rules are the Quick Design and the Advanced Design options. Tables 11-1 and 11-2 list the specifications for these two options.

 We strongly recommend you always use the Quick Design numbers for the design of your NDS tree. You should only use the Advanced Design recommendations in extremely large network environments. Your NDS tree will work better and more efficiently if you always use the Quick Design rules.

TABLE 11-1 **Quick Design Option Specs**

| Specification | Value |
| --- | --- |
| Partition size | 1,000–1,500 objects |
| Number of child partitions per parent | 10–15 partitions |
| Number of replicas per partition | 2–5 replicas (typically 3) |
| Number or replicas per server | 7–10 replicas |
| Number of replicas per Replica Server | 30 replicas |
| Minimum server hardware | Pentium 100MHz (64MB RAM) |

TABLE 11-2  Advanced Design Option Specs

| Specification | Value |
| --- | --- |
| Partition size | 3,500 objects |
| Number of child partitions per parent | 35–40 partitions |
| Number of replicas per partition | 10 replicas (typically 3) |
| Number or replicas per server | 20 replicas |
| Number of replicas per Replica Server | 70–80 replicas |
| Minimum server hardware | Pentium 200MHz (128MB RAM) |

A Replica Server is a NetWare 4 server dedicated to storing only NDS replicas. This type of server is sometimes referred to as a DSMASTER Server. This configuration has become a popular choice for some companies with a lot of single server remote offices when a need for storing a second replica for each remote server arises. The Replica Server provides a place for you to store additional replicas for the partition of a remote office location.

The replica synchronization process on the server must be completed in 30 minutes or less, making this the ultimate limiting factor for the number of replicas on any server. The factors that affect the time it takes to complete a synchronization are:

♦ CPU speed of the Replica Server hardware

♦ Number of replicas stored on that server

♦ Number of objects in each replica stored on that server

♦ Number of servers in each replica ring

♦ Location of replicas in the replica ring (local or remote)

♦ Speed of the WAN links connecting remote replicas

♦ Amount of RAM on the Replica Server hardware

♦ Frequency of inbound replica synchronization

# Designing the NDS Tree for NDS for NT

When you configure the NDS for NT software, you select a specific context in the tree where the current NT Domain objects are to migrate. The migration is performed using the Domain Object Wizard. During the execution of the Wizard, you are asked to provide a name for the NT Domain object that is created in the selected context. This Domain object in NDS represents the NT domain. As we mentioned in the previous chapter, the Domain object behaves similarly to Group and Container objects in that it holds information about the domain and users that are members of the domain, but it also contains Member objects such as computers and groups, as would an actual domain. Figure 11-1 illustrates how the Domain object placed in the NDS tree represents the NT domain.

Figure 11-1: The Domain object (in this case, NTDOMAIN) created in the NDS tree represents the NT domain. Users added to the Domain object in NDS are immediately visible to the NT Server domain.

Because the NT Domain object in NDS acts as a group with a list of domain members, it takes on the NDS design characteristics of an NDS Group object. However, the NT Domain object is also a special NDS Container object that holds the following objects:

◆ NDS for NT Local Group objects

◆ NDS for NT Global Group objects

◆ NDS for NT Workstation objects

◆ NDS for NT Alias objects

These are objects migrated from the original NT domain. Figure 11-2 illustrates how the NTDOMAIN object contains the NDS for NT Local Group objects, NDS for NT Global Group objects, and NDS for NT Workstation objects that have been migrated.

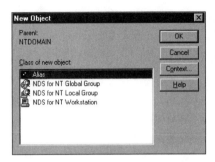

Figure 11-2: The NTDOMAIN object in the NDS tree contains the NDS for NT Local Group objects, NDS for NT Global Group objects, and NDS for NT Workstation objects that have been migrated.

Because the NT Domain object acts as both a group and a container, it has some unique design characteristics. For instance, you can create an NDS partition at the Domain object. In other words, the NT Domain object in the tree can become its own partition. Figure 11-3 illustrates how a Domain object can be partitioned using the NDS Manager utility. In this case, the NT Domain object called NTDOMAIN in ATL.ACME is being created as an NDS partition.

Figure 11-3: The NT Domain object, NTDOMAIN.ATL.ACME, is being partitioned using the NDS Manager utility.

Users migrated from the original NT domain are not part of a partition created from the NT Domain object in NDS. Rather, those users are members of the NT Domain object. By making user objects members of the domain, rather than having them actually reside within the domain, administrators can place the NDS User objects anywhere in the tree and still give them access to specific domains. Because NDS for NT stores each user's Relative Identifier (RID) in the NT Domain object and not in the User object, one NDS User object can be a member of more than one NT Domain object. This provides a way for a single NDS user to access resources in multiple domains without having to set up the complicated trust relationships found with ordinary domains.

Because the Domain object represents the original NT domain, one of the first design decisions to make is where to create or place the Domain object in the NDS tree. We recommend the object be placed in a container that is local to the majority of domain users. For example, if the Atlanta site has an NT domain, the NTDO-MAIN object should be created within the ATL.ACME container of the NDS tree, as shown in Figure 11-4.

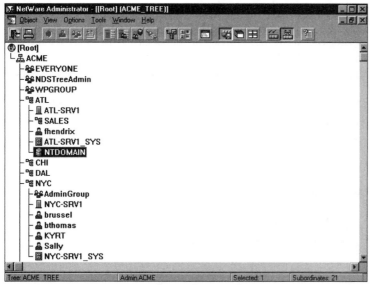

Figure 11-4: The original NT domain users are located at the Atlanta site and have been migrated to the NDS tree under the ATL.ACME container. The object called NTDOMAIN represents the NT domain. Users that have been added to the Domain object in NDS are immediately visible to the NT Server domain.

## Consulting Experience

The Domain object in NDS can only be partitioned using NDS Manager. NDS Manager version 1.25 is currently the only version that enables you to make this partition change. Previous versions of NDS Manager shipped with NetWare 4 do not let you perform the operation. Version 1.25 of NDS Manager ships with the NDS for NT product and is installed automatically on the server that you select to install NDS for NT. Make sure you are using the correct version of NDS Manager before trying to perform the partition operation.

The version of NDS Manager that ships with Novell's latest NetWare 4 support pack (INWSP4.EXE) is Version 1.24. To help reduce confusion, you can copy the NDS Manager version 1.25 to all your NetWare 4 servers.

In addition, the User objects should be migrated to the appropriate department container or containers under ATL.ACME. In the previous example, the NT Domain object is placed in the ATL.ACME container. The users for the original NT domain have been moved into the SALES.ATL.ACME container. Figure 11-5 illustrates how the users can be moved using the Domain Object Wizard. In this case, the users are being migrated to the SALES.ATL.ACME container, even though they are managed through the NTDOMAIN.ATL.ACME Domain object in the tree. You want to place the users in the container with the network resources they use most frequently. Most users from the migrated NT domain also use servers and printers in the SALES.ATL.ACME container, therefore we've placed the users in that container.

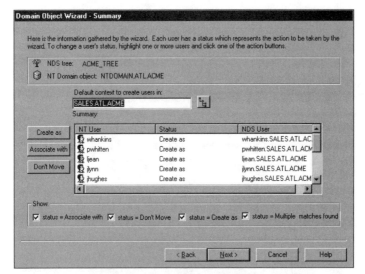

Figure 11-5: The original NT users are migrated to the NDS tree using the Domain Object Wizard. The SALES.ATL.ACME container has been chosen as the default destination for these users.

After the users have been migrated to the tree, they become true NDS user objects, as illustrated in Figure 11-6. In addition, they obtain all the rights and benefits of being a part of NDS. Therefore, any rights assigned to the SALES.ATL.ACME container are automatically granted to all users in the container through security equivalence.

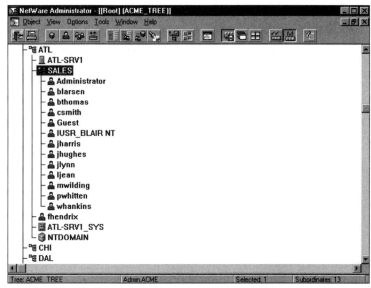

Figure 11-6: The NT users have been migrated to the SALES.ATL.ACME container.

After you decide where in the NDS tree the Domain object and users are to be placed, consider the following design rules for NDS for NT:

♦ Limit the number of members in the membership list of the NT Domain object to a maximum of 3,000. This implies that you limit the number of users in the original NT domains to less than 3,000 users.

♦ If possible, keep the users associated with the NT domain in the same partition. The result is you minimize external references and their associated traffic.

♦ If you have multiple NT domains in your NDS tree, place each NT domain and its associated users in separate partitions.

♦ Create the NT Domain object as its own partition when the number of objects already in the container is greater than 1,500.

♦ Always have the NDS for NT NDSDM.NLM running on the master replica of the partition holding the NT domain.

♦ The NT domain PDC or BDC must be in the same SAP domain as the NDS domains supporting the user objects.

# Managing NDS for NT

The NT Domain object you create in the NDS tree represents the original NT domain. With NDS for NT, all administration for both the NDS and NT systems can be done from a single point using NWAdmin. For example, you can manage all the NT domain users from NWAdmin. Figure 11-7 illustrates how the NDS users can be associated with an NT domain by making them members of the NT Domain object in NDS. These users are typically the original NT users you have migrated to NDS.

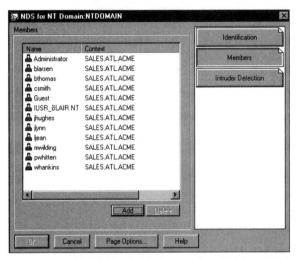

Figure 11-7: The NDS users can be associated with an NT domain by making them members of the NT Domain object in NDS.

In order to associate the user with the NT domain, you add the user as a member (which is similar to a group). As mentioned previously, you make User objects members of the domain rather than having them actually reside within the domain. This gives you the flexibility to place the NDS user objects anywhere in the tree and give them access to one or many NT Domain objects. However, keep in mind that the best performance for NDS comes when you have the NT Domain object and the NDS users for that domain residing in the same partition.

# Creating NT Users in NDS

NWAdmin is used to create a new user and associate it with the NT Domain object in the tree. Because NWAdmin is the primary utility used by administrators to manage the information in the NDS tree, and all NT requests are redirected to NDS, NWAdmin provides a single point of administration for both worlds. As an example, if you need to add a new user with access to an NT Server using NDS for NT, you first use NWAdmin to create the user, and then associate it with the NT Domain object. In addition, using the provided NWAdmin, you can grant the user in NDS rights to the NT Server. Figure 11-8 illustrates how you add a new user to the NT domain using NWAdmin.

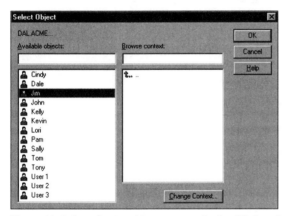

Figure 11-8: In order to add a new user to the NT domain, the user must first be created in NDS.

Alternatively, you could use Microsoft User Manager to create the user. User Manager sends requests to the NT Server to create the user in the domain. NDS for NT directs those requests to the NDS database. The user is created in NDS with the same properties and access restrictions available from the domain itself. Any subsequent modifications made to that user with User Manager or any other domain administration utility is serviced in the same way. Figure 11-9 shows the main screen for Microsoft's User Manager utility, which can be used to create and modify users. With NDS for NT installed the request is redirected to NDS.

Creating a user with the User Manager utility and having the request redirected to NDS is possible because NDS for NT is installed only on the NT Server. No workstation components or configurations are needed. So for the workstation running the User Manager utility, nothing has changed. In fact, nothing has changed for any regular Microsoft clients or applications using the domain. The domain requests are simply redirected to NDS to service them. All workstations and applications will continue to function as they did before the installation. For this reason the User Manager utility can be used without modification.

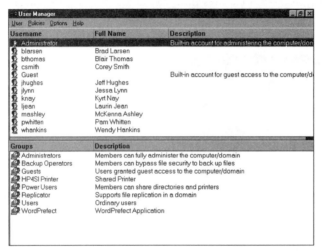

Figure 11-9: With NDS for NT installed on the NT Server, you can use the Microsoft's User Manager utility to create and modify users, because the request is redirected to NDS.

## Consulting Experience

All NT clients and applications communicate to the NT Servers using Remote Procedure Calls (RPC). Any request passed from the workstations using RPCs is extracted and passed to the SAMSRV.DLL layer. Normally, the SAMSRV.DLL accesses the Windows NT Security Accounts Manager (SAM) where the domain namebase is stored and performs the requested operation. However, NDS for NT replaces the SAMSRV.DLL, and the request is forwarded to NDS instead of the local SAM namebase. Using this method, NDS becomes the single directory where everything is stored. By replacing just the SAMSRV.DLL, this ensures the level of compatibility is 100 percent, except for passwords that may be different on the NetWare and NT Servers. The SAMSRV.DLL is the only DLL replaced on the NT Server when NDS for NT is installed. The Microsoft SAMSRV.DLL is renamed SAMSRV.OLD.

Once a Windows NT domain has been brought in to the NDS tree, the NT domain controller must be able to authenticate to the NDS tree. The NT Server that is a PDC or BDC needs to store, modify, and retrieve domain information from the Domain object placed in NDS. In order for the NT Server to authenticate, the NDS Domain object is used. The Domain object is given the appropriate administrative rights to create and modify all containers holding the NDS user objects of the domain membership. This may require you to grant trustee rights to the Domain object where future domain members may exist. You can configure the NT Domain object in NDS with a default location in NDS to which all new objects created with the User Manager utility are redirected. Figure 11-10 illustrates how you can select a default location for creation of all new NT users. You can set the Default User Creation Context for the NT Domain object using NWAdmin and going to the Details page. The result of setting this value is all new users created with the User Manager utility are automatically created in the NDS tree at the selected container location.

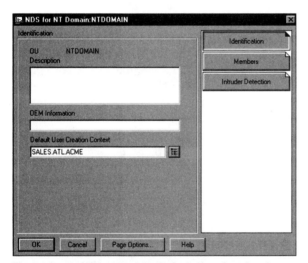

Figure 11-10: You can set the Default User Creation Context for the NT Domain object in Details. Setting this value allows you to create new users with the User Manager utility and have them automatically created in the NDS tree at the selected container location.

For NT Servers you want brought into the NDS tree, but that already have a large number of users and computers defined, NDS for NT provides a utility that allows the NT Server administrator to easily migrate Windows NT domains to NDS. This utility guides the administrator easily through the process of creating the Domain object in NDS and then proceeds to create all previously defined Local

Groups, Global Groups, and Workstation objects. User objects from the domain can either have new NDS User objects created for them or they may be associated with existing NDS User objects. This greatly simplifies the task of moving an existing domain to NDS. For more information on how to migrate new NT domains to the NDS tree, refer to Chapter 10.

## User Authentication and Single Login

Single login is one of the major benefits of having the NT domain integrated into NDS. In this situation, single login means that when a user needs to access network resources from intraNetWare or Windows NT, the user only enters one username and password. When an NT domain is migrated to NDS, the hashed user passwords are also migrated. This allows a user to log in to the domain using the same password that was defined before the migration took place. NDS holds both hashed passwords for the user, one encrypted using the MD4 algorithm (Microsoft) and one encrypted using RSA (NDS).

Windows NT uses an MD4 password encryption algorithm, whereas NDS uses the more robust RSA encryption. When user passwords are created, they are hashed (encrypted, or scrambled) by the respective algorithms, after which these hashed values are stored on the respective servers. Because no modification occurs to the workstation, the login process used to authenticate to NDS and the NT Server does not change. The login process hashes the user password with RSA and sends that directly to the NetWare 4 server for authentication to NDS. When a user logs in, the password is passed through the RSA encryption algorithm at the workstation, and the encrypted value is sent to NDS for verification. If the hashed value of the entered password matches that stored in NDS, the user is authenticated to NDS.

At the same time, the password is also hashed with the MD4 algorithm and sent to the Windows NT domain controller. This hashed value is compared to that stored in the domain User object; if they match, the user is authenticated to the NT Server. This authentication process is secure because the encryption process performed on each password is nonreversible. This means that even though the hashed value is sent on the wire, there is no way to reverse the encryption process to determine the clear text password from the encrypted value.

Figure 11-11 illustrates how the workstation running the intraNetWare Client is responsible for password and authentication to both the NetWare 4 and Windows NT Servers.

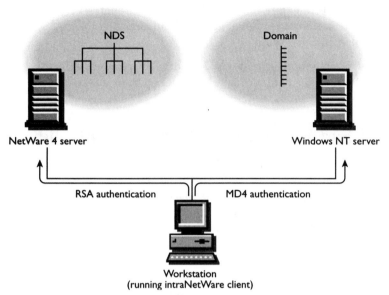

**Figure 11-11:** The workstation running the intraNetWare Client is responsible for hashing the password and using it to authenticate to both the NetWare 4 and Windows NT Servers.

## Maintaining Password Synchronization

Because Novell maintains Microsoft's security, it is necessary to keep the NDS and NT passwords synchronized. Most users change their password when prompted or when they have forgotten it and have to call their network administrator. In either case, the passwords are easily changed and synchronized. The methods used to maintain this synchronization are identical to those used when authenticating users to standard NT domains.

The best way to maintain synchronized passwords involves setting up the client workstation to authenticate to both NDS and Windows NT simultaneously. The following methods and utilities will help you maintain password synchronization:

- ◆ Use the intraNetWare Client for Windows NT and check the Automatically Synchronize Passwords check box at login if the passwords are not currently synchronized. The intraNetWare Client change password feature is accessed through the NWGINA module.

- ◆ Use the NWAdmin and the snap-in provided with NDS for NT to change user passwords. This snap-in provides a change password option that will change both the NDS and NT passwords. Using the snap-in for NWAdmin instead of User Manager, NETADMIN, or SETPASS ensures password synchronization.

◆ Set the passwords to expire through NDS and not through NT. This ensures an NT password is not changed without changing the corresponding NDS password.

◆ Make sure those users that need both NDS and NT resources authenticate to both NDS and NT simultaneously. This method helps avoid any rare password synchronization issues.

## NDS for NT and Windows NT Domain Controllers

Windows NT networks are installed with a primary domain controller (PDC) and one or more backup domain controllers (BDCs). The NT domain namebase is stored on each of these domain controllers in a single master configuration. This means that each domain controller can provide information requested by workstations, but all changes to the domain must be made at the PDC. The PDC then replicates the changes down to each of the backup domain controllers.

NDS for NT moves the domain namebase into NDS, where it is referenced by both primary and backup domain controllers. In order for all domain controllers to have access to the domain information stored in NDS, all primary and backup domain controllers must have NDS for NT installed. In addition, each of the domain controllers need to be associated with the same NT Domain object in NDS. Next, make sure the NT Server is installed with the Novell intraNetWare Client for Windows NT. The client is installed by default. The client enables the NT Servers to connect to the NetWare 4 servers and NDS, which allows the domain redirection to NDS.

NDS for NT upgrades the Windows NT domain system to a true directory service and gives you single login, single point of administration, and full NT application support for mixed intraNetWare and NT networks. NDS for NT alleviates the need to manage users on both systems. Thus, NDS for NT greatly reduces the amount of time network administrators spend managing the mixed server networks. It allows administrators the flexibility of managing all Windows NT domains and their resources in NDS using either NWAdmin or the Windows NT utilities. NDS for NT also allows a single NDS User object to become a member of multiple domains, doing away with the complexity of trust relationships.

# Managing NDS Users with Other Novell Utilities

In addition to providing a mechanism for managing NT domains with NDS for NT, Novell provides other utilities that allow you to deliver applications to your users' desktops, upgrade their systems, and manage their workstations. In this section you'll read about how to configure users to receive applications at their desktops through the Novell Application Launcher and how to manage NT Workstations via NDS with the Workstation Manager.

# Managing User Objects with NAL

The Novell Application Launcher reduces administration significantly and eliminates complexities associated with networked applications in mixed environments. It also provides for fault tolerance and load balancing among application servers and supplies true location independence, which it does from a single point of administration. This is accomplished by storing the application information required to execute the application on the workstation within a directory object. Administrators can then assign the right to use applications by user, group, or organization, and thereby have the appropriate applications dynamically appear on users' desktops.

Software assignment can be done once for a company group or department so that current and future members of the group gain automatic access to a standard desktop configuration. The end user can have access to all applications assigned to him or her on both NetWare and Windows NT Servers, while the administrator can easily support this demand from their management console.

NAL works with Windows 3.x, Windows 95, and Windows NT to automatically determine the desktop operating system platform upon which it is running. The NetWare Application Launcher also lets the network administrator physically distribute software to the desktop through automated installations or allows users to pull applications to their desktop by providing them with setup programs. For installation of this product, refer to Chapter 10.

Network applications can either be pulled or pushed to the user's desktop. NAL provides administrators with either option. A pull distribution implies user intervention and provides an application icon on the user's desktop delivered via NDS. In this scenario, the user clicks on the application icon at their desktop to either launch the application from the server or run an installation program that places the application on the user's hard drive. In both cases NAL makes any necessary workstation configuration changes.

Push distribution implies no user intervention; it does the same as pull distribution, but it is known as a "force run." For operating system updates, network client updates, or virtually any client updates, the push approach works best.

Let's look at two approaches for using the NAL utility; a simple distribution and a complex distribution of an application.

## MANAGING A SIMPLE DISTRIBUTION

A simple distribution is one which does not require any Registry changes, INI file changes, or DLLs at the workstation. A simple distribution requires you to create the application object name and specify a path to the executable file.

Using NWAdmin, create the NDS Application leaf object (see Figure 11-12). Your installation of the NAL snap-in adds the Application object class to the list of available objects in NDS. After you have created the NDS object by giving it a name, you need to specify a path to the executable file, either a drive mapping or a UNC path, as shown in Figure 11-13. The last step is to associate the application object to a container, group, or user (see Figure 11-14). Once associated, those containers, groups, or users receive the application when they run either NAL.EXE (NAL Windows) or NALEXPLD.EXE (NAL Explorer) at the desktop. A configurable refresh parameter provides a time interval when applications appear and are refreshed at the desktop.

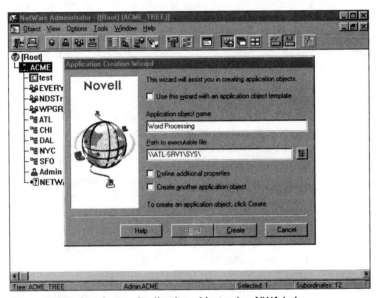

Figure 11-12: Creating an Application object using NWAdmin

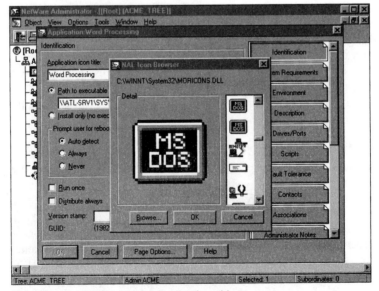

Figure 11-13: Configuring the Application object

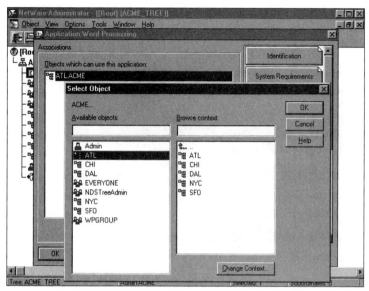

Figure 11-14: Associating the Application object with a container

## MANAGING A COMPLEX DISTRIBUTION

A complex distribution makes use of the NAL's component utility snAppShot (SNAPSHOT.EXE) and is used in cases that require Registry changes, INI file changes, and DLL distribution to the workstation. Basically, the snAppShot utility takes two snapshots of your workstation configuration. The first snapshot is taken before you install an application on the workstation. The second snapshot is taken after you install the application to the same desktop. The configuration differences between these two snapshots are compared, and the difference is stored in a file known as the Application Object Template file, or AOT file. This file, which represents specific configuration changes the application made to the desktop, is stored in NDS. During the distribution of the application the AOT file is used to make updates to the workstation, Windows Registry, and so on.

Here's a brief example of how this process works for distributing an application to the desktop. After running SNAPSHOT.EXE from the administrator's workstation, follow the prompts and fill in the required information. The snAppshot configuration screens guide you through the process. Keep in mind that if you are attempting to use snAppshot for the client component of a network application, you need to run a complete network installation of the application first before using snAppshot. Once the application is installed on the server, use snAppshot to distribute the client portion of the application to your workstations. Figure 11-15 shows the AOT configuration screen, one of the screens you configure before running snAppshot.

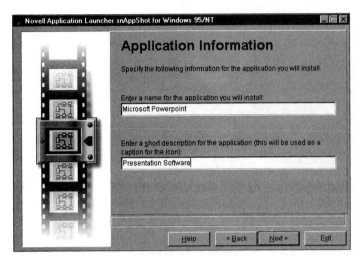

Figure 11-15: The AOT configuration screen

After running SNAPSHOT.EXE, follow these steps:

**STEP 1. ENTER A NAME FOR THE APPLICATION YOU WANT TO INSTALL.** This will be the Application leaf object name in the NDS tree.

**STEP 2. ENTER A SHORT DESCRIPTION OF THE APPLICATION.** The short description is used as a caption for the icon and is viewed by the users when running the NAL or NAL Explorer windows.

**STEP 3. NAME THE DIRECTORY AND FILENAME FOR THE TEMPLATE YOU PLAN TO CREATE.** This is where the AOT file will be created and stored. Installing to a network drive allows others to use this AOT file and is easier for centralized management.

**STEP 4. SPECIFY A DIRECTORY FOR APPLICATION FILES (NETWORK DIRECTORY RECOMMENDED).** This is where the application FIL files will be stored. The snAppShot utility keeps track of all the files an application's Setup program installs to the workstation, copying and storing them as a series of FIL files. Additionally, a FILEDEF.TXT file will be created here, which is a complete listing of the application files that will become part of the AOT.

Recognize that Windows 95 and Windows NT applications may not need to be placed in separate directory structures.

We do not recommend placing the FIL files on the SYS volume, as they can be very large (depending upon the size of the application you're distributing) and could fill the SYS volume.

We recommend that you put the application's AOT file in the same directory as the corresponding application's FIL files for organizational purposes. Here is a suggested directory structure:

```
\\file_server_name\<volume>\AOTFILES\Windows31\<appname>
\\file_server_name\<volume>\AOTFILES\Windows95\<appname>
\\file_server_name\<volume>\AOTFILES\WindowsNT\<appname>
```

**STEP 5. MODIFY THE LINES FOR YOUR WINDOWS DRIVE AND BOOT DRIVE, IF NECESSARY.**   The default for both is the C drive.

**STEP 6. REVIEW THE INCLUDE/EXCLUDE SCREEN.**   Modify these settings to set the scope of discovery for snAppShot. For example, if you were installing this application to a network drive, you would include the drive mapping in the Drives to Include box. By default, snAppShot only views drive C for files copied. If you don't want snAppShot to track certain files, such as DLLs that may already be more current on user workstations, you simply specify these files in the Exclude Files box. Carefully review your application's files and test your process before running it on your user's network.

You are at the last configuration screen and ready to have snAppShot take a pre-installation picture of your workstation, including or excluding the discovery parameters you set above. You will see the screen indicating that a snapshot is being taken. Once this process is completed, you are ready to run the application's Setup program.

**STEP 7. RUN THE APPLICATION'S SETUP PROGRAM.**   This can be accomplished within this utility or by going to the Windows Start Menu or anywhere else and running the application's SETUP.EXE. Install the application on your workstation with the same configuration characteristics you want to appear on all your users' desktops. Once you see the Application Complete screen, you are almost ready to take the second picture of your workstation.

**STEP 8. SELECT AN INSTALL DIRECTORY.**   You need to specify the path where the software was just installed, as we recommend. This is required for the creation of installation macros. Macros are a property of application objects. Although macros are not required, they are a very powerful component of NAL.

The snAppshot utility now performs a post-installation snapshot and discovers the changes made during the application's setup, taking into account the scope of discovery you set in Include/Exclude screen and any macro information. This information is stored in the AOT file.

The snAppShot process is finished when a Completed window is displayed, showing you a summary screen of where the AOT file and the application files have been placed. Now the Application object needs to be created in NWAdmin using this AOT file.

The last step in this process is to create the Application object in NWAdmin and select the option Use This Wizard with an Application Object Template, which results in incorporation of the AOT file you just created into the application object.

## Inheriting Applications

At some point a network administrator will want to know what applications are being delivered to a user and by what associations. This is accomplished by highlighting a User object and then selecting the Show Inherited Applications option under the Tools menu in NWAdmin. An example of this is shown in Figure 11-16.

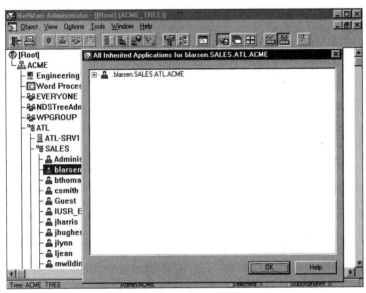

Figure 11-16: Viewing Inherited Applications with NWAdmin

NAL calculates the applications to be distributed to users in this order:

1. All applications associated directly with the user object.

2. All applications from groups of which the user is a member.

3. All applications from parent containers above the user. This last calculation is dependent upon the Inherit Container Applications setting in the Launcher Configuration property (see the section that follows, "Container Association Considerations").

Currently the network administrator has no way to prioritize applications as they are distributed to users; however, this prioritization could be somewhat controlled based on the calculation order just described.

This Show Inherited Applications option categorizes the applications into the different areas they will show up in (Launcher, Start Menu, desktop, or System Tray). Remember, users need to be running the NAL Explorer to have applications distributed to the Start Menu, desktop, or System Tray. This option also shows if the application is a push application.

If you want an application to show up in a user's Start Menu, you would go back to where the association was made (either to a container, group, or user) and set this up under this object's Applications Property page. This is also where you would set up a force run distribution.

# Container Association Considerations

When calculating applications to be distributed to users, NAL by default only looks in the user's immediate parent container for container-associated Application objects (the actual Application objects can reside anywhere in the tree). This default is based on setting either the container's Launcher Configuration property to Use Default Settings or the user's Launcher Configuration property to Use Parent Container Settings.

If you do associate an Application object with a container that is at a level or levels higher in the tree than the user's immediate parent container, you need to adjust the Inherit Container Applications property by entering an appropriate value in the Levels box:

| | |
|---|---|
| 0 | NAL won't look for container-associated Application objects. |
| 1 | NAL looks at the immediate container for container-associated Application objects (default). |
| 2 | NAL looks up two containers for container-associated Application objects. |
| 3 | NAL looks up three containers for container-associated Application objects, and so on. |
| −1 | NAL looks up to the [Root] for container-associated Application objects. |

As an example, if an Application object has been associated with a container one level above a user's immediate parent container, the user's immediate parent container's Inherit Container Applications property would need to be modified to a setting of 2 before the application would be distributed to any user in that container. Optionally, you could make the setting at the User object level to control this for just a specific user.

**TIP** Users will not see NAL-delivered applications associated with parent containers unless this is set correctly! This is a good troubleshooting tip to remember.

You need to be careful with this inheritance. Even though you could associate Application objects at the highest container in the tree (for example, O=) and let these flow down to all users by having NAL search up to the [Root], this could cause additional traffic on your LAN/WAN, depending on your partitioning and replica placement.

## NDS Design Considerations

As with any other NDS object resource in the tree, you should try to place Application objects close to the users who will be accessing them. Ideally, these Application objects should be within the same NDS partition as the user. It is not recommended to have users access Application objects in remote NDS partitions (that is, partitions across WAN links) for performance and accessibility reasons.

Application objects have a Schedule property so you can control when users are delivered applications. This is useful in the scenario where you want to distribute a large service pack to all users. You probably would not want this to occur at 8:00 a.m., when all users may log in. Additionally, you may not want this distribution to occur on weekends, when no technical support people are on-site. In this scenario, you could make the Application object available Monday through Friday at 8:00 a.m. To avoid all users downloading the service pack at 8:00 a.m. when they log in, you could set the Spread from Start Time option to 120 minutes. The application then becomes available on a random basis between the hours of 8:00 a.m. to 10:00 a.m. Refer to context-sensitive help for more information on an Application object's Schedule property.

## Application Object Properties

Let's take a look at other Application object properties, remembering to use the context-sensitive help for additional information. This section is intended to give you a description of each property and some possible implementation ideas. However, it's important to understand your application and test the application in a lab environment before you distribute it. Even if this testing process were to take three to five days, think of the time you'll save not having to visit hundreds or thousands of desktops.

### IDENTIFICATION PROPERTY PAGE
**Application Icon Title** (mandatory property). This text appears as the caption beneath the NAL-delivered application. The default is the name you used when you

created the Application object; however, this can be changed and can be different from the name of the Application object in the tree.

**Path to Executable File.** This points to where an application's executable file is located. This can be edited if you later move the application to another location. This option distributes any Registry or INI changes, if necessary, the *first time* the user launches this application before launching the executable file. Successive launches of this application simply launch the executable file.

**Install Only** (mutually exclusive with Path to Executable File). This option is used for updating or installing applications, service packs, and other items on a workstation.

**Prompt User for Reboot.** This option allows you to control if and when a workstation reboot should occur after an application has been installed.

**Run Once.** This option is useful when you are distributing a service pack that only needs to be installed once. The Application object disappears from the NAL or NAL Explorer Window after it has been run once. In this scenario, you might also consider setting up this service pack Application object as a force run so that it runs once without user intervention.

**Distribute Always.** This forces a distribution, along with any Registry or INI settings, every time a user launches the application (versus how the distribution works with the Path to Executable File property). Distribute Always is useful when you want to ensure certain Registry or INI settings are present or updated every time an application is run, not just the first time.

**Change Icon.** A default NAL icon is used unless one is selected here.

**Version Stamp.** This is a tool to assist with upgrading applications. This stamps the workstation with a text string (in the Registry) that represents the version of the application (although this text string may or may not have anything to do with the actual version of the product). As an example, you could type in a string to coincide with the first distribution of this application. Then if you later change some property of the Application object, you could enter a different string, and these new property changes will become effective the next time the user launches the application. This process would not need to be used if the application was set up as Distribute Always. You would change the version stamp if you wanted to do any of the following:

◆ Have the distribution retriggered

◆ Have a Run Once application reappear/run

◆ Retrigger a scheduled application during the current scheduled period

**GUID** (Globally Unique Identification). This is how NAL tracks information about Application objects and is displayed for informational purposes only.

## ENVIRONMENT PROPERTY PAGE

**Command Line Parameters.** For special start-up switches for the application's executable file.

**Working Directory.** Path to the application's working directory. This will be the default directory when users save within the NAL-delivered application.

**Run.** The options for this are Normal (Default), Minimize application when run, or Maximize application when run.

**Windows NT 16-bit Windows on Windows "WoW" Support.** Only applies to Windows NT:

◆ **Shared** (Default) – Runs the Windows 16-bit application in a shared (unprotected) 16-bit virtual DOS machine (VDM). If this application crashes, all 16-bit applications sharing this space will also crash. This option allows 16-bit applications to communicate with each other.

◆ **Separate** – Runs the Windows 16-bit application in its own protected 16-bit VDM. If this application crashes, it will not affect any other application. 16-bit applications cannot communicate with each other.

**Enable Error Logging to File.** The path to a file where any errors are logged if an application fails to launch or install. No status is tracked here except for errors (although this will be enhanced in the future). Users need file system rights to write to this file in order for it to work. This log file records the time, date, workstation, user, and error text.

**Clean Up Network Resources.** When left at the default (On), NAL cleans up resources allocated, such as drives mapped, printer ports captured, and connections made to file systems for accessing the application. In essence, NAL is cleaning up licensed connections.

**Monitor Module Name.** This option is effective when Clean Up Network Resources is on. Some applications, like WordPerfect, are actually wrappers – for example, WPWIN.EXE runs WPWIN7.EXE and then terminates, while WPWIN7.EXE continues to execute. In this case, NAL would be monitoring WPWIN.EXE and would quit monitoring it before the application is really done. Monitor Module Name allows the network administrator to type the name of the actual executable file that is going to run (WPWIN7.EXE in this case), and NAL can then monitor it for termination. Knowing your application (as mentioned earlier) is important here. Generally speaking, the condition Monitor Module Name addresses is this: The application runs fine outside of NAL but generates errors when run within NAL.

## DRIVES/PORTS PROPERTY PAGE

Any drive mappings or printer ports captured here are set when a user launches the application and are automatically cleaned up when a user exits the application, assuming the Clean Up Network Resources option (discussed previously) is on. This is useful for eliminating unnecessary licensed connections versus a licensed connection always being used if these commands are set within a NetWare login script. You could potentially eliminate all application drive mappings and printer port captures within a login script if you are using all NAL-delivered applications!

## DESCRIPTION PROPERTY PAGE

This gives users more detailed information on the application other than what they see as the caption (from the Application Icon Title property mentioned previously). Users would right-click on the NAL-delivered application and then select Properties to view this description.

## FAULT TOLERANCE PROPERTY PAGE

**Enable Load Balancing.** You can enable this feature for a site that has several applications servers. You set up separate Application objects for the applications that reside on these different servers. NAL then uses a random number to distribute the load among the applications on these servers; NAL does not distribute the load based upon server CPU utilization. You would probably design load balancing for servers on the same side of WAN links. Load balancing assumes fault tolerance. Remember, you currently have to assign file system rights to the applications on these different servers.

    **Enable Fault Tolerance.** There are design considerations here. If your client has its primary NDS connection on one of the servers to which the Application object is pointing and that server crashes, you will get error messages when you try to relaunch another Application object on a different server in the Fault Tolerant List. (This is actually a client software issue, as opposed to a NAL issue.) So when designing this feature, your Application objects in the Fault Tolerant List should not be on the server where you have your primary NDS connection *if* you want fault tolerance to protect you from a server crash. It will still work if something happens to the application but the server still remains up. If you have more than two Application objects in the Fault Tolerant List, NAL simply selects the next object by going down the list in order. Fault Tolerant servers might be positioned across WAN links. Remember, you currently have to assign file system rights to the applications on these different servers.

## SCRIPTS PROPERTY PAGE

Both prelaunch application and post-termination application scripts are available. The commands used here are the same as the ones used in NetWare login scripts. However, you should view context-sensitive Help for the login script commands not supported. All login script variables will work. Any drive mappings or printer ports captured here are *not* cleaned up, even if Clean Up Network Resources is turned on.

## CONTACTS PROPERTY PAGE

Users can access this page to see who to contact if they are having a problem with their application. They do this by right-clicking the NAL-delivered application, and then selecting Properties to view the Contact person, Phone Number, and E-mail

Address (assuming these properties are set on the contact user's NDS object and that users have been assigned the read object right to view these NDS properties).

## ASSOCIATIONS PROPERTY PAGE

As discussed earlier, this controls which containers, groups, or users receive the application. If the bottom level of your tree is set up based on functional areas (Accounting, Sales, and so on), container-based application distribution becomes a very powerful feature. You could associate an Accounting application to the Accounting container. As a result, any new users hired (and therefore added) to the Accounting container would *automatically* receive the Accounting software distribution!

## SCHEDULE PROPERTY PAGE

An example for use of this property was discussed earlier. Refer to the context-sensitive help for additional examples.

## SYSTEM REQUIREMENTS PROPERTY PAGE

This page controls the operating system on which the NAL-delivered application appears (i.e., Windows 3.x, Windows 95, and Windows NT) and effectively replaced the need for the three separate Application objects in earlier versions of NAL. This property can also control application delivery based upon type of processor, amount of physical RAM (on Windows 95 and Windows NT), and free disk space. This is a good Property Page to check out for troubleshooting purposes if a NAL-delivered application does not appear on a certain workstation.

# Managing NT Workstation Objects in NDS

For some network administrators, managing the Windows NT Workstations is a primary concern and can be quite time consuming. A user who needs to access his or her NT Workstation and a NetWare network must have access to two separate user accounts. Therefore, Novell's Workstation Manager product was created to provide central administration to both the NetWare and NT Workstation accounts. This product is well suited for accounts running Windows NT at the desktop with NetWare servers.

The Workstation Manager product eliminates the need for an NT domain because you can store workstation information (profiles and policies) in NDS. Users then only need to remember their NDS username and password. The Workstation Manager grants the appropriate access to any properly configured NT Workstation. Once attached to the network, a user's unique profiles and policies can be downloaded to provide a consistent desktop, regardless of the workstation being used.

As mentioned in the Workstation Manager installation discussion in the previous chapter, the product consists of two components: the Novell-created Graphical Identification and Authentication module for Windows NT (NWGINA) and the snap-in DLL for the NetWare Administrator. The installation renames Microsoft's NWGINA module and replaces it with the NWGINA module from Novell.

The NWGINA module provides the login prompt for the user, collects the user's username and password, and performs the authentication to NDS and the NT Workstation. NWGINA runs on the workstation with administrative privileges. This level of access allows NWGINA to dynamically create and delete NT user accounts.

The snap-in DLL provides the necessary functionality to the NetWare Administrator so that a supervisor can create NT Workstation objects within NDS. As shown in Figure 11-17, you can create a Workstation object preconfigured for the engineering workstation. After installing the Workstation Manager product, you simply highlight a container in the tree, select Object, Create in the pull-down menu, and then select the NT Workstation object found in the list.

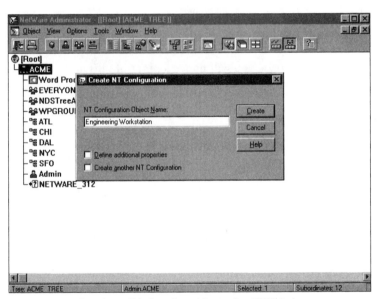

Figure 11-17: Creating a Workstation object using NWAdmin

Once the object is created, you can view it in your NDS tree. As shown in Figure 11-18, we created the Engineering Workstation object and then selected Details on that object.

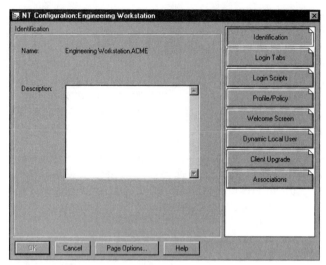

Figure 11-18: A view of the Details screen for the Engineering
Workstation object

Once you are in the Details screen, you will notice a series of tabs at the right. In this section we discuss each of the available tabs.

## Creating Associations

The next step is to select Associations and to associate NDS users, groups, or containers with the NT Workstation object in NDS. By creating this association you are granting access to those users for that NT Workstation object. You have the option to select a single user to be associated with the Workstation object or multiple users. As shown in Figure 11-19, you can associate a user, group, and container with the newly created Engineering Workstation object. In this example, the user and users in the group and container selected can log in using this NT Workstation object.

After you have associated a user with an NT Workstation object in NDS, NWGINA can obtain user information from the Workstation object to create an NT Workstation account at the workstation.

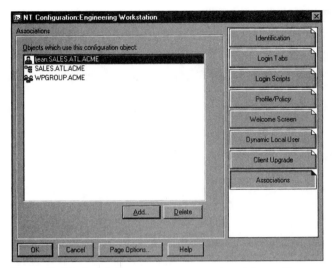

Figure 11-19: Associating a user, group, and container with an NT Workstation object

# Configuring Dynamic Local Users

The next step is to select the Dynamic Local User tab in the Details screen. This important page defines the specifics of this NT Workstation user. The first selection, Enable Dynamic Local User, tells NWGINA whether it needs to create the local user at all. Selecting this option causes NWGINA to retrieve the NT username from the Workstation object and queries the local Security Access Manager (SAM) to see if the username already exists. If it does exist, NWGINA authenticates the user to the NT Workstation. If the username does not exist, the local user is created in the local Security Access Manager (SAM) database. Not selecting the option causes NWGINA to attempt to find an existing NT user with the credentials (username and password) indicated in the Windows NT tab of the login screen.

# Volatile User Accounts

In the same Dynamic Local User screen you should also notice a selection for a volatile user account. A user at the local workstation can be either volatile or non-volatile. A nonvolatile user is created and remains in the local SAM after the user logs out of the workstation. This type of user can log in again and again because this user remains defined in the local SAM.

## Consulting Experience

The first issue to resolve as an administrator is the dual administration and login for user accounts. Your goal should be to synchronize the login for the NT desktop and the intraNetWare network with a single username and password. For an existing user with the same name on both systems, let the client software automatically change the NT desktop password to match the one on the network. For a new user, create the new user account in NDS, and when the user enters the login username and password for NDS, the Workstation Manager software generates a new user account on the NT Workstation. This is provided by default through an associated NT Configuration object on the Dynamic Local User page and Enable Dynamic Local User check box. No travel to the NT Workstations to set up user accounts is needed. No NT domains are needed. The net result is two systems, one login.

A volatile user does not remain in the local SAM. Upon logging out of the workstation, the volatile user account is deleted by NWGINA. Employing volatile accounts prevents a large number of user accounts from accumulating at the workstation. With this configuration, users cannot gain access to the workstation without first going through NDS.

The next option on this screen is Use NetWare Credentials. When the box for this option is checked, NWGINA queries the user's NDS user account for the login name, full name, and description. The password for the NT user account is the same as the NDS account. If the check box is not selected, other credentials must be specified in the fields below the check box. You must enter the username in the NT Username field. The Full Name and Description can also be included to provide complete user descriptions.

The last selection on the Dynamic Local User page is to specify whether this Workstation object will be a member of any NT-defined groups. By default, the Workstation object is a member of the User and Administrator groups. You can specify additional group types by using the Add button at the bottom of the screen. An example of this is shown in Figure 11-20.

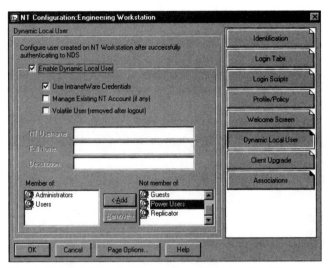

Figure 11–20: Adding the Workstation object to other NT groups
in NWAdmin

# Defining Profiles and Policies

Windows NT user profiles are the desktop settings automatically created and maintained on the local PC. They allow multiple users sharing a single computer to customize their desktops and have those custom settings loaded during login. Conversely, a single user can move between computers using the same profile if the administrator stores that profile in NDS. Once the roaming user attaches to the network, the profile is retrieved and the user is presented with the normal settings for his or her desktop. This enables you to customize the user's profiles and policies to provide a consistent desktop environment regardless of physical location or workstation being used.

Using the Profile/Policy page of an NT Configuration object, you can implement NT user profiles and system policies centrally and en masse. All users load the user profiles and system policies from the NT Configuration object with which they are associated. To use these options, select the Enable Roaming Profile and Enable Policy check boxes on this page and specify the exact directories in which the appropriate user profile and policies reside. Each user associated with the NT Configuration object will use this profile and policy during login.

Using NT system policies, you can control what users can do on their desktop. For example, you can restrict certain options in the Control Panel and prohibit access to account information such as passwords, rights, auditing, and trust relationships. You can customize parts of the desktop and configure network settings. Like the user profiles, when the NT system policies for each user is held in an associated NT Configuration object, the local values currently set in the registry of the workstation are overwritten upon user login.

## Using Login Tabs

The NWGINA module included with this product provides flexibility for your users when logging into NDS and the NT Workstation. As shown in Figure 11-21, the NWGINA login utility has multiple tabs to display different login and configuration options. As an administrator, you can define and centrally control which tabs are displayed on the NT Workstation.

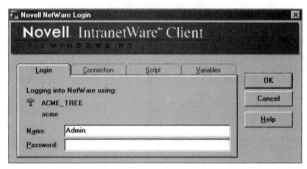

Figure 11-21: An example of the NWGINA utility with multiple tabs enabled

To enable or disable the tabs, simply go to the Login Tabs screen in Details for the selected NT Workstation object and select or deselect the desired tabs. An example of this process is shown in Figure 11-22.

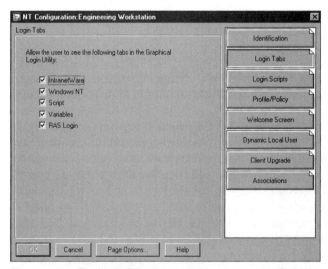

Figure 11-22: The Login Tabs screen enables you to specify which tabs the user sees while logging in at the NT Workstation.

# Using Login Scripts

The GUI login can also be configured to control login script processing. You can manage the execution of login scripts by selecting the Login Scripts page in Details for the Workstation object you have selected. You control login script processing by selecting the Enable Login Scripts option at the top of the screen. By default, you'll notice that when a script executes, the script is shown in an open window. When completed (without errors), the window is automatically closed. You can control the viewing of the script through the Open Script Window and Automatically Close Script Window options.

Through the use of this page you can also specify whether a user is able to execute alternate user and profile login scripts instead of those defined in the NDS User object. The Alt.Login Script and the Alt.Profile Script options define alternative scripts.

This page also allows you to define custom login script variables to meet a particular need in your scripting. You have the ability to define values for variables %2, %3, %4, and %5.

# The NWGINA Welcome Screen

As a network administrator, you can modify the Welcome screen that all your NDS managed NT users see when they log in to their workstation. Because you are using the NWGINA module from Novell, you have the ability to add your own bitmapped image to this login screen. Select the Welcome Screen tab. In the area next to Title Message, you can add text that you want displayed at initial login to the workstation. Under the section Bitmap to Display, you can change the current bitmap or delete and replace it with one of your own.

# Client Upgrades

The last option we discuss in this section is the client upgrade, or what is known as the Automatic Client Upgrade (ACU), which is performed during the login process. This feature pushes the NetWare (intraNetWare) client to the workstation from a central location.

Because the NT Workstation is a secure system, the ACU can only work when an administrator-level user is authenticating to the workstation. The Workstation Manager can create this temporary administrator user at login and then cause the client upgrade to take place. Rather than creating a dynamic user, NWGINA creates a temporary administrative user with administrator access and logs into the workstation. After the login, the login script for the ACU is run, the client upgrade is performed, and a workstation reboot is performed. NWGINA then logs out and deletes the administrative user.

The Workstation object is instructed to upgrade the workstation with the latest client software when the next administrator-level user logs into the workstation. Use the following steps to perform this operation:

1. Create a login script that performs the ACU you want placed on the network.

2. Enable the NT Workstation object to perform a client upgrade by selecting the Enable Automatic Upgrade check box. You specify the ACU login script to run as the Alternate Login Script Location.

By using the NetWare Client for Windows NT and the Workstation Manager, you have flexibility and control over your Windows NT desktops. You gain a single point of administration for NT Workstation accounts and NDS user accounts. You also have the ability to centrally configure and control user desktops using profiles and policies.

NDS for NT provides management of NT domains within NDS. The Novell Application Launcher delivers applications to the user's desktop via NDS and can easily update applications as well. The Workstation Manager allows you to manage NT Workstations via NDS without the need for NT domains.

With these three products you have a comprehensive solution for managing your mixed NetWare and NT environments.

# Index

## A

abort partition operation, 139-140
access methods
    bindery services establishment, 225-232
    client software for network connections,
      218-225
    design rules, 218
    mobile user access, 245-252
    user environment setup with login scripts,
      232-245
    using NetWare Application Launcher,
      252-255
    *See also* user access
ACU (Automatic Client Upgrade), 394-395
add replica operation, 180
additive licensing, 224
ADMIN password, 204
ADMIN user, security issues, 204-205
administering the network. *See* network
    administration
administration utilities, 332-333, 341-343. *See
    also specific utilities*
administrative objects
    in centralized management approach, 91-92
    in combined approach, 94-95
    in decentralized management approach,
      92-94
Advanced Design rules, 22, 362
AFP Server objects, 212
Alias objects, 209, 249-250
Application objects
    associating with containers, 381-382
    creating samples, 352
    NDS design considerations, 382
    properties, 382-386
applications
    bindery calls made by, 105
    complex distribution, 377-380
    distributing using NAL, 255, 375-380
    inheriting, 380-382
    push vs. pull distribution, 375
    simple distribution, 375-377
    supplying using NAL, 252-254
    *See also* bindery services; Novell
      Application Launcher (NAL)

Associations property page for Application
    objects, 386
authenticated client software connection state,
    223
authenticating users, 372-373
Automatic Client Upgrade (ACU), 394-395

## B

BACKEND.DLL, 354
backslash (\) as reserved character, 194
backup domain controllers (BDCs), 374
banks, NDS tree design for, 75-77
BDCs (backup domain controllers), 374
bindery objects, 206, 226, 227-230
bindery path. *See* server bindery context
Bindery Queue objects, 212
bindery services
    applications making bindery calls, 105
    bindery emulation services, 36
    bindery-based login scripts, 233-235
    dynamic bindery objects, 228-230
    enabling, 102-103, 105
    establishing, 225-232
    multiple bindery contexts, 226
    NDS connection vs. bindery services
      connection, 224-226
    as NDS tree design criterion, 102-105
    planning, 157
    replication and, 102, 104, 157-160, 167
    server bindery context, 157-160, 225
    static bindery objects, 227-228
    Supervisor account, 231-232
blueprint for NetWare 4 rollout, 19
booting time servers, 300, 325
bottom level NDS tree design, 83-108
    bindery services and, 102-105
    creating common resource containers,
      88-90
    creating containers, 85-86
    design criteria, 90-108
    determining depth of the tree, 86-87
    login scripts and, 100-102
    network administration and, 91-95
    organization chart for, 30-31, 33

*(continued)*

bottom level NDS tree design *(continued)*
overview, 33-35
partitioning, 120-121
partitions and replicas and, 105-108
placing network resources, 96-100
placing NT users, 100
representing company organizational units, 83-85
broadcasts, 42, 43
buildings, representation in NDS tree, 59-61

## C

C=Country object, 45-47, 201, 212-213
campus networks, 59
building representation in NDS tree, 59-61
design guidelines, 66
function designation in NDS tree, 61-62
geographic containers with high-speed links, 62
in hub and spoke network infrastructure, 68-70
maps for NDS tree design, 26-27, 28, 31
NDS tree design for, 59-66
as network infrastructure, 50-51
network infrastructure representation in NDS tree, 63-64
O=Organization object, 66
[ROOT] object name, 66
student representation in NDS tree, 64-65, 89-90
centralized management, 91-92
change replica type operation, 182-183
child (subordinate) partitions, 126-130, 169-171
cities, OU=Organization Units for, 70-72
Client 32, 220-221, 253
Client for Windows NT, 221-223
client software, 218-225
connection states, 223-224
DOS/Windows Requester, 219-220
NDS vs. bindery services connections, 224-226
NetWare Client 32, 220-221
Novell Client for Windows NT, 221-223
client upgrades, 394-395
comma (,) as reserved character, 194
CommExec object, 213
commonly used objects, 202, 206-212
complex distribution, 377-380

computer objects, 213
CONFIG command, 159
configured lists communication, 290-293
requirements, 262
SET TIMESYNC Configured Sources command, 310-311
TIMESYNC.CFG file examples, 292-296
connected but no identity established state, 223
connection states for client software, 223-224
Contacts property page for Application objects, 385-386
containers
associating Application objects with, 381-382
for banks and similar companies, 75-77
container administrators, 92-95
creating at bottom of tree, 85-86
creating common resource containers, 88-90
geographic containers with high speed links, 62
group objects in, 208
login scripts, 100-101, 236-237
maximum subordinate containers, 77-78
moving, 138-139
network resource organization using, 200-201
for partitioning, 105
peer-level containers in same partition, 118-119
regional containers to distribute physical locations, 73-74
regional containers to distribute remote or branch offices, 74-75
types of, 201
for university students, 64-65, 89-90
*See also* OU=Organization Units
Country object, 45-47, 201, 212-213
create partition operation, 135-136

## D

daylight savings time settings, 319-321
debugging time synchronization, 305-307
decentralized management, 92-94
dedicated NDS replica servers, 153
deleting
replicas, 181
time sources, 313
timestamps and, 268
departments, in LAN-only network, 56-58, 69

depth of NDS tree
   centralized vs. decentralized administration
     and, 95
   determining, 86-87
Description property page for Application
   objects, 385
design criteria, 90-108
   bindery services, 102-105
   login scripts, 100-102
   network administration, 91-95
   partitions and replicas, 105-108
   placing network resources, 96-100
   placing NT users, 100
design guidelines
   for campus networks, 66
   for LAN infrastructure, 59
   for MAN infrastructure, 66
   for naming standard, 192, 196-198
   for NT domain, 24
   for subadministrator access, 94
   *See also* design rules
design objectives. *See* objectives of NDS tree
   design
design principles, 11
design rules
   for access methods, 218
   for containers at the bottom of the tree, 86
   maximum subordinate containers, 77-78
   for NDS for NT, 367
   for NDS objects, 23, 189
   for NDS tree design, 20-21, 360
   for partitions, 21-22, 111, 360, 361-362
   for replicas, 21-22, 144, 361-362
   time synchronization configuration, 23-24
   for top level NDS tree design, 40-41
   *See also* design guidelines
designing NDS for NT, 360-367
   Advanced Design options, 362
   design rules, 367
   NDS partition guidelines, 360, 361-362
   NDS replica guidelines, 361-362
   NDS tree design, 362-367
   NDS tree guidelines, 360
   Quick Design options, 361
designing partitions
   administration, 121
   characteristics or rules of NDS partitions,
     117-119

minimizing partition size, 125
minimizing replicas, 121
minimizing [ROOT] partition size, 126
naming partitions, 118
NDS partitions vs. file system partitions,
   128
network infrastructure as basis, 105-106,
   115-117
not spanning WAN links or physical
   locations, 123
overlapping and, 119
partitioning around local servers in each
   geographic area, 124
partitioning bottom layers of tree, 120-121
partitioning top layers of tree, 119-120
partitions as subtrees, 119
peer-level containers in same partition, 118
pyramid-shaped design, 122
[ROOT] partition, 112-115, 126
subordinate partitions, 126-130
Device objects, 213
Directory Map objects, 99, 208
disabling logins, 168
DISPLAY SERVERS command, 44
distributing software
   complex distribution, 377-380
   push vs. pull distribution, 375
   simple distribution, 375-377
   using NAL, 255, 375-380
divisions, in LAN-only network, 56-57
documentation
   campus network maps, 26-27, 28, 54
   naming standards document, 195-200
   network resources list, 29-30, 97
   organizational chart, 30-31
   Partition and Replica Matrix, 141, 162
   sites (locations) list, 27-29
   WAN diagrams, 26, 27, 54
domain controllers, 374
Domain object for NT. *See* NT Domain object
Domain Object Snap-In, 332
Domain Object Wizard, 4, 332, 337, 362-363
DOS Requester, 219-220
Drives/Ports property page for Application
   objects, 384-385
DSMERGE utility, 45
DS.NLM version, 304

DSREPAIR
    aborting partition operations, 140
    checking partition status, 178-179
    checking replica status, 133, 137
    Receive Updates operation using, 184-185
    Send Updates operation using, 183-184
    viewing replica synchronized up to values,
       174
DSTRACE, 134-135, 176, 179
dynamic bindery objects, 228-230
dynamic local users, 389

**E**

e-mail post office server, 97
Environment property page for Application
    objects, 384
equal sign (=) as reserved character, 194
event ID, timestamp component, 267
Exchange. *See* Mail Box Manager for Exchange;
    Microsoft Exchange
Exchange ADMIN, 2
execution order for login scripts, 210, 233, 234
extending NDS schema. *See* NDS schema
    extensions
External Entity objects, 214

**F**

fast synchronization, 173
fault tolerance, 107, 144-146, 278, 385
file servers
    naming, 98
    placing in NDS tree, 98, 152
    Volume object, 205-206
file system rights, 349
filtering broadcasts, 43
flat tree design, 32-33
flexibility in NDS tree design, 20, 33, 34-35
forcing replica synchronization, 175-176

**G**

global login scripts, 210-211
group objects, 207-208
guidelines. *See* design guidelines; design rules

**H**

heartbeat for replica synchronization, 176

hub and spoke network infrastructure, 51-52
    institutions with many remote or branch
       offices, 75-77
    maximum subordinate containers, 77-78
    NDS tree design for, 66-78
    regional containers to distribute physical
       locations, 73-74
    regional containers to distribute remote or
       branch offices, 74-75
    top of tree based on hubs and campus
       spokes, 68-70
    top of tree based on hubs and city spokes,
       70-72
    top of tree based on hubs only, 66-68

**I**

Identification property page for Application
    objects, 382-383
IGRATE.EXE, 357
IMPORT.EXE, 353, 355
infrastructure. *See* network infrastructure
Inherit Container Applications property, 381-382
inheriting applications, 380-382
installing NDS for NT, 331-358
    adding NT domain to NDS, 337
    administration utilities, 332-333, 341-343
    core components, 332
    finding duplicate NT and NDS users, 338-339
    installation files, 334
    log file, 339, 340
    Mail Box Manager for Exchange
       installation, 352-355
    NAL installation, 346-352
    Novell Administrator for Windows NT
       installation, 356-358
    Novell Workstation Manager configuration,
       343-345
    requirements, 334
    running WINSETUP.EXE, 334-340
INSTALL.NLM, 232
intraNetWare Client for Windows NT, 6, 8-10,
    332, 373

**L**

L=Locality objects, 201, 213
LANs. *See* local area network (LAN)
    infrastructure
layers in NDS tree, 44, 86-87

leaf objects, 210
  commonly used objects, 202, 206-212
  less commonly used objects, 202, 212-215
  placing physical network resources in NDS,
    202-215
  required objects, 202, 203-206
  types of, 202
  for user access, 201-202
less commonly used objects, 202, 212-215
licensed client software connection state, 223
List objects, 214
local area network (LAN) infrastructure, 50, 56
  design guidelines, 59
  NDS tree design for, 56-59
  network resources, 56-58
  O=Organization object name, 59
  [ROOT] object name, 59
  time synchronization option, 260
local replication, 146-151
locality objects, 201, 213
location login scripts, 211
locations. See sites
locking partitions, 131, 165
log file for NDS for NT installation, 339, 340
login process
  disabling logins, 168
  NDS for NT advantages, 3
  single login, 3, 12, 221, 372
  user object properties updated, 169
login scripts, 232-245
  bindery-based login scripts, 233-235
  container scripts, 100-101, 236-237
  default, 245
  Directory Map objects and, 208
  global scripts, 210-211
  GUI login, 393
  location scripts, 211
  minimizing need for, 254
  for mobile users, 251-252
  NDS login scripts, 235-236
  NDS tree design and, 36, 100-102
  NetWare GUI Login utility, 253
  order of execution, 210, 233, 234
  profile scripts, 101-102, 210-211, 239-245
  special function scripts, 211
  user environment setup using, 232-245
  user scripts, 102, 243-244

Windows 3.1 and script execution, 233
  See also profile login scripts
logout process, 169

**M**

M (master) replica, 131, 164-165, 166
Mail Box Manager for Exchange, 6, 11, 333, 352
  components, 353
  installing, 352-355
  requirements, 354
managing NDS for NT, 368-374
  associating users with NT domain, 368
  creating NT users in NDS, 369-372
  password synchronization, 373-374
  user authentication and single login,
    372-373
  Windows NT domain controllers, 374
managing NDS users, 374-386
  complex distribution, 377-380
  container associations, 381-382
  inheriting applications, 380-382
  NDS design considerations, 382
  simple distribution, 375-377
  User object management with NAL, 375-380
managing NT Workstation objects. See Novell
    Workstation Manager
managing partitions. See partition operations
managing replicas. See replica operations
managing time synchronization. See SET
    TIMESYNC commands; time
    synchronization
MANs. See metropolitan area network (MAN)
    infrastructure
master (M) replica, 131, 164-165, 166
maximum layers in NDS tree, 87
maximum replicas per partition, 107, 121,
    151-152
maximum replicas per server, 152-153
maximum subordinate containers, 77-78
maximum subordinate partitions, 126-130
merge partition operation, 133, 136-138
merging NDS trees, naming standard and, 193
meshed network infrastructure, 52-53, 78-82
Message Routing Group objects, 214
Messaging Server objects, 214
metropolitan area network (MAN)
    infrastructure, 50-51, 59

(continued)

metropolitan area network (MAN) infrastructure
*(continued)*
building representation in NDS tree, 59-61
design guidelines, 66
function designation in NDS tree, 61-62
geographic containers with high speed
links, 62
NDS tree design for, 59-66
network infrastructure representation in
NDS tree, 63-64
O=Organization object, 66
[ROOT] object name, 66
*See also* campus networks
Microsoft Exchange, 2. *See also* Mail Box
Manager for Exchange
MIGRATE.EXE, 232
mobile user access, 245-252
design approach, 246
login scripts, 251-252
NDS name context, 247-251
remote users vs. mobile users, 246-247
types of access required, 245, 246-247
move subtree partition operation, 138-139
moving
containers and contents, 138-139
subtrees, 138-139, 209
multiple bindery contexts, 226
multiple NDS trees, 44
multiple O=Organization objects, 48-49
multiple reference servers, 280, 298-299
multiple time provider groups, 288-289

**N**

NAL. *See* Novell Application Launcher (NAL)
NAL Explorer, 7, 348, 375-376
NAL Snap-In, 333, 347-348
NAL snAppShot, 7, 348, 377-380
NAL Window, 7, 348, 375-376
NAL.EXE. *See* NAL Window
NALEXPLD.EXE. *See* NAL Explorer
name context for mobile users, 247-251
changing manually, 248-249
setting in workstation configuration file,
250-251
using alias objects to set, 249-250
name resolution, 160-162
naming
file servers, 98

multiple NDS trees, 44
NDS objects naming standard, 190-200
NDS tree ([ROOT] object), 41-45, 66, 69
O=Organization object, 47-49
partitions, 118
printers and print queues, 98
renaming NDS tree, 45
naming standard, 190-200
document production, 195-200
example guidelines, 192, 196-198
goals, 191-195
reserved characters, 193-195
using, 190
navigation, naming standard and, 191-192
NCP (NetWare Core Protocol) server object, 205
NDS browsing, naming standard and, 191-192
NDS for NT, 3-6, 331-332
advantages of, 2-3, 11-13
bundled administration utilities, 332-333
core components, 332
design objectives, 11-20
design principles, 11
designing, 360-367
installing, 331-358
managing, 368-374
need for, 1-2
other NT integration products, 6-11
requirements, 334
*See also* designing NDS for NT; installing
NDS for NT; managing NDS for NT
NDS inactivity synchronization interval, 176
NDS Manager, 130-132, 333
aborting partition operations, 139-140
adding replicas, 180
changing replica type, 182-183
checking replica status, 133
creating new partitions, 135-136
Domain object partitioning, 365
merging partitions, 133, 136-138
moving subtrees, 138-139
NetWare 4 support pack version, 365
rebuilding replica information, 183-185
removing replicas, 181
NDS objects, 189
commonly used objects, 202, 206-212
design rules, 23, 189
less commonly used objects, 202, 212-215
naming standard, 190-200

network resource organization using
    container objects, 200-201
placing physical network resources using
    leaf objects, 202-215
required objects, 202, 203-206
unique names, 193
user access using leaf objects, 201-202
*See also* containers; O=Organization objects;
    OU=Organization Units
NDS rights, NAL requirements, 349
NDS schema extensions
    Mail Box Manager, 353
    NAL, 352
    NDS for NT, 337
NDS tree design
    basing on network infrastructure, 20-21
    benefits of good design, 11-13
    bottom level design, 33-35, 83-108
    depth of the tree, 86-87
    design rules, 20-21, 360
    essential steps, 20-24
    gathering corporate documents, 26-31
    maximum layers, 87
    maximum subordinate containers, 77-78
    modifying for organization's needs, 35-36
    for NDS for NT, 362-367
    NT domain guidelines, 24
    NT Domain object placement, 364-366
    objectives, 11-20
    pyramid design, 31-33
    tasks, 25-36
    top level design, 31-33, 34, 39-82
    *See also* bottom level NDS tree design;
        design rules; top level NDS tree design
NDS users, managing. *See* managing NDS users
NETADMIN, 235-236, 240
NET.CFG file, 45, 250-251
NetWare 2
    bindery emulation services, 36
    bindery login scripts, 233
NetWare 3
    bindery emulation services, 36
    bindery login scripts, 233
    migrating servers to NetWare 4, 232
NetWare 4
    blueprint for rollout, 19
    support pack, 365
    time synchronization features, 303

NetWare 4 servers
    additive licensing, 224
    connection states, 223-224
    dedicated NDS replica servers, 153
    disabling logins, 168
    e-mail post office server, 97
    file servers, 98, 152
    finding NDS tree, 43
    locating, 42-43
    maximum replicas per server, 152-153
    migrating from NetWare 3, 232
    naming standard for, 199
    NetWare Core Protocol (NCP) server object,
        205
    partitioning around local servers, 124
    Replica Servers, 362
    replica synchronization cycle, 176-177
    replicas for remote offices with one server,
        149-150
    replicas for remote offices with two servers,
        150-151
    time servers, 269-281
    viewing time periodically, 304-305
    Volume objects, 205-206
NetWare Administrator utility. *See* NWADMIN
NetWare Client 32, 220-221, 253
NetWare Core Protocol (NCP) server object, 205
NetWare GUI Login utility, 253
network administration
    centralized management approach, 91-92
    combining centralized and decentralized
        management, 94-95
    decentralized management approach, 92-94
    naming standard and, 192-193
    NDS tree design and, 35, 91-95
    subadministrator access guidelines, 94
network infrastructure
    designing NDS for, 55-82
    determining, 49-53
    first level of OU=Organization Units and,
        53-55
    partitioning based on, 105-106, 115-117
    *See also* campus networks; local area
        network (LAN) infrastructure;
        metropolitan area network (MAN)
        infrastructure; wide area networks
        (WANs)

network resources
  creating common resource containers, 88-90
  LAN-only networks, 56-58
  list for NDS tree design, 29-30, 97
  organizing, 13-19, 200-201
  placing in NDS tree, 96-100
  placing using leaf objects, 202-215
NETX.EXE shell, 219
Novell Administrator for Windows NT, 6, 10, 333
  compatibility issues, 358
  installing, 341-343, 356-358
  integrating and synchronizing users, 357
  prerequisites, 341
  requirements, 356-357
Novell Application Launcher (NAL), 6-8,
    252-255, 332-333
  administrator components, 346-348
  components, 7-8
  creating sample application objects, 352
  directory structure for files, 350-351
  extending NDS schema, 352
  features, 253
  inheriting applications, 380-382
  installing, 346-352
  managing User objects, 375-380
  minimizing need for login scripts, 254
  NAL Explorer, 7, 348, 376
  NAL Snap-In, 333, 347-348
  NAL snAppShot, 7, 348, 377-380
  NAL Window, 7, 348, 376
  readme file, 352
  rights requirements, 349
  setting up applications, 254
  software distribution using, 255, 375-380
  supplying network applications using,
    252-254
  system requirements, 346
  user components, 348
Novell Client for Windows NT, 221-223
Novell Directory Service for NT. See NDS for NT
Novell Web site, 253
Novell Workstation Manager, 9-10, 333, 386-388
  client upgrades, 394-395
  components, 343-344, 387
  configuring dynamic local users, 389
  creating associations, 388-389
  defining profiles and policies, 391

  enabling NT Workstation Manager settings,
    345
  enabling NWADMIN snap-in settings, 345
  installing, 341-343, 344-345
  login scripts, 393
  login tabs, 392
  prerequisites, 341
  volatile user accounts, 389-391
NT Domain object, 4-5, 206
  adding during NDS for NT installation, 337
  container contents, 363
  creation, 362-363
  design characteristics, 364
  making NDS users members of, 368
  partitioning, 365
  placing in NDS tree, 364-366
NT users
  creating in NDS, 369-372
  duplicate NDS users, 338-339
  placing in NDS tree, 100
  user profiles, 391
NT Workstation objects. See Novell Workstation
    Manager
NWADMIN, 333
  enabling profile login scripts for users, 240
  Mail Box Manager snap-in, 333, 353
  managing NDS login scripts, 235-236
  NAL snap-in, 333, 347-348
  Novell Workstation Manager snap-in, 344
  password synchronization, 373
  profile login script creation, 239
  Show Inherited Applications option, 380-381
  simple distribution, 375-376
  viewing replica synchronized up to values,
    174
NWAPP (NAL Library), 7-8
NWGINA. See Novell Workstation Manager

## O

O=Organization objects, 201, 203-204
  C=Country object and, 45-46
  for campus or metropolitan area networks,
    66
  for LAN-only network, 59
  naming standard for, 199
  using more than one, 48-49
  using one only, 45-46, 47

objectives of NDS tree design, 11-20
    benefits of good design, 11-13
    organize network resources, 13-19
    provide blueprint for NetWare 4 rollout, 19
    provide flexibility to reflect corporate
        changes, 20
objects. *See* NDS objects
order of execution for login scripts, 210, 233,
    234
organization objects. *See* O=Organization
    objects
organization units. *See* OU=Organization Units
organizational chart, 30-31, 33
Organizational Person objects, 214
Organizational Role objects, 207
organizing network resources, 13-19, 200-201
OU=Organization Units, 201, 206-207
    building representation in NDS tree, 59-61
    C=Country object replaced by, 45-47
    campus network infrastructure
        representation in NDS tree, 63-64
    for campus or metropolitan area networks,
        59-66
    first level and network infrastructure, 53-55
    function designation in NDS tree, 61-62
    geographic containers with high-speed
        links, 62
    group objects vs., 207-208
    for hub and spoke networks, 66-78
    for institutions with many remote or branch
        offices, 75-77
    for LAN-only networks, 56-59
    maximum subordinate containers, 77-78
    for meshed networks, 78-82
    naming standard for, 199
    regional containers to distribute physical
        locations, 73-74
    regional containers to distribute remote or
        branch offices, 74-75
    representing company units, 83-85
    student representation in NDS tree, 64-65,
        89-90
    top of tree based on hubs and campus
        spokes, 68-70
    top of tree based on hubs and city spokes,
        70-72
    top of tree based on hubs only, 66-68
OU=RESOURCES, problems with, 88

# P

parent (superior) partitions, 126-130
Partition and Replica Matrix, 141, 162
partition operations, 131-135
    abort partition, 139-140
    checking partition status, 134-135
    checking replica status before, 133, 137
    create new partition, 135-136
    locking partitions before, 131
    merge partitions, 133, 136-138
    move subtree, 138-139
    Partition and Replica Matrix, 141, 162
    subordinate references' effect on, 156
    utilities, 130-131, 132
partitions, 111-141, 143
    adding replicas, 180
    administration, 121
    Advanced Design rules, 22, 362
    bottom layers of tree, 120-121
    characteristics or rules of, 117-119
    checking partition status, 134-135, 178-179
    container objects for, 105
    creating, 135-136
    design issues, 36
    design rules, 21-22, 111, 360, 361-362
    designing partitions, 112-130
    fault tolerance, 107, 144-146
    file system partitions vs. NDS partitions,
        128
    locking before partition operations, 131
    managing partitions, 130-141
    maximum replicas per partition, 107, 121,
        151-152
    merging, 133, 136-138
    naming, 118
    as NDS tree design criterion, 105-108
    network infrastructure as basis, 105-106,
        115-117
    not spanning WAN links or physical
        locations, 123
    NT Domain object partitioning, 365
    overlapping and, 119
    Partition and Replica Matrix, 141, 162
    partition operations overview, 131-135
    partitioning around local servers in each
        geographic area, 124

                                    *(continued)*

partitions *(continued)*
    peer-level containers in same partition,
        118-119
    pyramid-shaped design, 122
    Quick Design rules, 22, 361
    removing replicas, 181
    [ROOT] partition, 112-115, 126
    size of, 106-107, 115, 125-126
    subordinate, 126-130
    as subtrees, 119
    top layers of tree, 119-120
    *See also* replicas
PARTMGR utility, 131, 132
passwords
    ADMIN password, 204
    bindery Supervisor account, 231-232
    synchronization, 222-223, 373-374
    user passwords with Client for Windows NT,
        221-222
    Windows NT, 1
PDC (primary domain controller), 374
peer-level containers in same partition, 118-119
performance
    local replication and, 146
    master replica placement and, 166
    name resolution, 160-162
    replica synchronization and, 144, 152
    replica synchronization time requirements,
        362
period (.) as reserved character, 193
Person objects, 215
physical locations. *See* sites
placeholder containers. *See* regional containers
plus sign (+) as reserved character, 194
polling process
    primary time servers, 273-275
    reference time servers, 277
    SET TIMESYNC commands, 312-313, 322
PREFERRED TREE statements, 45
primary domain controller (PDC), 374
primary time servers, 272-275
    changing secondary time servers to, 301-302
    characteristics, 272-273
    polling process, 273-275
    reference time servers vs., 275-276
    for time provider group configuration,
        285-286
    as time providers, 273

Print Queue objects, 210
print queues
    naming, 98
    naming standard for, 199-200
    placing in NDS tree, 98
    Print Queue objects, 210
    Print Server objects, 209
    Volume objects and, 205
Print Server objects, 209
Printer objects, 209-210
printers
    naming, 98
    naming standard for, 199-200
    placing in NDS tree, 98
    Print Queue objects, 210
    Print Server objects, 209
    Printer objects, 209-210
profile login scripts, 101-102, 239-245
    creating, 239
    default login script, 245
    enabling for users, 240
    for entire company, 241
    global scripts, 210-211
    location scripts, 211
    NDS user login scripts, 243-244
    for one location, 241
    spanning NDS containers, 242-243
    special function scripts, 211
    for special group of users, 241-243
Profile objects, 210
    for global login scripts, 210-211
    for location login scripts, 211
    for special function login scripts, 211
properties
    Application object properties, 382-386
    Inherit Container Applications property,
        381-382
    login/logout modification of, 169
    naming standard for, 197-198
    replica synchronization modification of, 173
    replica synchronization property flags, 172
property rights, NAL requirements, 349
pull distribution, 375
push distribution, 375
pyramid-shaped design, 31-33, 122

**Q**

Quick Design rules, 22, 361

# R

read/write (R/W) replicas, 165-167
READNAL.TXT file, 352
read-only (RO) replicas, 167-169
rebuild replicas operation, 183-185
Receive Updates operation, 184-185
reference time servers, 275-280
    changing type of, 301-302
    characteristics, 275
    designating, 301
    fault tolerance and, 278
    multiple reference servers, 280, 298-299
    polling process, 277
    primary time servers vs., 275-276
    single reference time servers, 280-281
    for time provider group configuration, 287
    as time providers, 275
    time source for, 278-279
regional containers
    for banks and similar companies, 75-77
    to distribute physical locations, 73-74
    to distribute remote or branch offices, 74-75
    in meshed network design, 81-82
Registry, PREFERRED TREE statements in, 45
Remote Procedure Calls (RPCs), 5, 370
remote user access, 246
remove replica operation, 181
renaming. See naming
replica number, timestamp component, 267
replica operations, 131-135, 178-180
    add replica, 180
    change replica type, 182-183
    checking partition status, 178-179
    rebuild replicas, 183-185
    Receive Updates, 184-185
    remove replica, 181
    Send Updates, 183-184
Replica Servers, 362
replica synchronization, 143, 171-177
    cycle on server, 176-177
    fast synchronization, 173
    heartbeat or trigger, 176
    master replica and, 165
    NDS inactivity synchronization interval, 176
    performance and, 144
    performing, 175-176
    properties changed, 173
    property flags, 172

    Receive Updates operation and, 184
    replica characteristics, 164
    scheduling, 174-175
    Send Updates operation and, 183
    slow synchronization, 173
    time required, 362
    timestamps and, 266
replicas 143, 164
    across WAN links, 146-148
    adding, 180
    Advanced Design rules, 22, 362
    automatic creation of, 146
    for bindery service access, 157-160
    bindery services and replication, 102, 104
    changing type, 182-183
    checking status before partition operations,
        133, 137
    dedicated NDS replica servers, 153
    design issues, 37
    design rules, 21-22, 144, 361-362
    for fault tolerance, 107, 144-146
    installation process and, 146
    local replication, 146-151
    managing partitions, 130-141
    managing replicas, 178-185
    master (M) replica, 131, 164-165, 166
    maximum per partition, 107, 121, 151-152
    maximum per server, 152-153
    for name resolution improvement, 160-162
    NDS replica characteristics, 163-164
    as NDS tree design criterion, 105-108
    Partition and Replica Matrix, 141, 162
    purposes and benefits, 143-144
    Quick Design rules, 22, 361
    read/write (R/W) replicas, 165-167
    read-only (RO) replicas, 167-169
    rebuilding, 183-185
    for remote offices with no servers, 151
    for remote offices with one server, 149-150
    for remote offices with two servers, 150-151
    removing, 181
    replica operations overview, 131-135,
        178-180
    Replica Servers, 362
    of [ROOT] partition, 112, 113
    subordinate reference (SR) replicas,
        153-156, 169-171

*(continued)*

replicas *(continued)*
  synchronization, 143-144, 164, 165, 171-177
  viewing depth for server, 304
  *See also* partitions
required objects, 202-206
  NCP server object, 205
  NT Domain Object, 206
  O=Organization objects, 203-204
  [ROOT] object, 203
  Top object class, 203
  User objects, 204-205
  Volume objects, 205-206
reserved characters, naming standard and,
    193-195
resource containers, 88-90
resource objects, 215
resources. *See* network resources
restarting time synchronization, 314
rights, NAL requirements, 349
RIP (Router Information Protocol), 43
RO (read-only) replicas, 167-169
[ROOT] object, 201, 203
  keeping the NDS tree name unique, 43-44
  layer counting and, 44
  locating NetWare 4 servers, 42-43
  multiple NDS trees, 44
  naming, 41-42, 59, 66
[ROOT] partition, 112-115
  creating child partitions, 113-114
  replicating across WAN links, 161-162
  replication of, 112, 113
  size of, 115, 126, 161
Router Information Protocol (RIP), 43
RPCs (Remote Procedure Calls), 5, 370
rules. *See* design guidelines; design rules

**S**

SAMSRV.DLL, replacing, 3-4, 5
SAP. *See* Service Advertising Protocol (SAP)
scalability of NDS for NT, 13
Schedule property page for Application objects,
    386
scheduling replica synchronization, 174-175
Schema Manager, 333
Scripts property page for Application objects, 385
secondary (read/write) replicas, 165-167
secondary time servers, 270-272
  changing to primary time servers, 301-302

characteristics, 271
  configuring to follow other secondary
    servers, 296-298
  as time consumers, 271
seconds, timestamp component, 267
security
  bindery Supervisor account safeguards,
    231-232
  protecting NDS tree access, 204-205
  user authentication, 372-373
Send Updates operation, 183-184
server bindery context, 157-160
  multiple bindery contexts, 226
  setting, 158-160
  verifying setting, 102, 103, 159
servers. *See* NetWare 4 servers
service accounts, 6
Service Advertising Protocol (SAP), 41
  directory tree mode for, 311
  filtering broadcasts, 43
  locating NetWare 4 servers, 42-43
  multiple NDS trees and, 44
  NDS tree name and, 41, 43-44
  requirements, 261-221
  SAP types that must be supported, 42
  service type for NDS tree SAP, 42-43
  time synchronization using, 261-262, 290,
    310-311, 314
SERVMAN utility
  changing time server types, 301-302
  modifying time synchronization parameters,
    308-309
  running, 281
  setting server bindery context(s), 102-103
  Time option, 281
  time provider group setup, 285-286
  verifying bindery context setting, 102, 103
SET NDS INACTIVITY SYNCHRONIZATION
    INTERVAL command, 176
SET SERVER BINDERY CONTEXT command,
    102, 103, 158-159
SET TIMESYNC commands, 307-323
  Add Time Source, 309
  Configuration File, 310
  Configured Sources, 310-311
  Correction Floor, 323
  Daylight Savings Time Offset, 319-320
  Daylight Savings Time Status, 319

DEBUG commands, 305-307
Default Time Server Type, 318
Directory Tree Mode, 311
End of Daylight Savings Time, 320-321
Hardware Clock, 311-312
Immediate Synchronization, 322
Maximum Offset, 322
New Time with Daylight Savings Time
    Status, 321
Offset Ceiling, 323
Polling Count, 312
Polling Interval, 312-313
Remove Time Source, 313
Reset, 314
Restart Flag, 314
Service Advertising, 314
Short Interval, 322
Start of Daylight Savings Time, 320
Synchronization Radius, 315
Time Adjustment, 315-316
Time Source, 316-317
Time ZONE, 319
Type, 317
Write Parameters, 318
Write Value, 318
SETUP.EXE, 354
SETUPNAL.EXE, 349, 350
SETUPNW.EXE, 344-345
SETUPSNP.EXE, 350
simple distribution, 375-377
single login, 3, 12, 221, 372
single reference time servers, 280-281
single reference time synchronization, 282-284
    advantages and disadvantages, 283-284
    default configuration, 282
    requirements, 260
    uninstalling Directory Services and, 284
sites
    building representation in NDS tree, 59-61
    function designation in NDS tree, 61-62
    geographic containers with high speed links,
        62
    institutions with many remote or branch
        offices, 75-77
    list for NDS tree design, 27-29
    meshed network design, 78-82
    partitioning around local servers in each
        geographic area, 124

partitions not spanning, 123
profile login script for one location, 241
regional containers to distribute physical
    locations, 73-74
regional containers to distribute remote or
    branch offices, 74-75
top of tree based on hubs and campus
    spokes, 68-70
top of tree based on hubs and city spokes,
    70-72
top of tree based on hubs only, 66-68
size
    maximum layers in NDS tree, 87
    maximum replicas per partition, 107, 121,
        151-152
    maximum subordinate containers, 77-78
    maximum subordinate partitions, 126-130
    of partitions, 106-107, 115, 125-126
    of [ROOT] partition, 115, 126, 161
slow synchronization, 173
SNAPSHOT.EXE, 7, 348, 377-380
software. See applications; distributing software
spaces
    NDS tree name and, 44
    in user names, 194-195
special characters, reserved, 193-195
special function login scripts, 211
SR (subordinate reference) replicas, 153-156,
    169-171
static bindery objects, 227-228
students
    containers for, 89-90
    representation in NDS tree, 64-65
subadministrators, 94-95
subordinate partitions, 126-130, 169-171
subordinate reference (SR) replicas, 153-156,
    169-171
subordinate references
    effect on partition operations, 156
    replicating to reduce, 153-156
subtrees
    moving, 138-139, 209
    partitions as, 119
superior partitions, 126-130
Supervisor account, bindery, 231-232
synchronizing passwords, 222-223, 373-374
synchronizing replicas. See replica
    synchronization

synchronizing time. *See* time synchronization
synthetic time, 326
System Requirements property page for
    Application objects, 386

# T

TIME command, 264-265
time provider group configuration, 284-289
    changing time server types, 301-302
    multiple time provider groups, 288-289
    primary time servers, 285-286
    reference time server, 287
    requirements, 260-261
    setting up, 285-288
    time source, 286-287
time required for replica synchronization, 362
time servers, 269-281
    adding, 300
    booting, 300, 325
    changing type, 301-302, 317
    classes of, 270
    correcting local time, 325-326
    default configuration, 271
    default type, 318
    multiple reference servers, 280, 298-299
    primary time servers, 272-275
    reference time servers, 275-280, 298-299
    secondary time servers, 270-272, 296-298
    single reference time servers, 280-281
    time zone specification, 319
    *See also* time synchronization
time source
    adding time providers, 309, 316-317
    for reference time servers, 278-279
    removing, 313
    setting hardware clock, 311-312
    time provider group configuration, 286-287
time synchronization
    checking, 264-265
    communication methods, 261-262, 290-296
    configuration rules, 23-24
    configured lists communication, 262,
        290-296, 310-311
    daylight savings time settings, 319-321
    design options, 259-261, 281-289
    immediate synchronization, 322
    managing, 303-327
    multiple time provider groups, 288-289

for NDS operations, 327
polling process, 273-275, 277, 312-313, 322
purpose of, 263-269
resetting to defaults, 314
restarting, 314
SAP communication, 42, 261-262, 290,
    310-311, 314
SET TIMESYNC commands, 307-323
setting network time, 268-269
single reference configuration, 260, 282-284
synchronization radius, 315
synthetic time, 326
time adjustments, 315-316
time provider group configuration, 260-261,
    284-289
time servers, 269-281, 296-299, 300-302
timestamps assignment, 265-268
TIMESYNC DEBUG commands, 305-307
traffic considerations, 299-300
troubleshooting, 324-327
UTC and local time, 263-264
viewing time periodically on all NetWare 4
    servers, 304-305
*See also* SET TIMESYNC commands; time
    servers
time zone, specifying, 319
Time_Not_Synchronized error, 325
timestamps
    components of, 267
    synthetic time, 326
    uses of, 264-266, 268
TIMESYNC commands. *See* SET TIMESYNC
    commands
TIMESYNC.CFG file, 307
    defining path for, 310
    examples, 292-296
    modifying, 308
    writing time synchronization parameters to,
        318
TIMESYNC.NLM, 263-264
top level NDS tree design, 31–34, 39-82
    C=Country object and, 45-47
    for campus or metropolitan area network,
        59-66
    design rules, 40-41
    determining network infrastructure, 49-53
    first level of OU=Organization Units, 53-55
    for hub and spoke network, 66-78

for LAN-based network, 56-59
for meshed network, 78-82
naming the O=Organization object, 47-49
naming the [ROOT] object, 41-45
partitioning, 119-120
Top object class, 203
traffic, time synchronization and, 299-300
tree design. *See* NDS tree design
trigger for replica synchronization, 176
troubleshooting time synchronization, 324-327

# U

UNATTEND.TXT file, 344, 345
underscore (_) for spaces in names, 194
uninstalling
    Directory Services, 284
    NAL Explorer, 348
unique object names, 193
Universal Coordinated Time (UTC), 263-265, 268
unknown objects, 211-212
user access
    ADMIN user, 204-205
    container login scripts, 100-101
    leaf objects for, 201-202
    for mobile users, 245-252
    profile login scripts, 101-102
    remote user access, 246
    simplifying, 23
    user authentication, 372-373
    user login scripts, 102
    *See also* access methods; login scripts
user accounts
    naming standard for, 198-199
    volatile, 389-391
user authentication, 372-373
user login scripts, 102, 243-244
User Manager for Domains, 1, 2
User objects, 204-205
    inherited applications, 380-382
    managing with NAL, 375-380
    protecting NDS tree access, 204-205

user profiles, Windows NT, 391
UTC (Universal Coordinated Time), 263-265, 268

# V

verifying server bindery context setting, 102,
    103, 159
viewing
    DS.NLM version, 304
    inherited applications, 380-381
    log file for NDS for NT installation, 339, 340
    time periodically on all NetWare 4 servers,
        304-305
Virtual Loadable Modules (VLMs), 219-220
volatile user accounts, 389-391
Volume object, 205-206

# W

/W switch, SETUPNW.EXE, 345
wide area networks (WANs)
    diagrams for NDS tree design, 26, 27, 31
    hub and spoke network infrastructure,
        51-52, 66-78
    meshed network infrastructure, 52-53,
        78-82
    partitions not spanning links, 123
    replicas not spanning links, 146-148
    [ROOT] partition spanning links, 161-162
    time synchronization option, 260
Windows 3.1, login script execution and, 233
Windows NT domain controllers, 374
Windows NT user profiles, 391
Windows NT users. *See* NT users
Windows NT Workstations, managing. *See*
        managing NT Workstation objects
WINSETUP.EXE, installing NDS for NT, 334-340
workgroups, in LAN-only network, 56-57
WORKMAN.REG file, 345
workstation configuration file (NET.CFG), 45,
        250-251
Workstation Manager. *See* Novell Workstation
        Manager

# my2cents.idgbooks.com

## Register This Book — And Win!

Visit **http://my2cents.idgbooks.com** to register this book and we'll automatically enter you in our fantastic monthly prize giveaway. It's also your opportunity to give us feedback: let us know what you thought of this book and how you would like to see other topics covered.

## Discover IDG Books Online!

The IDG Books Online Web site is your online resource for tackling technology — at home and at the office. Frequently updated, the IDG Books Online Web site features exclusive software, insider information, online books, and live events!

### 10 Productive & Career-Enhancing Things You Can Do at www.idgbooks.com

- Nab source code for your own programming projects.

- Download software.

- Read Web exclusives: special articles and book excerpts by IDG Books Worldwide authors.

- Take advantage of resources to help you advance your career as a Novell or Microsoft professional.

- Buy IDG Books Worldwide titles or find a convenient bookstore that carries them.

- Register your book and win a prize.

- Chat live online with authors.

- Sign up for regular e-mail updates about our latest books.

- Suggest a book you'd like to read or write.

- Give us your 2¢ about our books and about our Web site.

You say you're not on the Web yet? It's easy to get started with IDG Books' *Discover the Internet*, available at local retailers everywhere.